IT'S NOT WHAT YOU MAKE— IT'S WHAT YOU KEEP

HOW TO KEEP AS MUCH AFTER-TAX MONEY AS THE LAW ALLOWS
1995 EDITION

The only tax book chosen by *Money* magazine as one of the "Nine Best Personal Finance Books."

"Offers numerous short money-saving tips, as well as sophisticated strategies . . . one of the best books . . . has a clear, personable writing style devoid of legalese or IRS jargon. . . . A reader might never guess he is a tax lawyer."
NEW YORK TIMES

"Provides more depth than the other books."
WALL STREET JOURNAL

"Easily the best available."
FORBES

"Reading about taxes can be almost as unpleasant as paying them, but this book is an exception . . . all the earmarks of a well-written and well-researched book."
LIBRARY JOURNAL

"Block's book covers all the bases on tax planning, including year-end tax tips, filing tips. . . . The language is easy to understand and the examples are plentiful."
NEW YORK DAILY NEWS

"This book is written for the consumer, but the professional planner will also find it to be a good reference. . . . It's no wonder why it has received critical acclaim. . . . You will reach for it often."
TAX MANAGEMENT FINANCIAL PLANNING JOURNAL

How to Order:
Single copies may be ordered from Prima Publishing, P.O. Box 1260BK, Rocklin, CA 95677; telephone (916) 632-4400. Quantity discounts are also available. On your letterhead, include information concerning the intended use of the books and the number of books you wish to purchase.

ABOUT THE AUTHOR

Julian Block is a nationally recognized attorney. Block has been singled out by the *New York Times* as a "leading tax professional" and by the *Wall Street Journal* as "an accomplished writer on taxes." He is frequently quoted by these and other publications such as *Business Week*, *Money* magazine, and *U.S. News & World Report*. Block is well known for his ability to translate complicated tax laws into plain English and for the concise, entertaining way he alerts readers of his nationally syndicated column, "The Tax Report," to simple, perfectly legal, tax-saving strategies. His column also can be retrieved on the PRODIGY on-line service.

In addition to writing and practicing law in Larchmont, New York, he conducts programs on retirement planning for major corporations and professional associations and is a frequent guest on television and radio shows, including "Today" on NBC and "Wall Street Journal Reports." Bryant Gumbel complimented him as "a frequent guest, whose insights are always great fare." He holds an accounting degree from Roosevelt University, a law degree from DePaul University, and a master of laws degree in taxation from New York University Graduate Law School and is a member, and former officer, of the American Society of Journalists and Authors, a national organization of nonfiction writers.

Formerly, Block was with the Internal Revenue Service as a special agent (criminal investigator) and as an attorney. He has taught tax planning at such schools as Adelphi University (for a course held on a commuter train), Long Island University, Mercy College, New York University, Pace University, and The New School.

IT'S NOT WHAT YOU MAKE—
IT'S WHAT YOU KEEP

HOW TO KEEP AS MUCH AFTER-TAX MONEY AS THE LAW ALLOWS

1995 EDITION

Julian Block

Prima Publishing
P.O. Box 1260BK
Rocklin, CA 95677
(916) 632-4400

Copyediting by Elizabeth von Radics
Production by Melanie Field, Bookman Productions
Typography by Graphic Sciences Corporation
Interior design by Judith Levinson
Cover design by The Dunlavey Studio, Sacramento

Library of Congress Cataloging-in-Publication Data
Block, Julian.
    It's not what you make—it's what you keep : how to keep as much after-tax money as the law allows / Julian Block.
      p.   cm.
    Includes index.
    ISBN 1-55958-580-3
    1. Income tax—United States—Deductions. 2. Tax shelters—United States. 3. Tax planning—United States. I. Title.
HJ4653.D4B58 1994
343.73′0523—dc20   94-19863
                                                    CIP

Printed in the United States of America

95 96 97 98   RRD   10 9 8 7 6 5 4 3 2

CONTENTS

INTRODUCTION

The art of taxation consists in so plucking the goose as to obtain the largest amount of feathers with the least possible amount of hissing.
—Jean Baptiste Colbert (1619-1683) finance minister for King Louis XIV

If geese are to be plucked with the least squawking, which is the aim of all taxation, the fatter ones will always tempt politicians more because they have more feathers and there are fewer of them to screech.
—*The Wall Street Journal,* July 28, 1982

If you're NOT worried about the tax bite on your income, perhaps you SHOULD be! Everyone in the middle-income bracket owes it to him- or herself to protect hard-earned dollars from the tax takers . . . not just at filing time, but *all through the year.*

The key to getting the full benefit from the many opportunities that are available to lessen the amount siphoned off by the Internal Revenue Service is to consider the tax consequences beforehand as you make those everyday financial decisions, whether they be buying, borrowing, saving, investing, or giving.

To make a tough job tougher, the rules of the game change annually. Thus, memorizing last year's rules may be the worst kind of preparation for this year's return. But that only means this is as good a time as any to get started. No matter how little you have

learned about taxes in the past, you can lower your next tax tab by following this wholly revised twelfth edition of *It's Not What You Make—It's What You Keep.*

This book offers detailed help, in language that everyone can understand, on how to keep more of what you earn. It is a guide to use throughout the year for advance planning that alerts you to new and frequently overlooked changes in the tax rules and explains how to take advantage of them and steer clear of pitfalls—all completely legally.

Back in 1986, Congress enacted a top-to-bottom overhaul of the Internal Revenue Code, known officially as the Tax Reform Act. But that was only Act I. Congress passed wide-ranging legislation in each of the following years. The historic Tax Reform Act and subsequent refinements included provisions that kayoed or curtailed a vast array of long-cherished deductions, credits, exemptions, exclusions, deferrals, and other breaks that you had learned to count on.

What forces our lawmakers to keep going back to the drawing board? The need to raise more taxes to offset spiraling budget deficits—a predicament that means we can look forward to more changes in the immediate future.

This brand-new 1995 edition of *It's Not What You Make—It's What You Keep* incorporates key law changes, as well as significant court decisions, IRS rulings, and other announcements made during the past year. It provides clear, uncomplicated, and immediately helpful advice on how to choose and implement strategies to cope with these recent developments.

As part of its broad coverage of practical and effective tax angles, this book takes you step by step through special year-end strategies that can not only save taxes for this year, but also provide a head start on next year. For instance, it shows how to time the payment of deductible expenses or the receipt of income for maximum benefit, and explains why advancing or postponing payments for deductibles, or the date of a marriage or divorce, by merely a single day at year's end can cost, or save, many tax dollars.

This year-round guide also provides a straightforward look at many of the money-saving techniques long used by the wealthy, and how they can be used by those with average incomes. It gives advice on how to shield income from the tax collectors through safe and sensible arrangements that can eliminate, reduce, or postpone the amount that goes to the IRS.

To help highlight important tax-saving opportunities, several of the chapters are presented in question-and-answer form. They alert you to the steps to take, for example, to hang on to a dependency exemption for a college student or to get maximum mileage out of your medical expenses. Many difficult problems are made simpler for you because the questions are presented in much the same order in which you would ask them yourself.

Julian Block
Larchmont, New York

1 YEAR-END TAX TIPS

The Firm, John Grisham's best-selling thriller, became a 1993 film that starred Tom Cruise as a young lawyer seduced into working for a snazzy law firm that launders money for the Mafia. In the movie version, a mob mouthpiece describes tax law as "a game we teach the rich how to play so they can stay rich. The IRS keeps changing the rules so we can keep getting rich teaching them."

Judge Learned Hand of the Second Circuit Court of Appeals in New York, who is renowned for having served longer—and perhaps with more distinction—than any other federal judge in history, was often called the "tenth justice of the Supreme Court." In the course of his legendary career, Hand displayed a talent that is rare among judges: He wrote all of his four thousand opinions without committees of law clerks.

Ask tax professionals what judge did the most to interpret, unravel, and explain our labyrinthian Internal Revenue Code, and the runaway winner is Hand, who wrote this definitive analysis: "The words of such an act as the income tax merely dance before my eyes in a meaningless procession: cross-reference to cross-reference, exception upon exception—couched in abstract terms that offer no handle to seize hold of— leave in my mind only a confused sense of some vitally important, but successfully concealed, purport, which it is my duty to extract, but

which is within my power, if at all, only after the most inordinate expenditure of time. I know that these monsters are the result of fabulous industry and ingenuity, plugging up this hole and casting out that net against all possible evasion; yet at times I cannot help recalling a saying of William James' about certain passages of Hegel: that they were no doubt written with a passion of rationality; but that one cannot help wondering whether to the reader they have any significance save that the words are strung together with syntactical correctness."

Back in 1947, tax planning was something that concerned only the wealthy. That year, they received often-quoted words of encouragement from Judge Hand: "Over and over again courts have said that there is nothing sinister in so arranging one's affairs as to keep taxes as low as possible. Everybody does so, rich and poor; and all do right; for nobody owes any public duty to pay more than the law demands; taxes are enforced exactions, not voluntary contributions. To demand more in the name of morals is mere cant."

Nowadays, financial planning throughout the year, with an eye particularly on taxes, is not just for the wealthy. Advance planning is also rewarding for most middle-income individuals.

Spend a few hours plotting how to choose and implement your year-end strategies, and you may be pleasantly surprised to discover how many IRS-blessed opportunities there are to save on your taxes for this year and even gain a head start on next year.

The main thing is to act before December 31 while there is still time to take advantage of tax angles that can generate a dramatic savings if you understand how to get the full benefit of what the law allows. Once beyond December 31, it is too late to do anything but fill out your tax forms, except for contributing to an IRA or Keogh.

Caution. Beware of generalizations, including mine. Our patchwork quilt of tax laws has become so complicated that some advice that could move your brother-in-law into a lower tax bracket could put you into a higher one.

Consider, for instance, the traditional advice to accelerate the payment of deductions and defer the receipt of income, whenever possible—a decision that should never be made without a thorough review of the numbers. Though still right for most people, that tactic can be inappropriate and even result in a bigger tax tab if you overlook the AMT (alternative minimum tax; Chapter 14). The AMT is a complex levy structured to ensure the payment of at least some taxes by even the wealthiest individuals able to avail themselves of the most sophisticated tax breaks.

If you are hit by the AMT, some otherwise worthwhile year-end tactics need to be rethought. Among other things, medical expenses (discussed later in this chapter and in Chapter 7) are allowable only if they top 10 percent of your adjusted gross income, not 7.5 percent. No AMT deductions at all for: interest on home equity loans obtained for reasons other than to acquire, construct, or substantially improve first or second homes (discussed later in this chapter and in Chap-

ter 9); state and local income taxes (discussed later in this chapter); and for miscellaneous deductions (discussed later in this chapter and in Chapter 9).

Tip. In your zealous quest for tax savings, you ought not to get so carried away that you fail to ask yourself an important question: Is it worth the time or effort to get the answer to whether you ought to speed up or postpone income or deductions? Even worse, the cost of your time, not to mention the dent in your checkbook if you rely on high-priced professional help to do your planning, could prove to be greater than the savings you reap.

Marital Status

As part of your year-end planning, you need to consider an expected change in your filing status for this year or next. The often-overlooked strategy is that the advancement or postponement of the date of a marriage or a divorce by a single day at year's end can make a sizable difference in the amount of your tax tab for both years.

Usually, your marital status as of December 31 determines your filing status for the entire year. (There is an exception: If your spouse died during the year, you can still file a joint return.) Therefore, the Internal Revenue considers you a married person for the entire year in question, even if you should get hitched as late as December 31. Similarly, the IRS considers you a single person for the entire year although your divorce or legal separation takes place as late as December 31.

Suppose, for example, that you and your prospective mate both earn roughly the same. In that event, matrimony before the close of this year may be costly. *Reason:* The taxes that the two of you become obligated to pay as marrieds on your combined incomes can turn out to be a good deal more than they would be as two unmarrieds who share lodgings and report exactly the same incomes—a law quirk known as the "marriage penalty." But if you delay the ceremony until next year, you get a reprieve from the marriage penalty for this year.

Conversely, a marriage this year is a smart move when one of you earns the bulk of the income or considerably more than the other. Your taxes as a couple filing jointly will be less than if you remain unmarried.

Similar rules apply to couples who cut their ties. A divorce near the end of the year means that you forfeit the benefits of joint filing for the entire year. To save taxes, you have to grin and bear it beyond December 31. What if being single provides an advantage? You can achieve that goal only if you shed your spouse by December 31. (See "Marriage or Divorce as a Tax Shelter" in Chapter 4.)

Tip. Your marital status as of a particular date also can be significant for the following: whether you are eligible for the over-55 exclusion of as much as $125,000 gain from a home sale (see "Special Breaks for People over 55" in Chapter 3); how much of a credit you are entitled to claim for child- or dependent-care expenses (Chapter 6); the amount you can deduct for money put in Individual Retirement Accounts (Chapter 10); your allowable deduction for losses from rental properties (Chapter 10); determining your top marginal tax bracket (see "What Is Your Real Tax Bracket?" in Chapter 14); the amount of itemized deductions you forfeit when you have an adjusted gross income

above a specified amount that is adjusted annually to reflect inflation—$111,800 for tax year 1994—(see "Curtailment of Most Itemized Deductions for Individuals with Adjusted Gross Incomes above a Specified Amount," in Chapter 14); how much you are taxed on Social Security benefits (Chapter 15); and the amount of your annual exclusions from gift taxes for lifetime transfers of money or other assets to family members and other persons, as well as the availability of the unlimited marital deduction for estate taxes when property is left to a surviving spouse (see "Minimizing Gift and Estate Taxes" in Chapter 16).

RETIREMENT PLANS

One tax decision you do not have to make before the year closes is how much to contribute to your IRA (for more on IRAs, see Chapter 10) or Keogh. If you are eligible to take a deduction for money put into an IRA, you have until the filing deadline of April 15 in the following year to *start* the plan, as well as deposit the money. Note that if you obtain an automatic four-month extension from April 15 to August 15 to file Form 1040 (for filing extensions, see Chapter 13), this does *not* extend the deadline to set up an IRA and make a deductible payment.

Different rules apply if you have self-employment earnings and put money in a Keogh retirement plan. You must *open* the plan by December 31 of the year in which you want to take the deduction; otherwise, no deduction is allowed. But, unlike an IRA, the Keogh contribution can be made as late as the filing deadline in the following year, *including* extensions.

Tip. All is not lost if you miss the deadline for a Keogh. You have until the filing deadline, including extensions, to establish and fund a SEP (simplified employee pension plan), which is like an IRA, but without a $2,000 cap on deposits. With a SEP, you can put away either (1) approximately 13.04 percent of your self-employment earnings or (2) $22,500, whichever is less.

DEPENDENCY EXEMPTIONS

Claiming dependency exemptions is not always a cut-and-dried procedure. Too often exemptions are needlessly lost because of inattentiveness or failure to take advantage of special rules.

For instance, you need to familiarize yourself with the rules if you are contributing to the support of a parent or other relative who receives Social Security benefits or other forms of government assistance or a college-going son or daughter who receives educational loans. Who pays for what kinds of expenses controls whether you meet the support test for a dependent—in most cases, over half of the total support for the year in question—and qualify for an exemption that slices $2,450 off your taxable income on a return for 1994 to be filed in 1995. You might have to closely monitor spending to make sure you furnish over half of the dependent's total support before the year comes to a close. See Chapter 2 for a detailed discussion of before-year-end steps to take to preserve your right to an exemption.

START TO SAVE NOW

Where feasible, a key part of your planning should be to time the payment of deductible expenses and the receipt of income to your best advantage and gain the benefit of special breaks that involve year-end time limits, such as lifetime gifts that reduce estate taxes. (See "How to Play Santa and Trim Taxes, Too" later in this chapter.)

Though some of these proven strategies only delay the day of reckoning, you might be able to continue delaying that day by employing similar tactics year after year. In the meantime, you enjoy the interest-free use of the money that you would otherwise have surrendered to the tax collectors.

If you get an early start on your planning and leave enough time to familiarize yourself with the steps that must be taken by December 31 if they are not to be lost forever, you still have the opportunity to save hundreds—maybe thousands—of dollars in taxes. Here are some reminders on practical steps that you can take to exploit opportunities and avoid pitfalls. Check with your tax adviser if you are unsure about the best moves.

ITEMIZING VERSUS STANDARD DEDUCTION

Recent law changes may require some careful calculating before you can tell whether to base your year-end strategies on itemizing or the standard deduction. You get one or the other, but not both.

Itemize on Schedule A of Form 1040 and you are able to write off outlays such as contributions and home-mortgage interest. The standard deduction is the no-proof-required amount that is automatically available without having to itemize.

Standard deduction

Your standard deduction depends on your filing status. Moreover, the standard deduction amount is indexed—that is, adjusted upward each year to provide relief from inflation—as measured by increases in the Consumer Price Index.

For tax year 1994, the normal standard deduction is $6,350 for married couples filing jointly or $3,175 if they file separately. The law requires marrieds filing separately to handle their deductions the same way; if one spouse itemizes, so must the other.

A frequently overlooked break is that the normal standard deduction is also $6,350 for someone who qualifies as a "surviving spouse"—a widow or widower who has a dependent child and is entitled to use joint return rates for two years after the death of a spouse in 1992 or 1993. (See "Joint-Return Rates for Surviving Spouses" in Chapter 4.)

The normal deduction amounts are $3,800 for an individual with the filing status of single and $5,600 for a head of household.

Extra-large standard deductions for elderly and blind nonitemizers

Individuals who are at least 65 by the close of the year in question are allowed higher deductions. For tax year 1994, the standard deduction goes up by $750 for a married person (whether filing jointly, separately, or as a surviving spouse) and $950 for an unmarried person.

Individuals considered blind (vision cannot be better than 20/200 in the better eye

with glasses, or the field of vision must be limited to 20 degrees or less) also are entitled to the additional $750 or $950 and more if they are both 65 and blind.

Example. For tax year 1994, the deduction rises from $3,800 to $5,700 for a single person who is at least 65 and blind.

Caution. Special rules lessen the deduction amounts allowed individuals (children and elderly parents mostly) who can be claimed as dependents on the returns of other persons. For tax year 1994, the standard deduction can be as little as $600. (See the discussion of the kiddie-tax rules in Chapter 10.)

Strategy. Should your tax planning be based on using the standard deduction or itemizing? For many of you, there is no easy answer because the law imposes nondeductible floors for several categories of itemized deductibles.

Itemize and you continue to enjoy full deductions for interest on most home mortgages (discussed later in this chapter), charitable contributions (discussed later in this chapter and in more detail in Chapter 8), as well as for state and local income taxes and real estate taxes (discussed later in this chapter). But you get only partial deductions for other expenses.

For starters, medical expenses (discussed later in this chapter and in more detail in Chapter 7) are deductible only for the amount above 7.5 percent of AGI, short for adjusted gross income. (AGI is the figure you report at the bottom of page 1 of Form 1040 after listing salaries and other sources of income and claiming certain deductions such as alimony payments and money placed in IRAs. The AGI amount is before itemizing and claiming dependency exemptions.) Casualty and theft losses (discussed in Chapter 9) are allowable only to the extent such uninsured losses exceed $100 (for each casualty or theft), plus 10 percent of your AGI.

Tax reform scaled back deductions for most miscellaneous expenses (discussed later in this chapter and in more detail in Chapter 9). This category includes such write-offs as return-preparation charges, safe deposit box rentals, and unreimbursed employee expenses, such as union and professional association dues. For miscellaneous expenses, only the portion in excess of 2 percent of AGI is allowable.

There is no deduction for interest on consumer loans (discussed later in this chapter) —car payments, credit card charges, and college tuition, for example. Between 1987 and 1990, the deduction was phased out.

Also, there are restrictions on deductions for interest on money borrowed to finance investments, such as margin accounts used to buy stocks. Investment interest expenses are allowable just to the extent of investment income, a category that includes dividends, interest, and, subject to restrictions, capital gains.

For this purpose, grudgingly ruled the IRS, investment income includes interest on an overdue tax refund (Ruling 9307005). But a long-standing, pre–tax-reform rule bars any deduction for interest on loans used to buy tax-exempt securities.

Forget about any deduction for state and local sales taxes. That break became extinct at the close of 1986.

Partial disallowance of certain deductions for persons with AGIs above a specified amount, which is adjusted annually to reflect inflation—$111,800 for tax year 1994. You suffer a partial disallowance of your allowable write-off for most itemized deductibles.

The disallowance is 3 percent of the amount by which your AGI surpasses a specified amount—$111,800 for 1994, which is up from $108,450 for 1993, $105,250 for 1992 and $100,000 for 1991, the year this restriction first went on the books. Put another way, you lose $300 in total deductions for every $10,000 of AGI above $111,800. The $111,800 figure drops to $55,900 if you are married and file a separate return; going that route does not raise the threshold for a couple to a combined $223,600. (See "Curtailment of Most Itemized Deductions for Individuals with AGIs above a Specified Amount" in Chapter 14.)

Tip. If you go the standard-deduction route and later discover that itemizing would have saved you more money, you can switch by amending your return on Form 1040X. (For more information, see "Refund Claims" in Chapter 14.)

TIMING PAYMENTS OF DEDUCTIBLE EXPENSES

Tax planning involves a good deal more than just knowing which items are deductible. In plotting your moves, remember that timing the payments for your deductibles also has a bearing on the size of your tax bill. Advancing or postponing those payments by only a day at the end of the year can save you a bundle in 1995 and future taxes.

To illustrate, let's suppose that you will reap a greater savings for 1995 by using the standard deduction rather than itemizing. Thus, you garner no tax benefit from payments in 1995 for state income taxes or other deductibles. Instead of losing these potential deductions, you can trim taxes for 1996 if you delay these payments beyond December 31 and itemize next year.

The law also allows you to reverse your strategy, should that prove more beneficial. Within limits, you can shift payments for itemized deductions from next year to this year and take the standard deduction next year.

In summary, you bunch itemized deductibles, such as charitable contributions, into one of two years so that they top your standard deduction. Then, for the other year, use the standard deduction if that is more advantageous than itemizing.

Example. You plan to claim the standard deduction for this year and next; you expect payments for itemized expenses to be just below the standard deduction for this year. If you pay no mind to the calendar, the cap on your total deductions for both years will be the standard deduction for each year.

But an extra $1,000 in payments by December 31 would raise your itemized deductions to $1,000 more than the standard deduction for this year and still entitle you to claim the standard deduction next year. That bit of foresight would give you a two-year total of $1,000 more in deductions than if you had routinely taken the standard deduction for both years. Assuming you are in a total tax bracket (federal, state, and, perhaps, city) of 35 percent, that would mean a savings of $350—not big bucks but more than enough to pay for a sumptuous night on the town. (For instructions on how to determine your tax bracket, see "What Is Your Real Tax Bracket?" in Chapter 14.)

Suppose instead that, for this year and next, you expect that payments for itemized deductibles will run to more than the standard deduction. But you also expect earnings

for next year to decline substantially as you plan to stop moonlighting or to retire. Under either assumption, you should pay for deductibles by December 31 instead of waiting until next year, thereby getting more mileage out of your payments because they offset income taxed at a higher rate.

Here are some tips on ways to maneuver deductibles into the year in which they will do you the most good.

Medical Expenses

The law makes it difficult for itemizers to deduct their medical expenses. To reap any write-off, you must pay bills that are not covered by insurance, reimbursed by your employer, or not otherwise satisfied. The big limitation is that those outlays are allowable only for the portion that tops 7.5 percent of your AGI.

You stand little chance of a break at filing time for medical costs unless your reportable income is modest or you suffer the misfortune of incurring unusually high expenses—for instance, because of uninsured surgery, severe chronic disease, or a catastrophic illness.

Example. You and your spouse have an AGI of $50,000 and unreimbursed medical expenses of $5,000. The 7.5 percent floor shrinks your deduction to just $1,250—what is left after the $5,000 is offset by $3,750, which is 7.5 percent of $50,000.

Tip. If you have sizable medical expenditures, your goal should be to concentrate payments into a year in which they top the 7.5 percent threshold. Otherwise, they are nondeductible.

A special rule applies when you use credit cards to pay for medical services and other deductibles such as donations. You get a deduction in tax year 1995 for the amount charged, even though you do not pay the credit card tab until 1996. See "Dating and Delivery of Checks" later in this chapter.

Tip. Be mindful of these tactics when your payments for tax year 1995 are close to, or already over, the 7.5 percent hurdle and you will incur charges in tax year 1996 for services that can be scheduled at your convenience. Examples are dental cleanings, routine physical checkups, hearing aids, extra pairs of eyeglasses or contact lenses, or medically required home improvements, such as wider doorways and lower kitchen cabinets to accommodate persons in wheelchairs. To avoid the possible loss of a deduction for 1996 for those payments and to boost your deduction for 1995, just have those services performed and pay for them by December 31 of 1995. This strategy is even more advantageous when you anticipate an increase in AGI for 1996 and, therefore, a higher 7.5 percent threshold.

Caution. Ordinarily the feds prohibit deductions for payments made this year for services that will not be performed until next year by doctors, hospitals, and the like. But the IRS does allow 1995 prepayments when you have to shell out now for long-term work to be done in 1996 and future years—for instance, orthodontic work on your child. (For more information on how to time the payment of medical expenses, see Chapter 7.)

Tip. In figuring your allowable medical expenses, count the payments you make for the care of your children, parents, and any other dependents for whom you provide more than half (more than 10 percent if you qual-

ify under a multiple support agreement) of the total support for the year in question. This tax break remains available even if you are ineligible to claim an exemption for, say, your father because his reportable income exceeds the ceiling on the income that a dependent can receive. The cap is $2,450 on a return for tax year 1994, a figure that is scheduled to be adjusted upward for 1995 to reflect inflation. (See Chapter 2.)

Partial disallowance of certain deductions for persons with AGIs above a specified amount—$111,800 for tax year 1994. Medical expenses are not subject to this partial disallowance. (See "Curtailment of Most Itemized Deductions for Individuals with AGIs above a Specified Amount" in Chapter 14.)

Special rule for medical insurance payments by self-employed persons. Under this rule, self-employeds get a deduction on page 1 of Form 1040 (from gross income to arrive at adjusted gross income) for 25 percent of the premiums that they pay for medical insurance for themselves and their dependents. This deduction is not subject to the 7.5 percent threshold for all other medical expenses on Schedule A of Form 1040. (See "Insurance Costs" in Chapter 7.)

Alternative minimum tax. For AMT purposes (see Chapter 14), medical expenses are allowable only for the portion that tops 10 percent of your AGI.

Charitable Contributions

They provide the greatest flexibility for most people. This is because their timing is completely discretionary. Remember, though, that gifts to charitable organizations are deductible when paid; pledges don't count.

One strategy is to accelerate payments by taking care of pledges to religious groups, schools, and other charities this year, instead of next, as well as by donating before year-end the entire amount that you expect to give to your favorite charity next year. Keep in mind that a check mailed as late as December 31 is deductible for this year. See "Dating and Delivery of Checks" later in this chapter.

You might even consider borrowing to accelerate the deduction. The tax savings may more than offset the interest expense of a short-term loan.

Get a jump on spring cleaning.   Yet another way to lower taxes is to clean out and donate the contents of your closets, attic, and garage now, rather than waiting until next spring. Just make sure to get a receipt showing the fair-market value of what you donate. Otherwise, the tax takers may disallow all or part of your deduction. If the charity doesn't give a receipt, prepare your own detailed description listing clothing, furniture, and so forth. Ask the charity to receipt the list.

Caution.   When you claim a deduction of over $500 for noncash gifts of property like clothing and toys, complete Form 8283 and submit it with your return.

How to be philanthropic in a way that simultaneously increases Uncle Sam's take and lowers your taxes.   Surprisingly, this break comes to you courtesy of the IRS itself. The instruction booklet that contains the tax forms offers this tax-saving tactic: "You may make a gift to reduce the public debt. If you wish to do so, enclose a separate check with your income tax return. Make it payable to

'Bureau of the Public Debt.' You may be able to deduct this gift on your next year's tax return if you itemize your deductions. Do not add your gift to any tax you may owe. If you owe tax, include a separate check for that amount payable to 'Internal Revenue Service.'"

So far, the response has failed to noticeably dent the debt. Since 1961, Americans have voluntarily kicked in $20 million, while the debt has swelled to better than $4 trillion, as this book goes to press in the summer of 1994.

The largest single contribution so far: $1 million from the unspent funds of former president Reagan's second inaugural committee.

Alternatives to writing checks.   A tax-savvy way to make donations is with appreciated properties—stocks, real estate, or other investments that have gone up in value since their purchase and that you have owned for more than 12 months.

Here's the benefit: Besides getting a deduction for the property's full market value, you also escape paying taxes on the accumulated gain in value since you made your investment.

To illustrate this break, assume your long-term stock holdings include some shares acquired for $3,000 that are now worth $9,000. Donate the stock to charity this year and reap a double break: a charitable deduction of $9,000, without having to pay taxes on the appreciation of $6,000. Had you sold the stock for a $6,000 gain, that would have meant an additional tax of $1,680 in the 28 percent bracket. Your deduction for the full $9,000 lowers taxes by $2,520 in the 28 percent bracket.

Caution.   You must obtain a written appraisal if you claim a deduction of more than $5,000 for any gift of property (over $10,000

in the case of stock in a closely held company), except for stock of publicly traded companies. (See "Appraisal Rules for Sizable Donations of Property" in Chapter 8.)

Caution. It's a good idea to check with a tax expert before you make sizable contributions, especially if you plan to donate appreciated property. In general, you can deduct up to 50 percent of your AGI for gifts of cash to most charities, such as churches and schools. But there can be limitations of 30 percent or even 20 percent of your AGI on the amount you can claim for contributions of appreciated investments. Remember, too, that donations of stock or similar property do not count as deductions for this year unless you complete those gifts by December 31, and it can take time to do the legal paperwork. (For more planning details, see Chapter 8.)

Partial disallowance of certain deductions for persons with AGIs above a specified amount—$111,800 for tax year 1994. Charitable contributions are among the itemized deductions subject to this partial disallowance. The disallowance is 3 percent of the amount by which your AGI exceeds $111,800. (See "Curtailment of Most Itemized Deductions for Individuals with AGIs above a Specified Amount" in Chapter 14.)

Interest Deductions

Under the rules applicable to tax year 1994 (the most recent year for which information is available as this book goes to press), most homeowners remain entitled to deduct all of their interest payments on mortgage loans. They can deduct 100 percent of their interest charges on up to $1,000,000 of mortgage loans to "acquire, construct or substantially improve" first or second homes, plus up to $100,000 of home equity loans.

Tip. These limitations apply to loans obtained after October 13, 1987. Generally, there are no ceilings on interest deductions for loans obtained by October 13, 1987.

Prepayment penalty. Will an early payoff of a home mortgage mean you get socked with a prepayment penalty? Remember to include the penalty with your other itemized deductions for mortgage interest.

Mortgage points. Special rules apply when you make a prepayment of "points" (a term used to describe fees for organizing or processing loans) to obtain a mortgage loan to buy or improve your "principal residence" (that is, your year-round home, as opposed to a vacation retreat or property for which you charge rent), with the loan secured by that home. Your deductible interest includes the full amount you pay as points in the year of payment, if certain conditions are met.

At a loan closing, you likely will receive a Uniform Settlement Statement. The statement must clearly identify the amount that the lender charges as points and must calculate the points as a percentage of the loan. Moreover, the charging of points has to conform to an established business practice in your area, and the deduction cannot exceed the number of points generally charged in your area.

Example. On a $100,000 mortgage, 2 points equals a $2,000 deduction that saves $600 if you are in a total tax bracket (federal, state, and, perhaps, city) of 40 percent.

Caution. In most cases, there is no immediate deduction for points paid to *refinance* (with none of the proceeds used to pay for improvements) a mortgage on your principal residence. The points are deductible over the life of the loan. (For more information, see " 'Points' for Home Mortgages" in Chapter 9.)

Caution. If you refinance, check on whether you need to increase the amount taken out for taxes from your paychecks or to increase estimated payments. To revise your withholding, file a new Form W-4 (Employee's Withholding Allowance Certificate) with your employer. (See the section on withholding in Chapter 14.)

Personal interest. If you do better by cramming deductions into 1995, consider this strategy. Where possible, pay off interest charges on personal or "consumer" loans. There is no longer any deduction for consumer interest payments, a wide-ranging category that includes charge account and credit card balances, college tuition, car loans, and other personal debts, such as overdue federal and state income taxes.

Example. For someone in the 31 percent bracket, an investment would have to yield a whopping 26 percent before taxes to match the benefit available from just paying off a credit card costing 18 percent.

Tip. If it makes sense to sidestep the deduction restrictions, one way to pay off personal loans is with funds obtained through home equity loans; as explained earlier, the interest on up to $100,000 ($50,000 for married persons filing separate returns) of home equity loans remains 100 percent deductible with no restrictions (other than the purchase of tax-exempt obligations) on how you can use the loan proceeds.

Caution. A different rule applies if you are subject to the alternative minimum tax (Chapter 14). There is no deduction for interest on home equity loans obtained for reasons other than to acquire, construct, or substantially improve first or second homes. (For more information, see "Interest on Home Equity Loans" in Chapter 9.)

Proposed legislation. As this book goes to press in the fall of 1994, Congress is considering proposals to curtail deductions for interest on home mortgages and restore deductions for interest on student loans.

Caution. My advice is to consider carefully the risk that you assume when you put up your residence as collateral for home equity loans used to eliminate personal debts or to finance purchases of cars, boats, or other goodies that you have dreamed of for years. Also shop around: Banks and other lenders charge widely varying rates for these loans.

Partial disallowance of certain deductions for persons with AGIs above a specified amount—$111,800 for tax year 1994. Itemized deductions subject to this partial disallowance include interest on home mortgages but not investment interest, that is, interest on money borrowed to finance investments, such as margin accounts used to buy stocks. The disallowance is 3 percent of the amount by which your AGI exceeds $111,800. (See "Curtailment of Most Itemized Deductions for Individuals with AGIs above a Specified Amount" in Chapter 14.)

State and City Taxes

One widely recommended tactic to build up itemized deductions for tax year 1995 is to pay property taxes and the fourth-quarter installment of 1995 estimated state and local income taxes before 1995 comes to a close, instead of waiting until they become due in 1996. This maneuver saves taxes if you expect to be in a lower federal bracket next year; the deductions are worth more this year.

Tip. If it seems clear that the amount now being withheld will not be enough to take care of your 1995 state and local income taxes, you can ask your employer to withhold more for those levies from your final paychecks for the year or make an estimated payment to cover the shortfall, regardless of whether you usually make estimated payments. (See the section on withholding in Chapter 14.)

Prepayment in 1995 also is advantageous if you expect to be subject in 1996 to the alternative minimum tax (AMT, Chapter 14), which applies only when it produces a higher bill than the tax figured the regular way. For AMT purposes, state and local income taxes, along with property taxes, are among the write-offs that are not deductible.

Caution. Don't try to game the system with an overpayment. An IRS ruling warns that a payment of estimated state income taxes in December of 1995 cannot be deducted for 1995 where a person did not reasonably expect to owe any additional state tax liability at the time he submitted the payment and received a refund for this overpayment in 1996 (Rev. Rul. 82–208).

Partial disallowance of certain deductions for persons with AGIs above a specified amount—$111,800 for tax year 1994. State and city income taxes and property taxes are among the itemized deductions subject to this partial allowance. The disallowance is 3 percent of the amount by which your AGI exceeds $111,800. (See "Curtailment of Most Itemized Deductions for Individuals with AGIs above a Specified Amount" in Chapter 14.)

Miscellaneous Itemized Deductions

By bunching your miscellaneous expenses, you stand a better chance of getting a deduction for them. Most of these expenses are deductible only to the extent that they, in the aggregate, exceed 2 percent of your AGI. (For a detailed discussion of miscellaneous expenses, see Chapter 9.) If your AGI is, say, $50,000, the 2 percent floor wipes out any deduction for the first $1,000 of expenses.

Your goal should be to speed up or postpone payments into a year when you anticipate that they can surpass the 2 percent floor, just as you maneuver payments for medical expenses to overcome their nondeductible floor of 7.5 percent. It is difficult to overcome the 2 percent hurdle. But if you are close to, or already surpass, the barrier, it makes sense to maneuver into 1995 what would otherwise be 1996 payments for write-offs such as tax advice, safe deposit box rentals, IRA custodial fees, union and professional association dues, and other employee expenses.

Prepaid expenses. You have to play the payment game according to the IRS rules. For instance, forget about boosting your 1995 itemized deductions by December prepayments of expenses that span several years. The possibilities include union dues, safe deposit box rentals, and purchases or renewals of multiple-year subscriptions to business or investment publications. Generally, warns the IRS, your 1995 deduction cannot exceed the cost applicable to 1996. The cost attributable to, say, 1997 is not deductible until 1996 and can be claimed only if it surpasses the 2 percent hurdle. Another no-no for 1995 is to prepay for services that will not be performed until 1996—preparation of a return for 1995, for instance.

Example. You pay $600 in December of 1995 for a three-year subscription to an investment newsletter to begin in January of 1996. The cap on your 1995 deduction is $200 (one-third of $600, the portion representing the first year of the subscription, and assuming, of course, that your total miscellaneous deductibles are above the 2 percent stipulation). The ceiling stays at $200 even if the one-year subscription rate is higher. As for the remaining $400, you get a deduction, if at all, of $200 for 1996 and a similar amount for 1997.

There is a further limitation if the subscription is an extension of one that does not expire until, say, the end of March 1996. Your 1995 deduction decreases to just $150—three-fourths of the annual rate of $200, covering the months April through December 1996. You can deduct the $450 balance, if at all, as follows: $200 for 1996, $200 for 1997, and $50 for 1998.

Partial disallowance of certain deductions for persons with AGIs above a specified amount—$111,800 for tax year 1994. Miscellaneous deductions are among the itemized deductions subject to this partial disallowance. The disallowance is 3 percent of the amount by which your AGI exceeds $111,800. (See "Curtailment of Most Itemized Deductions for Individuals with AGIs above a Specified Amount" in Chapter 14.)

Alternative minimum tax. For AMT purposes (see Chapter 14), no miscellaneous deductions are allowed.

Dating and Delivery of Checks

The IRS has some tricky regulations that can upset the plans of individuals who make end-of-year payments to move deductions into tax year 1995 because they are more advantageous this year than next. Contrary to what people scrambling for last-minute breaks prefer to believe, dating your checks "December 31" does not automatically entitle you to claim the expenses for 1995 instead of 1996.

Instead, cautions the IRS, whether a deduction falls into this year or next depends on a check's date of delivery, which is not necessarily the date written on the face of a check. Fortunately, "date of delivery" does not mean that you have to depend on an unpredictable post office to actually deliver your checks by December 31. Just as long as you actually drop the letters in the mailbox by December 31 and they are postmarked by midnight that day, you nail down deductions for this year, even if your checks are not cashed until after the start of next year. That requirement applies to payments of charitable contributions, medical bills, interest expenses, and all other deductions.

Caution.   You garner no deductions for this year by mailing checks that are postdated to prevent cashing until next year.

Tip.   If the feds audit your return, odds are that they are going to look closely at large year-end checks dated December 31 and made out to charities, doctors, state tax collectors, and others. Clearly, you had deductions for this year in mind. So it is advisable to send such checks by certified mail. Request return receipts and staple them to your canceled checks. The receipts will back up your deductions for payments made with checks that may not clear the bank until well beyond the close of the year.

Credit Cards

They come in handy should you be without enough cash to pay for the deductions that you would like to take by December 31. However, the write-off rules can be complex if you pay with plastic.

The rules are helpful when you pay for deductibles like charitable donations, medical services, or business expenses with bank or similar credit cards issued by third parties such as Visa and MasterCard. You get 1995 deductions for the amounts charged. It is immaterial that the credit card bills do not arrive until 1996.

But write-offs may be unavailable for this year when you use charge cards issued by stores and are billed directly. No deductions are allowed until you pay the bills.

Paying bills by telephone or at your bank on the last business day of 1995, which is Friday, December 29? Those payments are deductible in the year your account is debited, a rule that shifts the deduction to 1996, if, as can happen, the bank does not actually debit your account until the next business day.

Tip.   File credit card slips for donations and other deductibles with your tax records to avoid overlooking them at filing time.

There is no deduction for interest charges on credit card loans for personal items. See "Interest Deductions" earlier in this chapter.

TIMING RECEIPT OF INCOME

As noted previously, an important element in your year-end tax planning should be, when feasible, to time the payment of deductible expenses and the receipt of income to get the greatest savings for this year and later. Generally, it is much more difficult to shift income from one year to another than to maneuver deductibles.

The effort, though, can be worthwhile because of the spread between the tax brackets. For tax year 1994 (the most recent year for which information is available as this book goes to press in the summer of 1994), the brackets are 15, 28, 31, 36 and 39.6 percent. (See "What Is Your Real Tax Bracket?" in Chapter 14.)

Tip.   Reducing your income might bring additional benefit by preserving some of your deductions and personal exemptions. As discussed previously, you suffer a partial disallowance of certain itemized deductions to the extent of 3 percent of the amount by which adjusted gross income (AGI) is above a specified amount that is adjusted annually to reflect inflation—$111,800 for tax year 1994. (See "Curtailment of Most Itemized Deductions for Individuals with AGIs above a Specified Amount" in Chapter 14.)

As for dependency exemptions, they start to phase out when AGI surpasses certain levels that are adjusted upward each year for inflation. For tax year 1994, exemptions phase out when AGI is above $111,800 for singles, $167,700 for joint filers, $139,750 for heads of households, and $83,350 for marrieds filing separately. (See Chapter 2.)

Lowering your AGI could also increase allowable deductions for three categories of itemized deductions that are based on AGI: (1) casualty and theft losses (allowable only to the extent such uninsured losses exceed $100 for each casualty or theft, plus 10 percent of AGI—see Chapter 9); (2) medical expenses (deductible only for the amount above 7.5 percent of AGI, discussed earlier in this chapter); and (3) most miscellaneous expenses (allowable just for the portion above 2 percent of AGI, discussed earlier in this chapter).

Moreover, trimming AGI could increase the amounts deductible for contributions to Individual Retirement Accounts (Chapter 10) and losses on rental properties (Chapter 10). On the income side, it could decrease the amount you are taxed on Social Security benefits (Chapter 15).

Earned Income

Employees.   Most employees can do little to control when they report their salaries. According to what are known as the "constructive-receipt" rules for reporting income, you are considered to have received your salary as soon as it is made subject to your control or set aside for you. It is immaterial that you choose not to take it. Therefore, paychecks that arrive in December count as taxable income this year.

Caution.   You are not able to defer income to next year simply by, say, stashing paychecks in a drawer rather than cashing or depositing them, or arranging with your employer to hold them back until after December 31. Those constructive-receipt rules require you to arrange for the deferral before you become entitled to the pay. (For more on constructive receipt, see "When Income Is Reportable" in Chapter 13.)

Self-employeds.   Do you run a business, either full-time or as a sideline to a salaried job? Unlike the typical employee, you have a good deal of flexibility on the year in which to report income from free-lance extra jobs or professional services.

Here are some year-end moves that might help if you expect a significant drop in your top rate for federal and state taxes next year. (See "What Is Your Real Tax Bracket?" in Chapter 14.) That drop could occur because you or your spouse no longer moonlight at a second job, go on maternity leave, are the victim of a corporate cutback, decide to take early retirement, move out of a state with a high tax rate into one with a low rate or without any tax at all, as in the case of a California-to-Texas transfer, or an upcoming marriage or divorce will put you in a lower bracket next year (see "Marriage or Divorce as a Tax Shelter" in Chapter 4.)

To push the receipt of income past New Year's Eve, simply delay the mailing of bills to clients until after December 31, or bill them so late in December that payment this year is unlikely. Don't press clients for payment in this year of money owed to you. Also, pay business expenses this year, rather than deferring payment until next year. Similarly, you can wait until next year to realize profits from the sale of stocks or other investments.

Going the reverse route. Whether you are an employee or are self-employed, do the opposite if you anticipate a significant increase in your top tax rate next year. Maybe you are switching to a job that pays a good deal more, your spouse is returning to work after a jobless period, you are moving out of a state with a low or no tax rate to a state with a high rate, as in the case of a Texas-to-California move, or an upcoming marriage or divorce will put you in a higher bracket next year. Accelerate income from the next year into this year, while you remain in a lower bracket. Delay payments of as many deductibles as possible until next year.

Caution. If you choose to accelerate income or defer deductions, make sure your estimated tax payments and/or withholding cover your additional income tax to avoid estimated tax penalties (Chapter 14).

Investment Income

Usually, you have little flexibility on when to report dividend or interest income. For instance, you have to count as this year's income a dividend check that you receive on December 31 or interest credited to your savings account that day, despite your inability to get to the bank to cash the check or withdraw the interest until January. Never-

theless, there are a number of ways to defer other types of investment income. For example, you can time voluntary, as opposed to required, withdrawals from IRAs (discussed in Chapter 10) and other retirement plans.

To aid in your tax planning, here are some other strategies for you to keep in mind. (For more tax-planning opportunities for investors, see Chapter 10).

United States Savings Bonds. You have several options. One is to declare the interest from U.S. Series E or EE bonds (Es were issued before 1980 and EEs have been issued since 1980) as it builds up each year without cashing in the bonds. Alternatively, you can delay reporting the interest that has accumulated until you cash in the bonds. This deferral break provides you with some valuable leeway in reporting your interest; with careful planning, the deferral can become the equivalent of an exemption from taxes.

Example. You need to redeem some bonds to cover various expenses. Consider whether you want to report the income this year or next when you plan to retire, and your tax bracket is likely to be much lower. Then time your collection trip to the bank accordingly, either before or after December 31.

To illustrate the possible savings, suppose you are now in the 28 percent tax bracket, but will be in the 15 percent bracket next year after you retire. You plan to cash in bonds at that time and use $3,000 of the accumulated interest for a postretirement trip early next year. If you forget the calendar and cash them this year, the IRS takes $840 and you keep $2,160. If, however, you bide your time until after December 31, that tactic trims the tax tab to $450; you keep $2,550. And if your tax bracket plummets to zero, you keep the entire $3,000. (For how to determine your tax bracket, see "What Is Your Real Tax Bracket?" in Chapter 14.)

Trading EE bonds for HH bonds.   What if you need to increase current income but still want to delay a final reckoning with the IRS on the interest from your holdings of U.S. Series E or EE bonds? You are able to do so by combining the deferral option with yet another long-standing break that is especially popular with retired persons—the tax-free swap of those Es or EEs for cash-yielding Series HH bonds.

HH bonds are available in denominations that range from a minimum of $500 to a maximum of $10,000. These bonds pay interest (at an annual rate of 4 percent, as this book goes to press in the summer of 1994) twice a year by Treasury check or by direct deposit to your bank account.

You are liable for current taxes on the money received from the HHs after you acquire them. But you continue to postpone payments of taxes on the accumulated interest on the Es or EEs you traded in until such time as the HHs are cashed, otherwise disposed of, or reach final maturity (HHs have an initial term of 10 years, and are guaranteed to earn interest for 20 years), whichever occurs first. Meanwhile, you use the tax-deferred dollars on the interest earned up to the time of the trade to earn more money in HH interest.

Example.   You trade EEs with a redemption value (the sum of the original price and the accrued interest) of $7,830 for HHs. You get $7,500 in HHs and $330 in cash. You must report the $330 as taxable income in the year of the trade to the extent that you did not report the interest on the EEs you traded.

Note, too, that there is a modest bit of tax relief when the redemption value of the EEs to be swapped for HHs is more than $500, but not enough for the next-larger-size HH. You can add enough cash to purchase an HH of the next-higher $500 multiple. For instance, sticking with the numbers in the example, you can add $170 in cash ($500 minus $330) to obtain $8,000 worth of HHs, thereby deferring taxes on the $330.

At the time of the exchange, the EE interest is stamped on the face of the HHs. There is no limit on the amount of bonds that you can swap without paying taxes on the accumulated interest.

To swap bonds, ask your local bank for Form PD F 3253 (Exchange Subscriptions for United States Savings Bonds of Series HH).

Special rules for EE bonds bought in 1990 and later years.   These rules exempt some individuals from taxes on interest from EEs cashed in to pay educational expenses. The interest-exemption break is for bonds bought after 1989 by persons who are at least 24 years of age at the time of issue and cashed in by them during a year when they pay tuition and fees at colleges and universities for themselves, children, or others for whom they can claim dependency exemptions. You get no break for EEs purchased in the name of a child under the age of 24 or redemption proceeds used to pay charges for room and board. Moreover, the interest exemption begins to phase out when adjusted gross income is above a specified amount that is adjusted annually to reflect inflation. For tax year 1994 (the most recent year for which information is available as this book goes to press), the amount is $61,850 for joint filers and $41,200 for singles and heads of households.

(For more on this special exemption, see "The Kiddie Tax" in Chapter 10.)

Tip.   The phase-out figures are for adjusted gross income when the EEs are redeemed for tuition and fees, not when bought.

Help from the Treasury Department.   Need more detailed information on income, gift, and estate taxes, and other aspects of Savings Bonds? There is an excellent guide you can get free. Write to the Office of Public Affairs, U.S. Savings Bond Division, Treasury Department, Washington, DC 20226. Ask for *Legal Aspects* (Publication SBD-2035).

Treasury bills.   There is an easy way to move some interest income out of this year and into the next. Just switch funds from, say, money market mutual funds or bank accounts, which generate interest that is reportable this year, to Treasury bills with maturity dates beyond December 31. T-bills are available with maturities of three, six, or twelve months.

Your return is the difference between what you pay for the bill, which is sold at a discount from its face value, and the full face value that you receive at maturity. The cash that you get back shortly after you buy the bill is a refund on the purchase price, not income. The discount, or interest, does not count as reportable income until maturity. Moreover, like interest on other U.S. government securities, T-bill interest, though subject to federal taxes, is completely exempt from state or local taxes. That exemption is a particular advantage in high-tax states such as California, Massachusetts, and New York.

Example.   You put $10,000 (the minimum investment) into a one-year T-bill with a quoted discount rate of 8.6 percent. Within a week or so, you receive a check for your discount of $860. When the bill matures, you receive $10,000. Because of the prepayment of interest in the form of a discount, the true yield is not 8.6 percent, but 9.4 percent. What's more, if your state and local taxes run around 10 percent, that 9.4 percent yield is equivalent to a yield of 10.4 percent on a fully taxable investment.

Capital gains and losses.   The rules applicable to tax year 1994 authorize a break for long-term capital gains from sales of stocks and other investments owned more than 12 months—a top rate on such gains of 28 percent, versus as high as 39.6 percent for ordinary income, such as your salary. (See "Capital Gains and Losses" in Chapter 10.)

As for capital losses, they can be fully offset against any capital gains. When losses exceed gains, up to $3,000 of the excess can be offset against ordinary income. You can carry forward any unused loss over $3,000 into the following year and beyond, should that prove necessary.

Caution.   It can be dangerous to your financial health to make decisions to sell some investments and purchase others solely on the basis of tax considerations. You also need to consider the prospects for your present portfolio, your overall financial position and where to stash the proceeds from the assets you unload.

Tip.   To nail down a loss deduction for worthless stock, be prepared to show that the stock is *entirely* worthless. It matters not that the stock is no longer traded on a market and is *practically* worthless for all intents and purposes. The burden is on you, not the IRS, to establish that there is no current liquidating value, as well as no potential value. (See "Losses on Worthless Stocks" in Chapter 10.)

Special rules govern nonbusiness bad debts, such as loans to relatives or friends. When those kinds of loans become worthless, you get to deduct them under the rules for short-term capital losses. (See "Lending Money to a Relative or Friend" in Chapter 9.)

Wash sales.   Be mindful of a limitation when you sell shares to establish a tax loss and want to maintain a position in the same company—no current deduction for the loss unless the repurchase takes place more than 30 days after the sale of the original stock. Of course, the 30-day wait exposes you to an adverse move in the stock price; but in tax avoidance, as in life, there is almost always no free lunch, observes the *Wall Street Journal.* (See "Wash Sale Rule" in Chapter 10.)

Tip.   Forget about violating the wash sale rule if you need to sell a stock you like in order to register a capital gain, something you might want to do if your losses surpass the $3,000 cap on the deduction against ordinary income. When you sell for a *profit,* you are free to immediately reinvest in the same stock.

Stock sales of shares you bought in the same company at different prices and at different times.   Make sure to clearly indicate to your broker which shares of stock you want to sell. Otherwise, you might not reap the most favorable gain or loss when you sell only part of your holdings. To create the biggest loss, sell the shares that you bought for the highest prices. (See "Keep Good Records of Stock Purchases" in Chapter 10.)

Year-end stock gains.   Sell some shares during the last week of December and you probably will not receive payment until early in the following year. This kind of sale often straddles the year end because the New York Stock Exchange and other securities markets generally require five full trading days from the trading date (when you order the sale to be executed) to the settlement date (when you receive the sales proceeds and have to turn over the shares).

Under prior law, you could choose to report the gain from a last-week-in-December sale in the year of the trade date or the year of the settlement date. Now, however, you have no choice. You must report the profit in the year the trade takes place, regardless of when the settlement takes place. To shift the gain from this year, delay the sale until next year.

As for capital losses, the rules are unchanged. Report a loss in the year the trade occurs. (For more on capital gains and losses, see Chapter 10.)

Short sales.   There is a different rule for a "short sale," which is stock exchange jargon for a sale of stock *not* from your own portfolio but of identical stock borrowed from your brokerage firm. Report the transaction in the year that the short sale is closed out by delivery of the shares you own to your broker to cover the sale.

Example.   At the start of this year, you buy 1,000 shares of Krypton for $15 a share. Near the close of the year, the price climbs to $25. Assume, too, that you expect to be in a lower bracket next year, but fear that Krypton will fall in value if you wait to sell until then. To safeguard the $10,000 gain on the Krypton, you unload 1,000 shares at $25 through a short sale and deliver 1,000 shares in the following year. *Result:* You lock in that $10,000 gain, but need not declare the profit until next year. However, you will not share in the gain if the shares you actually own increase in price before you use them to replace the borrowed stock.

Caution. For an investor with a small amount of stock, a short sale might not be worth the effort, after considering commissions.

Reevaluate your investments from a tax standpoint. Do you fall into a lofty combined federal, state, and, perhaps, city tax bracket because you live or work in a high-tax place like California, Massachusetts, or New York? (For how to determine your bracket, see "What Is Your Real Tax Bracket?" in Chapter 14.) If so, it might make sense to switch from fully taxable investments, such as certificates of deposit, to municipal bond funds or other tax-exempt investments. (See "When Tax-Exempt Investments Make Sense" in Chapter 10.)

Home Sales

Eye the calendar carefully if you plan to sell your home and are near age 55. You may get a tax bonus by putting off the sale until after you become 55.

Under-55 sellers are able to postpone taxes on the profit from the sale of a year-round home only if they buy another dwelling that costs at least as much as the sales price of the old one, whereas over-55 sellers have the option to permanently exclude from tax up to $125,000 of the gain without the need to buy a replacement residence. To claim the over-55 break, you have to own and use the property as your principal residence for at least three years out of the five-year period ending on the sale date. (See "Special Breaks for People over 55" in Chapter 3.)

You get the exclusion only once (per couple, not per person). So if you have a well-below-$125,000 profit, you can postpone tax by buying another principal residence and saving the exclusion for a later, more profitable sale.

Do you have an above-$125,000 profit? After you exclude that much, it is possible to postpone tax on the balance of the profit. The law expressly allows you to combine the exclusion and postponement breaks, provided you meet a deadline. Within a period that spans from two years before to two years after the old home's sale date, you can buy another home that costs at least as much as the old one's sales price (after allowing for broker's and attorney's fees and other selling costs) reduced by the $125,000 of excluded gain.

Caution. In the case of married couples, either you or your spouse can be at least 55, but neither of you can have used the exclusion before, such as in a previous marriage.

Tip. A much misunderstood point is that the tax postponement, assuming you qualify, is *mandatory,* not optional. Suppose you want to report a gain because you have investment losses that can offset it. To do so, at least 24 months have to elapse before you can replace the home.

Proposed legislation. As this book goes to press in the summer of 1994, Congress is considering a proposal to index for inflation the once-in-a-lifetime $125,000 exclusion for a gain on the sale of a principal residence.

How to Play Santa and Trim Taxes, Too

For many individuals, a key part of their investment and estate planning is to write year-end checks for gifts to family members. The following reminders will help put your tax planning in perspective for 1995 and beyond.

Unlike charitable contributions, you get no income tax deductions for gifts to individuals. Nevertheless, these gifts can be advantageous because they shift investment income from yourself to family members in lower brackets, as well as reduce the value of your assets subject to estate taxes at your death.

As part of your planning, you need to consider gift taxes when you make sizable lifetime transfers of money or other assets. Fortunately, gift taxes present no problems for most persons. Usually, it is possible to get around these taxes, courtesy of annual exclusions of $10,000 ($20,000 when you are married and your spouse joins in, even if all of the gift comes from your assets) for gifts in any single year to any one person. These annual exclusions permit you to pass along as much as $10,000 (or $20,000) a year to each of as many of your relatives or friends as you like, without payment of gift taxes or using up part of your exemption of $600,000 from gift and estate taxes.

Tip. The law authorizes another way to give away a lot more without incurring any liability for gift taxes—pay someone else's school tuition or medical care. Note, though, that you have to pay the educational institution or medical-care provider *directly*, rather than reimburse the person you want to assist. (See "Unlimited Exclusion for Payments of Educational and Medical Expenses" in the discussion of "Minimizing Gift and Estate Taxes" in Chapter 16.)

Caution. In 1990, Congress considered, but did not enact, changes that would have substantially affected gift and estate planning. The proposed legislation included a provision that would have ended your unlimited annual exclusions of $10,000 and limited you to an annual exclusion of $30,000, with the cap doubling to $60,000 when you are married and your spouse agrees to gift splitting. As this book goes to press in the summer of 1994, budget pressures might cause Congress to resurrect and enact some type of curtailment on annual exclusions. (Gift and estate taxes are covered in Chapter 16.)

Use it or lose it. You are able to take advantage of the exclusions each year, even if you write checks or transfer other assets to the same recipients, but only if you make those gifts by December 31. Miss that deadline and you lose out on your exclusions for that year. For instance, you are not allowed to carry forward any unused portion of exclusions for 1995 to 1996 or any subsequent year.

Caution. If you intend to give by check close to the end of 1995, remind the object of your generosity to deposit your check in sufficient time for it to clear your bank by December 31. The penalty for ignoring this requirement is that the check has to be treated as a gift for 1996 and applied against your exclusion for that year.

Tip. There is an easy, IRS-approved way to steer clear of this pitfall. All you need to do is instruct your bank to certify the check; that instantly takes the funds out of your account.

Kiddie tax. Whenever you make gifts to youngsters, be mindful of tightened rules that drastically curtail your ability to shift income-earning assets to lower-bracket, under-age-14 children. The law still taxes an over-14 son or daughter at his or her, not your, rate on investment income. Now, though, investment earnings above a specified amount received by an under-14 child generally are taxed at your top rate—not, as before, at the child's typically lower rate.

For tax year 1994 (the most recent year for which information is available as this book goes to press in the summer of 1994), the kiddie-tax rules kick in when investment income is above $1,200. There will be an upward annual adjustment of that income amount for 1995 and later years to reflect inflation.

Tip. There remain ways to divert some of an under-14 child's investment income into a lower bracket. Your strategy should be to give assets that postpone taxable income until beyond the child's 14th birthday, when the earnings begin to be taxed at his or her rate.

Example. You have a four-year-old daughter for whom you set up a custodian account that holds gifts of growth stocks or mutual funds that currently pay only modest dividends but are expected to appreciate substantially. After she hits 14, you could unload her stocks; the gain is then taxed at her rate, not yours. (The kiddie-tax rules are covered in Chapter 10.)

Step up in basis for inherited property. Lifetime gifts might be inadvisable for older investors whose holdings include appreciated stocks and other assets that they can leave to their children and other heirs, because the basis of an asset is stepped up to its value at the date of death.

Example. A father paid $20,000 for stock that was worth $200,000 at his death when he left it to his daughter. On a later sale, she benefits from a step up in basis for the stock from $20,000 to $200,000. *Result:* She escapes paying any income taxes on the amount the stock appreciated between the time her father bought it and the time he died. The daughter is taxed only on post-inheritance appreciation. However, any *estate* taxes (Chapter 16) due are figured on the stock's date-of-death value, not the original cost. (For more information on the step up in basis, see "Sale of Inherited Property" in Chapter 10.)

Suppose, instead, that he makes a father-to-daughter lifetime gift of stock that cost him $20,000 and is now valued at $200,000. Unlike inherited property, there is no step up in basis for property that he gave away during his life. In figuring gain on a later sale, the sales price is measured against his original cost of $20,000—in tax jargon, a carryover of basis.

Nevertheless, the gift route shifts the capital gain from the father to the daughter—a maneuver that remains advantageous as long as she is in a lower bracket and, as explained above, the kiddie tax is not applicable because she has attained the age of 14.

Tip. It is unwise to make a gift of property that has gone down in value since you bought it. Rather, you should sell it so you can get the benefit of the tax loss.

Phaseout of dependency exemptions for some high-income persons. Exemptions start to phase out when adjusted gross income exceeds certain amounts that are revised upward annually to reflect inflation. (See Chapter 2.) When the phaseout causes you to lose exemptions, sometimes it becomes beneficial to transfer assets to an older child or an elderly parent or other relative, instead of claiming him or her as a dependent. Then that person would get the benefit of the exemption, as well as the standard deduction (see "Itemizing versus Standard Deduction" earlier in this chapter), or he or she might be able to qualify for a medical deduction that is unavailable to a more affluent person because of the nondeductible 7.5 percent floor (see "Medical Expenses" earlier in this chapter).

Prepare a will or make sure an existing will is up-to-date. When you die without a will (intestate, in legalese), your assets pass in accordance with your state's intestacy laws. The absence of a will often means that your estate will be burdened with unnecessary administrative expenses and taxes.

When you make out a will or update an existing one, also prepare a letter of instructions. This is the legal term for an informal document in which, among other things, you list the location of your important personal papers and assets.

Your heirs need to know what your assets are—Individual Retirement Accounts, 401(k)s (see Chapter 10), and other retirement plans from your employer or your business; insurance policies; bank accounts; mutual funds; brokerage accounts and other holdings like real estate; jewelry or art works—and how to dispose of them. Advance planning can help ensure that your intentions are carried out and that your heirs are not taken advantage of by incompetent or dishonest advisers during a vulnerable time.

(For more on why you should have a will and a letter of instructions, see Chapter 16.)

Make Tax Planning a Year-Round Job

Taxes are by far the biggest item in your household budget, says the Tax Foundation, which keeps tabs on how much of your income is siphoned off by federal, state, and local governments. The latest available figures reveal that the average American spends almost three times as much for government as for food. (For more on Tax Foundation statistics, see "Your Share of the Tax Burden" in Chapter 14.)

That disheartening statistic underscores just how costly a mistake it is to think of federal income taxes as simply a once-a-year affliction caused by the need to grapple with Form 1040. Instead, despite the title of this chapter, what you ought to do is crank taxes into your financial planning throughout the year. You might be pleasantly surprised to discover the scores of tax-saving opportunities that most individuals overlook each year. The savings can add up to thousands of dollars.

Strategy

The first step for effective tax planning is to organize that ever-growing accumulation of records in your desk drawers, closets, and other storage spaces. Also, if you have been remiss, resolve now to reconstruct missing or incomplete records before they become hazy in your mind.

Caution.   Haphazard records can cause you to needlessly lose money to taxes. The better the records you keep, the easier it is to search for—and seize—opportunities, which is what tax planning is all about.

Tip.   When it comes to sorting through financial papers, my advice to clients is to err on the side of caution in deciding which ones to save and which to toss out. To make the chore manageable—and, incidentally, to reduce the likelihood of mistakes—limit yourself to a single category of records at each sitting. For example, tackle all records dealing with investments one evening, insurance another, and so on.

Incidentally, this do-it-yourself undertaking provides valuable side benefits: less-cluttered storage spaces and a clearer picture of your financial affairs.

As part of the organizing task, treat yourself to a nice notebook or computer program. That will make it easier to stick to your resolution and continue to keep careful and complete records throughout the year. Good record keeping is the key to mapping out strategies that you can employ year after year to sidestep, decrease, or postpone the federal indenture—for instance, as discussed earlier, timing the receipt of income and the payment of deductible expenses to your best advantage.

Develop your own system.   Each month, set aside the time to bring your records up-to-date. A good time to do that is when you are reconciling your checkbooks and bank statements. Go through that accumulation of checks, receipts, and whatever else might help you to uncover all your deductions and to determine the correct amounts of income items, such as gains or losses on investments.

Your record-keeping system should be well organized, but it need not be elaborate. You might well be able to make do with those lined sheets that accountants use, on which you enter column headings that reflect your particular tax-deductible spending and income sources.

Under the appropriate worksheet column heading, enter the details for each item. They would include the check number, date, payee, and other information that you think might be helpful later.

What follows are examples of the kinds of questions to ask yourself when you look over receipts and canceled checks: Do you volunteer to help raise money or to perform other chores for religious, educational, or charitable organizations? If you do, remember to keep track of unreimbursed out-of-pocket expenses, such as the cost of transportation, telephone calls, stamps, stationery, and uniforms. These outlays are commonly missed. (See "Volunteer Workers" in Chapter 8.)

Have you made home improvements? They yield no current deductions but are added to your home's cost basis and, therefore, reduce any taxable profit when you eventually sell. Improvements include adding a room or paving a driveway, as opposed to routine repairs or maintenance that adds nothing to the dwelling's value, such as painting or papering a room or replacing a broken windowpane. (See "Keeping Good Records" in Chapter 3.)

To hold down a job, do you pay someone to provide care for your child under age 13, a disabled dependent of any age, or a disabled spouse? You may be entitled to a tax credit for a percentage of the first $2,400 of your expenditures for the care of one qualifying person and the first $4,800 spent for the care of two or more persons. In calculating your credit, be sure to include your payments of

Social Security taxes for care providers. (See Chapter 6.)

The reward for your record-keeping efforts comes at tax time. The annual reckoning will be less time-consuming, whether you do the job yourself or use a paid preparer, as well as less costly if you turn the task over to someone else. (See "Get the Right Help at Tax Time" in Chapter 13.)

Revised withholding.   Actually, your reward might come much sooner in the form of increased take-home pay. Check on whether you should file a revised Form W-4 (Employee's Withholding Allowance Certificate) with your employer, on which you indicate the number of withholding "allowances" (exemptions) that you want to claim. The W-4 allows you to lower the taxes subtracted from your pay when, among other things, you have sizable itemized deductions for contributions, medical expenses and the like, alimony payments, credits for child- and dependent-care expenses, or other adjustments, such as deductible payments to Individual Retirement Accounts. On the W-4's back, a worksheet translates these and certain other expenses into exemptions that can be claimed in addition to the regular exemptions for yourself and your dependents.

Tip.   You need to change your W-4 only if you want to boost your take-home pay because you are entitled to take extra exemptions. You need not do so if you prefer to stay overwithheld until you file and obtain a refund. (See the discussion of withholding in Chapter 14.)

Audits.   Good records are also essential if you are audited. Unlike in a criminal trial, where you are presumed to be innocent until the government establishes your guilt, the burden of proof in a tax dispute usually is on you, not the IRS. (See Chapter 11.)

For example, only a partial deduction was allowed for charitable contributions where the donor neglected to get receipts and the only substantiation was kitchen-wall-calendar notations that, observed a dubious Tax Court, were not made contemporaneously with the contributions and were largely self-serving.

United States Savings Bonds.   The Treasury Department advises owners of United States Savings Bonds to maintain records of serial numbers (including prefix and suffix letters), issue dates (month and year), denominations, names and addresses on the bonds, and Social Security or taxpayer identification numbers of the owners. To help you compile these records, Savings Bonds District Offices have a free form available, *Personal Record of Ownership, United States Savings Bonds.* That list will make it possible for the Treasury to speed up the usual waiting period of at least six weeks for free-of-charge replacement of bonds that are lost, stolen, mutilated, or destroyed. Just make sure to keep that list in a safe place separate from the bonds, such as a safe deposit box.

Use Form PD F 1048 to apply for replacement of lost, stolen, or destroyed bonds, and Form PD 1934 for replacement of mutilated or partially destroyed bonds. Most banks have these forms; if not, the best bet is the nearest Federal Reserve Bank or branch. Send the forms to the Bureau of the Public Debt, Parkersburg, WV 26106-1328.

Educate yourself.   Establishing up-to-date records is the first step toward gaining control over your tax tab. Educating yourself on the current tax opportunities and pitfalls can be an important second step. Ideally, you should be equipped to weigh the tax consequences before you make decisions on whether to invest, borrow, or spend.

In these increasingly tough times, it is more vital than ever that you assume greater responsibility for your financial future. You ought not to rely exclusively on paid advisers to keep on top of tax-law changes or other legislation that might make it necessary to revise your plans. At the very least, you should be knowledgeable enough to raise good questions and evaluate answers when you deal with a professional. The informed client gets the best advice.

On a personal note, I passed a bar exam better than 30 years ago; throughout that time, I have often been called in to help lessen the damage caused clients who blindly relied on faulty advice provided by my fellow lawyers and other professionals.

Those circumstances prompt me to offer this advice: Enroll in adult education courses on taxes, investing, and other aspects of personal finance. They are well worth a modest amount of your time and money.

You can select sessions tailored to your interest from among the offerings available at high schools, community colleges, and YMCAs. The instructors are individuals with hands-on experience—financial planners, attorneys, CPAs, and enrolled agents (EAs). (EAs are people enrolled to practice before the IRS, who are not attorneys or CPAs, but who are former IRS employees or have passed a rigorous examination on taxes administered by the IRS. For more on EAs, see "Get the Right Help at Tax Time" in Chapter 13.)

Done properly, adult education courses deliver a lot of useful information at little cost. For starters, the instructors will alert you to those law changes that I previously mentioned.

Another advantage is that a course provides your best chance to ask questions of a professional at a fraction of what it would otherwise cost to meet that person on a one-to-one basis. Along with the other students, you get the opportunity to discuss the implications of important events in your life— say, the start or end of a marriage (Chapter 4); the purchase or sale of a home (Chapter 3); the receipt of an inheritance or a severance package from an employer; the withdrawal of funds from an IRA, 401(k), Keogh plan, or other retirement arrangement (Chapter 10); a job-related move (Chapter 5); or the start or finish of a business venture, to cite just some of the laundry list of possibilities. Also, you learn money-saving techniques that you can apply yourself or test out on your advisers.

Caution.   The adage that there is no free lunch is particularly apt when it comes to seeking financial advice. You need to be wary of no-charge seminars sponsored by brokerage houses, insurance companies, and the like. Far too often, these outfits use the talks mainly as marketing tools to promote themselves, certain products that generate lucrative commissions, or both.

2 DEPENDENCY EXEMPTIONS

From a 1919 article on income taxes by P. G. Wodehouse:

As I sit in my poverty-stricken home, looking at the place where the piano used to be before I had to sell it to pay my income tax, I find myself in a thoughtful mood. The first agony of the separation from my hard-earned, so to speak, income, is over, and I can see that I was unjust in my opinion of the United States Government. At first, I felt toward the U.S.G. as I would feel toward any perfect stranger who insinuated himself into my home and stood me on my head and went through my pockets. The only difference I could see between the U.S.G. and the ordinary practitioner in a black mask was that the latter occasionally left his victim carfare.

Gosh! I was bitter.

Now, however, after the lapse of weeks, I begin to see the other side. . . . Think how differently the head of the family regards his nearest and dearest in these days of income tax. Many a man who has spent years wondering why on earth he was such a chump as to link his lot with a woman he has disliked from the very moment they stepped out of the Niagara Falls Hotel, and a gang of children whose existence has always seemed superfluous, gratefully revises his views as he starts to fill up the printed form.

His wife may be a nuisance about the home, but she comes out strong when it is a question of married man's exemption. And the children! As the father looks at their grubby faces, and reflects that he is entitled to knock off two hundred bones per child, the austerity of his demeanor softens, and he pats them on the head and talks vaguely about jam for tea at some future and unspecified date. . . .

————————————

High on the taxpayers-the-IRS-will-never-forget list is a Miamian, a recent immigrant from Cuba, who found out from a newspaper that her children were worth $2,450 apiece as exemptions; so she hastened to the closest IRS office, with her two tykes in tow, and asked how quickly her $4,900 would be sent.

For many persons, a key part of their planning is to take maximum advantage of dependency exemptions that lower the amount of income subject to tax. Each exemption reduces your taxable income by $2,450 on a return for 1994 to be filed in 1995. (The amount of the exemption on returns for later years is scheduled to be indexed—that is, adjusted upward to provide relief from inflation, as measured by increases in the Consumer Price Index.) If you contribute to the support of a parent who receives Social Security benefits or a child who is in college, you should be watching the tax rules with particular care. A simple shift in who pays what expense can determine whether you keep or lose an exemption. To help in your year-end planning, here are answers to some of the commonly asked tax questions.

Some General Rules

Q. *How has tax reform changed the rules for dependency exemptions?*

A. For starters, tax reform ended exemptions for individuals (mostly children) who are claimed as dependents on other people's returns. Previously, the law allowed a double benefit: The exemption for, say, a college-going child could be claimed by the student on his or her own return, as well as on the return of the parent or some other family member, such as a grandparent.

Now, though, no exemption for a child on the child's return is allowed when he or she can be claimed on the parent's return. It is immaterial that the parent does not actually claim the child.

Elderly and blind. Tax reform abolished additional exemptions for the elderly and blind. However, elderly and blind persons who are nonitemizers get higher standard deductions. (See "Itemizing versus Standard Deduction" in Chapter 1.)

Phaseout of exemptions for some high-income persons. Deductions for exemptions are phased out (that is, reduced) for persons with adjusted gross incomes (AGIs) above certain levels. The phaseout affects all exemptions that can be claimed on a return, including those for a spouse and dependents. It is one of a number of special provisions designed to take tax benefits away from high-incomers, thereby limiting the windfall that they may reap from lower tax rates.

For tax year 1994, exemptions are phased out when AGI is between:

- $111,800 and $234,300 for singles;
- $167,700 and $290,200 for joint filers;
- $139,750 and $262,250 for heads of households; and
- $83,850 and $145,100 for marrieds filing separately.

All high-incomers completely lose the benefit of their exemptions when their AGI exceeds the top figures. These figures are scheduled to be adjusted upward for tax year 1995 to reflect inflation.

More paperwork. Think again if you thought tax "simplification" (the quotation marks are mine) would make it easier to file tax returns. The law now says you must report Social Security numbers for children and other persons one year or older who are claimed by you as dependents.

Failing to report the numbers or listing incorrect ones could subject you to a penalty of as much as $50, as well as the possible disallowance of an exemption. Even worse, you might be audited.

Need to start the paperwork for issuing numbers? Contact your local Social Security office (the IRS does not issue numbers) for Form SS-5. Social Security wants you to return the SS-5 with proof of your child's age, identity, and citizenship.

Obtaining a number usually takes about two weeks. If your dependent will not have a number by the time you are ready to file your return, ask Social Security to give you a Form SSA-5028 (Receipt for Application for a Social Security Number).

If you or your dependent does not receive a number by the time you are ready to file, you should file your return and write "Applied for" in the space provided for the number. If you have a Form SSA-5028, attach a copy to your return.

Why do the feds insist that Form 1040s list children's Social Security numbers? To curtail an abuse uncovered by IRS spot checks of returns. The probe revealed that a sizable and steadily swelling number of taxpayers, mainly parents, played games at filing time. Some claimed exemptions for children they never had or had deserted and no longer supported; others, who were divorced or lived apart and filed separate returns, claimed the same child twice, once for mom and again for dad.

Disappearing dependents. It was in 1987 that a law first required taxpayers to report Social Security numbers for virtually all dependents. The following year, notes *Money* magazine, "7 million children vanished from the nation's tax returns, representing a 9 percent drop in the 76.7 million dependents claimed on the previous year's returns. Some 11,627 families reported a decrease of seven or more dependents. People [had been] listing their dogs, cats and birds as dependents."

Aliens. You can claim exemptions for aliens (persons who are not U.S. citizens) only if they are residents of the U.S., Canada, or Mexico. It makes no difference that you pass the support test (discussed below) because you provide over half of their total support for the year in issue.

For instance, Malgozata Camilo of New York was unable to claim her parents and brother, all three of whom were Polish citizens visiting in the U.S. on six-month visas. The Tax Court agreed with the IRS that the visit was insufficient to establish that the trio had become U.S. residents.

Q. *What tests must I pass to deduct a dependency exemption?*

A. Tax reform leaves the basic rule for exemptions largely unchanged. The key requirements continue to be the "support" and "gross income" tests.

To claim *anyone* as a dependent, the general rule is that you must furnish over half of his or her total support for the year in question.

The over-half-support rule is subject to two important exceptions. The first exception, discussed later in this section, imposes a less stringent, over–10 percent requirement for someone who claims a dependent under a multiple support agreement. Under the second exception, there are special rules for children of divorced or separated parents. These rules are discussed in the next section of this chapter.

Caution. Even if you satisfy the support test, you lose the exemption for a dependent who receives gross income in excess of $2,450 (the limit in the case of a return for tax year 1994, a figure that is scheduled to be adjusted upward for 1995 to reflect inflation). There is, however, no ceiling on the gross income received by your child, provided he or she (1) will not reach the age of 19 this year, or (2) is a full-time student for at least five months (not necessarily consecutive) and will not reach the age of 24 this year. Put another way, the income ceiling *does* apply to a son or daughter who is a full-time student and 24 or older.

Q. *How strictly does the IRS define "student"?*

A. Your son or daughter must be enrolled on a full-time basis for a minimum of five months in the calendar year in an educational institution with a regular faculty, an established curriculum, and an organized student body.

Tip. The IRS authorizes no exceptions to the five-month rule, but your child need not be enrolled for five consecutive months or even five full months. Also, less-than-five months' attendance is okay, as long as he or she registers and attends classes for a total of five months.

Example. Katherine Holzgraefe registers for a full-time course load in January, with classes to run from February through May. With that time span, Katherine satisfies the time requirement, provided she completes the semester.

Suppose, though, that Katherine attends school exclusively at night. She fails to qualify as a full-timer. However, it is okay for her to include some night attendance as part of a full-time course of study.

Caution. Just how inflexible the agency is on the time stipulation is underscored by an IRS ruling that was sought by the parents of a 19-year-old student who dropped out of school after four months following hospitalization for a nervous breakdown. She was unable to return to school for the remainder of the year. The verdict: No exception from the five-month requirement, regardless of the daughter's reason for leaving school. Consequently, the parents could not claim an exemption for her.

Q. *What may I consider as "support" in figuring whether I furnished over half the support for a dependent so I can claim an exemption?*

A. Among the items the IRS counts as support of a dependent are food, shelter, clothing, medical and dental care (including premiums on health insurance), education, church donations, transportation, recreation, and similar necessities. Support does *not* include scholarships (see the later discussion in this chapter, "College Students as Dependents"), Medicare receipts, life insurance on the dependent's life (no matter who pays), or the value of services you or a member of your family provide without cost to a dependent (for instance, housecleaning or nursing care), among other things.

An IRS ruling says that a parent can count as support what the parent lays out for the wedding of a daughter (where the daughter does not file a joint return with her husband; see the later discussion in this chapter, "College Students as Dependents") in computing whether she is a dependent of the parent for that year. Qualifying outlays include payments by the parent for her wedding dress and accessories, a reception, flowers, and church rental (Rev. Rul. 76–184).

Q. *In computing whether I contribute over half the support for a dependent living with me, how do I figure the value of his or her lodging?*

A. Include as support the "fair rental value" of the lodgings you provide, which should take into consideration a reasonable allowance for the use of the furnishings, telephone, electricity, and so on. "Fair rental value" is the amount you could reasonably expect to receive from a stranger for the same lodgings, not the rent or real estate taxes, mortgage interest, etc., paid by you that are attributable to the space involved.

Tip. Count the value of a year-round room you maintain for a child away at college and the food you provide while he or she is home during a college recess.

Q. *We pay our housekeeper a salary and also provide her board and lodging. Aside from what we pay her, she has no other income. Are we able to take her as a dependent?*

A. You fail to satisfy the main requirements to claim someone who is not your relative by blood or marriage: that you furnish over half her support and she is a member of your household for the entire year. What you provide is payment for her work, not support.

Q. *Do I get the full exemption for a child born late in the year?*

A. Yes, even if your child won't be on the scene until December 31 or lives only momentarily. No exemption, though, for a stillborn child (Rev. Rul. 73–156) or, apparently, for an aborted child (Rev. Rul. 85–118).

Q. *Do I get the full exemption for a spouse who died early this year?*

A. Yes. You do not lose out on the exemption, even if he or she died on January 1. But you cannot claim an exemption for a deceased spouse if you remarry during the year.

Q. *How long do I need to keep records in case the IRS questions my dependency exemptions?*

A. Until the statute of limitations runs out for an IRS audit. Generally, that is three years from the filing deadline—for example, April 1998, in the case of a return for 1994. (For more on how long to keep records, see Chapter 11.)

PARENTS AS DEPENDENTS

Q. *I contribute most of my mother's support. But she earns small sums from occasional jobs, and those earnings are likely to be $2,400 somewhere around November or December. Should I ask her to work fewer hours for the rest of the year?*

A. Absolutely. Once her gross income (count total salary *before* any deductions for Social Security, etc.) hits $2,450 (in the case of a return for 1994, a figure that is scheduled to be adjusted upward for 1995 to reflect inflation), you forfeit your exemption for her. You will come out way ahead if you supplement your support contributions, rather than letting her earn $2,450. For instance, if you fall into a 34 percent federal and state tax bracket, another $50 earned by her will cause you to lose an exemption of $2,450, thereby increasing your taxable income by $2,450 and boosting your tax bill by $833.

Q. *My mother refuses to stop working. But she has told her boss to hold her December check until next year. Can I still claim her?*

A. This last-minute maneuver will not salvage your exemption. Like most taxpayers, your mother reports her income to the IRS on a cash basis: This means, as a general rule, that she does not have to declare her salary until she receives the check. But you still flunk the gross income test because the IRS's "constructive-receipt" rule requires her to count as income for this year the check that was held back on her instructions.

Caution. That constructive-receipt rule means she also has to count a dividend check received on December 31, or interest credited to her savings account that day, even if she is unable to get to the bank to cash the check or withdraw the interest until January. So you need to watch that gross income ceiling closely for a parent or any other dependent. Check now on whether he or she will receive some year-end investment income. (For more on constructive receipt, see "When Income Is Reportable" in Chapter 13.)

Q. *How do the support rules work when a parent or other dependent receives tax-free items, such as Social Security (see Chapter 15 for a discussion of Social Security) or welfare benefits, life insurance proceeds, inheritances, and gifts?*

A. Any money spent by, say, your father for his own support counts as part of his total support, even though the money comes from Social Security or some other untaxed source that need not be counted toward the ceiling on income ($2,450 on a return for 1994) that can be received by a dependent parent. But you have to count only money actually *spent* by him for his support, rather than money *available* for his support. So when your dependent receives tax-free income, it may be necessary to figure things very carefully to make sure you furnish more than half of the dependent's total support before the year closes.

Tip. Be certain, for example, that any money you contribute is allocated to things that the IRS counts as support. Your dependent should, where possible, either save his money or earmark it for nonsupport items.

Q. *My father lived with me for five months and will stay with my sister for the remaining seven months. Does this mean she will automatically get the exemption for him?*

A. Not necessarily. The answer depends on which one of you furnishes over half his *total* support for the *entire* year, not which one furnishes the lodgings. For instance, your payments for his hospitalization for several weeks could easily top the cost of her outlays for the period when he resides with her. In other words, it's *dollars,* not *time,* that counts.

Q. *What's the tax situation if the total cost of support for my mother amounts to $13,000, and she receives and spends $6,700 from Social Security and other tax-free sources, while I contribute $6,300?*

A. You cannot claim her as a dependent because you failed to contribute over half of her total support. But it's possible to tip the support scales back in your favor. If she were to save more than $400 of her tax-free money, or spend more than $400 on nonsupport items like life insurance or gifts to her grandchildren, you would wind up contributing over half her total support and thus could claim the dependency exemption.

Caution. To protect your deduction, you should check the situation well before year end. If, for example, you discover that she'll fall $100 short of the $400, you can still save the exemption by spending another $100 on support items yourself.

Tip. There is a last-minute maneuver that can help if your mother's support contributions appear to be outpacing yours as the year nears its end. In calculating what you spend on support during the year, include the cost of items that you provide by December 31, even though you hold off paying for them until next year—say, a Christmas gift that you pay for with a check sent in January.

Q. *My parents live apart from me; their total support outlay comes to $14,000—$7,000 each. The breakdown of the $14,000 is that I contribute $4,600 and the remaining $9,400 comes from their Social Security benefits and other tax-free sources. How should I handle my support payments?*

A. With that set of numbers, make sure to designate one of your parents as the specific recipient of your payments. Otherwise, you lose out on any exemption for either parent because you flunk the support test, which requires you to contribute more than half of their total support for the year.

Caution. It makes no difference that your $4,600 contribution is well over half the $7,000 support for either one of your parents. The snag in this situation is that an IRS auditor, in the absence of a designation by you of one parent as a specific recipient, routinely splits your contribution between your father and mother and will assume you provided $2,300 for each. Under that approach, you are not entitled to an exemption for either parent, unless you are able to overcome the IRS assumption with after-the-fact proof that your $4,600 was actually on one of them alone.

By the time the IRS gets around to an audit of your return, of course, it is usually impossible to show such proof. But there is an easy way to avoid the problem. An IRS ruling allows you to make a before-the-fact designation of your contributions as intended specifically for the support of, say, your mother. Usually, you do not have to prove that the designated amount was spent only on her.

Odds are, though, that an IRS examiner will refuse to go along with a verbal agreement between you and your mother that is not backed up by some written memo or other record that you prepared at the time you made your support contribution. So if you're paying only for your mother's support, be sure to note this in your checks to her.

Tip. Whenever possible, you should make the payments directly for things that the IRS counts as her support, such as clothing and medical bills. Remind her to have the bills made out to you; then pay them by check and keep the bills and checks as proof.

Q. *I won't be able to claim my father as a dependent because he already received reportable income of over $2,450 (the limit in the case of a return for tax year 1994, a figure that is scheduled to be adjusted upward for 1995 to reflect inflation). Does this also mean I won't be able to include my payments for his medical expenses under my medical deductions?*

A. Not necessarily. Even though you are ineligible to take an exemption for a dependent because you flunk the gross income test, you still can include your payments for a dependent's medical expenses among your own, so long as you pass the support test. (For more information, see Chapter 7, "Medical Expenses.")

Q. *I know that there is an exemption to the "over half the support" rule for families that share support of a dependent, such as a parent or grandparent. Suppose some of my brothers or sisters join me in contributing over half the support of our parent during the year, but no one of us contributes over half the support. I've been told that they can designate me to claim the exemption, so long as I contribute over 10 percent of our parent's total support for the year, and they waive* *their claim to the exemption by signing IRS Form 2120 (Multiple Support Declaration), which must accompany my return. How should I handle support payments for a parent that I intend to claim under such a multiple support agreement?*

A. Let's assume, for instance, that you and your two sisters each put up one-third of the support for your father. (Remember, under a multiple support agreement, each of you must contribute at least 10 percent, but no one contributor can give more than 50 percent of your parent's support.) Each year, you decide who gets to claim a dependency exemption for him. This year, it's your turn. But if one sister were actually to furnish over half his support, she would have to claim him, even if you fall into a higher bracket and could save more with his exemption. During the year in which you wish to qualify under a multiple support agreement, your tax strategy calls for making sure that neither sister furnishes over half his support.

Caution. As discussed at the start of this chapter, there is a phaseout of exemptions for some high-income persons. Exemptions start to phase out when adjusted gross income surpasses certain levels that are adjusted upward each year for inflation. Therefore, in a multiple support agreement, it could prove inadvisable for your father to be claimed by you if you are subject to the phaseout and your sisters are not.

Are there substantial medical costs for your father? You might need to consider the rules for medical expenses if you are claiming your father under a multiple support agreement. You can include your payments for his medical expenses among your own, even if you do not furnish over half his support. But if your sisters reimburse you for part of the medical-expense payments, you get no deduction for the reimbursed payments. Moreover, your sisters cannot deduct anything, as they did not pay the medical bills. *Result:* No one gets the deduction. To avoid losing medical deductions, pay all the medical expenses yourself and have your sisters pay for other expenses. For example, they can earmark their support payments for his food or clothing.

Tip. Ordinarily, the tax saving is greater when the exemption for your father is claimed by you, assuming you are in a higher bracket than your sisters. But this may not be so when a substantial part of the support payments are for medical care. It can prove more advantageous for a lower-bracket sister to take care of the medical bills and claim the exemption for your father, while you direct your support to nondeductible items. Why? Because such expenses must amount to 7.5 percent of a person's adjusted gross income before they provide any tax advantage. Consequently, your sister's lower income entitles her to a greater medical-expense deduction. (For more on the 7.5 percent rule, see "Computing the Deduction" in Chapter 7.)

Q. *I get several tax breaks because my father came to live with me after his retirement. Besides claiming a dependency exemption for him and including my payments for his medical expenses under my medical deductions, I cut my tax bills some more by filing as a "head of household" instead of as a single person. However, I have to be away frequently, and he's had a prolonged illness. So I plan to place him in a nursing home. I've been told that I'll still be entitled to the dependency exemption and* *can deduct my payments for his nursing care. But can I continue to take advantage of the lower head-of-household rates?*

A. Yes. Generally, the household of which you claim to be a head must be your own home, but there's an important exception. Parents can be supported in a household outside your home and still qualify you for this tax break. The IRS says you also continue to qualify as head of household when you support a parent in a nursing home.

Caution. You can't use the head-of-household rates if you claim your father under a multiple support agreement.

Nor can the head-of-household exception for a dependent parent be availed of when the dependent is someone other than a parent. For instance, Lillie B. McDonald, a single parent, disqualified herself from filing as a head of household after she followed a physician's advice to set up a separate home for her mentally ill son to help him become self-sufficient. His home was just a mile from hers; Lillie frequently spent time at his place and he sometimes resided at hers. Nevertheless, an unsympathetic IRS and Tax Court held that she could not be excused from the requirement that her home be her son's main home.

Q. *My mother lived with me all of last year, but I cannot claim her as a dependent because she has a small pension of $3,000 a year. Can I file as head of household? I pay all of the expenses on the house, and I am not married.*

A. No. Your mother must qualify as your dependent for you to claim head-of-household status.

COLLEGE STUDENTS AS DEPENDENTS

Q. *My son attends college full-time and plans to work part-time. What about my exemption for him?*

A. Claim him if you provide over half his support and he will not reach the age of 24 this year, no matter how much income he receives. But if he is 24 or older, there is a ceiling on the amount of income he can receive and still be your dependent—$2,450 for tax year 1994, a figure that is scheduled to be adjusted upward for 1995 to reflect inflation.

Tip. Be mindful of the cap if your son's income will not significantly top $2,450. It can be more advantageous for him to stop working before his income reaches that figure, thereby allowing you to keep the exemption.

Q. *What if some relative other than a parent picks up the tab for a youngster's college expenses and he works part-time?*

A. Only a parent is excused from the gross income test. For example, even though a grandmother furnishes over half the total support for her college-going grandson under the age of 24, she cannot take an exemption for him if his income tops $2,450 (a figure that is scheduled to be adjusted upward for 1995 to provide relief from inflation).

Q. *Will I lose a dependency exemption if my youngster receives a scholarship, GI Bill benefits, or a college loan?*

A. It depends on whether the benefits from such programs are counted and actually used for his or her support. For example, a scholarship that is received by a son or daughter who attends college full-time does not count in calculating total support, even though it is used for education and other support purposes. But GI Bill benefits and the proceeds from the student's own college loans count as support that he or she provides. On the other hand, any education loans *you* take out count as support that you provide.

Tip. Frequently, the difference between your own and your offspring's contributions to his or her total support is small. In some cases, it may be possible to swing the balance in your favor by urging your youngster either to save money or to earmark his expenditures for nonsupport items.

Example. The total support outlay will come to $14,000 for the year for your college student son, who is under the age of 24. You kick in $7,000 and he will provide $7,000 through a student loan. Or suppose you contributed $7,000 until his graduation in June, and his earnings for the rest of the year will total $7,000. You cannot take an exemption for him in either case, because you will fail to furnish over half his support. But if he puts some of his earnings in the bank this year or spends some on nonsupport items, you wind up furnishing over half of his support for the year and are entitled to the exemption.

Q. *I provide far more than half the support for my college-student daughter, who is under the age of 24. But she plans to marry another student at Christmas (1995). Am I entitled to claim her as a dependent if they file jointly for 1995?*

A. Yes. Many parents overlook this tax break. Ordinarily, you cannot claim someone who files jointly with another person. But the IRS says you can still claim her if she and her husband are not required to file a re-

turn and do so merely to get a refund of withheld taxes.

Tip. When parents provide over half the support for a daughter who marries during 1995, they may even save enough on their taxes, by claiming her as a dependent, to make it worthwhile for them to ask the couple to skip a joint return and file separately.

EXEMPTIONS FOR CHILDREN OF DIVORCED OR SEPARATED PARENTS

The previously discussed over-half-support test does not apply to three categories of parents who claim exemptions for children who did not live with them during the year in question. A different set of rules comes into play when the parents are (1) divorced, (2) legally separated, or (3) though they do not divorce or legally separate, living apart at all times during the last six months of the calendar year.

General Rules on Custody of Exemptions

These no-questions-asked rules automatically award the exemption for a child (or children, as the case may be) to the parent who has custody for the greater part of the year. In most cases, that is the mother. It does not matter whether she actually provides over half of the support.

How custody is determined. According to the filing instructions for Form 1040, custody is usually determined by the terms of the most

recent decree of divorce or separate maintenance, or a later custody decree. If there is no
decree, use the written separation agreement.

What if neither a decree nor agreement
establishes custody? Then the parent who
has the physical custody of the child for the
greater part of the year is considered to have
custody of the child.

The filing instructions also tell you to follow this approach when the validity of a
decree or agreement awarding custody is uncertain because of legal proceedings pending
on the last day of the calendar year.

Suppose the parents are divorced or separated during the year and had joint custody
of the child before the separation. Then the
parent who has custody for the greater part
of the rest of that year is considered to have
custody of the child for the year.

Exceptions to general rules. Assume there
is no decree or written agreement that gives
custody to the mother and the exemption to
the father. (If there is, the exemption belongs
to the father, not the mother.) In that case,
assuming the mother with custody is willing
to, she can sign IRS Form 8332 (Release of
Claim to Exemption for Child of Divorced
or Separated Parents). By doing so, she gives
the exemption to the father without custody.

To qualify for the exemption, the father
must submit Form 8332 with his Form 1040
or Form 1040A. His paperwork is just beginning. He has to list on his return the number
of dependent children who do not live with
him because of divorce or separation, along
with their Social Security numbers.

Tip. It might be worthwhile for the father
to negotiate for the exemption. That could
save more tax for him if his bracket is higher
than the mother's.

She has two options. The first is to sign
Part I of Form 8332 and release the exemption for only the year in question. The second is to sign Part II and release it for either
(1) a specified number of years or (2) all future years. In most cases, the first option
makes more sense for her. A one-year-at-a-
time release mandates an annual renegotia-
tion, a tactic that might help ensure that
child support payments are timely made.

**Exception for pre-1985 divorce or legal
separation.** There is another important exception for parents who divorced or legally
separated *before* 1985. The exception applies where there is a divorce or separation
decree or a written agreement signed before
the start of 1985 that gives custody to the
mother and the exemptions to the father. In
that case, the exemptions belong to him for,
say, 1995, provided he contributed at least
$600 toward the support of *each* child. A fa-
ther who is entitled to an exemption because
of a pre-1985 agreement must so indicate by
checking a box on Form 1040 or 1040A.

Caution. The rules for divorced or legally
separated parents apply only if they pass a
two-step test: (1) Their child received more
than 50 percent of his or her total support
from them during 1995 and (2) spent more
than half of the year with one or both of
them. Otherwise, the exemption can go
only to the person who furnishes more than
50 percent of the child's support or qualifies for the exemption under a multiple
support agreement.

Example. Neither the father nor the
mother is entitled to the exemption when a
doting grandparent, whether out of generosity or necessity, provided more than 50 per-

cent of the child's support or had custody of the child for more than six months.

Medical Expenses

At one time, a child's medical expenses paid by a divorced or separated parent were deductible by that parent only if the parent could claim an exemption for the child. Now, though, it no longer matters which parent gets the exemption. If either parent claims an exemption for a child under the rules for divorced or separated parents, each parent can deduct those medical expenses that he or she pays for the child. (For medical-expense deductions, see Chapter 7.)

Help from the IRS

Need more information than the instructions that come with Form 1040? Get IRS Publication 504, *Tax Information for Divorced or Separated Individuals*. For a free copy, call 1-800-TAX-FORM (allow at least 10 work days for mailing) or stop by the IRS office serving your area to obtain one immediately. Many libraries also have copies of this and other IRS tax guides. IRS Publication 910, *Guide to Free Tax Services,* provides a complete list of booklets and explains what each one covers. (For a discussion of IRS publications, see "Get the Right Help at Tax Time" in Chapter 13.)

Tip. Don't rely absolutely on IRS advice, whether it is information that employees give to telephone or walk-in inquiries or instructions that the agency prints in its publications. Mistakes in instructions or advice are inevitable, and the IRS is not bound by them.

DEPENDENCY EXEMPTIONS FOR LIVE-IN LOVERS

The inimitable Charles Osgood on POSSLQs
There's nothing I wouldn't do
If you would be my POSSLQ.
You live with me, and I with you,
And you would be my POSSLQ.
I'll be your friend and so much more,
That's what a POSSLQ is for.

And everything we will confess,
Yes, even to the IRS.
Someday, on what we both may earn,
Perhaps we'll file a joint return.
You'll share my pad, my taxes joint,
You'll share my life, up to a point!
And that you'll be so glad to do,
Because you'll be my POSSLQ.

Come live with me and be my love,
And share the pain and pleasure of
The blessed continuity
Official POSSLQ-ity
And I will whisper in your ear
That word you so love to hear.
And love will stay forever new,
If you will be my POSSLQ.

— THE OSGOOD FILE
CBS Inc.
All Rights Reserved

As part of the general easing of sexual attitudes in most sections of the country, there has been a sharp increase in the number of unmarried couples who live together. So common has the practice of sharing bed and board without a marriage license become that the Census Bureau coined the acronym POSSLQ (pronounced "possell cue"; it is governmentalese for "persons of opposite sex sharing living quarters") in the late 1970s. According to the most recent Census

Bureau survey, there are about 3 million such households, way more than in 1970, when the feds began to keep count.

These housing statistics also interest another federal agency, the Internal Revenue Service. Why? Because the Revenue Service suspects many POSSLQs improperly claim dependency exemptions for their live-in lovers.

The tax laws allow you to take an exemption for an unrelated person who is a member of your household for the entire year. A special rule applies, though, to an exemption for an unmarried mate. There is no exemption when your relationship violates local law. What the feds have in mind are those rarely enforced state statutes that absolutely prohibit sexual relations between unmarried individuals.

The local-law rule has been upheld by several courts that threw out exemptions claimed for mistresses. These courts agreed with the IRS that the local taboos were automatically violated when an unmarried couple lived together. It made no difference that their relationship was ignored by the local authorities.

Consider, for example, the unusual case of the man who neglected to check the validity of his divorce decree before he moved in with what he thought was his "second wife" and her mother. At tax time, he found out the expensive way about the local-law rule when he claimed his second wife and her mother. The tax gatherers threw out his claim for the supposed wife, but allowed his "mother-in-law," presumably because his relationship with her did not violate any local laws.

Another local-law dispute involved Sheral Martin, a trucker who moved around a lot. It all began, as Sheral later told the Tax Court, when he met Addie Lou one night at the Trailways Terminal in Tallahassee, Florida. They hit if off well immediately; after a couple of days, Sheral "took up housekeeping" with Addie Lou and her seven-year-old daughter, Nancy Sue.

Their arrangement continued for a little over a year. The three of them stayed in Florida for several months, moved to Illinois for about two months, and then went to Alabama, where they lived with Addie Lou's mother. But this last arrangement "became a little awkward" and all three returned to Florida. Shortly after that, Sheral and Addie Lou had a falling out, and he sent her and Nancy Sue back to her home in Georgia.

When filing time rolled around, Sheral claimed Addie Lou and Nancy Sue. However, the IRS objected to any deduction for Addie Lou, as did the Tax Court. For one thing, the judge pointed out that Sheral's relationship with Addie Lou during the time they lived together violated the laws of at least three states—Florida, Illinois, and Alabama. Their relationship "was on a day-to-day basis without the sanctity even approaching that of a common law marriage." Nevertheless, Sheral emerged a partial winner. An understanding IRS raised no question about the legal niceties of his relationship with little Nancy Sue; the agency went along with a deduction for her.

Nevett Ensminger also ran afoul of the local-law rule when he decided to maintain a young lady in his North Carolina home. Nevett supported her, and she had no income of her own; that, he reasoned, not only entitled him to an exemption for her, but to file as a head of household.

Unfortunately for Nevett, both the Tax Court and an appeals court concluded that the IRS properly used the higher rates for single persons to recalculate his taxes. His case went down the drain because, at the time of his arrangement, North Carolina still enforced a statute that made it illegal for an unmarried couple to live together. Therefore, Nevett forfeited an exemption for his companion and was ineligible to use the lower rates for head of household.

As is usually the case, the trial rules favored the government. It was not burdened with the troublesome chores of proving that Nevett and his bosom buddy bedded down together. Nevett was obliged to show that the relationship stayed strictly platonic; he failed to do so, and the dispute was laid to rest.

Fortunately, the courts do not always side with the IRS. In a dispute involving Missouri law, an understanding judge came to the rescue of Mary Margaret Shackelford, an unmarried woman who resided with and supported a male acquaintance. Their arrangement was that she turned over her paycheck to him for the payment of bills, groceries, and so forth. At no time did they hold themselves out as married persons.

The snag was a Missouri statute that makes it a misdemeanor when a "person, married or unmarried, is guilty of open, gross lewdness or lascivious behavior, or of any open and notorious act of public indecency." Moreover, Missouri law does not, in any event, recognize a common law marriage. Their relationship never attained even the level of a common law marriage; therefore, any lesser relationship, argued the IRS, made Mary Margaret ineligible to claim her companion.

The judge disagreed. An unmarried man and woman setting up housekeeping did not transgress Missouri's taboos. Taking note of today's moral climate, the judge pointed out that merely living together is not open, gross lewdness, or lascivious behavior. Nor does it openly outrage decency or injure public morals.

Caution. This case is not the final word. In those states that have kept statutes that forbid sexual relations between unmarried persons, the IRS can continue to disallow exemptions for girlfriends (or boyfriends, depending on who foots the bills). Residents of those states who opt to claim such exemptions should be prepared to face court battles. Presumably, however, the IRS would not balk at an extra exemption if the parties reside within a state that is without a statute that punishes unmarrieds who share the same quarters.

Tip. Is there a way to sidestep these restrictions legitimately? Perhaps, if you are willing to adopt your girlfriend (or boyfriend), or she adopts you. Once the adoption takes place and you become related, the local-law rule no longer stops you from claiming her. Instead, you come under an entirely different set of rules for relatives; it makes no difference that your affair still violates local law or that the local authorities successfully press charges against you.

Caution. Be aware that the IRS lays down some strict rules when it comes to taking an exemption for your new daughter or new mother, depending on who did the adopting. To claim her, you must pass a two-step test. First, you must contribute over half of her support for the entire year. Second, there is a ceiling on the amount of reportable income that a dependent can receive—$2,450 in the case of a return for tax year 1994 (the most recent year for which information is available as this book goes to press). What if you get past the first hurdle, but your new relative has income in excess of the limit? In that case, the rules twist and turn. If you did the adopting, you are able to take advantage of a special break for parents and can still claim that new daughter, even though her income tops the limit, provided she is under 19 or is a full-time student for at least five months and will not reach the age of 24 this year.

A final thought, at a time of unending discussion of further tax reform and simplification. Although Congress clamped down on dependency deductions for mistresses, it has yet to get around to other kinds of sinners.

In fact, our lawmakers remain unwilling to close a loophole that, among other things, authorizes a tax break for persons who commit incest—a failure to take corrective action that may reflect Congressional self-interest or that is simply unwitting. In any case, the IRS has no authority to question an exemption claimed by a parent for a child, or vice versa, merely because their relationship is incestuous. Nor, for that matter, can the IRS challenge an exemption claimed by a parent for a child merely because the child is illegitimate.

3 SELLING YOUR HOME

BASIC RULES

You get more than just the chance to be your own landlord when you come up with the down payment for a house or apartment. You get an asset with built-in economic advantages and tax breaks.

Home ownership is not just one of the better hedges against the ravages of long-term inflation, given the appreciation of residences in most parts of the country. It is also one of the best tax shelters that remain available after the changes introduced by tax reform. Besides itemized deductions for mortgage interest and real estate taxes to help alleviate the anguish at Form 1040 time (see Chapter 1), a profit on the sale of your house or condominium qualifies for special tax breaks that allow you to postpone or even escape taxes.

At any age, you can defer taxes on the gain from the sale of a "principal residence," which is legalese for a year-round home, as opposed to a vacation retreat or property for which you charge rent.

For a complete deferral of taxes, you must buy another dwelling that costs at least as much as the sales price of the old one. Generally, you have from two years before to two years after the sale date of your old home to buy an existing replacement or build a new one and move into the new residence. (If the second home costs less than the first, only the portion of the profits you invest in the second home is tax deferred.) The postponed profits will be taxed when you sell the second house, unless you again reinvest the proceeds in a home.

Another break becomes available if either you or your spouse is 55 or over when you finally sell. You completely escape taxes on up to the first $125,000 of profit (including deferred gain from the prior sale of a home or homes), provided you own and use the property as your principal residence for at least three years out of the five-year period ending on the sale date.

Those breaks, however, may become traps that snare a good part of your profit unless you make sure to qualify under the deferral or over-55 rules or some of the other ways available to reduce the tax gobble to a nibble. What follows are some reminders on how to capitalize on tax-saving opportunities and to avoid pitfalls.

Proposed legislation. As this book goes to press in the fall of 1994, Congress is considering a proposal to index for inflation the once-in-a-lifetime $125,000 exclusion for a gain on the sale of a principal residence.

POSTPONING THE TAX ON PROFIT FROM SALE

Whether you are under or over age 55, you can put off paying any capital gains tax on a profit from the sale of your home, provided you acquire another residence (it can also be a cooperative apartment or condominium) that costs more than what you received for your old one. But to qualify under the "rollover" rule, you must do so within a set period of time. The time limit (discussed in the next section of this chapter) is generous, generally 24 months.

If you have a tax-deferred gain on a former home because you acquire a replacement home that you then sell, you are still entitled to postpone taxes on the entire profit so long as you buy a higher-priced home and occupy it within the deadlines imposed by the IRS.

Caution. The tax is merely deferred, *not* eliminated. The deferral ends if you (1) eventually replace your old home with a less expensive one that does not soak up the entire gain or (2) move into an apartment and become a renter. You then have to settle with the IRS for the taxes due on the gain from the sale of your home *plus* any deferred gain from the sale of previously owned homes. (If you own the house when you die, your heirs are excused from income taxes on the profit, thanks to a "step up" in basis, which is the figure from which gain is measured, for the dwelling to its date-of-death value. See "Sale of Inherited Property" in Chapter 10.)

Tip. You can increase the cost of your replacement, thereby cutting your taxable gain, by adding the cost of improvements made to the replacement within two years of the sale of your old home. (See the discussion of improvement later in this chapter under "Keeping Good Records.")

Example. You bought a house some years ago for $100,000, added improvements of $20,000, and sell it today (when you're still under 55) for $190,000. Your profit is $70,000. You then buy and move into a $140,000 condominium within 24 months after the sale. You pay tax now on $50,000 of your profit—the difference between the $190,000 sales price and the $140,000 replacement price. The remaining $20,000 of your profit stays tax deferred, at least until you sell your replacement residence.

But if you move from your $190,000 house to a much less expensive dwelling (for example, to a $120,000 condominium) or a rented apartment, you pay tax now on your entire profit of $70,000. How you calculate the tax on the gain is explained in the discussion of the over-55 rules later in this chapter.

Tip. The IRS bestows a handy gift on newlyweds who both own homes, sell them, and buy a new one when they marry. Both can take advantage of the postponement break when each invests more than the sales price in one new residence that they hold jointly (Rev. Rul. 75–238). The IRS also says this break is available on the sale of a jointly owned home when a couple splits up and then purchases separate homes. Each new home must cost at least half the value of the old one (Rev. Rul. 74–250).

Caution.   Assuming you acquire a replacement home and qualify for the deferral, the law *requires* you to defer taxes on the gain. You do *not* have the option to count the gain as reportable income. That is something you might want to do when, for instance, the gain can be offset by investment losses that are not otherwise currently deductible because of the ceiling of $3,000 in any one year on the amount of net capital losses that can be deducted from "ordinary income," such as salaries or other compensation. (See "Capital Gains and Losses" in Chapter 10.) The gain counts as reportable income only if you delay the purchase of a replacement home until after the end of the replacement period, that is, at least two years after the sale date.

Second Sale during Replacement Period

To qualify for the postponement of tax on the entire gain from the sale of your old home, all that you need to do is buy or build a costlier replacement within a period (discussed in the next section of this chapter) that spans from two years before to two years after the sale date. Moreover, as a general rule, the law imposes absolutely no limit whatever on the number of times that you can take advantage of the postponement rule.

Caution.   Beware of a potential complication if you plan to sell a home and have sold another one within the past two years. Generally, you are able to defer the tax on the gain from only *one* home sale within a two-year period. When there is more than one sale and

replacement during the two-year period, the *last* home purchased is considered the replacement home for the first one sold.

Exception to the general rule for a job-related move.   As the law now stands, there is just one reprieve: The general rule does not apply when a second sale becomes necessary because you switch job locations and qualify for a deduction for moving expenses (the key requirement being that the new job location adds at least 50 miles to your commute; for a discussion of moving expenses, see Chapter 5). When that is the script, the law permits you to postpone the tax on the gain from the second sale.

Example.   In March 1992, Lawrence Talbot realized a profit of $50,000 from the sale of Home 1 for $150,000. That same month, he paid $225,000 for Home 2, thereby enabling him to postpone the tax on the profit of $50,000. His adjusted basis for Home 2 is $175,000 (cost of $225,000 minus postponed profit of $50,000). In February 1994, Lawrence sells Home 2 for $240,000 and buys Home 3 for $250,000.

What gums things up is that he sells Home 2 within two years after his sale of Home 1. Because of his inattention to timing, Lawrence has to treat the profit from the sale of Home 1 as having been reinvested in Home 3, *not* Home 2, the intermediate residence. So there is no deferral of tax on the gain from the sale of Home 2. This holds true even though Lawrence purchases Home 3 within two years of the sale of Home 2. *Result:* For tax year 1994, he winds up with a reportable gain of $15,000 from the sale of Home 2 (sales price of $240,000 minus cost of $225,000). Home 3's adjusted basis becomes $200,000 (cost of $250,000 minus deferred gain of $50,000 from Home 1's sale).

Strategy. The hitch is that Lawrence sells Home 2 too soon. Assume instead that he delays its sale until April 1994, that is, more than two years after Home 1's sale. *Revised result:* He gets to postpone the tax on the gain from Home 2's sale. Home 3's adjusted basis becomes $185,000 (cost of $250,000 minus deferred gains of $50,000 and $15,000 from the sales of Homes 1 and 2).

Proposed legislation. As this book goes to press in the fall of 1994, there is bipartisan Congressional support for a rules simplification to abolish this tax trap by ending the job-related-move requirement for a second sale within the two-year period after the first sale.

DEADLINES FOR BUYING OR BUILDING

You do not qualify for the postponement break merely because you reinvest the proceeds in another home of equal or greater cost. You must buy or build within a set period of time. This holds true even though an illness or unavoidable construction delays gum up your plans. You have from two years before to two years after the sale date of your old home to buy an existing replacement or build a new one and move into the new dwelling.

The location of the replacement residence does not matter. It can even be in a foreign country.

The deadlines are suspended in certain cases for members of the armed forces on extended active duty after the sale of the old residence and for persons employed abroad.

You are eligible for the postponement break only if you physically occupy your new home within the required time. You flunk the occupancy test if you merely move furniture or other personal belongings into that new home without actually occupying it.

The IRS is unyielding when the deadline is not met. This was underscored in the following situations where the taxpayers lost:

1. A close relative of the taxpayer moved in within the replacement period, but the taxpayer did not actually move in until shortly thereafter.
2. The taxpayer spent the proceeds from the sale of his old home on a guest house, which he built and occupied within the required time, and a main house, which wasn't completed and occupied within the required time. Only the cost of the guest house counted as reinvestment funds.
3. Completion of a replacement residence was delayed because of a fire.
4. The taxpayer wanted to construct a seaside house and first had to build a seawall that was stalled for almost a year until a state agency's stop order halting work on the seawall was held void.

Proposed legislation. As this book goes to press in the summer of 1994, Congress is considering a special relief provision that would suspend the usual two-year deadline, that is, authorize additional time for homesellers who have substantial deposits frozen in bankrupt or insolvent financial institutions. The proposed change would authorize a suspension for up to five years for such homesellers.

Special Breaks for People over 55

All is not necessarily lost, however, if the replacement break does not defer the entire tax on your gain. Yet another relief provision becomes available if you sell after you reach age 55. For one time only, you can "exclude" (a term that means you pay no taxes) up to $125,000 of gain. That $125,000 figure can include deferred gains from prior home sales.

This break stays available even if you buy a less costly replacement or if you do not buy another one at all and become a renter. If your profit is above $125,000, you are liable for taxes on the amount above $125,000.

Proposed legislation. As this book goes to press in the summer of 1994, Congress is considering several changes in the once-in-a-lifetime $125,000 exclusion for a gain on the sale of a principal residence, the most significant of which would index for inflation the $125,000 cap on the exclusion. Moreover, the exclusion would become applicable to farmhouses plus as much as 160 acres adjacent to the house. And the special exclusion for a home seller who is older than age 55 and disabled (discussed later in this section) would apply to a home seller who becomes disabled before age 55.

Tip. The over-55 exclusion adds flexibility to your financial planning. For instance, the exclusion is a real boon if you are an "empty nester"—someone whose children have moved out and left you with a house that is too big and too expensive to maintain. You can sell your dwelling for a sizable gain, switch to smaller quarters and the lower maintenance expenses that go along with it,

and channel the inflation-swelled profit, undiminished by taxes, into a business venture or into a retirement fund to supplement Social Security benefits, instead of being compelled to acquire another home or pay a tax on the profit.

But what if you expect to dispose of your dwelling for a gain of more than $125,000, a profit not uncommon today? In many cases, taxes still can be sidestepped by combining the exclusion and deferral provisions.

Example. You sell for $315,000 (after allowing for a real estate agent's commission and other selling costs) and realize a net profit of $265,000. The exclusion will allow you to escape taxes on the first $125,000 of profit. Moreover, you can postpone taxes on the remaining $140,000 of your profit if you buy a new home that costs at least $190,000. Why $190,000? Because that is the difference between the $315,000 that you unload your home for and the $125,000 of excluded gain. That $140,000 stays tax deferred, at least until you sell your new home and replace it with a lower-priced one.

If the price of the new place is under $190,000 but over $50,000, the currently taxed part of your $140,000 profit is the difference between $190,000 and the cost of the new home. For instance, say you spend $175,000 for a replacement. The IRS gets to exact its share of $15,000 ($190,000 minus $175,000), but you can still defer any reckoning with the IRS on the $125,000 ($140,000 minus $15,000) balance.

If the cost of the new home is less than $50,000, the entire $140,000 of taxable profit is taxed currently. Under the rules applicable to tax year 1994, there is a top rate of 28 percent for long-term capital gains.

Basis of Replacement Home

You must subtract the deferred (but not the excluded) gain on the sale of your old home from the cost of your replacement home for purposes of determining its basis (the figure from which gain or loss is measured) on a later sale, thereby increasing whatever gain you reap.

Example.   As in the illustration above, you sell for $315,000 and realize a profit of $265,000, of which you exclude $125,000. Your deferred gain is $140,000. You buy a $200,000 replacement. Its basis is $60,000 ($200,000 minus the deferred profit of $140,000). Subsequently, you sell the second home for $230,000 and do not acquire a replacement. You are taxed on a profit of $170,000 ($230,000 minus $60,000), the combined deferral of $140,000 from the sale of the first residence and $30,000 from the second one. For how to determine the basis of a home, see "Keeping Good Records" later in this section.

Tip.   A special rule applies if you own the home when you die. Your heirs escape income taxes on the profit, courtesy of a step up in basis for the dwelling to its date-of-death value. (See "Sale of Inherited Property" in Chapter 10.)

One-Time Election

You are allowed only one crack at this once-in-a-lifetime bonanza for homeowners. That limitation deserves careful consideration before using the exclusion, if you have a gain from a sale that is substantially under $125,000 and you still have years of potential house changes ahead.

Taking part of the exclusion is the same as taking it all. Suppose, for instance, that you exclude $20,000 of profit. You forfeit forever the opportunity to use the remaining $105,000 of your exclusion to shelter a subsequent profit that may be far more than $20,000. So should you take it or let it ride? Saving it for later means that you must pay taxes now on any gain you do not roll over because you buy a less expensive home or do not buy one at all. But going the exclusion route now also means you must pay taxes on all of your gain when you sell subsequently, unless you buy another replacement home. The decision on whether to use the exclusion now or squirrel it away for later is a difficult one to make; you may need to check with a tax pro.

Age, Ownership, and Use Rules

There are some other strings attached to the exclusion. You have to own and use the property as your principal residence for at least three years out of the five-year period ending on the sale date.

Caution.   The sale date must be after the date on which your 55th birthday falls, not just after the start of the year you reach 55. However, you become 55 a day early for sale purposes. Say you were born on December 12; you turn 55 on December 11, the way the IRS keeps count.

Tip.   The law does not require you to postpone signing the sales contract until after your birthday. What controls whether you are eligible for the exclusion is the date of the closing, not the signing of the contract. Legally, the sale does not take place until the transfer of title at closing. So if someone makes you an offer that you cannot refuse, you do not disqualify yourself for the exclusion by signing the contract in advance of your birthday, provided you reach age 55 by the date of the closing.

Ownership and use. In calculating whether you satisfy the requirement that the residence be owner-occupied for at least three out of the five years just before the sale, you cannot count as part of those three years the time you spent in a previous home (or homes) on which the gain was tax deferred. Those three years, though, need not be consecutive; they can be off and on for a total of three full years.

Tip. Short temporary absences for vacations or other seasonable absences count as periods of owner use. This is so even if you rent your home out during those periods of absence.

According to an IRS ruling, the ownership and use tests are figured *separately.* Under this pro-taxpayer approach, the exclusion is available when, for example, an apartment dweller buys his apartment after the building goes condominium and he moves elsewhere before he sells the apartment. The law does not require him to own and use the dwelling *simultaneously* for at least three years. For exclusion purposes, the period of apartment use and condominium ownership need not involve the identical period of years (Rev. Rul. 80–172).

Another IRS ruling tightens the eligibility rules slightly for a married couple who own their home jointly and file a joint tax return for the year of sale. Previously, they quali-

fied for the exclusion when only one spouse satisfied the age test and only the other spouse satisfied the ownership and use tests. Now, however, *one* spouse must meet *all three* requirements (Ruling 8352023).

Example. Arlene, who is under 55, weds Bernie, who is over 55. She then switches the title to a dwelling in which she has lived for five-plus years from her name to the names of the two of them, as joint owners. The couple intend to sell the residence for a substantial profit and take advantage of the exclusion.

No gift, though, for these newlyweds from the IRS. The exclusion is theirs, the agency says, only if they delay the sale until after Bernie has lived in the home for three years. As of now, Arlene's report card shows a Pass for ownership and use and a Fail for age, while Bernie's grades are P for age and F for ownership and use.

Tip. Arlene and Bernie do not have to wait three years to qualify for the deferral break. At any age, the couple can defer tax on their profit if they purchase a replacement that costs at least as much as the sale price of their home.

Special Rule for Someone Who Is Disabled

There is an exception to the requirement that the home be used for three out of five years in the case of a seller who becomes physically or mentally incapable of self-care (that is, disabled). The use test is met if the seller uses the home for at least one year and during any of the remainder of the five years becomes disabled and has to live in a nursing home or other facility for disabled individuals. Put another way, up to two of the three years can be spent in a nursing home without losing the exclusion.

For exclusion purposes, *disabled* has its own definition. It means a seller with physical or mental disabilities that prevent him from dressing or feeding himself or tending to personal hygiene without the help of another or who needs constant attention to prevent him from injuring himself or others.

Converting Residence to Rental Property

Rent out your home without forfeiting your $125,000 exclusion.   As noted in the previous discussion of a disabled person, the three-out-of-five requirement does not mean that you must live in your home on the sale date. Actually, up to two years can elapse between the time you move out and the sale takes place.

Tip.   This frequently overlooked provision allows you to derive a greater benefit from the $125,000 exclusion if you decide against a sale now because you anticipate additional appreciation and are willing to take your chances on being a landlord.

Example.   You could sell now for $200,000 and realize a gain of $95,000 that is erased by the exclusion of $125,000. Instead, you move out and become a landlord for an under-two-year period. Then you unload the home for $215,000 and reap a gain of $110,000 (without taking basis-lowering depreciation into account). Because your profit remains below $125,000, the exclusion eliminates the entire tax on the transaction. Such attention to timing, notes *Money* magazine, "will keep money in your pocket and out of

the IRS's till, which is, after all, what tax planning is all about."

Tip.   As long as you sell within two years after moving out from a dwelling that was your principal residence for the three years before the move, you can avail yourself of the exclusion to eliminate taxes on a profit of as much as $125,000. It makes no difference that a portion, or even most, of the appreciation occurs during the rental period or that some of the gain is attributable to rental-period depreciation lowering the basis of property.

Caution.   Make sure the rental period does not exceed two years. Otherwise the home ceases to be your residence for three out of the past five years. *Result:* You flunk the owner-occupied test and forfeit the exclusion.

Married Couples

For exclusion purposes, the IRS treats married couples as a unit. There is only one exclusion of $125,000 for a married couple; the tax break does not apply to each spouse. Moreover, once they use the exclusion, that's it.

There are additional complications when a couple weds late in life after one spouse has used the exclusion during a previous marriage. For as long as they remain hitched, the other spouse loses his or her right to the exclusion.

Tip.   Be particularly mindful of this rule if you are considering marriage and it will not be the first time around for you or your mate-to-be.

Example.   Before their marriage ended, Stan and Samantha sold their home and claimed the exclusion. She plans to wed Walter, who has never used the exclusion, and move into his home. With that scenario, Walter can use the exclusion only if he sells his residence *before* the wedding. As soon as they marry, Walter becomes ineligible for the exclusion because Samantha already used hers.

In tax jargon, Samantha's prior use "taints" her for life and that taint gums things up for Walter. But that restriction lasts only while he is wed to her. The exclusion that Walter surrendered because of his marriage may be regained by him if he sheds Samantha or she dies.

Two exclusions for mates-to-be. Before-marriage sales similarly make sense for two people who own homes that have substantially appreciated and have yet to use their exclusions. Selling both homes prior to their wedding entitles them to combined exclusions of as much as $250,000, as opposed to a single exclusion of no more than $125,000 on one of the after-marriage sales.

Special relief provision. The exclusion is available for a widow (or widower) who does not meet the ownership and use tests for the sale of a home that she inherits from her late husband, who had met those tests.

Suppose that Jane is age 56. She wed John in 1992 and he died in 1993. John left Jane the home that they lived in, which had been his residence since 1984. Jane, who has not remarried, sells the home in 1994. Neither one had previously used the exclusion. Since John had met the ownership and use requirements on the date Jane sold the property, she is eligible for the exclusion.

Loophole for Nonmarrieds

As much as $250,000 can be tax-free on the sale of a residence owned jointly by individuals who are not husband and wife—for example, a parent and child, a brother and sister, or an untainted, unmarried couple sharing quarters without a marriage certificate. As long as each unmarried joint owner passes the age, ownership, and use tests, each one gets to exclude up to $125,000 of his or her share of the profit. But when one is under 55 and the other over 55, only the older owner is eligible for the break (Ruling 8942008).

Sale Must Be of Entire Interest

An IRS ruling cautions that the exclusion is available only when a person disposes of his or her *entire* interest in the dwelling. But the ruling also authorizes use of the exclusion by someone who owns less than the entire interest in the property.

The ruling uses the example of a woman who is over 55 and whose residence for many years is a home in which she owns only the right to live in for life, a limited interest that is known as a "life estate." A sale of her life estate meets the requirements for the exclusion, as she is disposing of her entire interest (Rev. Rul. 84–43).

An earlier IRS ruling is bad news for elderly homeowners who want to cash in on the increased value of their homes, but not move out of them. The IRS prohibits use of the exclusion by a person who sells his residence while retaining the right to live in it for the rest of his life. Here, a woman plans to sell her dwelling under an agreement that entitles her to rent-free possession of the property until her death. No exclusion, says the

IRS; the sale is only of a partial interest, not her entire interest (Ruling 8029088).

Tip. A more common arrangement would be one where a person sells his residence but agrees with the purchaser that he will remain in possession for some period of time under a lease arrangement. Although the IRS has not ruled on this question, it has informally indicated that the exclusion would probably be available if the lease called for payment of the fair rental value.

KEEPING GOOD RECORDS

When you are in the midst of remodeling or improving your home, the last thing on your mind is the possibility that you may someday sell it and have to reckon with the IRS. But unless you keep adequate records of those improvements, you will have a tough time proving your profit or loss if and when that day arrives.

A home sale could cause those relentless IRS computers to select your return for an audit. In the event that the IRS challenges your postponement break or over-55 exclusion, the audit will be less traumatic and less expensive if you have kept good records. Those records should include what you originally paid for your home, plus settlement or closing costs, such as title insurance and legal fees, as well as what you later shell out for improvements, as opposed to repairs.

Improvements versus Repairs

The IRS distinguishes between repairs and improvements. Repairs and improvements are both nondeductible personal expenses. But unlike repairs, improvements are added to your home's basis—the figure used to determine gain or loss on a sale of the property. Therefore, improvements ultimately reduce any profit.

The IRS says expenditures qualify as improvements only if they "add to the value of your home, considerably prolong its useful life or adapt it to new uses." Some examples of outlays that pass muster as improvements: putting a recreation room in an unfinished basement, adding another bathroom or bedroom, putting up a fence, putting in new plumbing or wiring, putting on a new roof, and paving a driveway. Do not, however, count the value of your own labor.

As for repairs, the feds forbid their inclusion in the cost of your dwelling. Repairs merely "maintain your home in good condition." They do not add to its value or prolong its life. Some examples of expenses that are classified as repairs: repainting your house inside or outside, fixing your gutters or floors, mending leaks or plastering, and replacing broken windowpanes.

Tip. Often there are no clear-cut answers on whether particular items are repairs or improvements. Each situation depends on its own facts—and that can be to your advantage.

Example. An IRS examiner may agree with you that a major repair, such as extensive patching of a roof, qualifies as an improvement. Perhaps what proves convincing is the sizable amount of money that you have spent.

Tip. Sometimes it pays to defer repairs and have them done later on as part of an extensive remodeling or restoration project. That way, the cost of some items that would ordinarily count as repairs, such as painting rooms, can be included in the cost of the larger job and be added to the cost of your home.

Condominiums and cooperative apartments. There is an often-overlooked break for owners of co-ops and condos. Typically, the cost includes more than just what is spent for improvements within your *own* apartment. Owners should count their share of maintenance charges or special assessments that are spent on improvements for the benefit of *all* apartments. Common examples of basis-increasing improvements are putting in a new heating system, installing permanent storm windows, or replacing the roof.

Caution. No addition to basis for an assessment used to cover a shortfall in regular assessments—perhaps because some of the owners are delinquent in paying those assessments.

Energy Credit Adjustment

Count on more paperwork if you were one of the many individuals who previously claimed energy-saving tax credits. You need to keep track of what you spent before 1986 for energy credits. At one time, the law authorized a tax credit of up to $300 (15 percent of the first $2,000 spent) for part of what you spent on installing insulation, storm windows, and certain other items to make your home more energy efficient. There was another credit of up to $4,000 (40 percent of the first $10,000 spent) if you installed equipment that produces renewable energy from such sources as the sun and wind. Both tax breaks went off the books at the close of 1985. Nevertheless, they remain one of your record-keeping chores. The law requires you to keep track of what you claimed before 1986 for energy credits. Why? Because the cost of your home must be reduced by credits for what you spent on energy-saving items that increased the tax basis of your home.

IRS Audits

Figuring your profit or loss on the sale. Whether you are under or over age 55 when you sell your dwelling, the net sales price (the price after allowing for broker's and attorney's fees and other costs) can be offset by your previous outlays (what you originally paid for your home plus subsequent improvements). But without adequate records, you can, at best, rely only on estimates. Not surprisingly, when IRS agents uncover unsupported estimates that help cut taxes, their usual reaction is to disallow or reduce them.

Win some, lose some. More than one home seller has learned the expensive way about the importance of good records. Consider, for instance, what happened in a dispute that pitted the IRS against Marietta Cenedella, who kept scant records of how much she spent on her home in the preinflation 1950s, when a dollar was still worth 80 cents.

Marietta sold her home for $23,000, which was $10,000 more than she had paid for it. Still, Marietta thought it unnecessary to declare any gain. The way she saw things, no taxes were due on her gain because it was entirely wiped out by extensive property improvements. By her estimate, those improvements must have run to more than $10,000, as she had increased her mortgage by $11,000, mostly to pay for them.

Unfortunately for Marietta, a skeptical IRS agent lowered the cost of her improvements by enough to arrive at a profit of $6,000. That prompted an outraged Marietta to try her luck with the Tax Court, where she gained almost a complete victory. Although the judge was unwilling to entirely accept her version of how she used the mortgage borrowings, he concluded that close to $9,000 went for improvements and cut her profit to about $1,000, on which she owed taxes and interest.

Poor record keeping also meant extra taxes for Roger Bayly. Back in 1964, Roger bought a modest dwelling in Glen Burnie, Maryland, for $11,000. By his estimates, he plowed $21,000 into major improvements over a 12-year period, adding two bedrooms and a family room with a fireplace and cathedral ceiling, along with wall-to-wall carpeting and hardwood floors in all three rooms. So when Roger sold his home in 1976 for $38,000, he subtracted total costs of $32,000 and declared a capital gain of $6,000.

But the IRS challenged those figures. Because Roger's records were incomplete, the agency refused to allow more than $7,000 for improvement outlays, put the total cost of the home at $18,000, and billed him for taxes on a gain of $20,000—more than three times the amount that he reported.

Roger took his case to the Tax Court. But the court's decision "bore heavily" against him because Roger lacked documentation. The court determined that he had improvement costs of $16,000 and a gain of $11,000—well below what the IRS claimed were the correct figures, but considerably more than what the figures might have been had he kept proper records.

Detailing spending. These cases have a clear moral: Go through your accumulation of invoices, contracts, and checks at the time the work is done or, if you have been remiss, resolve to do the job now. Make a running record of all home improvements: Prepare a worksheet showing the original cost of your home and improvements made since its purchase; leave space for those that you are likely to make in later years. Keep the sheet with your tax records. Then each year, when filing time rolls around, it will remind you to list the type and cost of improvements made during the year and to retain the bills, canceled checks, and whatever else might help substantiate your figures. (For more on keeping records, see "Make Tax Planning a Year-Round Job" in Chapter 1.)

A word to the wise. Retain these records even if you sell your home and are able to defer the gain because you acquire a costlier one. The law requires you to subtract the deferred gain on the sale of your old home from the cost of your replacement home to determine its basis on a later sale, thereby increasing whatever gain you reap.

Example. Gerald and Gail Robinson realize a $60,000 profit on a $240,000 sale and buy a $320,000 residence. The basis of their new residence is $260,000 ($320,000 minus $60,000). Subsequently, Gerald and Gail sell the second home (when they are still under age 55) for $400,000 and do not acquire a replacement. They are liable for taxes on a profit of $140,000 ($400,000 minus $260,000), the combined gain of $60,000 from the sale of the first dwelling and $80,000 from the second one.

When it is safe to deep-six records. Just how long do the Robinsons need to keep their records after they no longer are able to take advantage of the postponement break and must settle with the IRS? Unfortunately, there is no flat cutoff. But the couple should retain those records at least until the expiration of the statute of limitations (the limited period of time after which the feds are no longer able to come knocking) for an audit or for the Robinsons to file a refund claim, should they find an error after filing. In most cases, the deadline for an audit or a refund claim is three years from the mid-April filing due date—for example, April 1998, in the case of a return for tax year 1994. (For more on how long to keep records, see Chapter 11.)

Once the three-year period runs out, it is usually safe for you to dispose of your supporting records. An important exception: when individuals fail to report a home sale on IRS Form 2119 (Sale of Your Home), which should accompany Form 1040. In such cases, the three-year statute of limitations starts to run only *after* they notify the IRS of their profit.

Tip. You may not use expenses of purchasing a home, such as legal fees or title costs, that you have deducted as moving expenses (no longer deductible as moving expenses, starting with returns for tax year 1994) to increase the cost basis of the home for purposes of determining gain on a subsequent sale. (For more on moving expenses, see the discussion in Chapter 5.)

SALES AT A LOSS

Ordinarily, you get no deductions for a loss on the sale of your home. You may, however, be able to deduct part of your loss if, before selling, you have used your home for business or have rented it out.

You get no write-off even though you must sell because, for instance, you move to take a new job at a new location or your employer shifts you to a new location. If your employer reimburses you for the loss, you cannot offset the loss against the reimbursement. They are separate transactions. The loss stays nondeductible, and you have to report the reimbursement as income. Nor can the loss be used to increase the basis of your new home.

The loss is similarly nondeductible if you sell because a doctor recommends an immediate move for medical reasons.

Proposed legislation. As this book goes to press in the summer of 1994, Congress is considering a proposal to allow a loss on the sale of a principal residence to offset a taxable gain on the future sale of another principal residence.

HOME USED PARTLY FOR BUSINESS OR RENTAL

The tax rules on the sale of a home become rather complex in the case of a two-family home or when part of the property is used for business or investment reasons. Suppose, for instance, you used one room as an office or you rented it out. The law requires you to treat the sale as if you sold two pieces of property—one a residence and the other a business. You must make separate calculations for the residence profit and the business profit.

Let's assume you set aside one-fourth of your home as an office and claim office-at-home deductions for depreciation, utilities, and other expenses associated with the business use of your residence. You have to allocate one-fourth of the home's original cost and its selling price to the business sale. That's easy enough.

But then things become more complicated. To figure the profit on the office part of your home, you must increase the original office cost by the cost of the improvements allocable to the office. Next, you have to subtract the office depreciation you claimed in previous tax years. Then, to arrive at your profit, you need to subtract your adjusted cost from the net selling price allocable to the office. There is no deferral or $125,000 exclusion break for the tax on that profit. It becomes due in the year of sale.

However, you may still be able to postpone the tax on your residence profit. And since only three-fourths of your selling price is allocable to the residence part of your old home, only that three-fourths needs to be reinvested in your new home to qualify you for the tax deferral. You do not have to reinvest the one-fourth of the selling price allocable to the office part of your old home.

But another complication arises if you use part of your new home as an office. Then you must treat the purchase as if you were buying two pieces of property—one a residence and the other a business. Only the cost allocable to the residence part of your new home counts for reinvestment purposes. You lose out on the tax postponement to the extent the proceeds from the sale of the residence part of your old home are invested in the business part of your new home.

Discontinuance of Business Use Before Sale

Despite these rules, it remains possible for some homeowners to have a home office, yet defer or exclude the entire gain. This is because of the way the IRS determines whether it is necessary to allocate the old home's cost and sale price between its business and residential parts. The IRS limits its inquiry to how you use the property *at the time of sale*—an approach that allows you to avoid an allocation and continue to be entitled to defer or exclude the entire profit. Under this approach, all that you have to do is switch from business use to personal use of the office and thereby become ineligible to take an office-at-home deduction for the year in which you sell your home.

Caution. If you plan to take advantage of the over-55 exclusion, you must disqualify yourself for the office-at-home write-off at least three years before the sale date.

Tip. A prerequisite for an office-at-home deduction is that you use the room exclusively for work. To show that you ceased to do so, it should be sufficient, for example, if you place Fluffy's litter box in the room, unless you are in the cat business.

This maneuver is blessed by, surprisingly, the IRS itself. Revenue Ruling 82–26 includes the example of Harold Bottner, a schoolteacher who took work-at-home depreciation deductions for an office in his residence where he graded papers and prepared assignments. Harold took such write-offs through 1975. After that, he could not take a deduction because of a law change. The revised rules allow office-at-home deductions only if, among other things, the home is his principal place of business and he uses the office regularly and exclusively for work (Code Section 280A).

It was immaterial that he continued to use part of his home for business reasons at the time of sale. Because Harold did not qualify for the home-office deduction, he did not have to make an allocation between business and residential areas and remained entitled to defer or exclude the entire gain.

Revenue Ruling 82–26 also uses the example of a home sale by Dr. Serdakowska who, right up to the time of sale, uses part of her residence regularly and exclusively to see patients. Because the doctor qualifies for home-office deductions at the time of sale, she can defer or exclude gain only to the extent that it is allocable to the residential part of her property. The profit allocable to the medical office is taxed in the year of sale; it need not be reinvested in a replacement dwelling (Rev. Rul. 82–26).

Tip. The two examples in Revenue Ruling 82–26 deal only with the postponement or exclusion of tax on the profit, not with the reduction of basis caused by previously claimed depreciation. Both the teacher and the doctor must reduce the basis of their homes by allowable depreciation, even if not actually claimed.

Sale for a Loss

Ordinarily, the loss is nondeductible. Here, it is advantageous if you must make separate calculations for the residence loss and the office loss. The residence loss stays nondeductible; the office loss, however, is deductible.

THE "PRINCIPAL RESIDENCE" REQUIREMENT

To qualify for the postponement break or the over-55 exclusion, both the home you sell and the one you acquire to replace it must be used by you as your residence or, if you have more than one residence, as your "principal residence."

Example. You own and live in a house in town and also own beach property that you use in the summer months. The town property is your principal residence; the beach property is not. Say, instead, that you live in another home for which you pay rent and also own beach property. The rented home is your principal residence; the beach property is not.

What Is a Principal Residence?

The postponement break and the over-55 exclusion are not limited to the sale and purchase of a single-family home. Your principal residence can also be a cooperative or condominium apartment, a trailer home, or anything else that provides all the amenities of a home. It can be a houseboat, for instance, or even a yacht that has facilities for cooking, sleeping, and sanitation (Ruling 8337050).

Nor do the postponement rules require you to use the identical proceeds from your old home to buy your new home or to reinvest all the sales proceeds in that new one.

For instance, you can reinvest a lesser amount and get a mortgage loan for the balance. That means your profit is sheltered even when you channel part of the proceeds into another investment.

But the postponement opportunity vanishes when the proceeds go into a home in which you have no legal title. Therefore, no deferral was available where a parent invested the proceeds in a home held in a daughter's name. Similarly, the Tax Court balked when the taxpayer acquired a home in his mother's name, despite her testimony that title was taken in her name merely for convenience and that the son was the actual owner.

An IRS ruling barred a deferral when a couple sold their home and invested the proceeds in a retirement community that furnished living quarters and personal care but did not give them any ownership interest in their unit. It made no difference that they could transfer their membership interest or that it cost more than they received from the sale of their old home. To defer gain on the sale, the couple has to actually hold legal title to their new place (Ruling 8837022).

Proposed legislation. The principal-residence requirement can be a problem when a couple sells its jointly owned home as a result of a divorce or separation. As the law now stands, a spouse who moves out of the dwelling could be ineligible for the postponement break by the time the sale takes place because the place was not his or her principal residence at the time of the sale. As this book goes to press in the summer of 1994, Congress is considering a rules change that would help divorcing spouses qualify for deferral of gain. The proposed change treats the property as a person's principal residence as long as a two-step requirement is met. First, the sale is because of a divorce or separation. Second, he or she used the place as a principal residence at any time during the two-year period that precedes the sale. Doing so enables each spouse to roll over his or her profit into a new residence. Note, though, that this proposal does not help someone whose divorce proceeding takes more than two years to become final.

Sale of Land without Home

The IRS bars use of the deferral or the over-55 exclusion by a person who moves the house to a new lot and sells only the land. Without the sale of the house, there is no sale of a principal residence (Rev. Rul. 83–50).

Tip. You should also be aware that furniture, appliances, and similar items that are not "fixtures" under the law where you live do not count as part of your principal residence. Thus, a profit from the sale of a home cannot be reduced by a loss from a garage sale of furniture or other personal property. The garage sale is a separate transaction; you never get a tax write-off for this kind of loss.

Nor, for that matter, can you offset your profit by deducting a penalty charge for prepayment of your mortgage, though you can include the penalty with your other itemized deductions for interest payments. (See "'Points' for Home Mortgages" in Chapter 9.)

"FIX-UP" EXPENSES

There is a special tax break if you incur certain pre-sale "fixing-up expenses" to help make your home more attractive to prospective buyers and then replace it with a dwelling that costs *less* than the one you sell.

Under the deferment rules, the amount realized on the sale of your home, after allowing for a real estate agent's commission and other selling costs, can be further reduced by your outlays for fix-up work that otherwise would be considered nondeductible personal expenses. This "adjusted sales price" is then compared with the cost of the new home to find the deferrable profit.

You get the benefit of this break even though your outlays for, say, painting or papering count neither as improvements (see "Keeping Good Records" earlier in this chapter) that increase your cost basis nor as selling expenses that are deductible in determining the actual profit. But fixing-up expenses remain nondeductible. They do *not* cut down the amount that eventually goes to the IRS. That's because you must reduce the cost basis for your new dwelling by the gain postponement attributable to fix-up expenses on the old one.

There are other limitations. You must have the work done no earlier than 90 days before you sign a contract to sell your residence, and you must pay for the work no later than 30 days after the sale date. The value of your own labor is not taken into account.

Here is a simplified example of how fixing-up expenses can help when you sell your home and move into a less expensive one.

Let's assume that $80,000 covers (1) what you originally paid for your home, (2) settle-ment or closing costs, such as title insurance and legal fees, and (3) what you later paid for improvements that added to its value, such as new floors, plumbing, and the like. You also paid $3,000 for inside and outside repainting and some minor repairs several weeks before a sale that nets $84,000 after allowing for selling costs. You then buy a new residence for $83,000. That fix-up work entitles you to postpone the tax on your entire gain of $4,000 ($84,000 minus $80,000) because the adjusted sales price of $81,000 ($84,000 minus $3,000 for fixing up) for your old residence is less than the cost of $83,000 for your new one.

Caution. The IRS is inflexible on the requirement that you must contract to sell within 90 days after the fix-up work is performed. For instance, it wouldn't let a seller use fix-up costs to reduce the gain where a timely first contract fell through because the prospective purchaser couldn't get a mortgage and a second one did not contract until after the 90-day deadline. (Rev. Rul. 72–118).

INSTALLMENT SALE

If you expect to dispose of your home for a hefty profit, and the sale-and-replacement or over-55 breaks will not protect your entire profit, there are other ways to lower the amount that goes to the feds. So it can pay you to sit down with a tax expert beforehand to make sure you take advantage of tax-saving opportunities or steer clear of pitfalls.

One such tax-saving opportunity is the installment sale—instead of receiving the entire price up front, you agree to receive part of the price from the buyer in a year after the year in which the sale takes place. If you plan to sell between now and December 31, don't plan to reinvest in a new home or use the $125,000 exclusion, and prefer not to report the entire profit on your return for this year, an installment sale may be quite advantageous. With it, you can close your transaction this year and still spread out the tax bite on your profit over the years you report the installment payments, when, for example, you have retired and your tax bracket is likely to drop significantly.

Example. You realize a profit of $45,000 on a home you sell for $150,000 after deducting for a real estate agent's commission and other selling costs. Were you to receive the entire $150,000 in a lump sum, that $45,000 profit added to your other income could cause your taxes to soar. Suppose, though, that you agree to accept a down payment of $30,000 in December 1994, $45,000 in January 1995, and $75,000 in 1996, plus interest on the installment payments. Instead of reporting the entire $45,000 profit this year, you could report $9,000 in 1994, $13,500 in 1995, and $22,500 in 1996, the 30 percent portion of profit (profit of $45,000 divided by sale price of $150,000) in each installment, plus interest income.

Incidentally, the "unearned" income that you receive with the installment payments will not cause you to lose any Social Security benefits.

Even though you arrange the sale to qualify for installment reporting, you do not have to make your final decision on how to report the profit until you file your 1994 return. Thus, you can use a large amount of

hindsight. If, by the following April 15—or later if you obtain a filing extension—it seems wiser strategy to count your entire profit as 1994 income, you can do just that simply by not electing to use installment reporting. (For a discussion of extensions, see "More Time to File Your Return" in Chapter 13.)

Note that a deferred arrangement is treated as an installment sale unless you elect *not* to have it treated as such. You show your election on Schedule D (Capital Gains and Losses) of Form 1040.

Before you opt to use installment reporting or any of the other procedures that allow you to postpone or escape taxes, it would be wise to consult a tax adviser.

RAFFLING OFF A HARD-TO-SELL HOME

Some homeowners who have experienced difficulty selling because of unfavorable market conditions have worked out deals with charities to raffle off their homes. The tax results can be complex.

Consider, for example, this typical arrangement. Mr. and Mrs. Sirkman paid $30,000 for their dwelling and want $100,000 for it. The couple sells an option to a philanthropic organization to buy their home for $100,000. The charity sells 2,000 tickets at $100 each and raises $200,000. It turns $100,000 over to the Sirkmans and pockets the $100,000 balance. The house winds up with the Corrsins, who paid $100 for their winning ticket. An IRS ruling spells out the tax results of the raffle (Rev. Rul. 83–130).

The Sirkmans. The sellers have to declare a taxable long-term capital gain of $70,000 —the difference between the $100,000 they received and their $30,000 cost basis, exactly as in an ordinary transaction. But the usual rules provide possible relief for these home sellers. The rollover provision allows the Sirkmans to defer taxes on their profit of $70,000 if they purchase a replacement that costs at least $100,000. Alternatively, they can exclude up to $125,000 of gain on a sale that takes place after one of them has attained the age of 55 and used the property as a principal residence for at least three years out of the five-year period ending on the sale date.

No charitable deduction applies for this couple for the $100,000 kept by the philanthropy. The Sirkmans merely sold their house for its full market value. (Charitable contributions are discussed in Chapter 8.)

The losing ticket holders. They get no charitable deduction for raffle tickets bought from a philanthropic organization because those tickets gave them a crack at winning a house. Instead, the rules for gambling losses (Chapter 12) apply. The losses of $100 per ticket can be subtracted from any kind of gambling winnings, provided the ticket buyers itemize their deductions.

The Corrsins. Their reportable gambling winnings are $99,900, the difference between the home's fair market value of $100,000 and the raffle ticket's cost of $100. The $99,900 is taxed just like salary from a job. Their cost basis for the home is $100,000.

HOW TO REPORT SALE OF HOME

At filing time, you need to fill out Form 2119 (Sale of Your Home) to show the details if you (1) postpone taxes on the gain from the sale of your old residence by buying a new one or (2) qualify for, and elect to use, the $125,000 exclusion. Attach Form 2119 to your Form 1040. Form 2119 must accompany your tax return even if you can defer or exclude the entire gain or have a nondeductible loss. Use Schedule D (Capital Gains and Losses) if you have to report a taxable capital gain. Keep a copy of your Form 2119 and/or Schedule D.

You can make or revoke an election to exclude at any time during the period for amending the return for the year of the sale of your home. Generally, that is three years from the filing deadline for Form 1040, which is mid-April for most persons—for example, April 1998 in the case of a return for 1994. (For information on amended returns, see the discussion of refund claims in Chapter 14.)

Anticheating innovation. IRS investigations revealed that many sellers of homes failed to report their profits. To make it easier for the tax enforcers to uncover unreported gains, the law now requires the attorney, real estate broker, or other person handling the settlement to report the sale to the IRS. The sales price and date, along with the names of the seller and buyer and the seller's Social Security number, must be listed on Form 1099-S. These forms are sent to home sellers and, like other 1099 forms from banks and brokerage firms that report dividend and interest information, are also sent to the IRS for use by its computers, which compare 1099 figures with amounts listed on returns.

Tip.   The IRS can exact penalties for failing to provide the required information. There is a $50 penalty for failing to file a Form 1099-S and an additional $50 penalty for failing to give the seller a copy.

Help from the IRS

Need more-detailed information on the tax aspects of selling a home? See IRS Publication 523, *Tax Information on Selling Your Home.* For a free copy, call 1-800-TAX-FORM (allow at least 10 work days for mail-ing) or stop by the IRS office serving your area to obtain one immediately. Many libraries also have copies of this and other IRS tax guides. IRS Publication 910, *Guide to Free Tax Services,* provides a complete list of booklets and explains what each one covers. (For a discussion of IRS publications, see "Get the Right Help at Tax Time" in Chapter 13.)

Tip.   Don't rely absolutely on IRS advice, whether it is information that employees give to telephone or walk-in inquiries or instructions that the agency prints in its publications. Mistakes in instructions or advice are inevitable, and the IRS is not bound by them.

4 MARRIAGE AND DIVORCE

Ode to April 15th

Go back to work my dear?
Tho' I know you could hack it,
just think of what it will do to our tax bracket.
So she submerged the urge with nary a moan,
and 30 years later, she's filing alone.

—Ruth Wolfe

MARRIAGE OR DIVORCE AS A TAX SHELTER

A wedding is a solemn event that marks a personal commitment. So taxes are probably the last thing on your mind when you are on the threshold of marriage. But it might pay you to take them into account when you choose between a December or January wedding.

Be aware that postponing or advancing the date by a single day can make a big difference in the size of your tax bill for two years. The often-overlooked rule is that your marital status as of December 31 usually determines your filing status for the entire year. Therefore, the Internal Revenue Service considers you a married person for all of 1995 even if you should get hitched as late as December 31. Similarly, the Revenue Service considers you to be a single person for all of 1995, though your divorce takes place as late as December 31.

To illustrate the benefits of picking the right date for the ceremony taxwise, consider what can happen when, as is common nowadays, you and your prospective mate may have relatively equal earnings. In that event, marriage in December may prove to be a costly proposition.

Why does a walk down the aisle in December lead you into a tax trap? Because the tax that the two of you become obligated to pay as Mr. and Mrs. on your combined incomes can be considerably more than it would be as two swinging singles who share bed and board and report exactly the same incomes —a much-criticized quirk in the Internal Revenue Code that has come to be known as the "marriage penalty" or, depending on one's point of view, "sin subsidy."

But take heart. You receive a year's reprieve from the additional tax for 1995 if you opt to postpone the ceremony until January of 1996.

Is it still possible for a marriage in December to save taxes? Absolutely. A December marriage definitely is a smart move when one of you earns all the income or considerably more than the other. Your taxes as a couple filing jointly will be less than if you remain unmarried.

Here's an example of how our system increases the tax bite for 1995 when a working couple decides to get married before the close of the year. John and Mary each has taxable income (what is left after reportable income is offset by exemptions, deductions, and other subtractions) of $20,000. Had they delayed their marriage until next year, their total tax bill for 1995 as singles would have been about $6,000. But as marrieds filing jointly, their tax is about $6,300—a modest marriage penalty of approximately $300. Note, though, that the marriage penalty grows as their taxable income increases. The penalty is about $1,000 if each has taxable income of $35,000, and about $1,200 if each has taxable income of $50,000.

But nothing is entirely straightforward when it comes to taxes. The rules of the game change and a 1995 marriage is advantageous when taxable income is, say, $40,000 for one mate and $10,000 for the other. Then, the penalty becomes a bonus. Had they delayed their marriage until next year, their total tax for 1995 as singles would have been about $9,700. But as marrieds, their tax drops to about $9,100—for them, a marriage bonus of approximately $600.

Profiting from a Year-End Divorce

These tax quirks have not gone unnoticed by tax-savvy, dual-income couples. To the surprise of no one but the Internal Revenue Service, an increasing number of these couples have journeyed to Haiti, or some other equally obliging place, to get a divorce in December and then to remarry in January. Some affluent couples announced on "60 Minutes" and other national television programs that they slip into and out of marriage with annual quickie divorces just so they can

file as two unmarried persons and save a sizable sum in taxes. Even if their savings are largely offset by the divorce fees, their outlays also allow them to frolic for a week or so in the Caribbean sun and to buy some extra-nice Christmas presents for the folks back home, all courtesy of those obliging souls at the IRS.

These year-end arrangements prompted a public relations–conscious IRS to issue a prim warning: It will disregard a divorce obtained solely to save taxes and require the couple to recalculate their taxes as if they had stayed married for the entire year. That means they become liable for additional taxes plus interest and possible penalties.

Tip. A beleaguered IRS readily concedes that couples can file as single persons when they get a regular divorce and simply live together out of wedlock. This arrangement has become a socially acceptable way of life for more than 3.6 million couples who fit the Census Bureau's description of POSSLQs, the acronym for persons of the opposite sex sharing living quarters. (For more on POSSLQs, see "Dependency Exemptions for Live-In Lovers" in Chapter 2.)

No Escape from the Marriage Penalty

To stop another end run around the marriage penalty, the IRS also ruled that a pact entered into before marriage did not entitle a two-income couple to file as unmarrieds. It seemed that the couple who sought the ruling agreed to function toward each other as "fully independent, single individuals with none of the financial characteristics which are usually present in a marriage relationship." But this eminently practical arrangement got them exactly nowhere with an unsympathetic IRS, which ordained that a couple who enter into a valid marriage cannot escape the marriage tax merely by making a private agreement.

Some couples contend that our tax system is unconstitutional because it forces many working marrieds to pay more taxes than they would if they stayed single. But the IRS has been backed up by the courts, which consistently hold that it is immaterial that some pay more and some pay less because of marriage. That does not unreasonably interfere with the right to marry. All it does, concluded a federal judge, is "change the relative attraction of different prospective spouses. For the tax-minded young man or woman with a substantial income, the Internal Revenue Code adds to the attractiveness of a prospective spouse without taxable income and detracts from one with it." Taking note of the changes in our moral attitudes, the judge also observed that two-paycheck couples who cohabit without sanction of clergy "can enjoy the blessing of love while minimizing their forced contribution to the federal coffers."

How the Marriage Penalty Came and Stayed

It takes a little history to understand why marriage can mean higher taxes. The dilemma developed in 1948, when the one-breadwinner family was the norm, as opposed to the more prevalent two-earner arrangement nowadays. It was then that "income splitting" first became available to couples filing joint returns.

Joint filing provided a sizable savings for couples when one mate reported all the income or considerably more than the other; it allowed them to treat the income as though each had received half. If, say, a husband's taxable income was $20,000 and his wife had none, they calculated their tax on this income as though each had received $10,000; their levy was substantially less than the amount due from a single person with the same taxable income of $20,000.

Understandably, that fact made many singles unhappy. They never stopped complaining that it was flagrant discrimination to require a single to pay more than a married with the same income.

One response by Congress was to provide a measure of relief for persons who qualify as a head of household. Their rates fall about halfway between those for joint filers and those for singles.

Another bit of tinkering by Congress made income splitting available to a "surviving spouse" for two years after the death of a wife or husband, provided the survivor has a dependent child and maintains a home for the child. (See "Joint-Return Rates for Surviving Spouses" later in this chapter.)

Back in 1969, as part of its unending quest for tax fairness, Congress created the marriage penalty when it set up different rate schedules for singles and marrieds. The folks on Capitol Hill also sought to soothe singles by trimming their rates from as much as 40 percent to no more than 20 percent above those imposed on marrieds filing jointly. Far from settling the issue, the reduction of their burden failed to satisfy the singles, who remained unconvinced of the logic of a system that required them to pay a premium of up to 20 percent solely because they were unmarried.

Moreover, the advancement of more working wives up the pay scales swelled the ranks of the outraged because Congress left the rates for marrieds unchanged. That created an incentive for two-earner couples to consider the financial virtues of forgoing holy matrimony or obtaining a divorce and thereafter living a more prosperous life in unwedded bliss.

Fade to 1981 and a Congress that wanted to muffle complaints that it sided with promiscuity and opposed the sacred institution of marriage. That was the year Congress authorized a deduction designed to provide partial, not complete, relief from the federal marriage indenture for two-paycheck couples. The revised rules entitled working marrieds filing jointly to deduct 10 percent of the first $30,000 in earnings of the lower-paid mate, for a maximum deduction of $3,000.

Despite the deduction, many two-earner couples continued to feel that they were unfairly penalized by our tax system. Worse yet, marriage-penalty relief resulted in new "inequities." The full deduction became available only when each spouse earned a minimum of $30,000. No deduction was available when one spouse was unemployed, though he or she may have had substantial investment income from stocks, rental property, and so on.

An election-year Congress did some more tinkering in 1986, when it passed a top-to-bottom restructuring of the Internal Revenue Code that was supposed to make taxes fairer. The overhaul included a provision that abolished the special deduction for working couples after 1986.

How do things stand now? Unless Congress goes back to the drawing board, the law continues to require millions of dual-income couples to pay more than if they remained single, even without taking into account the increase in the top tax rate for 1993 and later

years. The snag is the long-standing one of bracket creep—higher income means a higher tax rate.

As singles, two people might have most of their separate incomes taxed at a top rate of 15 percent. For tax year 1994, the 15 percent bracket for singles applies to taxable income up to $22,750. (For how to determine your tax bracket, see "What Is Your Real Tax Bracket?" in Chapter 14.)

As marrieds, however, their incomes are combined, a consequence of which is that the top rate for the first dollar of the second income is the same as the rate for the last dollar of the first. *Result*: A larger slice of their incomes is taxed at the next higher rate of 28 percent, which starts at $38,000 for joint filers.

Example. Joey Evans and Vera Simpson each have taxable income of $22,500. As single taxpayers, their entire combined income of $45,000 is taxed at a 15 percent rate. But as a married couple who file jointly, they enter the 28 percent bracket at $38,000 and are stuck with taxes at that rate on the $7,000 balance of their income ($45,000 minus $38,000).

The 1993 tax act. There are winners and losers under this act, as is so of all tax legislation. Opening the envelopes reveals that those at a disadvantage include wealthier two-income couples; their marriage penalty is magnified by the new rules. The advantaged include affluent couples with only one wage earner; their marriage bonus is boosted.

For starters, there is the 36 percent bracket. For tax year 1994, it applies to joint filers after taxable income surpasses $140,000, whereas it applies to single persons after taxable income surpasses $115,000. Consequently, two unmarried individuals are comparative winners; they can have a combined taxable income of as much as $230,000 before both are ratcheted from the 31 percent bracket to the 36 percent bracket.

What befalls a married couple with the same combined taxable income of $230,000? They have to shell out $4,500 more (5 percent, the excess of 36 over 31, times $90,000, the excess of $230,000 over $140,000) than they would if they were unmarried.

The marriage penalty becomes positively painful after the 10 percent surtax hits taxable income over $250,000 for *both* single persons and married couples. Note that the threshold does not rise to a combined $500,000 for a married couple who file separate returns.

Example. Ray and Ruth Stone have taxable income of $300,000, divided evenly between the two of them. They are slapped with a surtax on $50,000 of their income—the part above $250,000.

The Stones might want to take a cue from Nathan and Adelaide, two singles living together out of wedlock. Nathan and Adelaide can have taxable income of as much as $250,000 apiece, for a combined total of $500,000, and remain unscathed by the surtax.

Strategy. Unquestionably, marriage is advantageous when one mate earns all the income or considerably more than the other. The right kind of script transforms the penalty to a bonus.

Example. For 1992, as was true for millions of other two-income couples, the marriage penalty increased the tax tab for William Jefferson and Hillary Rodham Clinton; as Arkansas' governor, he received a salary of $35,000, and his wife earned way more as a partner in a Little Rock law firm.

For his term of office, President Clinton receives a yearly salary of $200,000 and is the sole earner in the family unit; Ms. Clinton works without pay in her government post. *Result*: No penalty for the First Couple. Instead, they reap a marriage bonus of several thousand dollars—not megabucks but a start towards covering what they spend for care of the First Cat.

Ask not what your Congress can do for you. What is the morning line for yet another rewrite of the rules, this time one that would create a marriage-neutral system that imposes equal burdens on marrieds and singles? If history provides any guidance, it will be injurious to your health if you inhale and remain that way until Congress deals with this vexing issue. All previously introduced bills to abolish the added cost of true love were always DOA.

Why decades of inaction by Capitol Hill's denizens, who on frequent occasion solemnly recommit themselves to an unending search for tax equity and family values? Because to abolish the marriage penalty would either cost the United States Treasury billions and further fuel the deficit, or boost taxes for millions, including, by the way, members of Congress, many of whom, notes the *Wall Street Journal,* tend to be among the minority of American families with one wage earner.

SOME JOINT-FILING TAX TRAPS

One advantage of being married is that a couple can file joint returns and trim their tax tab. But many married persons have learned the expensive way that joint filing can turn out to be a tax trap if the Internal Revenue Service audits their returns and demands extra taxes. The hitch is that the IRS is free to dun either mate for the entire amount of any additional taxes that become due. It makes no difference that they have since separated, one spouse has died, or that the extra taxes are attributable to the business or income of only one of them.

Usually, the joint-filing trap closes on the unsuspecting wife or, after a marriage comes unglued, on the ex-wife. What she discovers is that the Revenue Service is not obliged to go after her husband for the unpaid taxes and can head straight for her assets if they are easier to grab, even if she has since remarried.

Signing under Duress

One way for a blameless wife to get herself off the hook for back taxes, interest, and penalties is to show that she was bullied by her husband into signing a return and didn't really intend to file jointly with him. But a New York City wife discovered how difficult it can be for a woman to prove that she signed under duress.

It seems that Martin had a drinking problem that often caused him to assault Caroline, as well as to destroy the furniture in their Fifth Avenue apartment. On one occasion, Martin even kicked their dog across the floor of the apartment.

Caroline testified about her ordeal at tax time when Martin came home loaded, ordered her to sign a return, and she refused. He tore her clothes, pulled out her hair, and forced her head under the bed. No slouch when it came to defending herself, Caroline counterattacked with a hat pin and had the police remove him from the apartment. But the next day, for reasons left unexplained by Caroline, she had a change of heart and went to Martin's office, where she signed the returns—a step that came back to haunt her when she testified that she signed only under duress. That, ruled a reluctant Tax Court, was not duress, and Caroline was liable for taxes on the income Martin had failed to declare.

On the other hand, the IRS got exactly nowhere when it claimed Lola and Thurston had filed jointly before their divorce and wanted to nail her for his hefty back taxes. Thurston was described by the Tax Court as a large man with a violent temper who assaulted his wife so often that she became a frail and nervous person. During their marriage, the family purse was in the tight grip of Thurston, who always bought everything and never gave Lola a personal allowance or let her write checks on their joint accounts. Luckily for Lola, she wound up before a judge who believed her testimony that Thurston ordered her to "sign it or else" whenever she questioned a return. The clincher was testimony by Lola that Thurston threatened to hit her unless she signed; at the time, she was confined to bed and suffering great pain after a back injury that left her partially paralyzed.

Then there was the unusual case of Rebecca and Sid. The way Rebecca told it to the judge, Sid showed her a blank tax return and ordered her to sign it. She said: "Of course not." He said: "If not, I will break your head open and smash your face in." But Rebecca refused to give in, and Sid signed her name himself. Next year, Sid made April 15 another day of terror for Rebecca. She testified: "It started as early as we got up in the morning and proceeded all day long. 'You sign it or I will break your head open. You sign it or I will smash your face in or I will kill you. You sign it or I will kill you.'"

Sid eventually forced Rebecca to sign. "While my husband and Millie together stood outside, I opened the door just a crack, still keeping the door on the chain, just enough so he could shove the tax return in to me about two inches, just enough to obtain my signature on the bottom line. And just as soon as he obtained this signature, he pulled it right back and said, 'Now I've got you.'"

The judge's decision doesn't identify Millie or tell what happened after Rebecca slid the chain off the door. But he decided Rebecca hadn't intended to file jointly with Sid for those two years.

Innocent-Spouse Rules

Another way for a wife to escape liability for her husband's taxes is to seek relief under the "innocent-spouse" rules. This relief is available when (1) the husband "substantially understates" the tax liability on their joint return, and (2) the understatement (that is, the additional tax owed) is attributable to "grossly erroneous items."

What is the magic number that makes an understatement substantial? The understatement has to be more than $500.

As for "grossly erroneous," that refers to income not reported by the not-so-innocent husband or deductions or credits that were claimed by him and subsequently disallowed. But the wife is excused from liability for taxes, interest charges, and penalties attributable to disallowed deductions or credits claimed by the husband only when he had "no basis in fact or law" for such claims.

It is wise to enlist the help of an attorney, accountant, or other tax professional when an audit gets into the complicated factual question of whether a person is entitled to relief under the innocent-spouse rules. (See "Get the Right Help at Tax Time" in Chapter 13.) Among other things, the burden is on the wife to establish that she did not know and had no reason to know there was a substantial understatement when she signed the joint return. The law further requires her to show that it would be inequitable to hold her liable for the additional taxes, taking into account all the facts and circumstances, including whether she significantly benefited from the hidden income or phony deductions.

The innocent-spouse rule has been successfully invoked by a number of women. For instance, an understanding Tax Court excused Patricia Mysse, the widow of a bank embezzler, when she showed that even the bank failed to discover his cheating until after he died and she received nothing from him other than her normal household allowance.

But a skeptical judge refused to believe Rose Most when she denied knowing that her husband, Louis, never reported a sizable amount of income from his law practice. For one thing, Rose sometimes worked in her husband's office, and she was aware he had received the omitted income. For another thing, the judge reasoned that Rose directly benefited from the omission because she and Louis used the money to cover their living expenses. Rose's case was thrown out when she refused to appear in court as a witness and risk cross-examination of her story by the government.

Even a husband can qualify as an innocent spouse. When the Hackneys decided to go into business on their own, Bill, an eighth-grade dropout, let his wife, Verna, handle the records. Verna also kept records for a lumber company, where she met Howard and joined in a scheme to swindle the company. Then things got sticky for Bill when the IRS tried to collect back taxes, interest, and a fraud penalty from him because Verna did not report her share of the swindle on their joint returns.

Fortunately for Bill, his case was heard by Cynthia Hall, then the Tax Court's only female member. Judge Hall accepted his claim that he knew nothing about the swindle and signed returns prepared by Verna without going over them. It was no problem for Bill to show he derived no benefit from the income hidden by Verna; she took the bulk of their property with her when she left him to marry Howard.

Tip. Congress did not enact the innocent-spouse-relief law just for spouses divorced, deserted, or separated. It is also available for still-married spouses.

LOWER RATES FOR SOME MARRIEDS FILING SEPARATELY

Joint filing usually trims taxes for married couples when one spouse earns all or considerably more of the income than the other—a long-standing rule that lots of couples cherish. (See the previous discussion in this chapter, "Marriage or Divorce as a Tax Shelter.") That break, though, can prove to be a trap if you and your spouse decide to split up, but do not obtain a divorce or legal separation.

Legally, you and your mate remain able to file jointly, assuming the two of you want to do so. However, it may be more advantageous to file separately.

For starters, an obscure provision in the tax code says that joint filers are jointly liable.

Translation: If the IRS examines a joint return and insists on additional taxes, the agency is empowered to nail one spouse for all of those taxes; it matters not that all of the income was earned by the other. (For liability on a joint return, see the previous discussion in this chapter, "Some Joint-Filing Tax Traps.")

However compelling the circumstances that justify shunning tax togetherness, both of you may be in for an unpleasant and expensive surprise at Form 1040 time. The taxes you will pay as married people filing separately often prove to be considerably greater than the taxes you would owe as joint filers or even as two unmarried individuals.

There are other disadvantages for a married couple that decides to file separately. For example, the law requires each of them to itemize their deductions for contributions and the like or to both use the standard deduction that people automatically get without having to itemize. In effect, the mate who itemizes compels the other one to follow suit. (See "Itemizing versus Standard Deduction" in Chapter 1.)

Moreover, filing separately when the spouses are not living apart eliminates or reduces certain tax breaks—for instance, the credit for child- or dependent-care expenses (Chapter 6) and the extent to which Social Security benefits are taxed (Chapter 15).

Special rule for married people living apart. Fortunately, there is a way out of this trap for many married people. An easily missed rule allows you to be treated as if you were unmarried for tax year 1994, provided you meet certain requirements. *Result:* Even though you are not divorced or legally separated, you are excused from having to use the rates for a married filing separately and get the benefit of the more favorable rates for a head of household.

To be considered unmarried, you have to pass a four-step test.

1. You file a separate return.
2. Your spouse did not live in your home during the last six months of 1994.
3. You paid over 50 percent of the cost of keeping up your home for 1994. (For which expenses to count or not to count, see the discussion in the next section of this chapter, "Joint-Return Rates for Surviving Spouses.")
4. Your home was, for more than half of 1994, the principal home of your child, stepchild, or adopted child, whom you could claim as a dependent.

Tip. You are not necessarily disqualified from filing as a head of household just because you are unable to claim the child. As the parent with custody (the mother, in most cases), you continue to be eligible if either one of these two exceptions apply:

- You sign IRS Form 8332, allowing the 1994 exemption to be claimed by your husband, the parent without custody, or
- A pre-1985 agreement grants custody to you and the exemption to your husband and he provided at least $600 in 1994 for the support of the child. (See "Exemptions for Children of Divorced or Separated Parents" in Chapter 2.)

Tip. When you and your spouse live apart by mutual agreement, you may be able to work out an arrangement whereby each gets a dependent child and each qualifies as a head of household. Congress enacted the special provision that treats marrieds as unmarrieds primarily for the benefit of abandoned wives (or husbands). But it worded the provision broadly enough to cover couples who have separated and who live apart by mutual agreement and without any actual abandonment.

Another break is that the standard deduction is higher for a head of household than for a person with the filing status of single. (See "Itemizing versus Standard Deduction" in Chapter 1.)

Mate must move out for you to qualify as head of household. The Tax Court ruled that a husband failed to qualify when he and his wife agreed to live in separate areas of the same residence. Living apart under one roof does not pass muster.

In another dispute, the court reminded Laurel Hopkins that sharing the same quarters for as little as one day during the last six months of the year can be fatal. Before more than six months had elapsed during the year in question, Laurel and her husband, William, had ceased to live together; but during the balance of the year, she sometimes let him stay overnight because he was unable to find a dwelling.

As she paid all the household bills and was the sole support of their two children, Laurel, not unreasonably, believed herself entitled to file as a head of household. Unfortunately, in the course of a subsequent IRS audit, Laurel let slip that William sometimes stayed in her apartment.

On the basis of that admission, the feds determined that her proper filing status was that of a married person filing separately. Though sympathetic to Laurel's predicament, the Tax Court agreed with the IRS that a wife who shelters a homeless husband at any time during the last six months of the year disqualifies herself for head of household status.

JOINT-RETURN RATES FOR SURVIVING SPOUSES

There is a special filing break for some widows and widowers. They may be entitled to the benefit of joint-return rates for two years after their mate's death.

Make sure to take advantage of this frequently missed tax trimmer for surviving spouses if your spouse died in 1992 or 1993 and you have a dependent child. To get the benefit of this break, check the box for "qualifying widow(er) with dependent child" on Form 1040 or Form 1040A (it's unavailable on Form 1040EZ, the shortest version of the tax return).

By way of background, the death of your spouse bars you from filing a joint return, unless you have remarried. Nor are you allowed to claim the personal exemption for your spouse as you are on a joint return. Nevertheless, you still may be able to figure your 1994 tax using the rates for a joint filer, which are lower than for a single person or a head of household.

To qualify as a surviving spouse and use joint-return rates for 1994, you must meet these four requirements:

1. You did not remarry before January 1, 1995.
2. For the year in which your spouse died, you were entitled to file jointly with him or her, whether you actually filed that way or not.
3. During all of 1994, your home is the principal residence of your child,

adopted child, stepchild, or foster child, whom you can claim as a dependent. (For the rules for dependency exemptions, see Chapter 2.) Your home need not be in the same location for the entire year.

Example. You do not disqualify yourself for joint-return rates merely because you move from one dwelling to another during the year.

Tip. In determining whether your child lived in your home, you are allowed to ignore temporary absences by your son or daughter because of vacations, sickness, school, or military service. But you do become disqualified if your child moves out permanently before the year end or fails to qualify as your dependent.

4. You furnish over half the cost of maintaining your home. In calculating the cost, note the instructions that accompany Form 1040. You are allowed to count such items as rent, property insurance, real estate taxes, mortgage interest, upkeep, repairs, utilities, telephone, domestic help, and food consumed within the home.

Caution. Do not count the cost of clothing, education, medical treatment, vacations, life insurance, transportation, or the value of work done in the home by you or your child. Nor are you permitted to count the rental value of a home that you provide for your child, even though you do count its value in determining whether you contribute over half of the child's total support for the year and are, therefore, entitled to an exemption for him or her.

Tip.   Another break is that the standard deduction is higher for a surviving spouse than for someone with the filing status of single or head of household. (See "Itemizing versus Standard Deduction" in Chapter 1.)

Tip.   All is not lost if you fail to qualify during 1994 as a surviving spouse who can use the joint-return rates. You still may be able to avoid the single-person rates and use the more favorable ones for a head of household. If you are no longer eligible for treatment as a surviving spouse, but you remain unmarried and your child lives with you, you may qualify as a head of household even if you are ineligible to claim an exemption for your child.

DIVORCE SETTLEMENTS: WATCH OUT FOR TAX TRAPS

The breakup of a marriage forces a couple to deal with many complex financial problems. In negotiating an agreement, the couple's main concerns may be alimony, child custody, and child support arrangements. However, they may also have to deal with dependency exemptions for children (see Chapter 2), legal fees (discussed later in this chapter), and transfers of property.

To add to their troubles, the complex tax rules can make it even harder to hammer out an agreement. But unless those rules are carefully considered while the settlement is still in the proposal state, one or the other of the splitting spouses may be in for an unpleasant surprise when it's too late to change anything.

Consider, for example, what happens when a divorce settlement involves a transfer of appreciated property. At one time the law, in effect, treated such a transfer in much the same way as if the property had been sold. Here's the background.

Frequently, the splitting spouses negotiate an agreement that requires one mate (usually the husband) to transfer stock, real estate, or other assets to the wife to obtain her release of support rights. It is unlikely that they will see any profit or loss in such a swap. The old law, however, treated the transaction as though he had sold the property for an amount equal to the value of her relinquished support rights, which were considered to be equal to the value of the property transferred.

Assume John and Mary worked out a deal that required the husband-to-wife transfer of stock that cost him $10,000 some years ago and is worth $150,000 in today's market. John had to report a long-term capital gain of $140,000. As for Mary, she did not have to count as income the property received for her release of support rights. For purposes of figuring gain or loss on a later sale, the stock was considered to have cost her $150,000. (For taxes on capital gains and losses, see Chapter 10.)

But the way the law now works, it is a much different story. John is excused from reporting a gain or loss on a transfer of property to Mary that is "incident to a divorce." This is a property transfer that occurs within one year after they cease to be married or that is related to the divorce. The current rules apply whether John transfers the stock to Mary for the relinquishment by her of her marital rights, which is what usually happens, for cash or other property, for the assumption by her of some liabilities, or for other consideration that she provides. Mary's cost (in tax jargon, her basis) for such property is John's basis ($10,000 in this example). *Result:* If she then sells the stock for its value of $150,000, the $140,000 gain is taxed to her.

Caution. My example underscores a point to keep in mind when there is a division of appreciated property in a divorce settlement. There might be an overstatement of the $150,000 value assigned to the shares of stock if that value fails to reflect the potential taxes that Mary would incur on the $140,000 appreciation if she subsequently sells her stock. Consequently, it is to Mary's advantage to seek inclusion in the divorce agreement of a provision that requires John to reimburse her for any tax liability triggered upon the sale or other disposition of the stock. Alternatively, Mary could negotiate for a settlement that assigns as the stock's value the amount of estimated after-tax proceeds that she would receive upon disposing of her shares.

A final thought on a stressful event like divorce that frequently results in painful negotiations: What prompts my suggestions is not that I want to provide tax strategies for Mary to employ *against* John; rather, all I have in mind is to explain a tricky problem and help both of them to compromise their competing interests.

Help from the IRS

Do you need additional information on property transfers and other concerns of couples contemplating divorce? The IRS has a helpful booklet, *Tax Information for Divorced or Separated Individuals,* known officially as Publication 504. For a free copy, call 1-800-TAX-FORM (allow at least 10 days for mailing) or stop by the IRS office serving your area to obtain one immediately. Many libraries also have copies of this and other IRS tax guides. IRS Publication 910, *Guide to Free Tax Services,* provides a complete list of booklets. (For a discussion of IRS publications, see "Get the Right Help at Tax Time" in Chapter 13.)

Tip. Don't rely absolutely on IRS advice, whether it is information that employees give to telephone or walk-in inquiries or instructions that the agency prints in its publications. Mistakes in instructions or advice are inevitable, and the IRS is not bound by them.

LEGAL FEES FOR A DIVORCE

Generally, the IRS will not allow a tax deduction to ease the pain for a couple who split and incur legal fees and other costs to obtain a divorce, separation, or decree of support. But they do get a deduction for legal fees specifically for tax advice in connection with a divorce or separation, as well as for legal fees to obtain taxable alimony. Here is a rundown of the rules.

Nondeductible Expenses

The IRS bars any deduction for the cost of personal advice, counseling, and legal action in a divorce. For example, a husband gets no write-off for the cost of resisting his wife's demands for more alimony or to set aside an antenuptial property agreement.

These expenses are nondeductible even though they are partly incurred in arriving at a financial settlement or to conserve income-producing property. This has been upheld by the Supreme Court. It is not enough, said the Court, that the outcome of a suit or claim may be loss of the income-producing property; the suit or claim against the property must also *arise* or *originate* out of the husband's profit-making activities, not from a purely personal matter. The wife's claims in a divorce action arise from a purely personal marital relationship, not from anyone's income-producing activities.

More than one taxpayer has learned the hard way that the Tax Court will not bend these rules to permit a deduction for divorce fees. In one case, the court threw out a deduction by a company for legal expenses paid on behalf of its principal shareholder in a divorce action in which his wife sought to acquire an interest in his stock. The company got nowhere with its argument that the wife suffered from mental problems and that her intrusion in its affairs would have jeopardized its continued success.

Nor would the court approve a husband's medical deduction for attorney's fees for a divorce that was recommended by his psychiatrist. The husband failed to prove that had it not been for the illness that the divorce was supposed to cure, he would not have incurred the fee. (Medical expenses are discussed in Chapter 7.)

Tip. There is no deduction for legal fees incurred in a divorce action to retain ownership of income-producing assets, such as a building. But those fees can increase the basis of the building for purposes of figuring gain or loss on a later sale.

Fees for Alimony

The portion of legal fees specifically paid (usually by the wife) to collect alimony that is taxable to her can be included in Schedule A of Form 1040 with her other itemized deductibles under "miscellaneous deductions," just as can the cost of preparing her return or the price paid for this book. This break is available for the original proceeding by which she procures taxable alimony, as well as for any subsequent proceeding to increase it or collect arrears. But these legal fees and most other miscellaneous itemized deductions are allowable only to the extent that their total in any one year exceeds 2 percent of her adjusted gross income. (For the rules on miscellaneous deductions, see Chapter 9.)

In no event can she deduct the cost of obtaining income that is *not* taxable to her—say, back child support or temporary alimony while a joint return was still being filed. Nor can a wife who seeks no change in an alimony arrangement write off the cost of a suit to acquire assets awarded her ex-husband in a former divorce action or money he received in exchange for those assets.

Fees for Tax Advice

Subject to that 2 percent floor for miscellaneous expenses, the husband can take an itemized deduction for fees paid to *his* attorney that cover tax research and advice on such items as property transfers (discussed in the preceding section of this chapter) and dependency exemptions for the children (see Chapter 2), as well as such nontax matters as child custody and visitation rights, but only if the bill specifies in a reasonable way how much is for tax counseling. Moreover, a husband gets no deduction for fees paid to his *wife's* attorney for tax advice to her. The deduction is allowed only for advice on his own tax problems.

Allocating Fees between Tax and Nontax Matters

These tax rules were made expensively clear to Howard Goldaper. He was charged $6,975 by a divorce lawyer whose fee statement allocated $2,750 for such tax services as valuation and analysis of his deferred compensation plan and other executive fringes. At filing time, Goldaper took a tax-advice deduction for the $2,750. But his return never made it past the computers. The IRS disallowed the entire deduction on the ground that Goldaper failed to prove that his outlay was for tax advice.

Goldaper decided to take the dispute to the Tax Court. Unfortunately for him, neither the bill nor testimony by the attorney provided specific information as to how much *time* was spent on tax counseling. The Tax Court concluded that he was entitled to a deduction of only $750.

According to an IRS ruling, the agency will accept a lawyer's allocation of his fee between tax and nontax matters where he does so primarily on the basis of the amount of his time attributable to each, the customary charge in the locality for similar services and the results obtained in the divorce negotiations (Rev. Rul. 72–545).

INVALID DIVORCE

Nowadays, most states have eased their divorce laws. But despite the general easing, it is not uncommon for a court of one state to invalidate a divorce obtained in another state. To the complications this can cause in your life, add some troublesome tax questions after you have gone.

For example, consider this estate tax problem. A married person's estate can completely sidestep federal estate taxes, thanks to a break known in legal lingo as a marital deduction. (Estate taxes are discussed in Chapter 16.) No estate taxes fall due on property left to a surviving spouse. For an estate to take advantage of a marital deduction, a person must leave a surviving spouse. But if a state invalidates a divorce obtained by someone who remarried in the meantime, who is the "survivor"?

Consider the case of Elizabeth and Charles Spalding, who lived in Connecticut until a disagreement prompted him to move to New York. Eventually, he went to Nevada; its divorce statute allowed him to obtain a divorce without an appearance there by her.

The divorce was ruled invalid by New York; but this did not dissuade Charles from a California marriage with Amy. The couple resided in California until the death of Amy, who left substantial property to Charles. Thanks to the marital deduction, the IRS was disinherited to the tune of about $400,000.

Somehow, the IRS got wind of the New York decision and insisted that Charles was still married to Elizabeth. Therefore, contended the feds, Amy Spalding's estate was ineligible for the marital deduction. But what counts, said a federal court, was how California, the state of both Amy's marriage and estate administration, viewed the relationship. Since their marriage went unchallenged by California, Charles and Amy were husband and wife there and her estate was entitled to the deduction.

But in other disputes, the IRS has triumphed. For instance, Gertrude and Leo Goldwater lived in New York when he obtained a Mexican divorce without an appearance by her—a maneuver that caused New

York to declare the Mexican divorce invalid. Leo, nevertheless, married Lee in Connecticut and the couple resided in New York until his death. *Decision:* Leo's estate could not claim a marital deduction for property left to Lee because his marriage to her was not recognized by New York, the state responsible for the probate of the estate.

The same approach was followed in another case that read like a script for "Dynasty." Here, Crockett and Priscilla Lane lived in Wisconsin when she obtained a Mexican divorce on grounds not recognized by Wisconsin. Priscilla wed Wesley Steffke, and they remained in Wisconsin until his death, when he left most of his property to her.

For state inheritance-tax purposes, Wisconsin determined that Priscilla wasn't Wesley's widow; she remained the wife of Crockett. The IRS then disallowed the marital deduction claimed by Wesley's estate for property left to Priscilla. *Decision:* For the IRS. It was immaterial that it was not until after the death of Wesley that Wisconsin invalidated Priscilla's unhitching from Crockett.

DIVORCE VERSUS ANNULMENT

According to the dictionaries, there is a difference between a divorce and an annulment. The courts grant a divorce to mark the end of a marriage that was valid when entered into, whereas an annulment is for a marriage that at no time was valid, as when one of the parties was under the age of consent at the time of the marriage.

To a couple interested only in the fastest way to untie the knot, the question may seem to be an unimportant technicality. Those watchful souls at the IRS, however, think that there is an important difference when Form 1040 time rolls around.

According to an IRS ruling, if an annulment is retroactive, the couple was never married. *Result:* They had no right to file joint returns (Rev. Rul. 76–255).

Example.   John and Mary married in 1994, filed jointly in 1995, and had their marriage annulled after the filing deadline. Because their marriage was declared null and void from its very inception by the annulment decree, they are considered to be unmarried at the end of 1994. Consequently, they were ineligible to file jointly for 1994 and must refile under the rules for unmarried persons, which can mean higher taxes.

Tip.   This ruling involved only a one-year marriage. Nevertheless, the theory would presumably apply regardless of the length of the marriage. On the plus side, refunds may be available to couples whose marriages were annulled and who would have paid reduced taxes as single persons. (For information on refund claims, see Chapter 14.)

5 TRAVEL AND MOVING EXPENSES

COMMUTING DEDUCTIONS: THE RULES ARE ROUGH

Usually, the Internal Revenue Service adamantly opposes deductions for commuting costs between home and work. The tax collectors consider those outlays to be nondeductible personal expenses, no matter how necessary.

It makes absolutely no difference if your work location is in a remote area not serviced by public transportation or that disability or illness rules out using public transportation.

This hard-nosed approach was underscored in a ruling that denied deductions for cab fares required to transport a physically disabled person to and from work. Similarly, no write-offs become available merely because you need a car to get to work more quickly or in emergencies.

Is it possible to get around these restrictions if you install a telephone in your car and make calls to clients or business associates or hold business discussions while driving to work? The IRS says that does not transform the trips from commuting to business.

Nor can commuting legitimately be called something else because someone suffers racial discrimination, a point of law on which the IRS has the backing of the Tax Court. The court held that racial bias did not entitle a black Californian to deduct his personal costs of commuting 17½ miles from his home in Huntington Beach to a job in Orange, where he had been transferred by his employer. Robert Brown cited racial discrimination against blacks as the reason for his inability to buy a home in Santa Ana, two miles from his job. But the court said it made no difference that he was forced to commute; the tax laws authorize no relief for someone whose nontax rights are violated.

Circuit court concludes commuting cop commanders can claim car costs. Federal court judges with lifetime tenures are, to the distress of the IRS, sometimes hostile to the agency's notion that its proclamations ought to be considered ukases. A case in point: The United States Court of Appeals for the Tenth Circuit rejected the pro-IRS reasoning of the Tax Court and allowed Salt Lake City police captains Jon R. Pollei and Harry W. Patrick to deduct driving costs from their homes to stationhouses.

The case was spawned by a cost-cutting campaign undertaken by Salt Lake City. As part of those efforts, Salt Lake City decided to require command-level officers to use their personal cars during expanded duty tours that began as soon as they left their homes and ended when they returned home. The city outfitted these unmarked cars with special gear, including sirens, emergency lights, and radios, equipment that made it possible for the two captains to monitor police calls, observe responses of subordinates to calls from dispatchers, and respond more quickly to emergency situations.

The Tax Court ruled that the IRS correctly characterized the between-home-and-stationhouse trips as commuting, not business, because the captains did not do any work, whereas the Tenth Circuit noted that the city gave them no choice, requiring commanding officers to perform supervisory and patrol duties during those trips. The appellate court gave short shrift to the IRS's entreaty that allowing write-offs by police captains under standing orders to keep in radio contact with headquarters would immediately result in hordes of other commuters deducting travel outlays—for instance, employees who use car telephones or portable dictaphones during between-home-and-job drives.

There was, responded the court, no foundation for the feds' fears of vastly decreased tax collections causing ballooning budget deficits and grass growing in the streets of America. After all, the overwhelming majority of employees voluntarily decide to forego public transportation and use their personal cars; that kind of personal convenience cannot authorize deductions. Moreover, unlike the two captains, virtually all employees are unable to validly assert that they hold public service or safety jobs that require them to use their personal cars.

Car Pools

These commuting restrictions also eliminate a deduction for payments to a car pool, whether each member takes a turn driving his or her own car or only one does all the driving. On the other hand, you need not report payments from riders unless they exceed your expenses.

Travel from Job to Job

When you work at two different places, you can deduct any unreimbursed cost of travel from one place to another. This holds true whether you work for the same employer or you moonlight at a second job. There is a cap on the business-travel deduction if you do not go directly from one job location to the other, because of some personal reason—say, a stop at home to check on the kids. Your deduction is limited to what it would have cost you to go directly from the first location to the second.

Caution. The trip from your second location back to your home is nondeductible commuting, as is the trip between your home and a part-time weekend job.

Tip. There is another stipulation that has to be satisfied before you can deduct unreimbursed employee business expenses, such as job-to-job travel, as well as most other miscellaneous itemized deductions. They are deductible on Schedule A of Form 1040 only to the extent that their total in any one year is above 2 percent of your AGI, short for adjusted gross income. Anything below the 2 percent of AGI floor is nondeductible. AGI is the amount of income subject to tax after subtracting such things as money put in IRAs and alimony payments, but before itemizing for such expenses as charitable contributions or claiming the standard deduction. (For the rules on miscellaneous deductions, see Chapter 9.)

Partial disallowance of certain deductions for persons with AGIs above a specified amount, which is adjusted annually to reflect inflation—$111,800 for tax year 1994. You suffer a partial disallowance of your allowable write-off for most itemized deductibles, including reimbursed employee business expenses and other miscellaneous itemized deductions. The disallowance is 3 percent of the amount by which your AGI surpasses a specified amount—$111,800 for 1994, which is up from $108,450 for 1993, $105,250 for 1992 and $100,000 for 1991, when this restriction first went on the books. Put another way, you lose $300 in total deductions for every $10,000 of AGI above $111,800. The $111,800 figure drops to $55,900 if you are married and file a separate return; going that route does not raise the threshold for a couple to a combined $223,600. (See "Curtailment of Most Itemized Deductions for Individuals with AGIs above a Specified Amount" in Chapter 14.)

Win some, lose some. The IRS persuaded the Tax Court that no exception should be made for Mrs. Raymond Theep, a housewife who journeyed from her home to her job and back. She was, observed the court, a commuter, not a job-to-job traveler; the snag is that housewifely chores fail to qualify as a profit-motivated activity.

But the IRS was bested by Margaret Green, a professional blood donor, on the issue of a deduction for her home-to-laboratory travel. The Tax Court concluded she was a business traveler, rather than a commuter to the lab. Said the court: "Unique to this situation, the taxpayer was the container in which her product was transported to market. Had she been able to extract the plasma at home and transport it to the laboratory without her being present, such shipping expenses would have been deductible as selling expenses."

Carrying Tools or Equipment to Work

The IRS does make some exceptions to its blanket ban on deductions for commuting expenses. One of those exceptions authorizes a limited measure of relief for someone who needs to haul bulky tools or equipment that cannot go in a car. You are allowed to deduct the *additional* costs for hauling equipment, such as the charge for renting a trailer that is towed by your car (subject to the 2 percent floor applied to unreimbursed employee business expenses and most other miscellaneous itemized deductions). The car costs, though, remain nondeductible commuting expenses.

The Tax Court agreed with the IRS that the additional-cost exception could not be invoked by Ila Beards, who drove from her home in suburban Westchester County to her job as a teacher at a college in New York City. Professor Beards used her car to transport books and other materials necessary to teach her classes, as the college did not provide storage facilities.

On teaching days, she left home at noon and school at 10 in the evening; the drive each way was one hour. A trip by public transportation would have meant a walk of 3 blocks to a bus stop, a bus ride of 10 to 30 minutes to a train station, a train ride from the suburban station to Grand Central Station in New York City, and a walk or taxi ride of 12 blocks to the college; in all, a one-way commute of about 90 minutes. On her return for the year in issue, Ms. Beards claimed a then-allowable investment credit of $462 for the car and an attention-grabbing $7,500 for car expenses.

This set of facts prompted the Tax Court to conclude that the teacher would have gotten behind the wheel even if it had not been necessary for her to transport her books. The court cited Fridays, when she still drove, though she had no classes and came in merely to attend meetings or take care of duties other than teaching. Therefore, taking the books along did not cause her to incur additional costs.

BUSINESS-CAR DEDUCTIONS

In most cases, the law gives you a choice of two methods for figuring deductions for business use of your car. You can claim actual expenses or a standard mileage rate.

Actual Expenses

Under this method, you get to write off your allowable operating costs. The list of deductible items includes gas, oil, tires, repairs, license tags, insurance, garage rent, interest to buy the car, property taxes, and depreciation.

Caution. There are restrictions on depreciation deductions for cars used less than 50 percent of the time for business driving. Also, if you use the car for both business and personal driving, you must split total costs between the two purposes; your deductions are limited to the percentage of costs attributable to business use.

Standard Mileage Rate

Instead of claiming actual expenses, you may be able to use a standard mileage rate that simplifies the paperwork. The standard rate encompasses depreciation, as well as other car expenses. Under the rule applicable to tax year 1994 (the most recent year for which information is available as this book goes to press in the summer of 1994), the standard rate is 29 cents a mile.

When Standard Mileage Rate May Be Used

The IRS restricts your use of the standard mileage rate. You must do so in the first year that you place your car in service in your business. In later years, you have the option to use the standard rate or actual expenses. If you do not choose the standard rate in the first year, you cannot use it for that car in any year.

Tip. Whether you claim actual expenses or use the mileage allowance, remember to deduct parking fees and bridge, tunnel, and turnpike tolls, as well, that you pay while you are on business.

Record Keeping

If the IRS questions your car expenses, it will not challenge a standard mileage deduction, provided you are able to substantiate the miles driven; your actual expenses are disregarded. So you need to keep a glove-compartment diary or other record in which you list the details of when, how far, and why you went, along with the cost of parking and tolls.

Tip. At the audit, those diary entries will be more convincing if they are made close to when the trips take place, not when the filing deadline looms. (For a discussion of audits, see Chapter 11.)

Form 1040 Paperwork

Which forms you use for listing car expenses depends on whether you are an employee or self-employed. Individuals who are employees must use Form 2106 (Employee Business Expenses) to list actual expenses and depreciation or the standard mileage rate. Those who are self-employed fill out other forms—Schedule C (Profit or Loss from Business) for the mileage rate or actual expenses and Form 4562 (Depreciation and Amortization) for depreciation. Note, though, that the IRS wants to lessen the paperwork. Someone who is self-employed and *not* claiming car depreciation (either because the mileage rate is used or the car is fully depreciated) needs to use just Schedule C and is excused from filling out Form 4562. But continue to complete Form 4562 when depreciation is claimed. Attach the required forms and schedules to your Form 1040.

GIVING A CAR TO YOUR YOUNGSTER

If you plan to give your youngster a car as a gift, you've doubtless resigned yourself to rising prices putting a bad dent in your wallet. But insurance premiums are another story. There is something you can do to cut your costs considerably, depending on how you handle the gift. Here are some points to keep in mind.

Insurance Premiums

If only one car is insured and your child is the principal driver, the insurance tab stays the same whether the car is registered in the name of your child or yourself. But if you already insure a car, registering the new car to be used by your child in your name can provide a savings because many insurance companies allow a discount on most coverage options on a second or third car.

Suppose, for example, that you are a three-car family. You and your spouse are the principal drivers for two cars, and your teenage son is the principal driver of the third one. You forfeit the discount if you register the car in your son's name.

Of course, registering the son's car in your name does expose you to the possibility of a lawsuit in case of an accident. But this drawback is relatively minor, provided you carry sufficient insurance to cover yourself for any possible liability and see to it that your children do the same for themselves.

Casualty Losses

Another fact that may make it advantageous to register ownership in your name is that a casualty-loss deduction is available only to the *owner* of the damaged property. Thus, even if you get stuck with the bill, you get no tax write-off for damage or destruction of a car registered in your child's name.

This was made clear to the Omans, a Maryland couple who gave their 20-year-old son the money to buy a sports car that he registered in his name. Before he even acquired collision coverage, one of his friends totaled the car. When filing time rolled around, the couple claimed a casualty loss. But the Tax Court sided with the IRS and threw out their deduction. Since they kept no strings on the gift to their son, the car—and the casualty loss—was his.

Note, though, that uninsured casualty or theft losses of cars not used in your business are deductible only to the extent such losses exceed 10 percent of your adjusted gross income, plus $100 for each casualty or theft. (For more information on deductions for damaged cars, see "Casualty and Theft Losses" in Chapter 9.)

Partial disallowance of certain deductions for persons with AGIs above a specified amount—$111,800 for tax year 1994. Casualty and theft losses are not subject to this partial disallowance. (See "Curtailment of Most Itemized Deductions for Individuals with AGIs above a Specified Amount" in Chapter 14.)

Business Travel with Your Spouse

Some kinds of deductions just drive the IRS up the wall. An unsurprising example of what always causes the tax collectors to become suspicious and demand a detailed accounting: business travelers who journey to meetings or conventions at plush resorts or exotic locales and (gasp!) decide to combine work with play and take their spouses along.

Consequently, regulations promulgated long ago by the agency set stringent guidelines for deductions of a spouse's travel expenses. Those rules, though, were insufficient to satisfy baleful bureaucrats, who repeatedly asked Congress to further toughen the deduction rules for a spouse's travel expenses.

The grinches were rewarded for their persistence. A complaisant Congress imposed far stricter requirements that took effect starting with returns for 1994 to be filed in 1995—yet another entry in the continually-growing list of write-offs that have been curtailed or completely kayoed since enactment of the Tax Reform Act of 1986, which overhauled the Internal Revenue Code from stem to stern.

To be sure, IRS apparatchiks always had to allow you to deduct part of the tab for the cost of tending to business chores. All was never forfeited just because your mate tagged along for no reason other than to see the sights, though, in that event, there were strict limits on what and how much qualified as a business-travel deduction.

The key requirement: Show that you attended, say, a convention primarily for business reasons. Then, there should be no problem about a write-off for what you spent to get yourself to and from the convention, as well as expenditures for hotels and meals during the meeting. (Travel and hotel outlays are 100 percent deductible, but meals are only 50 percent deductible; see "Deductions for Entertaining at Home" in Chapter 9.)

But even before the rules were tightened, the agency's sherlocks balked at any deduction for the portion of the outlays attributable to your spouse's travel, meals, and lodging unless you could show a genuine business reason for his or her presence at the convention.

Those expenses did not become deductible merely because your spouse performed some incidental services—for instance, typing notes, acting as a hostess at dances and receptions, or accompanying you to and remaining awake throughout convention gatherings. What counted was whether your spouse's presence was *necessary,* as opposed to *helpful,* to the conduct of your business, according to IRS regulations, though in a number of cases, the courts ruled against the agency.

Under current rules, no deduction whatever is allowed for travel expenses of your spouse. It makes no difference that he or she goes along for business reasons.

This blanket prohibition is subject to a limited exception, one that will allow relatively few travelers to salvage deductions for a mate's travel expenses. To qualify for the exception, these requirements must be met: (1) the spouse (or dependent, or any other individual) accompanying you on business travel is a bona fide employee of the outfit that pays for the trip; (2) the spouse undertakes the travel for a bona fide business reason; and (3) the spouse is otherwise entitled to deduct the expenses.

Tip. Some often-overlooked tax relief remains available for lodging costs even when your spouse, significant squeeze, or someone else tags along only for fun. Claim a deduction for lodging based on the single-rate cost of similar accommodations for you, not half the double rate you actually paid.

Example. You and your spouse go by car to a business convention in Philadelphia, where the two of you stay at a hotel that charges $130 for a double and $120 for a single room. In addition to a deduction for the entire round-trip drive (the driving costs the same whether your spouse accompanies you or not), claim a per-day deduction for your hotel room of $120, rather than half the double, or $65. To help safeguard your deduction if the IRS questions it, remember to have the hotel bill note the single rate, or get a rate sheet.

MARRIED COUPLES WORKING IN DIFFERENT CITIES

Most persons are well aware that their business-travel deductions include what they spend on lodgings and meals (100 percent deductibility for lodgings, but only 50 percent deductibility for meals), so long as they are on a trip that takes them away from home overnight. But the IRS defines "home" as where a person's principal place of business or employment is located, even though his or her family resides in another place.

For most persons, this should raise no problems since they work at one job in the same place in which they live with their families. But identifying their tax home and whether their outlays for meals and lodgings qualify as away-from-home travel expenses raises troublesome questions for the ever-growing number of two-career couples who now live apart in an effort to keep their jobs or advance their careers.

Researchers estimate that roughly 1 million wives work and maintain homes in one city, while their husbands do likewise in another city. With more women launching careers, the number is likely to keep growing.

To illustrate the tax problem, consider the case of Robert and Margaret Coerver, who each had separate jobs and residences: He was in Wilmington, and she was in New York City. During the first two years of their marriage, she kept her job and apartment in New York and made frequent trips to Wilmington. Margaret contended she was entitled to deduct her rent and food while in New York, as well as her New York–Wilmington travel, as she and Robert filed jointly and their tax home was in Wilmington where he lived.

But the Third Circuit Court of Appeals backed the Tax Court, which barred any write-off for these expenses. Because her stay in New York was "indefinite," her tax home didn't shift from New York to Wilmington, even though she filed jointly. Thus, Margaret was never "away from home" while in New York, and her rent and food there remained nondeductible. Nor could she deduct New York–Wilmington travel, since those trips also were for personal reasons.

Then there was the case of George and Mary Leyland who worked in New Haven and found out the expensive way how the rules can twist and turn. He was with the Census Bureau, and she was with IBM. It all began when the bureau sent George to Boston for a year's training at the Harvard Business School. The couple gave up their New Haven apartment and rented one in Boston. They also joined a New Haven club and took a room there for Mary, which George shared when he traveled to New Haven. While George was in Boston, Mary sometimes journeyed to Boston on business for IBM.

At filing time, the couple claimed their tax home was in New Haven and deducted their Boston expenses. But the IRS viewed the matter somewhat differently. The IRS readily conceded that Mary's tax home was in New Haven, as her job location was unchanged. This, of course, entitled her to deduct unreimbursed business expenses while in Boston on assignment by IBM.

But the Tax Court agreed with the IRS that New Haven was no longer George's tax home, as he gave up his apartment there and moved to Boston. True, his Boston assignment started out as "temporary," rather than "indefinite." Nonetheless, the court found that George chose to shift his tax home to Boston, as he was reimbursed by the Bureau when he took his furniture with him and he was paid a per diem allowance by the Bureau when he traveled from Boston to New Haven on assignments. Thus, he was never away from home while in Boston, and his rent and food there were nondeductible. But, of course, that finding entitled George to deduct unreimbursed business expenses while in New Haven on assignments.

The Tax Court also ruled against Marianne and Donald Felton, an Indiana couple. Marianne was on the faculty of a school located about 100 miles from the town in which Donald worked and where they both resided. Usually, Marianne stayed two nights a week at her job site; she spent about $1,700 on travel expenses for the year under review.

The Tax Court held that Marianne's tax home was where she worked. Her decision to live with her husband was made for personal reasons; hence, the travel outlays in issue were nondeductible personal expenses.

Marianne, said the court, "argues that failure to consider personal elements in a case such as hers puts undue strain on two-job families. While her point perhaps is appealing sociologically, it has no basis in law." *Translation:* The law is the law, and there can be no deduction.

EDUCATIONAL TRAVEL NOT DEDUCTIBLE

Tax reform restricts most deductions for education expenses. Also, it abolishes deductions for travel as a form of education—a break previously enjoyed by many persons, particularly teachers with time for lengthy trips to far-off spots during school vacation periods or while on sabbatical leave.

On the plus side, teachers and others are still able to take education-expense deductions for spending they undertake either to (1) maintain or improve skills required to perform their *current* jobs or businesses or (2) to meet the requirements of their employers or of laws or regulations for keeping their jobs. However, they cannot deduct courses that enable them to meet the minimum educational requirements for *future* occupations or to qualify in *new* endeavors.

Example. The law prohibits any deductions by Norma Bates for courses that she takes to meet the minimum requirements for obtaining a license to teach high school Spanish. It is a different story, though, if Norma already teaches that language at a school and wants to switch to teaching French.

The IRS unreservedly bestows its blessings on deductions for courses to qualify her as a teacher of a different language; she is still in the same line of work. Moreover, Norma's educational write-offs are not limited to her payments for the French courses. Her deductibles include travel to and from the schools at which she takes the courses, whether they are in the United States or in France.

Under prior law, the cost of the *travel itself,* including meals and lodgings, usually qualified as a form of deductible education because the trip enriched her teaching skills.

In most cases, this break was available to Norma, as well as other language teachers who spent their summer vacations in, say, Japan or Germany, where, though they took no courses, their travels enabled them to improve their understanding of the languages and cultures of these countries.

Now, though, absolutely no deductions are allowed for travel expenditures by teachers and others where their travel is a form of education. The prohibition applies to travel deductions that are allowable solely because the *travel itself* is educational.

These restrictions are subject to an important exception. Tax reform retained write-offs for trips that are necessary to engage in activities that give rise to deductible education.

Example. Fred Dobbs is a Russian teacher who uses a sabbatical leave from his school for a journey to Russia to brush up on his accent and to better his knowledge of the culture. He cannot deduct his travel costs as education expenses even if Fred spent most of his time visiting Russian families and schools and attending movies, lectures, and plays.

Example. Nadine Miller is employed by a school to teach courses on French literature. She goes to Paris to do specific library research that cannot be done elsewhere or to take courses offered only at the Sorbonne. Assuming her research or courses meet the deduction requirements, Nadine also gets to deduct her transportation, lodging, and 50 percent of her meals.

Caution. Just because Nadine takes courses that allow her to sidestep the educational-travel restrictions does not mean that she can count on a full deduction for her courses, travel, and other unreimbursed employee business expenses. Yet another restriction requires Nadine to include these employee expenses with her other miscellaneous itemized deductions, such as tax return–preparation charges. Most miscellaneous deductions are allowable only to the extent that their total exceeds 2 percent of her adjusted gross income. (For the rules on miscellaneous deductions, see Chapter 9.)

Partial disallowance of certain deductions for persons with AGIs above a specified amount, which is adjusted annually to reflect inflation. You suffer a partial disallowance of your allowable write-off for most itemized deductibles, including educational expenses and other miscellaneous itemized deductions. The disallowance is 3 percent of the amount by which your AGI surpasses a specified amount—$111,800 for 1994. (See "Curtailment of Most Itemized Deductions for Individuals with AGIs above a Specified Amount" in Chapter 14.)

Help from the IRS

For more information, see IRS Publication 508, *Educational Expenses.* For a free copy, call 1-800-TAX-FORM (allow at least ten work days for mailing) or stop by the IRS office serving your area to obtain one immediately. Many libraries also have copies of this and other IRS tax guides. IRS Publication 910, *Guide to Free Tax Services,* provides a complete list of booklets and explains what each one covers. (For a discussion of IRS publications, see "Get the Right Help at Tax Time" in Chapter 13.)

Tip. Don't rely absolutely on IRS advice, whether it is information that employees give as answers to telephone or walk-in inquiries or instructions that the agency prints in its publications. Mistakes in instructions or advice are inevitable, and the IRS is not bound by them.

MOVING EXPENSES

Are you among the millions who will move this year to take a new job or to work at a new location for the same employer or for yourself? You may be able to ease the pain of relocating with deductions for many of the expenses incurred in the shift, although, of course, you get tax relief only for expenses that you bear, not for those that are reimbursed by your employer. What follows is a close look at the often-misunderstood rules on how far you must move and how long you must work to qualify for the deduction, which outlays are allowed without limits, and which ones are allowable only within certain limits.

Mostly tighter rules for 1994 and later years. The 1993 tax act makes significant changes in the rules for deductions by anyone who is moving to a new job. Most of the revisions are unfavorable for employees and self-employeds.

There continues to be no ceiling on the deduction for "direct" moving expenses. These are the basic costs of shipping household goods and other belongings, as well as the trip to the new hometown. Congress had considered, but eventually thought the better of, perhaps in response to lobbying pressures, drastically scaling back the allowable deduction for direct expenses by enacting a cap of $10,000, which is well below the cost of many long-distance moves.

But starting with returns for 1994 to be filed in 1995, several breaks vanish or become curtailed. For openers, the most important revision is an increase in the distance test from 35 to 50 miles. *Translation*: No deduction whatever for your direct expenses unless your new job location is at least 50 miles farther from your old residence than your old job was.

Congress also thought about, but did not impose, a higher number. But budget pressures might force a revenue-hungry Congress to again increase the distance requirement.

Also, no longer is any deduction allowed for "indirect" expenses of as much as $3,000, of which no more than $1,500 can be for pre-move trips to find a home and temporary living expenses at the new location. Indirect expenses include three kinds of expenditures: (1) pre-move house-hunting expenses incurred while traveling between your old home and the area of your new job location, (2) temporary living expenses for you and your family for up to 30 days at the new job location while waiting to move into, or looking for, a house or apartment, and (3) certain expenses of selling a residence or settling an unexpired lease in the old location or purchasing a new residence or acquiring a lease in the new location.

Also deep-sixed are any deductions for meals on the road, whether while moving or living in temporary quarters at the new job location. So you have to count as reportable income any employer reimbursements for nondeductible meals.

Finally, some good news. Unreimbursed moving expenses become an "above-the-line" adjustment, that is, a subtraction from gross income to arrive at adjusted gross income at the bottom of page 1 of Form 1040, just like contributions to IRAs and other retirement plans. No longer are moving expenses a "below-the-line" subtraction from adjusted gross income to arrive at taxable income and, therefore, allowable only as an itemized deduction on Schedule A of Form 1040. *Result*: You get to write off those unreimbursed moving expenses, whether you itemize your deductions for charitable deductions and the like or use the standard deduction, the no-questions-asked amount that is automatically available without the need to itemize. (See "Itemizing versus Standard Deduction" in Chapter 1.)

Distance Test

This is the key requirement. You are eligible to deduct these expenses only if your new job location is at least 50 miles farther from your old residence than your old job was.

As an illustration, assume the distance between your old home and your old job is 10 miles. The distance between your old home and your new job must be a minimum of 60 miles.

Tip. Actually, you have some leeway on the 50-mile minimum. The law does not require you to measure the distance on the basis of a straight line on a map. It's okay to calculate the mileage on the shortest of the routes that you would ordinarily travel. As for the distance between your new home and either job location, it is irrelevant.

First job or return to full-time work. An *easier* distance rule applies when there is no "old job," as is the case when you go to work full-time for the first time because you are just out of college or when you go back to full-time work after what the IRS considers to be "a substantial period" of part-time work or unemployment. To pass the distance test, all you need to show is that your place of work is at least 50 miles from your old home.

When is a spell of unemployment sufficiently long to be "substantial"? Two months of unemployment is not long enough to qualify you for the easier rule, according to an Internal Revenue ruling (Rev. Rul. 78–174). The tax collectors have yet to say how long you need to be without work to qualify.

Home. The IRS has its own interpretation of "home." Your home means your "principal residence," that is, a year-round dwelling, as opposed to a seasonal place, such as a summer beach cottage. Of course, the tax break is not reserved exclusively for folks who live in single-family homes. For purposes of the distance test, your principal residence can also be a cooperative or condominium apartment, a trailer home, or anything else that provides all the amenities of a home—a houseboat, for instance, or even a yacht that has all the facilities for cooking, sleeping, and sanitation. (For more information, see "The 'Principal Residence' Requirement" in Chapter 3.)

Direct Moving Expenses

Assuming you pass the distance test, you are allowed to write off expenses that the IRS refers to as "direct," that is, the basic costs of moving belongings and the family's trip to the new hometown. There is no ceiling on deductions for direct expenses.

Household goods and personal effects. Tote up all charges for the cost of packing, crating, and transporting your furniture, cars, pets, and other belongings from your old home to your new one. Include charges for in-transit storage and insurance for up to 30 days.

Tip. One proviso here is that the deduction for moving property from a place other than your old home is limited to what the estimated cost would have been to move it from your old home to the new one. Another stipulation is that there is no deduction for moving furniture bought on the way to your new home.

Travel expenses. Deduct transportation and lodging for yourself, family members, and pets (it's not necessary that you travel together or at the same time) while traveling from the old to the new residence. An often-overlooked deduction is the cost of hotels for the day before the move, assuming you were unable to live in your old home because your furniture had been moved, and for the day you arrive at your new home. These outlays are also fully deductible.

Did you use your car to transport yourself, your family, or your belongings?

You have these options: Deduct the actual cost of gas and oil (but not depreciation) or a flat allowance of 9 cents a mile (under the rules applicable to tax year 1994, the most recent year for which information is available as this book goes to press). Whether you claim actual costs or use the mileage allowance, remember to deduct parking fees and bridge, tunnel, and turnpike tolls, as well.

There is no deduction, though, for any side trips taken for personal reasons, such as stopovers with relatives or sightseeing at

Yellowstone while relocating from the East Coast to California. Your route, cautions the IRS, should be "the shortest, most direct one available by conventional transportation."

Time Test

Besides satisfying the 50-mile distance requirement, you must work full-time for a specified period at the new location.

Employees. You must work full-time for at least 39 weeks in the new area in the 12-month period after the move. Those weeks need not be consecutive, and you need not work for the same employer. As explained below, your family does not have to arrive with you.

Self-employed. You must conduct your business full-time for at least 78 weeks in the 24-month period after the move, including at least 39 weeks during the first 12 months.

Temporary absences. In determining whether you pass the time test, you can ignore temporary absences from work, through no fault of your own, due to illness, strikes, layoffs, natural disasters, or similar causes.

Joint returns. If you are married and both you and your spouse work full-time, either of you can satisfy the full-time work test. But you cannot add the weeks your spouse works to those you work to satisfy that test.

Time test not met by filing deadline. You may deduct your moving expenses on Form 1040 for the year of the move even if you have not met the 39-week (or 78-week) test by the filing deadline for the return. What happens if it turns out that you are ineligible? You either have to amend your return (use Form 1040X; see "Refund Claims" in Chapter 14) or report the amount previously deducted as moving expenses as income on the return for the year you fail the time test.

Example. You arrive at the new location on September 15, 1994. You deduct your moving expenses on your 1994 return, the year of the move, even though you have not met the time test by the date your return is due. If you do not meet the 39-week test by September 15, 1995, you should either amend your 1994 return or report the amount you had deducted as moving expenses on your 1994 return as income on your 1995 return.

Exceptions to the time test. You satisfy the time requirement when, among other things, your new job ends because of your death or disability, if your employer decides to transfer you elsewhere, or if you are laid off for some reason other than willful misconduct.

The IRS persuaded the Tax Court to apply the 39-week rule rigidly to Wanda Rohwer, a social worker for a state agency. Wanda moved downstate for a new job with the agency and worked there for 37 weeks until her employer announced openings in another office and she again transferred—a second switch that, noted the Tax Court, the agency approved but did not *require*. Therefore, no moving-expense deduction for the cost of her first move was allowed.

Tip. Had Wanda delayed her second move for two weeks, the IRS could not have invoked the 39-week rule.

Closely-Related Test

You do not lose out on the deduction merely because your move takes place after, rather than at, the time you begin your new job. But there is a deadline. The IRS allows a deduction only for a move that is closely related in time to the start of work at the new job location. As a general rule, the closely-related requirement is satisfied only when those moving expenses are incurred within one year from the date you first report to work. When more than one year elapses between the start of the job and the move, the expenses are not deductible unless you can point to circumstances that prevented the move within that time. Although the tax collectors judge each case by its own facts, Revenue Service agents usually concede that extra time is justified to allow your spouse to fulfill job commitments in the old hometown or your children to finish a segment of their schooling.

Example.   You actually move to your new job location within one year. Your spouse and child remain at the old residence for 18 months so that your child can complete high school in the same school. Their later moving expenses, though incurred considerably more than one year after your move, should be deductible, just as yours are. In fact, a 1978 ruling allowed a deduction for a move delayed for 30 months to allow a teenager to complete high school in the same school (Rev. Rul. 78–200).

However, the IRS was unwilling to approve a deduction for a two-paycheck couple when job-related reasons caused them to postpone their move for more than a year. The wife obtained a teaching position that required her to commute 120 miles to another city. The couple delayed a move closer to her job because they feared an immediate move might hurt the husband's chances for tenure at the university where he taught. After he obtained tenure, they moved, as his schedule made commuting more practical for him than for her. According to a 1983 ruling, these circumstances did not prevent a move within one year (Ruling 8346039).

Tip.   On the other hand, another 1983 ruling approved a deduction for a move made during a period of several months in which the taxpayer temporarily ceased to operate his business (Ruling 8346023).

Nondeductible Expenses

The IRS draws the line at moving-expense deductions for meals, a loss on the sale of your residence, prepayment of rent, fixing-up expenses to assist in selling your old residence, any real estate taxes, any payments that represent interest (such as mortgage penalties), any portion of the purchase price of the new residence, the cost of auto tags and a driver's license that are required by the state to which you move, refitting carpets and draperies, losses sustained on the disposal of memberships in clubs, tuition fees, and similar indirectly related expenses. (For information on the rules for home sellers, see Chapter 3.)

Want to reach out and touch someone after the move? The IRS also prohibits a deduction for the cost of installing a telephone in your new residence.

Paperwork

Make sure to save receipts and other evidence of what you spend on a tax-deductible move. You will need them for the annual reckoning with the IRS.

Actually, the tax saving can come much sooner in the form of increased take-home pay, should you incur deductible expenses that are not reimbursed by your employer. You may want to file a new W-4 form (Employee's Withholding Allowance Certificate) with your employer. The W-4 form allows you to cut the amount taken from your pay if, among other things, you have qualifying expenses. A worksheet on the back of the W-4 translates these and certain other expenditures into "allowances" that can be claimed in addition to the regular exemptions for yourself and your dependents. (For more information, see the discussion of withholding in Chapter 14.)

Your reportable income does not include any reimbursements received from your employer for *deductible* moving expenses. But the law does require you to report as income any reimbursement by your employer of *nondeductible* moving expenses—for instance, reimbursements for meals or a loss on the sale of your home. Those kinds of reimbursements usually are listed on your W-2, and you enter that amount on the Form 1040 line for wages and salaries.

Compute your allowable deduction, if any, on Form 3903 and enter the allowable deduction on the Form 1040 line for moving expenses. Attach Form 3903 to your Form 1040.

If the IRS questions your deduction, be prepared to show that your payments qualify. Hang on to checks and other records that substantiate those payments at least until the statute of limitations runs out for an IRS audit. As a general rule, that is three years from the filing deadline, which is mid-April for most persons—April 1998 in the case of a return for 1994. (For how long to keep records, see Chapter 11.)

If you neglected to claim a refund on a return for which you are still eligible to claim a refund, you can do so on a Form 1040X that is accompanied by Form 3903. (For more information, see the discussion of refund claims in Chapter 14.)

Different rules apply to members of the armed forces and persons employed abroad.

Tip. If you move after filing this year's return and you are expecting a refund, notify the IRS. To report an address change, use IRS Form 8822 (Change of Address). It is easy to fill out: Just insert your old and new addresses, your full name, and Social Security number, as well as the full name and Social Security number of your spouse if you file jointly. To get the form, call 1-800-TAX-FORM or stop by an IRS office. Mail the form to the IRS Service Center that handled your last return. Notifying the post office is not sufficient. (See "Still Waiting for a Refund? If You Moved, Tell the IRS" in Chapter 14.)

Help from the IRS

Need more information on which moving expenses you can deduct? See IRS Publication 521, *Moving Expenses.* For a free copy, call 1-800-TAX-FORM (allow at least 10 work days for mailing) or stop by the IRS office serving your area to obtain one immediately. Many libraries also have copies of this and other IRS tax guides. IRS Publication 910, *Guide to Free Tax Services,* provides a complete list of booklets and explains what each one covers. (For a discussion of IRS publications, see "Get the Right Help at Tax Time" in Chapter 13.)

Tip.   Don't rely absolutely on IRS advice, whether it is information that employees give to telephone or walk-in inquiries or instructions that the agency prints in its publications. Mistakes in instructions or advice are inevitable, and the IRS is not bound by them.

6 CHILD- OR DEPENDENT-CARE EXPENSES

Do you pay someone to care for your child or other dependent while you hold down a job? Under the rules applicable to a return for tax year 1994, those expenses may entitle you to a valuable break in the form of a tax credit for part of what you spend.

To take advantage of this tax trimmer, you need to satisfy several requirements. First, you must earn income from a job or from self-employment.

Next, you have to maintain a home for:

- a child under the age of 13 (the cutoff age was 15 through 1988, when a Congress committed to the inconsistent goals of enhancement of family values and lower budget deficits decided to favor the latter and changed the cutoff from 15 to 13);
- a disabled dependent of any age; or
- a disabled spouse.

Finally, if you are married, both you and your spouse must work at least part-time, unless one of you is disabled or is a full-time student.

The credit is figured as a percentage of the first $2,400 of your household or personal-care outlays for the care of one child (or other qualifying individual) and the first $4,800 spent for the care of two or more. The percentage is on a sliding scale that ranges downward from 30 to 20 percent, and the allowable percentage depends on the amount of AGI (adjusted gross income) you show at the bottom of page 1 of Form 1040 after listing salaries and other sources of income and claiming certain deductions like alimony payments and money put in IRAs, but before itemizing for things like charitable contributions and real estate taxes and claiming dependency exemptions.

For someone with an AGI under $10,000, the top credit is $720 (a maximum of $2,400 expenses times 30 percent) for one dependent and $1,440 (a maximum of $4,800 expenses times 30 percent) for one or more dependents. The allowable credit, however, declines by 1 percentage point for each $2,000 (or fraction thereof) of AGI above $10,000, until it bottoms out at 20 percent if your AGI exceeds $28,000. Thus, assuming your income is above the $28,000 level, the credit is limited to $480 (a maximum of $2,400 expenses times 20 percent) for one dependent and $960 (a maximum of $4,800 expenses times 20 percent) for two or more.

Example. You have an AGI of $20,500 and spend $3,800 for care of two dependents. Your allowable credit is $912 ($3,800 times 24 percent).

The allowable percentages for persons with adjusted gross incomes in excess of $10,000 are as follows:

Adjusted gross income over	Credit percentage
$10,000	29
12,000	28
14,000	27
16,000	26
18,000	25
20,000	24
22,000	23
24,000	22
26,000	21
28,000	20

EMPLOYER-PROVIDED CARE

Revised rules require the amount of expenses eligible for the credit to be reduced dollar for dollar by the amount of expenses paid for by employer-sponsored dependent-care assistance programs (DCAPs)—also known as flexible spending accounts, salary-reduction plans, and set-aside plans. A DCAP is an employer-provided fringe benefit that allows you to use pre-tax salary set aside to pay for care costs. No longer can you claim both the credit and an exclusion from income (you are excused from paying taxes on the money) for DCAP funds used to pay your expenses.

Previously, the law allowed double dipping if your employer offered a DCAP. First, you could reduce reportable income by channeling up to $5,000 of salary reductions into a DCAP, from which an employer reimbursed care expenses; then, you could claim the credit for care expenses above $5,000. Now, when DCAP-covered expenses exceed $2,400 for one dependent or $4,800

for two or more, your credit completely disappears.

Example. You have one child under 13 and $5,000 of care expenses, $2,500 of which is DCAP-reimbursed and excluded from your income. The DCAP-covered $2,500 causes you to lose out on any credit for the remaining expenses. Had the DCAP reimbursements been only $1,000, then $1,400 (maximum expenses of $2,400 minus $1,000 reimbursements) would count toward the credit.

Tip. Many individuals who had claimed both the credit and the exclusion available through a DCAP now must decide which break saves more tax dollars. Which is better can be a close call.

Generally, it pays for higher-income employees to use the DCAP exclusion and skip the credit. To begin with, the DCAP dollar limit is higher—$5,000, compared to credit limits of $2,400 for one dependent or $4,800 for two or more. Also, the savings percentage is greater for someone with a DCAP and higher income—28, 31, 36, or 39.6 cents for every exclusion-eligible dollar taxed at a 28, 31, 36, or 39.6 percent rate, versus 20 cents for every credit-eligible dollar (under the rules for tax year 1994, the most recent year for which information is available as this book goes to press).

But the reverse is true for low-income employees. The credit is more advantageous—a savings of at least 20 cents for every credit-eligible dollar, versus only 15 cents for every exclusion-eligible dollar taxed at a 15 percent rate.

Partial disallowance of certain itemized deductions for persons with AGIs above a specified amount that is adjusted annually to

reflect inflation—$111,800 for tax year 1994. An AGI-lowering DCAP provides another advantage if you have an above-$111,800 AGI and thereby suffer a partial disallowance of certain itemized deductions. The DCAP lessens the disallowance, which is 3 percent of the amount by which AGI exceeds $111,800. (See "Curtailment of Most Itemized Deductions for Individuals with AGIs above a Specified Amount" in Chapter 14.)

Caution. In 1990, Congress considered, but did not enact, legislation that would have kayoed the credit and the DCAP exclusion for families with above-$89,000 AGIs. Under the proposal, there would have been a phaseout of both the credit and the exclusion, which would have remained available only for families with below-$70,000 AGIs. As AGI rose above $70,000, there would have been a gradual phasing out of both breaks. Only a partial credit or exclusion would have been allowed when AGI was between $70,000 and $89,000. For each $1,000 of AGI above $70,000, the credit would have declined by 1 percentage point and the exclusion by $250. As this book goes to press in the summer of 1994, budget pressures might cause Congress to resurrect and enact some type of curtailment on the credit.

How the Child- or Dependent-Care Credit Saves Taxes

You can take the credit even if you decide not to itemize your charitable contributions and other expenses. Unlike a deduction, which merely lowers the amount of income

on which you figure your tax, a credit is a dollar-for-dollar subtraction from the tax you would otherwise owe. Whereas a deduction of $400 is worth only $112 for someone in a 28 percent bracket, dropping to just $60 for someone in a 15 percent bracket, a credit of $400 reduces your tax tab by $400, whether your bracket is 15, 28, 31, 36, or 39.6 percent. (For how to determine your bracket, see "What Is Your Real Tax Bracket?" in Chapter 14.)

Although the credit is fairly straightforward as tax laws go, some of the rules can be tricky and call for careful study. For instance, special provisions apply to working couples and divorced or separated parents. What follows is a rundown on how to take full advantage of this tax break.

Daycare and School Expenses

You can count in-home or outside-the-home expenses that permit you to take, keep, or actively search for a job. The tax offset is available for a wider range of outlays than you might think. Here is a summary of what counts.

In-Home Expenses

For starters, your allowable outlays include the entire salary paid a housekeeper, maid, or cook, even though the household helper's duties do not include acting as a babysitter or companion for someone in your home.

All that you need to establish is that the helper's services partially benefit the person for whom care is being provided—for instance, a fourth grader who is away at school and never physically present while the cleaning of his or her room takes place.

You also gain a credit for the cost of, say, a companion, nurse, or caretaker, as well as for what you spend on their meals. But the list of acceptable expenses does not include the salary of a gardener or chauffeur. Nor does it include lodgings for a live-in housekeeper unless you can show that your out-of-pocket outlays directly attributable to her were greater than your normal household expenses—rent for an extra bedroom, for example.

Outside-the-Home Expenses

There are increased restrictions on these credits. You get a credit for care of children under the age of 13, whether they are cared for in or out of your home, and for care of disabled dependents and spouses in your home. But you get a credit for care of a disabled dependent or spouse outside of your home only if you satisfy certain requirements, as discussed in the following.

Care of children under the age of 13. You can include payments for care outside the home by a nursery school, daycare center, day camp, or the home of a babysitter. Do not include payments for transportation between home and the daycare facility.

The IRS will not second-guess you on the size of your outlays just because you decide to forgo a cheaper alternative. For instance, you can still count the cost of nursery school even though less expensive or even free care is available.

Education.   Outside-the-home expenses do not include the cost of education beyond kindergarten. Thus, the IRS forbids a credit for tuition payments in the first or higher grades. But the IRS will not disallow a credit for payments to a beyond-kindergarten school that are for child care, rather than education.

Let's assume your job requires you to be away from your seven-year-old between 8 and 6 and your public school operates between 9 and 3. To hold your job, you send your youngster to a private school that provides sitters before and after classes. You can take a credit for the school's charge for babysitting, but not for the charge for education. Just make sure the school itemizes its bill to show the tab for child care separately.

Similarly, the IRS concedes a credit for part of your expenses if you place your youngster in a boarding school. For credit purposes, acceptable expenses include room, board, and supervisory care before and after the normal school day, but not amounts spent for tuition, books, and supplies.

Suppose, though, that a mother could work and keep her son in a public school but enrolls him in a boarding school because she believes that he will receive a better education there. Are the expenses disqualified because holding on to a job is not the sole reason the parent places the child in a private school? Not according to the Tax Court. It sided with Goldie Brown, who transferred her son from a Philadelphia junior high to a boarding school. The boy had attended a junior high so plagued with classroom disorders, gang fights, and teacher strikes that Goldie had been unable to work as she had to remain constantly prepared to pick him up if things got out of hand.

Summer camp. A recent law change is bad news for many working parents with children who spend some of the summer at overnight camps. No longer can these parents claim credits for part of the cost of sending children to overnight camps.

Tip. The change does not apply to day camps or nursery schools. They continue to qualify for the credit.

What caused Congress to prohibit credits for overnight camp stays? A key factor was the pro-taxpayer position taken by the Tax Court in a dispute involving Edith Zoltan, an Ohio accountant. The court concluded the accountant was entitled to a credit for the entire cost of sending her 11-year-old son to Camp Adanac in Canada for two months while she worked. Alternative arrangements would have cost about the same amount.

Unlike a boarding school, no part of the cost had to be disallowed as education (as discussed previously, there is no credit for the cost of education beyond kindergarten), as Adanac provided only minimal educational services. The camp's swimming, archery, and other traditional activities were recreational, rather than educational; the youngster, the court noted, need not "be bored stiff" for camping expenses to be acceptable.

Not surprisingly, the IRS wanted to counter this adverse court decision, and Capitol Hill accommodated the tax collectors. That is why the ever-growing list of curtailed or kayoed tax breaks now includes a measure that disqualifies overnight camps for credits.

Care of a disabled dependent or spouse outside of your home. A credit is available only if you pass a two-part test. First, the disabled dependent or spouse must "regularly spend at least eight hours each day in your household," that is, live with you.

Second, your disabled dependent or spouse must be looked after at a "dependent-care center" that "complies with all applicable state and local regulations." A dependent-care center is a place that provides care for more than six persons (other than the persons who live there) and receives a fee, payment, or grant for providing services for any of those persons, regardless of whether or not the center is run for profit.

An IRS publication spells out the types of outside-the-home payments for which the credit is available. Among other things, you get no credit for the costs of institutionalizing someone on a round-the-clock basis.

Example. You live with your disabled father and hire someone to nurse him while you work. Your in-home nursing payments count toward the credit. But if you place him in a nursing home, payments to the nursing home do not count toward the credit, although the payments may qualify as a medical expense. (For information on medical expenses, see Chapter 7.)

Payments to Relatives

Your allowable care expenses do not include payments to someone for whom you claim a dependency exemption or to a son or daughter who is under the age of 19 at the end of the year. But allowable expenses do include payments to a relative, even someone who lives with you, provided you do not take a dependency exemption for the relative, or to a son or daughter older than 18, provided you do not claim an exemption for him or her. For example, you get credit for payments to your sister to look after your bedridden father, provided you don't list her as an exemption.

You also gain a tax break for payments to your mother or mother-in-law (who is not claimed as a dependent by you) to look after your child. Previously, no credit was allowed for payments to a grandparent—a restriction removed during an election year by a Congress bent on finally ridding itself of the damning charge that Capitol Hill was "anti-Granny." Of course, those payments to parents or other relatives must be reasonable—that is, not more than the going rate for sitters in your area.

Not surprisingly, what our legislators giveth, they also taketh away. You must pay Social Security taxes on the wages of a relative that you employ. You are not, however, liable for Social Security taxes on what you pay your parent or a son or daughter under the age of 21.

If you do employ a relative or someone else and are required to shell out for Social Security taxes, you have to file a Form 942 (Employer's Quarterly Tax Return for Household Employees) for your employee for each calendar quarter. Form 942 must be accompanied by your check for the tax due from the employee and the tax due from the employer. You can withhold the required amount from your employee's pay and pay the employer's share yourself, or you can choose to pay it all.

Tip. Whichever route you go, don't overlook claiming a child-care credit for your share of the payroll taxes. Remember, too, that these payments could cause you to forfeit a dependency exemption for the relative. (More information on Social Security taxes for household help is found in Chapter 15.)

QUALIFYING DEPENDENTS

A key requirement for receiving the child-care credit is that you must maintain as your principal residence a home that includes as a member at least one of the persons listed in the following three categories:

1. Dependent children under the age of 13 for whom you claim exemptions on your tax return.

    This simply means that you furnish over half (over 10 percent in the case of a multiple support agreement) of the child's total support for the year. Although you can take an exemption for your son or daughter no matter how much income your youngster receives, you cannot take an exemption for some other youngster, such as a grandchild, who receives reportable income during the year of more than $2,450. (The ceiling of $2,450 applies to a 1994 return, and will be adjusted to reflect inflation in subsequent years. For the rules on dependency exemptions, see Chapter 2.)

Tip. If your child reaches the age of 13 during the tax year, the credit is available only for outlays you incur before the birthday.

Example. Your daughter's 13th birthday falls on June 1. You can take a credit for what you spend on her care between January 1 and May 31, but not for what you spend afterwards, unless (as explained below) she is disabled.

Tip. There is a special rule for divorced or legally separated women who have custody of their children but cannot claim exemptions for them. For instance, the credit remains available to a divorced woman with custody of a child under 13 even though a divorce decree awards the exemption for her youngster to her former husband or she signs IRS Form 8332, which allows him to claim the exemption. (See the discussion in Chapter 2 of exemptions for children of divorced or separated parents.) To qualify herself for the credit, however, she or her former husband or the two of them together must furnish over half of their youngster's total support for the year and have custody for over half of the year. But the credit will still elude her unless she has custody for a longer period than he does.

2. Other dependents, regardless of age, who are physically or mentally incapable of self-care (disabled).

   You meet the dependency requirement so long as you pass the over-half support test (or over 10 percent in the case of a multiple support agreement). This holds true even though you are ineligible to take an exemption for, say, your disabled mother because her reportable income tops the amount that a dependent can have before the exemption is lost ($2,450 in the case of a return for 1994).

Tip. In figuring your mother's income, you do not have to count items that escape tax—for instance, any Social Security benefits that she may receive. But in figuring who provided over half of her support, you must count benefits that she actually spent on her own support.

3. Your spouse who is physically or mentally incapable of self-care.

   For credit purposes, incapable of self-care means a person who suffers from physical or mental disabilities that prevent him (or her) from dressing or feeding himself or tending to personal hygiene without the help of someone else, or who needs constant attention to prevent him from injuring himself or others.

Example. Even though your grandfather otherwise enjoys good health, he is disabled if an injury, whether permanent or temporary, confines him to a bed or to a wheelchair. Similarly, he is disabled if he has suicidal or other dangerous tendencies that may require another person to attend him constantly.

Tip. If you claim a credit for care of a disabled person, you do not have to submit proof of disability with your Form 1040. But to safeguard your credit, should the IRS ask questions, it's wise to get a certification from the attending physician regarding the nature and duration of the disability.

HOUSEHOLDS

Previously, the child-care credit was available to a couple only if both worked full-time, unless one spouse was disabled. Now the credit is available even when both work part-time or are "actively searching" for jobs or if one works part-time and the other is either a full-time student or is disabled. The special provisions for separated or divorced parents are also described in this section.

Earnings Restrictions for Working Couples

Besides the $2,400 or $4,800 ceiling on qualifying expenses, the IRS lays down a tricky rule that can cut the credit allowed some dual-income couples. The ceiling on qualifying expenses is tied to earnings of the *lower-paid spouse*. This means that if one of the couple's earnings are less than $4,800 and more than one dependent is involved or if that mate's earnings are less than $2,400 and one dependent is involved, the couple cannot get the maximum credit.

Take, for instance, marrieds who pay someone $4,500 to clean house and mind their two infants. While one spouse makes a hefty amount, the other works part-time and gets only $3,500. Because of the earnings ceiling, they can count only the first $3,500 of their expenses toward the credit.

On the plus side, this restriction does not automatically take the credit away from a couple just because one spouse has no earnings. Yet another tax wrinkle provides a break when the spouse without earnings is either a full-time student or is disabled.

For credit purposes, that spouse is considered, during each month of disablement or while a student, to have earned $200 a month if care costs for one dependent are incurred and to have earned $400 a month if care costs for two or more dependents are incurred. As a result, the couple is eligible for almost the full credit.

Here is how this rule can help when, say, one spouse works and the other is a full-time student for 10 months. They can count care costs of up to $2,000 ($200 times 10 months) for one child or $4,000 ($400 times 10 months) for two or more children, so long as

the employed spouse does not earn less than the care costs.

While a person qualifies as a full-time student only if he or she takes the required number of courses for at least five months during the year, those five months need not be consecutive. However, when *both* spouses are full-time students or disabled during the *same* month and neither works full- or part-time, none of their expenses for that month counts toward the credit.

Tip. You and your spouse need not have the same working hours to qualify for the credit. One of you can work days and the other nights.

Separated Couples

Ordinarily, the credit is available to a married couple only if they file a joint return. They cannot file separate returns and claim the credit. But there is a way around this for married couples living apart who opt to file separately, provided they satisfy *all* of the following requirements. You will be considered an unmarried person for the year and allowed the credit on a separate return if:

1. You file a separate return.
2. Your spouse did not live in your house during the last six months of the year.
3. For over six months of the year, your home was the principal residence for someone for whom you paid dependent-care expenses.
4. You paid more than half the cost to keep up your home for the year.

If you pass these four tests and qualify as unmarried, you are eligible for the credit regardless of whether your spouse is employed or of the amount he or she earns.

Household Maintenance Test

You (or you and your spouse together) must furnish over half the cost of keeping a home that is the principal residence for yourself and someone for whom you pay dependent-care expenses. In calculating the cost, count such items as rent, property insurance, real estate taxes, mortgage interest, upkeep and repairs, utilities, telephone, and groceries. Do not count the cost of clothing, education, medical treatment, vacations, life insurance, transportation, property improvements or replacements, mortgage principal, or the value of services you or some family member provide without cost, such as housecleaning. For example, maintenance expenses include the cost of *repairing* a water heater, but not the cost of *replacing* one.

In determining whether your dependent lived in your home, you can ignore temporary absences because of vacations, hospitalization, school, camp, custody agreement, and the like. Your home need not be in the same location for the entire year. Thus, you do not disqualify yourself for the credit merely because you move from one house or apartment to another during the year.

You need to do some paperwork if your household maintenance costs cover a care period of less than a year. You must prorate the entire year's costs over the number of calendar months that fall into the period during which you pay care expenses. Treat a period of less than a calendar month as a calendar month.

Example. Yearly maintenance runs to $14,400 and the care period is from January 1 to August 8, when your child becomes 13 or your dependent's disability ends. To meet the household maintenance test for this eight-month period, you must furnish over $4,800 ($14,400 times $\frac{8}{12}$ equals $9,600; 50 percent times $9,600 equals $4,800).

Tip. Two or more families who occupy common living quarters may each be entitled to qualify as a separate household. Take, for instance, two unrelated women, each with children, who occupy common living quarters. If each woman pays over half of her own share of the household costs, each would be entitled to a separate child-care credit.

CREDIT VERSUS DEDUCTION

Under the rules applicable to a return for 1994, some of your outlays for the cost of care of disabled individuals that could entitle you to a tax *credit* (a subtraction from taxes owed) could otherwise qualify as a medical expense *deduction* (a subtraction from taxable income; see the discussion of medical expenses in Chapter 7). But you do not get both breaks for the same expenses.

Of course, you can go the credit route if you forgo itemizing your medical expenses. There is no problem if you use the standard deduction. But if you are an itemizer, you may have to choose between a credit or a deduction.

Assume that it's advantageous to claim the credit and some expenses are not included because of the $2,400 or $4,800 credit ceiling. You can then include these uncredited expenses with your other medical deductibles, which are allowable to the extent they exceed 7.5 percent of your AGI.

If you first take a medical-expense deduction and some expenses go unused because of the 7.5 percent rule, these unused expenses do *not* count for credit purposes. Test the computation both ways to be sure that you choose the method that saves the most tax dollars.

Example. Your disabled father lives with you, and you hire someone to care for him while you and your spouse are at work. Your payment of $2,500 for in-home nursing care qualifies as either a creditable expense or a deduction, and you have an AGI of $40,000.

With those numbers, forget about a deduction that is subject to a 7.5 percent floor and claim the credit. The medical deduction fails to generate a tax benefit because the expenditure of $2,500 is below $3,000 (AGI of $40,000 times 7.5 percent), whereas a credit reduces your taxes by $480 (20 percent of the first $2,400 of the $2,500 spent on nursing).

PAPERWORK

When you incur expenses that count toward the credit, you may want to file a new W-4 form (Employee's Withholding Allowance Certificate) with your employer. The W-4 form allows you to cut the amount taken from your pay if, among other things, you have qualifying expenses. A worksheet on the back of the W-4 translates these and certain other expenses into "allowances" that can be claimed in addition to the regular exemptions for yourself and your dependents. (For more information, see the discussion of withholding in Chapter 14.)

At filing time, you compute your tax credit on Form 2441 and enter the amount

on the Form 1040 line for "credit for child- and dependent-care expenses." On Form 2441, you must list the names, addresses, and Social Security numbers of the care providers, unless a provider is a tax-exempt organization, such as a church or other charity. Attach Form 2441 to your Form 1040.

Make sure to read the instructions that accompany Form 2441 carefully, particularly if you are affected by any of the special restrictions, such as those for working couples or divorced or separated parents.

If the IRS questions your care expenses, be prepared to show that your payments qualify for the credit. Hang on to checks and other records that back up those payments at least until the statute of limitations runs out for an IRS audit. As a general rule, that is three years from the filing deadline, which is mid-April for most persons. (For how long to keep records, see Chapter 11.)

If you neglected to claim a credit for which you are still eligible to claim a refund, you can do so on a Form 1040X that is accompanied by Form 2441. (For additional information, see the coverage of refund claims in Chapter 14.)

Help from the IRS

For more information, see IRS Publication 502, *Medical and Dental Expenses,* and 503, *Child and Dependent Care Credit,* and *Employment Taxes for Household Employers.* For free copies, call 1-800-TAX-FORM (allow at least 10 work days for mailing) or stop by the IRS office serving your area to obtain them immediately. Many libraries also have copies of these and other IRS tax guides. IRS Publication 910, *Guide to Free Tax Services,* provides a complete list of booklets and explains what each one covers. (For a discussion of IRS publications, see "Get the Right Help at Tax Time" in Chapter 13.)

Tip. Don't rely absolutely on IRS advice, whether it is information that employees give to telephone or walk-in inquiries or instructions that the agency prints in its publications. Mistakes in instructions or advice are inevitable, and the IRS is not bound by them.

7 MEDICAL EXPENSES

Relatively recent law changes make it much harder for itemizers to deduct payments for medical expenses. To qualify for any deduction, your outlays must be for charges that are not covered by insurance, reimbursed by your employer, or otherwise satisfied. Also, those payments are deductible only to the extent that they exceed a nondeductible floor.

Under tax reform, the nondeductible threshold went from 5 percent to 7.5 percent of your AGI (adjusted gross income). AGI is the amount that you show at the bottom of page 1 of Form 1040 after listing salaries, dividends, and other sources of income and deducting such items as funds placed in IRAs and payments of alimony, but before itemizing for outlays such as charitable contributions and listing exemptions for yourself and your dependents.

As a result of the change, you stand little chance of a break at filing time for medical costs, unless your reportable income is modest or you have the misfortune to incur unusually high expenses—for example, because of uninsured surgery, severe chronic disease, or a catastrophic illness.

Example. Assume that you and your spouse have an AGI of $40,000 and medical expenses of $4,000. With a 7.5 percent floor, $3,000 (7.5 percent of $40,000) is nondeductible; you are able to deduct only $1,000.

Assuming you incur costs that surpass the 7.5 percent floor, your deductible payments cover many more items than just those obvious outlays to doctors and hospitals. Also, deductibility can depend on *when* payment is made and, in some cases, *who* makes the payment. For instance, advancing or postponing a payment by a single day at year end can cost or save you quite a few tax dollars.

There are steps you can take now that will help in case the IRS later questions your deductions. This chapter answers some of the commonly asked tax questions on what or how much is deductible, as well as how to avoid pitfalls.

COMPUTING THE DEDUCTION

Q. *Can I take the standard deduction and also take a deduction for medical expenses, interest payments, and the like?*

A. No. Your outlays for medical expenses are deductible only if you itemize and do not claim the standard deduction. (For more on the standard deduction, see "Itemizing versus Standard Deduction" in Chapter 1.) Note, though, that special rules apply to deductions by self-employed individuals for their payments of medical insurance premiums. Those rules are discussed in the next section of this chapter.

Q. *If I pass up the standard deduction and itemize, how much am I entitled to deduct for medical expenses not covered by insurance?*

A. Your payments are deductible only to the extent that their total in any one year exceeds 7.5 percent of your AGI. Moreover, the deduction for drugs is limited to prescription drugs or insulin.

Before 1983, a long-standing rule imposed a 3 percent floor on your write-off for payments of medical expenses. Then the folks on Capitol Hill opted to increase the nondeductible floor from 3 percent to 5 percent. The 5 percent floor lasted for only four years, applying to returns for 1983 through 1986. The latest in the series of increases is to 7.5 percent.

Partial disallowance of certain deductions for persons with AGIs above a specified amount—$111,800 for tax year 1994. Medical expenses are not subject to this partial disallowance. (See "Curtailment of Most Itemized Deductions for Individuals with AGIs above a Specified Amount" in Chapter 14.)

Tip. In calculating your deductibles, make sure to include the payments you make for medical expenses incurred by your children, parents, and any other dependents for whom you provide more than half (more than 10 percent if you qualify under a multiple support agreement) of the total support for the year. This holds true even though you are ineligible to claim an exemption for, say, your father because his reportable income tops the amount that a dependent can have before the exemption is lost. (For the rules on dependency exemptions, see Chapter 2.)

Alternative minimum tax. For AMT purposes (see Chapter 14), medical expenses are allowable only for the portion that tops 10 percent of your AGI.

Q. *My employer requires me to get a yearly physical for which I'm not fully reimbursed. Am I entitled to claim the doctor's fee as an unreimbursed business expense rather than as a medical expense?*

A. Yes (Rev. Rul. 58–382). That way, you avoid taking only a partial or no deduction because of the 7.5 percent rule. Include the fee on Schedule A (Itemized Deductions) of Form 1040. But unreimbursed business expenses and most other miscellaneous itemized deductions are allowable only to the extent that their total in any one year exceeds 2 percent of your AGI. (For the rules on miscellaneous deductions, see Chapter 9.)

INSURANCE COSTS

Q. *What are the special rules on deductions by self-employed persons for medical insurance payments?*

A. The law authorizes partial relief in the form of a deduction, *without* regard to the 7.5 percent threshold, for payments of medical insurance premiums by (1) self-employed individuals, whether they operate their businesses as sole proprietorships or partnerships or (2) S corporation shareholders owning more than 2 percent of the stock. (S corportions are companies, taxed much the same as partnerships, that pass profits through to their shareholders; see "Section 1244 Stock" in Chapter 10.)

Fortunately for self-employeds, this particular break refuses to become history. Originally, the Tax Reform Act of 1986 introduced the measure for just a three-year period, beginning with returns for tax year 1987 and ending with tax year 1989. Then, starting in 1989, it received several reprieves, including an extension through June 30, 1992, when it officially went off the books.

In the fall of 1992, Congress passed legislation that, among a broad range of provisions, included one that would have extended the deduction beyond June 30, 1992. However, for reasons that had nothing to do with extending the deduction, President Bush vetoed the legislation and Congress did not override his veto. But President Clinton and Congress agreed to retroactively extend this measure from July 1, 1992 through December 31, 1993.

Proposed legislation.   As this book goes to press in the summer of 1994, Congress is considering legislation that would extend the tax break beyond 1993. That is likely; after all, 1994 is an election year.

Tip.   The deduction is a valuable one for self-employeds (and more-than-2-percent owners of S corporations). It entitles them to deduct 25 percent of the premiums they pay for medical insurance for themselves and their spouses and dependents.

As noted earlier, this deduction for medical insurance payments by self-employeds is *not* subject to the 7.5 percent threshold for all other medical expenses. Instead, like write-offs for money stashed in IRAs or other retirement plans, the deduction is claimed as an "above-the-line adjustment" on Form 1040—that is, a subtraction from gross income to arrive at AGI, rather than as an itemized deduction. *Result*: The medical-insurance deduction for the first 25 percent

of payments is available even to someone who forgoes itemizing mortgage interest and the like and uses the standard deduction, the no-questions-asked amount that is authorized for someone who finds it more advantageous not to itemize.

Tip.   You are not entitled to any additional break for the first 25 percent that is deductible as payments to obtain medical insurance coverage for a self-employed. It might, however, be possible for you to deduct the other 75 percent, which is combined with your other payments for medical care by doctors, hospitals, etc. The combined expenses are deductible to the extent that their total is more than 7.5 percent of your AGI.

Self-employment taxes.   The first 25 percent deductible as insurance coverage does not count again when you fill out Schedule SE (Self-Employment Tax) of Form 1040 to compute net earnings from self-employment for Social Security tax purposes. Stated differently, that 25 percent does not reduce your self-employment income when you figure self-employment taxes. (For more information on the rules for self-employment taxes, see Chapter 15.)

You must be your own boss.   Tax reform bestows this break for medical insurance *only* on someone who is *self-employed*. Forget about the write-off if you are eligible to participate in a health plan maintained by your employer or your spouse's employer. The law continues to treat an employee's payments of medical insurance premiums as part of his or her regular medical expenses, deductible only for amounts in excess of 7.5 percent of AGI.

Some other reminders. The medical insurance deduction is subject to several limitations that might affect some self-employeds. Among other things, no deduction is allowed for medical insurance payments that exceed a self-employed's net (receipts minus expenses) earned income for the year in question.

Another snag arises if you are self-employed and you (or your spouse) performs chores as an employee on behalf of some organization. No deduction is allowed for any month during the year in question for which you are eligible to be covered by a medical insurance plan provided by an organization that employs you *or* your spouse. This holds true whether the employment is on a full- or part-time basis.

Yet another stipulation can kayo a deduction when a self-employed operates a business that has employees. No deduction is possible unless the self-employed provides coverage under medical insurance plans for all employees. Those plans must satisfy what the Internal Revenue Code refers to as nondiscrimination rules. That means the benefits available to the self-employed individual are available to his or her employees on a basis that does not discriminate against them.

Most self-employeds need not fret about the coverage-of-employees requirement. It is not applicable when the only employees are the self-employed and that individual's family members.

TIMING OF PAYMENTS

Q. *What are the tax rules on timing the payment of medical expenses?*

A. Your tax strategy depends on how much you expect to report as AGI and the amount of medical payments you've already made. This is because your payments are deductible only if they exceed 7.5 percent of your AGI (other than payments by self-employed persons for medical insurance, which are discussed in the previous section of this chapter). The result is that your payments in any single year are completely wasted taxwise unless they top the 7.5 percent figure. So your tax strategy should be to avoid wasting payments by accelerating or postponing them into a more than 7.5 percent year.

Example. For 1995 and 1996, you and your mate anticipate an AGI of $50,000 and itemizing deductions. Assume, too, that your medical payments will amount to $3,750 for this year and the same amount for next year. The payments you make in 1996 include a check for $500 sent in January to take care of a bill received before 1995 comes to a close. *Result:* The 7.5 percent rule eliminates any deduction for 1995 or 1996. The reason? In both years, payments fail to top $3,750 ($50,000 times 7.5 percent).

Now, assume that you date the check and put it in the mail by December 31. That bit of forethought, which has the blessings of the IRS, converts a nondeductible payment for 1996 into a $500 deduction for 1995, which lowers your income taxes by $200, in the event that you fall into a 40 percent federal and state bracket. It makes no difference that the check does not clear your account until 1996.

Tip. If the IRS selects your return for an audit, you can expect a revenue agent to take a close look at large, year-end checks dated December 31 and made to doctors, hospitals, and others. The agent is well aware that you had deductions for this year in mind. So it is advisable to send such checks by certified mail. Request return receipts and staple them to your canceled checks; the receipts will back up your deductions for payments made with checks that may not clear the bank until well after January 1. (See the discussion of dating and delivery of payments in Chapter 1.)

Credit cards.   There is also room to maneuver when you use a credit card to pay for medical services and other deductibles. Credit card outlays come under a special rule. You get an immediate deduction for the year that the charge is made. It makes no difference that the credit card company does not bill you until the following year.

Tip.   Keep these tax-trimming techniques in mind when your payments for 1995 are close to or already over the 7.5 percent threshold and you will still require services that can be scheduled at your convenience. Some likely possibilities include dental work, prescription refills, elective surgery, routine annual checkups, and extra pairs of eyeglasses or contact lenses.

Here is all you need to do to avoid the possible loss of a deduction in 1996 for those payments and to boost your deduction in 1995. Simply have those services performed and pay for them by December 31 of 1995. This strategy is even more advantageous when you foresee an increase in AGI for 1996 and, therefore, a higher 7.5 percent threshold.

Caution.   You have to play the advance-payment game according to the IRS rules. Ordinarily, the tax collectors prohibit deductions for payments made this year for services that will not be performed until next year by doctors, hospitals, and the like. But the IRS is not inflexible. It does allow prepayments when you *have* to shell out in 1995 for work to be performed in 1996 and future years—orthodontic work on your child, to cite a common example. (For more on timing the payment of other deductible expenses, see Chapter 1.)

Q.   *The medical expenses incurred by my father before his death in December of last year were not paid by his estate until July of the following year. Are they deductible only in the year of payment?*

A.   There is a special rule for the expenses of a deceased person. Post-death payments of medical expenses are treated as though they had been paid by the deceased in the year incurred, provided these requirements are met: They must be paid within one year after death, and Form 1040 must be accompanied by a statement that the medical expenses have not been claimed as an estate tax deduction and a waiver of the right to so claim them.

Yet another possibility is to deduct those outlays on the Form 706 estate tax return or to split them, claiming part on Form 1040 and part on Form 706, *so long as there is no duplication.* Any portion of the unpaid expense claimed as an income tax deduction is subject to the rule that limits deductibility to the amount in excess of 7.5 percent of a person's AGI. Moreover, no estate tax deduction is allowed for any portion that is disallowed as an income tax write-off because of the 7.5 percent rule.

Example.   Mr. Trinz had run up unpaid medical expenses of $2,000 in 1993 and $1,000 in 1994 before he died in May 1995. His executor pays the expenses in 1995. The executor can deduct the $2,000 on an amended Form 1040 for 1993 and deduct the $1,000 on the return for 1994.

Now, assume that Mr. Minderbo had an AGI of $100,000 before his death in 1994. Within one year after Minderbo's death, his estate paid $20,000 for medical expenses he incurred during his last illness. While the entire $20,000 can be claimed as an estate tax deduction, the 7.5 percent rule reduces the income tax deduction to $12,500—$20,000 minus $7,500 (7.5 percent of $100,000). If the deduction is split between Forms 1040 and 706, the 7.5 percent rule still limits the combined deduction to $12,500.

Tip. What the Internal Revenue provideth, it also denieth. To the extent the Form 1040 deduction generates an income tax saving, this will, in turn, increase the estate tax bite.

Paying Someone Else's Expenses

Q. *Suppose I pay for the medical expenses of a parent or some other close relative, but I am ineligible to claim a dependency exemption for that person. Does this mean that I lose my medical-expense deduction for such payments?*

A. Not necessarily. As a general rule, you can keep that write-off, provided you furnish over half of the total support for your dependent, (over 10 percent if you qualify under a multiple support agreement. Dependency exemptions are discussed in Chapter 2).

As long as you meet the support test for the year the medical expenses were incurred *or* for the year you pay them, you can include your payments for, say, your mother's

medical expenses among your own. This holds true even though you cannot take an exemption for your mother because her reportable income exceeds the ceiling on the income that a dependent can receive before the exemption is lost or because she filed a joint return. For instance, you can deduct your payment this year for surgery your mother underwent last year, provided you furnished over half of her support for either year.

In figuring whether you pick up over half of her support tab, the IRS counts such items as medical and dental care, including premiums on health insurance, as well as money actually spent by your mother for support, even though the money comes from her Social Security benefits or from some other tax-free source that need not be counted toward the ceiling on a dependent's income ($2,450 on a return for tax year 1994).

However, support does *not* include Medicare benefits received by your parent, whether those benefits cover hospital or doctor care. Nor, on the other hand, does it include the value of nursing care or other cost-free services that you or a member of your family provide for a parent.

Remember, though, that it's *dollars,* not *time,* that counts. You can chip in for less than the entire year and still qualify under the support rules.

Example. Your payments for a short spell of hospital and doctors' charges could easily top the cost of a parent's support outlays for the rest of the year. Consequently, your payments for medical expenses incurred by a dependent provide double mileage: They help you pass the support test, and if you pass, you then include them with your medical deductibles.

Tip. If your mother contributes to her own support and her contributions appear to be outpacing yours, here is a year-end move that can help. In calculating the amount of support furnished by you for this year, include in it medical care that you provide by December 31, even if you cannot include the item with your medical deductibles for this year because you hold off paying until next year.

Example. Count as support for this year a pair of glasses that you buy for her by December 31, but do not pay for until January.

Caution. The support rules were made expensively clear to a nephew who provided over half the support of an aunt in a nursing home. He used her pension checks, along with his own funds, to pay her medical and nonmedical costs. The Tax Court trimmed his medical deduction by the amount of the aunt's pension—a hitch that could have been avoided by merely earmarking her checks for nonmedical bills and using only his checks to cover medical bills.

Children of divorced or separated parents. If you are divorced or legally separated, be aware of special rules that apply when you pay for medical expenses for your child. The law allows you to include those payments with your own medical expenses, even if your ex-spouse is entitled to take the exemption for the child.

Previously, what you spent on your child's behalf was lumped together with your own expenses only if the child's exemption belonged to you. Now, though, it no longer matters whether the exemption belongs to you or your former mate. If the rules for divorced or separated parents entitles either one of you to claim the child, then you each are allowed to include your respective payments with your expenses. (For the rules on dependency exemptions, see Chapter 2.)

Q. *I know that there is an exception to the over-half-the-support rule for dependency exemptions, as when some of my sisters join me in contributing over half the support of our father during the year, but no one of us contributes over half the support. I've been told that my sisters can designate me to claim the exemption for our father, so long as I contribute over 10 percent of his total support for the year and they waive their claim to the exemption by signing IRS Form 2120 (Multiple Support Declaration), which must accompany my return. But does this also entitle me to include my payments for his medical expenses under my medical deductions?*

A. Yes. But if your sisters reimburse you for those payments, you must reduce your medical deduction by the amount of the reimbursement. Moreover, your sisters cannot deduct anything, as they did not pay the medical bills. Thus, no one gets the deduction. To avoid this deduction loss, pay the medical expenses yourself and have your sisters take care of other items—for instance, food or clothing.

Tip. Ordinarily, the exemption for a parent provides the greatest tax savings when he or she is claimed by the family member in the highest bracket. But this may not be so when a substantial part of the support payments are for medical care. In that situation, it may be more advantageous for a lower-bracket family member with a lesser income to pay the medical bills and claim the exemption, while the ones in the higher bracket direct their support to nondeductible items. Why? Because medical expenses are allowable only to the extent that they exceed 7.5 percent of a person's AGI. Therefore, the one with the lesser income and the lower 7.5 percent threshold qualifies for a greater medical-expense deduction.

Q. *My divorce decree freed me from my ex-husband's obligations. But I continue to use a physician who also treated my ex-husband before our split, and I consider myself obligated to take care of his unpaid bills. If I pay these bills, do I provide him with an undeserved tax break?*

A. Not at all. Medical expenses that were incurred by your ex-husband while married to you are deductible by you, though you make the payments after you divorce him and even if you have since remarried and are filing jointly with another husband. Ex-husbands, deserving or undeserving, get no tax break for medical expenses paid by ex-wives.

Q. *It's becoming increasingly difficult for my daughter to make do on her husband's salary, and they have accumulated several unpaid medical bills. What if I pay their bills? Will I be allowed the deduction?*

A. The deduction will be wasted. Your payment does not entitle you to a deduction for their expenses because they aren't your dependents. And they will lose out on the deduction unless they make the payment.

Tip. To sidestep this problem, all you need to do is give or lend the money to them and let them pay those bills.

Q. *Are adoptive parents entitled to deduct expenses of the natural mother in giving birth?*

A. No. Their deduction is limited to medical costs attributable to care of the unborn child, not those incurred to protect the health of the mother.

Q. *My dog depends on me for food, and I depend on my dog for protection from harm in the night. I think of him as a part of the family. Will the IRS growl if my medical-expense deductions include a payment to a veterinarian?*

A. Definitely. When Leland Schoen made that very argument, the Tax Court agreed with the IRS that "in no circumstances can man's best friend qualify as a dependent by blood, marriage, or adoption." So Fido's medical expenses were thrown out.

SPECIAL EQUIPMENT

Q. *How do the medical deduction rules work if I make an improvement to my home or apartment on doctor's orders?*

A. You cannot deduct the entire cost if the improvement adds to the value of your dwelling. Your write-off is limited to the difference between the cost and the increase in value.

Example. You spend $6,000 to put in a central air-conditioning system after your youngster's allergist recommends that you install the equipment to alleviate an asthmatic condition. If that boosts the value of your home by $5,000, your allowable deduction shrinks to only $1,000, the amount by which the cost exceeds the increase in value.

Examples of other improvements that

readily pass IRS muster are an elevator or a bathroom on a lower floor that makes mobility easier for a person with arthritis or a heart condition.

Less stringent rules apply in the case of a *tenant* who for medical reasons makes an improvement, such as a wheelchair ramp. The renter can claim the entire cost because the improvement adds nothing to the value of his or her property. Moreover, whether you are an owner or a renter, your deductibles include the entire cost of *detachable* equipment—for example, a window air conditioner that relieves a medical problem.

Tip. Even if you are ineligible to deduct medically required equipment because its cost is completely offset by the increase in your home's value, you nevertheless qualify for some kind of tax relief. Remember to include as part of your medical deductions what you spend for such operating and maintenance expenses as electricity, repairs, or a service contract.

Accommodating a personal residence to the needs of the handicapped. The following expenditures generally do not increase the value of a taxpayer's personal residence and are therefore eligible in full for the medical-expense deduction (subject to the nondeductible 7.5 percent floor) when made for the primary purpose of accommodating a personal residence to the handicapped condition of the taxpayer, the taxpayer's spouse, or dependents who live there:

- entrance or exit ramps
- wider doorways at exits or entrances
- wider hallways or interior doorways
- railings, support bars, or other modifications to bathrooms
- modifications to kitchen cabinets and equipment
- relocation of electrical outlets
- porchlifts and other lifts (generally not including elevators because they may add to a residence's fair-market value, and any deductions would have to be decreased to that extent)
- modified fire alarms, smoke detectors, or other warning systems
- modified stairs
- handrails and grab bars, whether or not in bathrooms
- modified door hardware
- modified areas in front of entrance and exit doorways
- graded ground for better access to the residence.

Note. The above list is not exhaustive. Other expenditures incurred to accommodate a personal residence to a handicapped person's condition may be fully deductible (subject to the nondeductible 7.5 percent floor) as long as they do not increase the value of the residence.

IRS audits. Just because something like an air conditioner makes you feel better does not mean that the IRS will share the cost. That's why the tax takers look closely at sizable deductions for installations of equipment. Still, there are steps you can take now that will help in case the IRS later indulges in some second-guessing. Make sure to get a statement from your doctor that explains the medical need for your expenditures. Hang on to bills and canceled checks that show what you paid for improvements. Remember also that you may need those records to figure the profit or loss when you sell your home. (For the rules on home sales, see Chapter 3.)

Appraisals. When a hefty deduction is at stake, it's also prudent to get a written opinion from a competent real estate appraiser that details how little or how much the installation raised the value of your residence. If a disputed deduction ends up in court, the IRS can bring in its own appraiser. But because of the time lag, usually their appraisals are less convincing.

Tip. You do not have to count those appraisal fees under the 7.5 percent rule that trims your deductions for medical expenses. Instead, you can include them in full on Schedule A of Form 1040 with your other itemized deductibles under "miscellaneous deductions," just the same as payments for preparation of returns or publications that help with your tax planning, such as this book. But most miscellaneous itemized deductions are allowable only to the extent that their total in any one year exceeds 2 percent of your AGI. (For the rules on miscellaneous deductions, see Chapter 9.)

Caution. More than one taxpayer has learned the hard way about the importance of before-and-after appraisals. For instance, the Tax Court completely disallowed $4,000 spent on air conditioning because the taxpayer failed to get an appraisal and was unable to show the air conditioning did not enhance the value of his home.

Q. *Because of my chronic back problems, I intend to install an indoor pool in my Chicago home to do the year-round swimming that a physician says I need. A pool that fits in best with the style of my dwelling would cost about $15,000 more than an ordinary one. I* *have been told that the law authorizes the IRS to disallow a deduction for the extra expense. Is that true?*

A. Yes, according to a court case on the issue of whether part of the cost of a luxury pool was a deductible medical necessity or merely a nondeductible personal convenience. The pool belonged to Bonnie Bach Ferris, whose doctor had recommended that she install one in her home and use it twice a day to prevent permanent paralysis from a spinal disorder that was causing her to suffer excruciating pain when she sat up. For the year under review, Bonnie and her husband shelled out nearly $195,000 (nowadays, that figure would be more than twice as much) to install an indoor pool that, as they eventually explained to the Tax Court, was "architecturally and aesthetically compatible" with the cut-stone construction of their Madison, Wisconsin, Tudor-style home, which was then valued at $275,000.

At filing time, the Wisconsin couple claimed a medical expense of $86,000, or the $195,000 cost minus $109,000 (about $22,000 for the cost of a sauna, a bathroom, dressing room, furniture, and other amenities not essential to the operation of a pool, plus $87,000 for the increased value of their dwelling due to the pool addition).

Not surprisingly, the computers caught that $86,000 write-off; the IRS proceeded to nix over half of the deduction. Although the agency readily conceded that installation of the pool was dictated by medical needs, it asserted that the Ferrises could have built one that was perfectly adequate for Bonnie's needs for only $70,000. That would have boosted their home's value by $31,000. Therefore, the permissible deduction should be only $39,000.

But the Tax Court ruled that the IRS was

all wet; the Ferrises did not have to install the least expensive type of pool to qualify for a deduction. There is no case, as far as the Tax Court was aware, that "limits a medical expense to the cheapest form of treatment." It cited the example of someone who opts to stay in a private hospital room instead of a ward, or to go to the most expensive medical institutions. That person does not forfeit a write-off for the full amount.

Moreover, even assuming the law requires "bare bones" spending for medical care, the Ferrises would have qualified for virtually the same deduction, said the Tax Court, which thought that the IRS estimate of $70,000 was too low by $10,000 and that an $80,000 pool would probably have decreased, rather than increased, the value of the property.

Unfortunately for the Ferrises, the Tax Court decision was reversed by the Seventh Circuit Court of Appeals in Chicago. The outlay for luxury features was nondeductible; the allowable deduction, concluded the Seventh Circuit, is the "minimum reasonable cost of a functionally adequate pool and housing structure" less any value added to the Ferris residence because of the pool.

Q. *I am allergic to dust. Am I allowed a medical deduction for the cost of a household vacuum cleaner?*

A. No. In a case similar to yours, an IRS ruling barred any deduction because there was no proof the vacuum cleaner was bought primarily for medical reasons. For one thing, the IRS could find no evidence that a vacuum cleaner actually alleviates an allergy —in contrast to an air conditioner that can be deductible if purchased primarily for medical reasons. For another thing, there was no doctor's prescription to show the vac-uum cleaner was bought primarily for medical reasons.

Q. *Is it possible to deduct telephone equipment or telephone calls?*

A. It all depends. Folks who are hard of hearing get deductions for the cost and repair of special equipment that enables them to communicate over regular telephones or that prints on TV screens what is being said (Rev. Rul. 80–340).

Suppose, though, that a telephone is installed in a car driven by a person with a serious heart condition. The installation cost is deductible only if it can be established that the telephone was put in primarily to contact a doctor in case of a heart attack.

An IRS ruling approved a deduction for long-distance calls to a psychologist when it would have been a hardship for the patient to travel the distance from his home to the psychologist's office for weekly counseling sessions (Ruling 8034087).

Q. *Can someone who suffers from a heart condition deduct a reclining chair prescribed to give him maximum rest?*

A. An IRS ruling approves the deduction, provided the chair serves no purpose other than relieving your problem. It must not be used generally as an article of furniture.

TRANSPORTATION EXPENSES

Q. *Just how much am I allowed to take as a medical-expense deduction for travel to doctors, dentists, and the like?*

A. When you travel to and from your treatment by bus or train, just make sure to keep track of your fares and claim them as medical outlays. If you use your own vehicle, you can deduct the actual cost of gas and oil or you can simplify the paperwork and deduct a standard mileage rate. Under the rules applicable to tax year 1994 (the most recent year for which information is available as this book goes to press), the standard rate is 9 cents per mile.

Tip. Whether you use the mileage allowance or drive a gas guzzler and claim actual costs, remember also to deduct parking fees and bridge or highway tolls.

Example. Each journey from your suburban home to a downtown dentist involves a round trip of 50 miles and a $2 parking fee. On top of the dentist's fee, you can deduct another $6.50 (50 miles times 9 cents equals $4.50, plus $2 parking) for each visit. Or, if greater, you can deduct actual gas and oil, plus $2 parking for each visit.

Tip. As in the case of travel on behalf of a charitable organization (charitable deductions are discussed in Chapter 8), it is a good idea to back up your deductions for medical travel with a glove-compartment diary in which you record why and how far you went, as well as what you spent on parking.

You do not have to use the same car each time. If you rent a car and drive it only for medical travel, include the entire rental charge with your other medical expenses.

Caution. Drive within the speed limit. The IRS refuses to go along with a medical deduction for a traffic ticket even if you were racing the stork to the hospital.

How the IRS and the courts define medical travel. It includes a good deal more than just those obvious trips to doctors. For example, the following trips qualify:

- Driving a person confined to a wheelchair to school (a doctor stated that attendance at regular school sessions was medically desirable).
- Driving to meetings of Alcoholics Anonymous or Narcotics Anonymous.
- Parents' trips to visit their medically ill child at an institution, where their visits were an essential part of the child's treatment.
- A wife's visits to her husband at a hospital, where her presence was indispensable because of his weakened postoperative condition.
- A parent's trip to Europe to bring back a son who became ill while vacationing there; the parent made the trip only because the son was incapable of traveling alone (Ruling 7813004).
- A wife's plane trip with her ailing husband to a hospital for surgery, because he breathed through a tracheotomy tube and was unable to speak.

Caution. The mileage rates differ when you use your car for charitable activities (Chapter 8) or for business reasons (see "Business-Car Deductions" in Chapter 5).

Q. *Because of my medical problems, I am unable to use public transportation and must drive to work. Does that mean I can deduct the cost of driving as a medical expense?*

A. The IRS says you get no deduction for the cost of driving between home and work. (See "Commuting Deductions" in Chapter 5.) It makes no difference that illness or disability rules out using public transportation. For example, it held that cab fares required to transport a physically disabled person to and from work are nondeductible (Rev. Rul. 55–261).

But the IRS does not always have its way. Consider the unusual case of Mary Bordas, whose face was disfigured when she was thrown through her windshield in an auto accident. Mary underwent 14 plastic surgery operations, and her facial injuries affected her mental condition. Her doctor advised against using public transportation, where she would be exposed to curious stares. He also insisted she drive an auto to visit friends as therapy for her mental condition. Therefore, Mary bought a new Chrysler that she drove extensively for social purposes, as well as between her home and her doctor's office. The IRS tried to limit her medical transportation deduction to driving to and from medical appointments. But she challenged the IRS in the Tax Court and won a partial victory. The court gave its blessing to a deduction for "all the driving she did to alleviate her mental condition." But there the court drew the line. It refused to allow any deduction for the actual cost of her car.

Q. *I'm aware that no deduction is allowed for insurance on an auto driven for personal use. But my auto insurance premium includes a separately stated charge that pays for medical coverage for accident victims. Is this portion of the premium deductible as medical insurance?*

A. An IRS ruling makes such a deduction next to impossible. According to the ruling, an itemized auto insurance bill would have to separate the amount paid to cover you and your dependents (the deductible part) from the amount paid to protect any other persons in your car or persons injured by it (the non-deductible part) (Rev. Rul. 73–483).

MEALS AND LODGINGS

Q. *I drove with my asthmatic child from our Iowa home to Denver for outpatient care. Of course, I get to deduct the cost of transportation. But what about our outlays for meals and lodgings during the time we are en route or in Denver?*

A. Special rules apply to medical-care deductions for lodging expenses while away from home.

As a general rule, meals and lodgings are deductible as medical expenses only if incurred in a hospital or similar institution. Formerly, that restriction eliminated any deduction for the cost of a stay at a hotel while away from home to obtain outpatient treatment at a hospital—for instance, chemotherapy treatment for cancer patients. This held true even when outpatient care was less expensive than inpatient care and also when the patient was incapable of traveling alone and had to be accompanied by another person, as in the case of an infant accompanied by a parent.

Now, however, the law allows a deduction of up to $50 per day for away-from-home lodgings to receive outpatient treatment. To qualify, such lodgings must be "primarily for and essential to medical care provided by a physician" in a hospital or a similar facility, such as the Mayo Clinic. But no deduction at all is allowed, says Congress, for hotel rooms or other lodgings that are "lavish or extravagant under the circumstances" or if there is any "significant element of personal pleasure, recreation, or vacation in the travel away from home." Put more plainly, no tax break is allowed for what is actually a vacation. Moreover, outlays other than lodgings, such as food, remain nondeductible.

Tip. The $50 ceiling is on a per-person basis. Take the situation of a parent who accompanies a dependent child on a trip for medical treatment. The per-day deduction for their stay at a hotel is a maximum of $100.

Q. *Does the IRS define illness to include alcoholism and drug addiction? I need to know whether it's possible to deduct payments for treatment of a dependent at a therapeutic center for alcoholics or drug addicts.*

A. Yes. Your deduction even includes meals and lodgings at the center that are furnished as a necessary part of treatment (Rev. Rul. 72–226 and 73–325). Note also that it's permissible to deduct transportation costs (discussed earlier in this chapter) to and from meetings of Alcoholics Anonymous or Narcotics Anonymous (Rev. Rul. 63–273).

Q. *To avoid severe allergic reactions caused by chemically treated foods, I buy only natural foods. The health food stores charge considerably more than the supermarkets do for ordinary foods. How much of the cost can I claim as a medical expense?*

A. To claim even part of what you spend, you may have to take the IRS to court. The IRS takes a tough stance when your doctor tells you to switch from the food that you would ordinarily consume to food that is free of salt, sugar, and chemicals or is otherwise specially prepared to relieve a specific ailment.

The way the tax collectors see things, you get a write-off for what you spend on specially prepared meals only if they are a necessary supplement, as opposed to a mere replacement for your normal meals. Thus, the IRS balks at any break for the additional cost of adhering to a sugar- or a salt-free diet and the like. But that approach got nowhere

with the Tax Court, which wanted to relieve some of the pain for people on a doctor-ordered diet.

You can deduct the difference between what you pay for the special food that you need and what you would have paid for regular food, provided you are able to prove that extra cost. After peeling off the legal lingo, that, in essence, is what the Tax Court told Theron and Janet Randolph, an allergy-ridden couple who dined exclusively on non-allergenic food.

Theron (himself a physician and an allergy specialist) and Janet (his patient before they wed) became ill if they ate ordinary food. Because of her extreme sensitivity to even minute amounts of various chemical additives used to grow or preserve food, Janet was plagued with nausea, bronchitis, headaches, colds, vomiting, difficulty in breathing, and had lapsed into unconsciousness several hundred times over a 20-year period. Theron experienced similar, though less severe, reactions to chemically treated food.

To avoid these adverse reactions, Theron and Janet limited their meals to chemical-free "organic" foods, bought mostly at health food stores. For the year in issue, the couple figured their food bill ran to about $6,000— $3,000 more than what the tab would have been for conventional groceries at a supermarket. (Currently, these amounts would be more than twice as much.) That, reasoned the Randolphs, entitled them to write off the extra $3,000 as a medically required outlay.

However, the IRS gagged, and the dispute ended up in the Tax Court, which sided with the taxpayers. Their $3,000 estimate was reasonable, said the court. It noted that the couple had provided a "wealth of evidence" to back up their deduction. Among other things, the Randolphs showed their figure corresponded with the Department of Labor statistics for the cost of food in their particular area.

Caution. The Tax Court remains as unsympathetic as the IRS to deductions for specially prepared food consumed just because you think it will keep you healthy.

Tip. The IRS is inclined to be more lenient when it comes to spirits. No deduction is allowed for a drink before dinner, though it relieves the day's tensions; but a doctor-recommended daily drink of wine or whisky provides an unquestioned deduction for someone with a heart condition.

SCHOOLING

Q. *Am I allowed a medical-expense deduction for schooling a child with a physical or mental handicap?*

A. The answer depends on whether your youngster goes to a "special" or "regular" school. Your child's schooling is special, and the cost qualifies as a medical expense when the "principal reason" for going is to use the resources available at the school or other institution to prevent or alleviate a handicap. Put another way, while the school can provide an ordinary education, the learning must be "incidental" to the medical care.

Some obvious examples of places that pass IRS muster are schools that teach braille to the blind or lip reading to the deaf. Besides the tuition, you get to deduct the cost of meals and lodging at the school, as well as travel expenses.

But regular schooling is another story. Unless you can show some portion of your payment is specifically for medical treatment, you get no deduction for costs incurred at a school without special facilities. The IRS remains unyielding, even though a doctor believes that your handicapped child will benefit from the curriculum, disciplinary methods, or other nonmedical advantages available at a conventional school.

The IRS takes a particularly hard line against allowing a medical deduction for a private school for a child with minor disciplinary problems. It refuses to go along with a deduction unless the child suffers from a "disease"—a term, that, for tax purposes, does not include minor disciplinary problems or adolescent upsets.

Of course, the IRS's factual approach is not necessarily the final word. But its restrictive definition of special schooling is usually upheld by the courts, although each decision generally turns on its own set of facts.

For example, a New York father thought himself entitled to a deduction for the cost of sending his son to a boarding school, because he did so on the advice of a psychiatrist who believed that the school's structure and environment would help the boy's psychological problems. But a federal district court agreed with the IRS that the school was "regular," because all it provided in return for tuition was a normal education. The court noted that the school did not specialize in problems like the boy's and had no psychiatrist or psychologist on its staff.

On the other hand, the Tax Court allowed Lawrence Fay to deduct the cost of sending two of his children to a regular school with a special program for pupils with learning disabilities, though neither child had a disability severe enough to require psychiatric or psychological treatment.

Mr. Fay had two children with learning disabilities—reading and writing problems that caused them to become underachievers and to suffer some emotional disorders. On the recommendation of educators who were specialists in learning disabilities, he enrolled his children in a private school that had a program for such children.

The school, which used the Montessori method and offered a regular curriculum plus a special program for those with a learning disability, had no psychologists or psychiatrists on its staff. For the year in issue, the school charged $5,100 for the regular tuition plus $1,800 for the special program. (Nowadays, these amounts would be more than twice as much.)

The Tax Court okayed a deduction by Mr. Fay for the $1,800, though he failed to prove that his children were afflicted with a specific mental disease or defect and that the services provided were proximately related to the disease or defect. Said the court: "While these mental disorders may not have been severe enough to require psychiatric or psychological treatment, they were severe enough to prevent the children from acquiring a normal education without some help. Any treatment, whether rendered by medical people or specially trained educators, directly related to the alleviation of such mental disorders so that the recipient may obtain a normal, or more normal, education qualifies as medical care. While the staff were not medically trained, they were all educators specializing in the field of learning disabilities." The $1,800 was paid to alleviate or mitigate the mental problems that had prevented the children from progressing in a normal education environment.

Q. *Ordinarily, no deduction is available for what I spend to send my child to a private school or college. Do I, however, get a medical insurance deduction for part of the school's fee for education, board, etc., if it includes a charge for health-care items—for example, counseling for emotional problems?*

A. Yes, provided there is a separately stated charge for health care (Rev. Rul. 56–457). If the charge isn't separately itemized, ask the school for a breakdown of your bill to back up this deduction in case the IRS later questions your return.

PLASTIC SURGERY

Q. *I plan to redo my appearance with the help of a plastic surgeon. Can I count on the IRS to help with the fee which may run in to thousands of dollars?*

A. Only if you qualify under tightened rules that took effect at the start of 1991.

Before 1991, the IRS conceded that your medical deductibles included the cost of purely cosmetic surgical procedures, whether they were face-lifts, nose jobs, tush trims, liposuctions to get rid of love handles or other unsightly bulges, or any other reshapings that "affected a structure of the human body." It made no difference that the operation was in no way necessary and had not been recommended by a doctor to alleviate a physical or mental problem.

Under these liberal IRS guidelines, relief at filing time was available for, among others, executives who had face-lifts to better their chances to move up the corporate ladder and would-be topless dancers who underwent breast enlargements to overcome hereditary deficiencies that impeded their careers.

Not anymore. Now, cautions the IRS, the cosmetic surgical procedures must be necessary to improve deformities arising from, or directly related to, congenital abnormalities, personal injuries resulting from accidents or traumas, or disfiguring diseases.

Unsurprisingly, the Internal Revenue Code provides a restrictive definition of cosmetic surgery: "Any procedure that is directed at improving the patient's appearance and does not meaningfully promote the proper function of the body or prevent or treat illness or disease." *Translation:* As a general rule, say *sayonara* to any deductions when vanity, not medical necessity, is what prompts people to have face-lifts, hair removal (electrolysis), hair transplants, liposuction, operations to correct baggy eyes or crow's feet, or similar kinds of cosmetic surgery.

Tip. Eventually, the IRS will announce guidelines for deductibility of costly procedures done for both medical and cosmetic reasons. The long list of potential conflicts includes nose reshapings that alleviate breathing problems, eyelid operations (no IRS challenge is likely for operations needed because heavy upper lids obstruct vision), breast reductions done to relieve back pain after childbirths, breast enlargements (no deductibility problems whatever for enlargements done after mastectomies or to correct congenital asymmetries), or ear pinnings (the IRS probably will allow pinnings performed because of congenital deformities).

Strategy. In the meantime, be prepared to establish medical necessity if you claim such deductions. Ask the physician for a written statement that supports the write-off, in case the IRS comes knocking.

Nurses and Companions

Q. *My husband is now at home recovering from an operation. The woman I hired as his nurse is not a registered or practical nurse, but she has some nursing experience. She also will do housework. Am I entitled to a medical deduction for her salary?*

A. Nursing care for you or your dependents is deductible even though the person you hire to attend a patient has no previous nursing experience at all. What counts is the type of work that is actually performed.

But the paperwork gets complicated when you hire someone who doubles as a nurse and housekeeper. You must make an apportionment between the time she spends on nursing care (for instance, changing dressings or bathing a patient) and the time she spends on nonmedical duties (such as cleaning, cooking, and caring for healthy children) (Rev. Rul. 76–106). You can take a medical deduction only for payments allocable to nursing care (including the amounts you pay as an employer for Social Security taxes; for the rules on Social Security taxes, see Chapter 15). But you get no deduction for payments allocable to household chores.

Meals. Don't overlook a deduction for the amount you spend on meals. But the cost of those meals must be apportioned in the same way as her wages. For instance, if she spends only half her time nursing, then only half her meals are deductible.

Lodgings. The rules are stricter when it comes to a deduction for the lodgings you furnish her. You get no deduction unless you can show you made out-of-pocket expenditures directly attributable to her that were greater than normal household expenses—say, rent for an extra bedroom or additional utilities.

Tip. The IRS apparently requires the allocation to be made strictly on the basis of the *amount of time* spent on medical care. It doesn't take into account the possibility that the going rate for medical services is higher than for household services.

Caution. The IRS may indulge in some second-guessing on how much is deductible. Keep a simple diary that breaks down on a daily basis what type of work was done.

Q. *The IRS is questioning my medical deductions. Though the agent readily concedes that my allowable expenses include the cost of cab fares for medical appointments, he absolutely refuses to allow a deduction for the sitter who minds my children while I'm at the doctor. What is the reason for this hard-nosed position?*

A. As of now, the IRS remains adamant in its refusal to bow to changing times when it comes to babysitters, and it has the backing of the Tax Court. The expense is considered to be personal in nature and, thus, nondeductible.

Tip. The IRS takes a dim view of another kind of deduction for a sitter. You get no charitable write-off for the cost of a sitter who frees you to perform volunteer chores for a charity, according to an IRS ruling which, fortunately, is not the final word. The Tax Court says you can count the cost of a sitter as a charitable contribution, though that decision is not binding on the IRS (see Chapter 8).

CHANGE OF RESIDENCE

Q. *If medical reasons make it necessary to permanently change my residence, am I entitled to deduct any of my expenses?*

A. Usually not. The Tax Court did allow a medical deduction to a woman for the cost of traveling from Maryland to Southern California because her doctor recommended a permanent move to a more healthy climate. But she was not entitled to a medical deduction for such items as breaking her lease or moving her furniture and other family members.

Nor did the court allow travel expenses claimed by a patient under psychiatric care who traveled about the United States seeking a place to live, on the advice of his physician to move to a new locality more suitable to him and his personality needs.

No deduction can be taken for a loss on the sale of a home (see Chapter 3) even though a doctor recommends an immediate move for medical reasons. Thus, no loss was allowed for a move made to avoid psychological damage to a child or for a move from a two-story home to a one-story home to allow a child the maximum use of his wheelchair (Rev. Rul. 68–319).

THE COST OF STAYING HEALTHY

Q. *I've heard that usually there is no tax relief for someone who wants to pursue the wholesome, slender life and signs up for a health club membership or weight reduction program. Is that actually so?*

A. Yes, for the most part. The IRS is well aware of the sales spiel used by some health club and weight loss outfits and hot-tub dealers to persuade people to sign up for memberships or tubs. All too often, these businesses assure their clientele that regular sessions at the club or in the tub will not just keep them in shape and shed excess flab but also trim the tab when filing time rolls around.

But the IRS warns that no medical-expense deduction is available for outlays that merely improve your appearance, general health, or sense of well-being (even though they are recommended by a doctor), as opposed to those that cure or alleviate a specific ailment or disease. Thus, the IRS forbids a write-off for a spa or hot tub, unless used to treat a specific illness or condition, though it will allow a deduction when you participate in a weight reduction program as specific treatment for hypertension, obesity, and other problems (Rulings 8004111 and 8251045).

A much-criticized ruling disallows deductions for courses that help smokers kick the habit, a doctor's recommendation notwithstanding (Rev. Rul. 79–162).

Tip. As this book goes to press in the summer of 1994, the IRS is reconsidering its long-standing position that stop-smoking courses are not deductible.

Earlier rulings disallowed payments to the Church of Scientology for courses that, according to the person requesting the ruling, cured him of gall bladder problems, nervous disorders, and ulcers. Because the church requires those who take its courses to sign statements disclaiming its ability to heal ailments, he did not receive "medical care" within the meaning of the tax code. The rulings also denied charitable deductions for the payments (Rev. Ruls. 78–189 and 78–190).

The IRS is equally unyielding when it comes to a business-expense deduction for a health club membership even though your employer requires you to stay in excellent physical condition. That's the gist of a ruling barring a deduction by a police officer (Rev. Rul. 78–128; see "Business Expenses Must Be Ordinary and Necessary" in Chapter 9).

Q. *How far can I go in deducting expenses for doctor-ordered exercise?*

A. Leon Altman, a Los Angeles surgeon who suffered from pulmonary emphysema, discovered that you can go just so far. The way Leon told it to the judge, his physician advised him to play golf. But smog and pollutants within the confines of Los Angeles made it impossible for him to get the recommended exercise of walking and swinging a golf club. So he was forced to drive 56 miles from Los Angeles to reach the clean air of his country club for three or four rounds each week.

The IRS threw out his medical deductions of several thousand dollars for the long drives between his home and the golf course, for a golf cart, and for playing fees. An unsympathetic judge also declared him out of bounds. While the smog problem did make outside exercise impossible for Leon, the judge thought it was stretching things to claim that a person needed a golf course to engage in the exercise of walking—or swinging a golf club, for that matter. By way of an additional unkind cut, his honor characterized golf as the "classic example of a personal rather than a medical activity."

Q. *Does a doctor's recommendation ensure deductibility of medical expenses?*

A. Not necessarily. Consider the case of Frank, himself a doctor, and his wife, Betty, whose medical problems included chronic anxiety neurosis and phobias of sudden death, heights, cars, and being alone. Frank sought the advice of two psychiatrists who concluded that Betty could be socially integrated and deterred from threatening to kill herself, her children, and her husband if she had certain possessions. Their recommended treatment ("milieu therapy" in medical jargon) called for, among other things, providing "a social environment without anxiety." So, during the year in issue, Frank footed bills to the tune of about $25,000 for such items as specially tailored clothing, unlimited department store charge accounts, boat trips, new furniture and appliances, remodeling a lake cottage, and improvements to a new apartment. That, reasoned Frank, entitled him to trim the tax tab with a medical write-off for the entire cost.

Predictably, his return never made it past the IRS's computers, and Frank then tried the Tax Court. But his contention that charge accounts were an essential part of his wife's therapy got exactly nowhere with the court, though it readily conceded that shopping with unlimited charge accounts is generally therapeutic for a housewife, especially one under treatment for an anxiety neurosis.

Moreover, his case was not helped when the two psychiatrists gave conflicting testimony. One remembered having recommended shopping excursions to strengthen Betty's "tenuous hold on reality." But the other testified that Frank was forced to go along with the purchases to prevent his wife from being provoked into violent anger.

While the Tax Court didn't deny that Betty's shopping sprees might generally have alleviated her problems, it sided with the IRS because Frank failed to tie the purchases directly to his wife's treatment. Nor did he prove that he wouldn't have spent as much without the recommendation of a psychiatrist.

TREATMENT OF MARITAL AND EMOTIONAL PROBLEMS

Q. *Can I deduct the cost of deprogramming a family member who joined a religious cult?*

A. Not according to an IRS ruling that disallowed a deduction for what a mother paid to deprogram her teenager (Ruling 802104).

Q. *My husband and I went to a counseling center run by our church. We spoke to a clergyman about some of our marital problems. Because of his counseling, both of us definitely feel that our mental outlook is improved and that we are enjoying a more pleasant relationship. We would, however, feel even better if we could be certain that the IRS would permit us to deduct the counseling fees. Will it?*

A. No. In a ruling that concerned a situation identical to yours, the IRS concluded that the counseling "was not to prevent or alleviate a physical or mental defect or illness," but to help improve the marriage. Thus, it makes no difference that both of you are healthier persons because of the counseling. The cost is not a deductible medical expense. Nor will the IRS allow you to write off the cost as a charitable contribution even though the counseling center is run by a church (Rev. Rul. 75–319).

Tip. The deduction should be allowable as a medical expense if the marriage counselor restyles himself or herself as a therapist in sexual inadequacy and incompatibility.

Q. *Because of my problems as a transsexual, I plan to undergo a sex-change operation. Can I count on a medical deduction for this expensive procedure?*

A. Yes. It's not likely that the IRS will challenge your deduction, so long as the operation is performed on doctor's orders. But make sure to get a written statement from your doctor to nail down the deduction. And don't overlook your transportation to and from the hospital. That's also deductible. See the discussion earlier in this chapter of transportation expenses.

Q. *Does the IRS allow an unmarried woman to deduct contraceptive pills?*

A. Yes. However, at one time, the tax takers thought that no deduction should be allowed for birth control pills unless they were prescribed by a physician because pregnancy would seriously endanger the woman's life. But the IRS has long since ceased to quibble about a medical-expense deduction for the pill or other such birth control measures as sterilization, contraceptive devices, and legal abortions, though it remains unyielding on a tax break for the cost of an illegal abortion.

Nor does the IRS insist that you must be married before you are eligible to take a deduction for these expenses, for outlays for psychiatric counseling to alleviate sexual inadequacy or incompatibility, or for what you spend on travel to and from the psychiatrist.

LEGAL FEES

Q. *My psychiatrist thinks that my emotional problems cannot be relieved so long as I remain married and that I should consider a divorce. If I do that, the legal fees and divorce settlement will be expensive. Will the IRS approve a medical deduction for these costs?*

A. Don't count on it. A divorce may make you feel better, but the cost of one is not deductible as a medical expense. That's what the IRS and the Tax Court told a Chicago taxpayer.

It seems that the breakup of Joel's first marriage left him with a feeling of anxiety and uncertainty about another go at marriage. Another source of anxiety for Joel was the woman he chose to be his second wife. As Joel later told the Tax Court, she "always expressed a great deal of hostility toward other people, especially men"—a line that sounds like it came right out of a Woody Allen movie. So Joel thought it prudent to check beforehand with a psychiatrist about his plan to remarry. But despite a warning from the doctor, Joel went ahead anyway, thinking that would solve his problems.

Unfortunately for Joel, remarriage only made things worse. In fact, several weeks with his new wife were enough to make him fall into a severe depression and develop an urge to commit suicide, prompting the psychiatrist to advise Joel to get a divorce and to get it fast.

To end the agony, Joel did just that. Joel also let his wife browbeat him into an overly generous divorce settlement, even though he had a fairly good case against her since she had physically attacked him on at least nine occasions over an eight-month period. In all, Joel laid out over $17,000 in legal fees and divorce settlement payments.

When tax time rolled around, Joel tried to ease the hurt with a medical deduction for the $17,000 outlay. Not surprisingly, the IRS computer went bananas; Joel had to take his case to the Tax Court. He testified that marriage made him sick and that his health showed marked improvement after he obtained a divorce on doctor's orders. But severe depression again engulfed him when the judge said that it made no difference taxwise because Joel was unable to show that treatment of his illness was the only reason for his divorce and that he wouldn't otherwise have incurred the expense. In fact, the judge reasoned that any sane man would have gotten a divorce in this situation.

Q. *We had to commit our mentally ill daughter to an institution. Are we entitled to deduct the legal fees that were involved?*

A. Yes (Rev. Rul. 68–320). Simply include them with your other medical deductibles.

The Tax Court, however, refused to allow the parents of Guy Levine, a mental clinic outpatient, to deduct what they paid an attorney to look after their son. Guy, unable or unwilling to live with other people or in a mental institution, needed to stay close to the Menninger Clinic in Topeka, Kansas, mainly because of a particular psychotherapist there with whom he had a relationship not reproducible elsewhere. For this reason, his parents, New York City residents, rented a Topeka apartment for him.

Guy was so limited in his ability to care for himself and the apartment that his parents hired a Topeka attorney to act as their son's "surrogate parent/social service worker/ lawyer." The attorney saw Guy at least once a week to help him manage his day-to-day affairs such as clothing purchases, apartment cleaning, and bill paying.

The verdict: No medical deduction; the attorney's services were not needed to "legitimate" Guy's medical treatment.

IRS AUDITS

Q. *I stand a good chance of being audited because of my above-average deductions for medical expenses and other itemized deductions. Can I head off an audit by attaching doctor bills, canceled checks, and so on, to my Form 1040?*

A. You might avoid the bother of an audit by submitting documents with your return that help explain items appearing on it. If you do so, attach copies and not originals, because the documents may become separated from your return. Don't submit originals until the IRS actually asks for proof of your deductions. (For a discussion of IRS audits, see Chapter 11.)

Tip. It might help to submit a statement that you have reduced your medical expenses by the amount of your insurance reimbursements and still have deductible expenses in excess of 7.5 percent of your adjusted gross income.

Example. Bill and Maxine Simon are self-employed. To hold down premium charges, they selected a policy with a high deductible. Their policy does not cover routine physical examinations and certain other recurring expenses. The Simons submit the following statement with their return for tax year 1994:

Bill and Maxine Simon   Social Security number
123-45-6789

We have not been reimbursed by our medical insurance for the medical expenses claimed on Schedule A. Medical expenses claimed include insurance premiums of $5,000. Our insurance policy has a $3,000 deductible before we can be reimbursed for covered expenses. Under our policy, there is no coverage for expenses such as prescription drugs, eyeglasses, contact lenses, dental work, and annual physicals.

Q. *I failed to declare all my income on last year's return. In case I'm questioned, what are my chances of convincing the IRS that medical problems caused me to file a return that was inaccurate, but not fraudulent?*

A.   It depends on the nature of your problem. But don't be surprised to find the IRS and the courts are skeptical. Consider, for instance, what happened when an executive suffering from diabetes contended that his condition justified overturning his conviction for tax fraud. This claim did not sway the judge. His Honor noted that a doctor testifying for the defense did not assert that his patient had any mental problems. And the judge thought it unlikely that the executive was "in insulin shock every time he signed a tax return."

Then there was Joseph Jalbert, a New Hampshire businessman with legal training who had been an FBI agent. Jalbert cited medical testimony that he was a chronic drunk as one reason why he should not have been convicted for filing false returns. But the court found "far more persuasive" the testimony of government witnesses that he had been sharp enough to run his business despite his alcoholism.

8 CHARITABLE CONTRIBUTIONS

As part of your planning on how to cut your income taxes, make sure to donate to your favorite charities in ways that will save taxes for you. Here are some tips on how to sidestep traps and take advantage of breaks.

VOLUNTEER WORKERS

Are you one of the many individuals who volunteer to help raise funds or perform other tasks on behalf of such charitable organizations as religious groups, schools, and hospitals? When the annual reckoning with the IRS rolls around, the reward for your do-gooding takes the form of write-offs for unreimbursed expenses incurred while you do volunteer work.

But be aware of revised rules. Your donations, whether they take the form of gifts of cash or property or volunteer expenses, are allowable only if you itemize your deductions for contributions, interest on home mortgages, and the like. Contributions are nondeductible if you use the standard deduction for nonitemizers. This distinction was introduced by the Tax Reform Act. Previously, both itemizers and nonitemizers could subtract contributions from taxable income. (For more on the standard deduction, see "Itemizing versus Standard Deduction" in Chapter 1.)

What follows is a summary of the many possibilities. Remember, though, that some are subject to restrictions and others are frequently disputed by the IRS.

Only Out-of-Pocket Outlays Count

Your volunteer efforts entitle you to deduct only what you spend to cover unreimbursed expenses. These items include the cost of telephone calls, stamps, and stationery, as well as other materials that you supply, say, to make posters or bake cakes. Forget about any deduction, though, for the value of the unpaid time that you devote to charitable chores. Nor does the law allow you to claim anything for the use of your home or office to conduct meetings.

Uniforms

Does your volunteer work require you to wear uniforms? Don't forget to claim the purchase price and cleaning bills for clothing not adaptable to ordinary wear. Some of the more common examples are Red Cross volunteer and Scout leader uniforms. (For business-expense deductions for uniforms, see "Work Clothes and Uniforms" in Chapter 9.)

Babysitters

The IRS takes a dim view of deductions for babysitters who watch children while the parents do charity work. The payments for sitters, concedes the IRS, are incurred to make the volunteer work possible. Nevertheless, the agency ruled that the payments are nondeductible personal expenses.

Take heart, though. An IRS administrative ruling is by no means the last word. It merely reflects the official IRS position on an issue and is not binding on the courts. The Tax Court has held that babysitting fees that enable you to get out of the house are allowable, the same as car expenses linked to charitable work.

Blood Donations

An IRS ruling says no deduction for donating blood, except for any travel expenses to and from the blood bank. How does the IRS justify this restriction? Easy; it says that you are performing nondeductible "services," not donating property. On the other hand, the IRS insists on its share of any payment that you receive for providing blood.

Travel

An often-missed outlay begins the moment that you leave your home. Your allowable deductions include travel expenses to get to committee meetings, fund-raising events, and so on. Whether you travel to and from your volunteer work by bus, train, or taxi, just make sure to keep track of your fares and claim them as travel expenses.

If you use your own auto, you have two options on handling the expenses:

1. You can deduct the actual cost of gas and oil. You cannot claim depreciation because that is not an actual cash payment. Nor can you claim insurance and repairs unless you use the car only for charitable driving or the repairs are directly attributable to that use.

2. You can make the paperwork simpler by claiming a standard mileage rate. Under the rules applicable to tax year 1994 (the most recent year for which information is available as this book goes to press), the standard rate is 12 cents a mile. The 12-cent mileage rate has remained unchanged since 1985. The mileage rates differ when you use your car to obtain medical care (Chapter 7) or for business reasons (see "Business-Car Deductions" in Chapter 5).

Tip. Whether you use the mileage allowance or drive a gas guzzler and claim actual costs, remember to deduct parking fees and bridge or highway tolls as well.

Example. In the course of your charitable work this year, you drive 1,000 miles and shell out $40 for parking charges. Your allowable deduction is $160 (1,000 miles times 12 cents equals $120, plus $40 parking). Or, if you pay more for gas and oil than the mileage allowance, you can deduct actual costs plus parking.

Tip. It is a good idea, in case an IRS examiner questions your charitable travel, to be able to support your deductions with a glove-compartment diary in which you record why and how far you went, as well as what you spend on parking. You do not have to use the same car each time and can use more than one car at the same time. If you rent an auto and drive it only for charitable travel, include the entire rental charge with your other charitable expenses. Incidentally, stay within the speed limit. The tax collectors draw the line at a deduction for a traffic ticket. It matters not that you were on the way to teach Sunday school.

Away-from-Home Overnight Expenses

Additional breaks become available if your volunteer work requires that you be away from home overnight. Your deductions include travel expenses and a reasonable amount for lodgings and meals.

For instance, you can deduct these expenses when you attend a church convention as a duly appointed delegate. But you cannot deduct for such personal expenses as sightseeing or theater tickets. Nor are you allowed to deduct travel or other expenses incurred by your spouse or children.

Tip. To back up your deductions, in the event of an IRS audit, save a copy of the convention program and check off the sessions that you attend as a delegate. Sign an attendance book for any sessions that provide one. Keep a diary of your convention-related expenses, along with hotel and restaurant bills.

Disguised Vacations

The Tax Reform Act includes a provision designed to end deductions for charitable trips that are disguised vacations. There are limita-

tions on charitable deductions for travel expenses, including lodgings and meals, that are incurred by volunteer workers who perform services away from their homes on behalf of charities. The deductions are allowable only if there is "no significant element of personal pleasure, recreation, or vacation" in the away-from-home travel.

The travel-expense disallowance rules apply to payments made directly by you of your own expenses or of someone associated with you, such as a member of your family, as well as indirectly through reimbursement by the charity. A reimbursement, warns the IRS, includes any arrangement for you to make a payment to the charity and its payment of your travel outlays. To stop an end run around the disallowance rules, the law also bars reciprocal arrangements, where two unrelated persons pay each other's expenses or members of a group contribute to a fund that pays for all of their expenses.

These limitations are subject to an important exception. The deduction remains available for payments you make to cover the expenses of other persons who participate with you in, for instance, a camping trip.

Example. Dan Creamer, a Boy Scout leader, takes his scouts camping. Dan is entitled to deduct his payment of expenses for boys who belong to the group and are unrelated to him, but not for expenses for his own children.

Having Fun Is Not Fatal. What if Dan has a dandy time whenever he takes kids camping? Does Dan's euphoria erase any write-off for his own expenses? Not necessarily. The IRS concedes that Dan's expenses are allowable, provided he "is on duty in a genuine and substantial sense throughout the trip." It matters not that he enjoys the trip or supervising children. Those outlays, however, become nondeductible if Dan (1) "only has nominal duties relating to the performance of services" for the group or (2) "for significant portions of the trip is not required to perform services."

Tip. The Tax Court has stated, albeit in a context other than that of charitable write-offs, that "suffering has never been made a prerequisite to deductibility." (See "Profit Versus Pleasure: Strict Rules for Losses" in Chapter 9.)

Help from the IRS

Need more information on the frequently misunderstood rules? See IRS Publication 526, *Charitable Contributions.* For a free copy, call 1-800-TAX-FORM (allow at least 10 work days for mailing) or stop by the IRS office serving your area to obtain one immediately. Many libraries also have copies of this and other IRS tax guides. IRS Publication 910, *Guide to Free Tax Services,* provides a complete list of booklets and explains what each one covers. (For a discussion of IRS publications, see "Get the Right Help at Tax Time" in Chapter 13.)

Tip. Don't rely absolutely on IRS advice, whether it is information that employees give to telephone or walk-in inquiries or instructions that the agency prints in its publications. Mistakes in instructions or advice are inevitable, and the IRS is not bound by them.

CASH CAN BE RASH

Those bills you drop into church collection plates or give in response to door-to-door appeals can quickly add up. But if you plan to deduct a sizable sum for cash contributions, get receipts whenever possible. In the event those deductions are questioned by the feds and your only proof is your own word, an unsympathetic IRS agent will routinely refuse to allow more than a skimpy sum—say, one or two dollars a week for the year. Even worse, the auditor may check closely for other shaky items.

To safeguard your charitable write-off, use the envelope system, if your church has one, instead of dropping dollars in the collection plate. Put your regular cash contributions in an envelope, with your name and amount. After the year ends, get a receipt from your church.

If your church has no envelope system, list donations as you make them in some kind of record. Even entries in a diary may be acceptable as long as they are not made just before an audit. But it is much better to write checks or get receipts for your donations.

VIRTUE IS ITS OWN REWARD
Tighter Substantiation Rules

Previously, IRS auditors usually accepted canceled checks as sufficient substantiation for donations to churches, schools, and other philanthropic organizations. Sometimes, though, the IRS required taxpayers to obtain receipts or other written verification from the charities.

Was the agency's angst justified? Absolutely, in my experience. Many individuals receive something valuable in return for their donations—books, videos, tickets to artistic performances or sports events, or vacation trips, to cite just some of the many items routinely available from charities. Also, some creative taxpayers have even been known to cash checks at church bazaars and list them as acts of charity.

To make it easier to curb these abuses, the IRS persuaded Congress to tighten the rules, starting with returns for 1994 filed in 1995. The restrictions apply to any charitable conribution of $250 or more.

You need more than canceled checks to prove that you made a *single* donation of $250 or more. No deduction is allowable unless you obtain and keep for your records a receipt or written acknowledgment from the charity.

The IRS does not ask the charity to use a specific form for the acknowledgment, which can be by letter, postcard, or computer-generated form. Nor, for purposes of determining whether an acknowledgment is necessary, does the IRS require the charity to aggregate your contributions.

Let's suppose that you make several donations of $200 each to your alma mater. The school is relieved of the need to send a written confirmation to you. It makes no difference that the aggregate amount greatly exceeds $250.

Not unreasonably, however, the IRS intends to issue regulations that require an acknowledgment when, say, a donor simply writes multiple checks on the same date. The IRS treats this as a single payment.

Caution. You do not have an unlimited time to obtain the confirmation. There is a deadline; flunk it and you forfeit the deduction. You have until the filing due date (usu-

ally April 15, unless you obtain an automatic four-month filing extension to August 15) for the Form 1040 for the year in which you made the contribution payment. Translation: Under no circumstances does the law grant you the option to first find out whether the IRS computers bounced your return and, should that happen, then tell the charity to provide the confirmation. Under no circumstances have you the option to first find out whether the IRS computers bounced your return and, in that event, then tell the charity to provide the confirmation.

Additional paperwork. Another stipulation kicks in when a charity gives any goods (books and the like, as I mentioned before) or services (say, sessions with experts on interior decorating or weight loss and other aspects of personal grooming) in exchange for your above-$250 contribution. The charity's acknowledgment has to include a good-faith estimate of the value of what you received. That is so your deductible contribution can be reduced by what you received.

This requirement is subject to some exceptions. Among other things, you are not considered to have received something of value when your donation entitles you to attend religious services or occupy a particular seat or pew.

Caution. Things can get sticky if you disregard the acknowledgment and deduct the entire amount and your ploy becomes known to the IRS. Expect the agency to assess a penalty in addition to back taxes and interest charges.

Help from the IRS. The information-reporting requirements for charities mean extra expenses for many of them and are bound to cause lots of confusion. IRS Publication 1771, *Charitable Contributions—Substantiation and Disclosure Requirements,* spells out the details on just what sort of information charities need to provide to donors. The IRS has mailed out copies to over 500,000 charities. To obtain a free copy, telephone 1-800-TAX-FORM (allow at least 10 work days for mailing) or go to your local IRS office. (For more on other free IRS publications and services, see "Get the Right Help at Tax Time" in Chapter 13.)

Charities that provide more than token goods or services in return for donations must inform a donor just how much of the donation is deductible. Charities have to provide value-received estimates for contributions of more than $75. This related provision also took effect beginning with returns for 1994 filed in 1995.

A charity that provides more than token goods or services in return for your above-$75 donation must tell you just how much of the donation is deductible. The cap on the deduction is the amount by which the donated money or property exceeds the value of what you received.

As in the case of substantiation requirements for above-$250 donations, there also are exceptions for above-$75 donations. One is for a donation that entitles you to attend religious services or occupy a particular seat or pew.

Example. Your favorite charity runs a theater party and charges $100 for a ticket that costs $60 at the box office. You get to deduct only $40—the difference between your payment and what you received in exchange. Even if you opt not to use the ticket yourself and give it away to a friend, your write-off is limited to $40. To claim the entire $100, ei-ther make an outright donation or return the ticket for resale by the organization.

Caution. The IRS does not have an unwavering faith in the truthfulness of taxpayers. For purposes of the $75 threshold, it generally is not going to aggregate separate payments made at different times of the year to separate fund-raising events, but will aggregate multiple checks written on the same day for a fundraiser.

Tickets for College Sports Events

Sports fans get the benefit of a special exception. You can deduct 80 percent of your donations to colleges or universities for the right to buy scarce seats at sports events. But no charitable deductions to the extent the payments are for the actual purchase of the tickets.

Raffles

There is no charitable contribution for raffle tickets bought from religious or other philanthropic organizations, because those tickets give you a crack at winning a prize. Instead, the IRS rules for gambling losses apply (see Chapter 12). Provided you are an itemizer, you can subtract the cost of the tickets from any kind of gambling winnings (lotteries, horse racing, cards, and so forth). But if there are no winnings, there is no deduction either.

Other Kinds of Donations

The Supreme Court agrees with the IRS that Mormon parents cannot deduct as charitable donations payments for expenses of their children while the children are living away from home on missionary assignments for the Mormon Church. How come? Because the parents make the support payments directly to their children and the church has no control over the funds. Hence, the court concluded, it is not enough that the payments are made at the direction of the church and that it has some ability to supervise how the funds are used.

An IRS ruling says no charitable deduction for a person who donates money to charity in lieu of paying a court-imposed fine. Nor is the payment deductible as a business expense, since it was in settlement of a potential fine and a fine is nondeductible (Rev. Rul. 79–148).

The IRS has issued guidelines on deductions for voluntary payments made by participants at weekend marriage seminars sponsored by a charitable organization. No deduction, according to an IRS ruling, unless and to the extent the participants can show that their payments topped the value of "all benefits and privileges received," such as room and board. The burden of proof, cautions the IRS, still falls on the participants even though the sponsor suggested a figure to cover its costs (Rev. Rul. 76–232).

An IRS ruling approves a deduction for the donation of reward money by the parent of a murdered individual to a police department. The ruling sets the following scenario. Charles Carlton's son, Sidney, was murdered. Charles contributes $10,000 to his local police department to be used as a reward for information leading to the conviction of Sid's killers. If the money is not used to pay the reward, the police department has to use it for "exclusively public purposes."

Charles gets a deduction for the $10,000, as the reward helps the police maintain public safety and assists the police in carrying out governmental functions. Any benefit that Charles expects to receive from the conviction of Sid's killers is incidental to the benefits accruing to the public at large (Rev. Rul. 81–307).

Tip. An essential factor in the ruling is that money not used to pay the reward must be used for some other exclusively public purpose. Absent that stipulation, odds are that the IRS would have ruled unfavorably. Without such a provision and because apprehension of the killer is uncertain, the IRS might say that the donation is too uncertain to be deductible.

Predictably, an ecumenical Tax Court upheld an IRS disallowance of a deduction for the amount by which the cost of kosher food exceeds nonkosher food. Also deep-sixed was the deduction claimed by a gentleman who founded his own church and used his contributions to pay his rent and electric bills. The "church" merely served his personal needs. (For more on church founders who receive personal benefits, see "Questions and Answers" at the end of this chapter and "Family Trusts and Other Tax Scams" in Chapter 11.)

CONTRIBUTIONS OF APPRECIATED PROPERTY

The easiest way to contribute to charities is, of course, to write checks. The charities get the cash; you get deductions for the same amounts. But there is another way that can save more in taxes if you plan to make sizable donations. Instead of sending checks, consider contributions of appreciated properties, such as stocks, real estate, or other investments that have gone up in value and would be taxed as long-term capital gains if you sold them. (As the law now stands, the required holding period is more than one year; taxation of capital gains is discussed in Chapter 10.)

A gift of appreciated property is an often-overlooked strategy that makes good sense. The measure of your charitable deduction is the appreciated value of the asset, undiminished by the tax that becomes due on the accumulated profit if you sell the property.

To illustrate, let's assume that you intend to give $30,000 to your favorite philanthropy. Also assume that your long-term stockholdings include some shares that you acquired for $12,000 and are about to unload for $30,000.

You reap a double benefit when you contribute stock worth $30,000, rather than the same amount in cash. Going the stock route makes no difference to the charity; as a tax-exempt entity, it incurs no capital gains tax on the sale of the shares and ends up with close to the same amount of cash. But under the rules applicable to a return for tax year 1994, it does make a considerable difference in the size of your tax tab. In addition to the savings generated by a deduction for a $30,000 cash gift, you also sidestep the tax that is due on the $18,000 gain if you sell the stock yourself.

Tip. Uncertain about whether to surrender your position in the stock? Then you should consider donating the appreciated stock and using the money that you would have other-

wise donated to buy back the shares for their current market price. That way, you still get a charitable deduction of $30,000, as well as escaping tax on the $18,000 gain. Moreover, brokerage commissions aside, repurchasing the stock means that you can measure any gain or loss on a later sale against a cost of $30,000, not $12,000.

Partial disallowance of certain deductions for persons with AGIs above a specified amount, which is adjusted annually to reflect inflation. You suffer a partial disallowance of your allowable write-off for most itemized deductibles, including charitable contributions. The disallowance is 3 percent of the amount by which your AGI surpasses a specified amount—$111,800 for 1994. (See "Curtailment of Most Itemized Deductions for Individuals with AGIs above a Specified Amount" in Chapter 14.)

Deduction ceilings. The IRS clamps some tricky ceilings on the deductions available for contributions. In general, you are allowed to deduct up to 50 percent of your AGI (adjusted gross income) for gifts of cash to most charities—churches, schools, hospitals, and the like. But there can be limitations of 30 percent or 20 percent of your AGI on your allowable deduction for contributions of appreciated investments. Any gifts in excess of the limits cannot be claimed on this year's return, although they can be claimed during the next five years, subject to the annual limits. Five years should be sufficient time unless you make sizable future donations or your income plummets. (AGI is the amount you list at the bottom of page 1 of Form 1040 after listing salaries, dividends, interest, and other sources of income and deducting such items as money put in Individual Retirement Accounts and alimony payments, but before itemizing for outlays like medical expenses and interest on home mortgages.)

Paperwork.   Gifts of stock or similar property are allowed as deductions for this year only if you complete delivery of those donations by December 31. Make sure to allow enough time for completion of the legal paperwork.

If you unconditionally deliver or mail a properly endorsed stock certificate to the donee or its agent, the donation is considered completed on the date of delivery or mailing, provided the certificate is received in the ordinary course of the mails. But if you deliver the certificate to your bank or broker or to the issuing corporation as your agent for transfer to the name of the charity, the donation is not completed until the date the stock is transferred on the corporation's books—a process that could take quite a while.

Example.   The need to eye the calendar carefully was made expensively clear to Joseph Alioto, a lawyer and former mayor of San Francisco, who donated real estate. The Tax Court held that Alioto didn't complete his donation by December 31 of the year under review; although he executed the deeds in December, he did not record and deliver them until well into the following year.

Contributions of shares of stock you bought in the same company at different prices and at different times.   To reap the most advantageous deduction, make sure to donate the shares that you bought for the lowest prices.

Are you going to be the one who does the selection? Carefully choose the appropriate certificates from your safe deposit box.

Are the shares held by your broker in "street name" (that is, registered in the brokerage firm's name and intermingled with shares held for other customers)? Specify to your broker which ones are to be donated. (See "Keep Good Records of Stock Purchases" in Chapter 10.)

Expenses incurred in making the contribution.   You get a deduction for such expenses—for instance, fees for drafting documents to transfer the property. (More information on timing the payment of other deductible items is found in Chapter 1.)

Caution.   These drafting fees and similar expenditures are not deductible as charitable contributions. Rather, they must be claimed as miscellaneous expenses on Schedule A of Form 1040. Most miscellaneous itemized deductions are allowable just to the extent that their total in any one year surpasses 2 percent of your AGI. (For more information on miscellaneous deductions, see Chapter 9.)

Depreciated property.   Never donate stocks or other investments that have dropped in value since you bought them. The measure of your charitable write-offs is the *current* value of the asset. Worse still, you forfeit the capital-loss deduction. Instead, sell the property, donate the proceeds, and claim both the charitable contribution and the capital loss.

Example.   Your long-term investments include some shares you bought for $10,000 that are now worth $7,000. If you donate the shares, your allowable charitable deduction is $7,000. By selling the shares, however, you are able to claim a long-term loss of $3,000, as well as the $7,000 donation.

Step up in basis for inherited property. Another way to escape income taxes on appreciated assets is to transfer such property to your heirs as part of your estate after your death. This is because the basis of an asset is stepped up to its value at the date of death. Only post-inheritance appreciation is subject to income taxes. (See "Sale of Inherited Property" in Chapter 10.)

Bargain Sale of Appreciated Property

Another way to contribute appreciated property owned more than one year is to make a "bargain sale," that is, sell the stock or other asset to the charity for less than its fair market value. You remain entitled to a deduction for the donated appreciation (the difference between the fair market value and the sales price); but a bargain sale entitles the IRS to share your gain from the sale to the charity. This is because the transaction is treated as though you sold part of the property for its fair market value and gave the rest to charity, with your cost allocated between these two parts.

Here is an example of how the tax rules work when you bargain-sell property to a charity. Assume that several years ago you paid $12,000 for 100 shares of stock that are now worth $20,000, or $200 per share. You want to recover your cost of $12,000 and to contribute only $8,000 to a school. There are two ways to accomplish the desired donation, with similar results from an income tax standpoint.

The first way is to contribute only 40 shares. At the $200 price, this equals the desired $8,000. Then sell the remaining 60 shares for $12,000 on the open market. Because the 60 shares cost you $7,200 ($12,000

times 60/100), this gives you a taxable gain of $4,800.

The second way is a bargain sale—sell the 100 shares to the school for $12,000 and donate $8,000. Here also, the $4,800 profit on the sale is the difference between the $12,000 sales price and the $7,200 cost of the shares sold ($12,000 total original cost times $12,000 selling price divided by $20,000 fair market value).

Caution. You cannot sidestep taxes on the $4,800 profit by first borrowing against the property and then giving the encumbered shares to the school. The IRS treats this maneuver as the equivalent of a bargain sale.

Tip. Some types of property can be readily divided for sale—shares of stock, to cite an obvious example. On a sale of stock, as explained in the previous illustration, the tax results are identical whether you bargain-sell all the shares to a charity or sell some of them on a stock exchange for an amount equal to your cost and then contribute the remaining shares. But it may not be possible to divide for sale other kinds of property—certain types of real estate, for example. As a practical matter, a bargain sale may be the sole way to donate such real estate when you want to recover part or all of your cost.

CONTRIBUTING CLOSELY HELD STOCK

Charity begins at home for persons who own shares of closely held companies (other than S corporations, as explained below). With the blessings of the IRS, there can be big tax savings when you contribute some of those shares to religious groups, schools, and other philanthropic organizations.

Done the right way, contribution-redemptions allow you to withdraw sizable amounts from your company without the withdrawals being taxed to you and without giving up any ownership interest in your business. To qualify a withdrawal as tax-free, you make a charitable contribution of your stock which, without any prearrangement, is then sold by the charity to your company.

Here is how this technique works. Lady Godiva Accessories (LGA) is a corporation, all of whose 1,000 shares are owned by Ethel DeVorkin. Her shares originally cost $1,000 and are now worth $100,000. Ethel wants to give $15,000 to Roosevelt University. She donates 150 shares, instead of sending a check.

Roosevelt receives these 150 shares free and clear to do with them what it pleases. LGA then offers to redeem the shares from the university for their fair market value of $15,000. Because Roosevelt has no other practical way to turn the shares into cash, it will accept the corporation's offer. *Net result:* Ethel gets a charitable deduction of $15,000, the value of her contributed stock, without laying out a penny of her own cash and escapes being taxed on the appreciation on the shares given away. Roosevelt winds up, in effect, with a cash contribution. As for LGA, the company has, in effect, paid out its funds on behalf of Ethel, who once again owns all the stock. The redeemed shares are simply carried at cost as treasury stock on LGA's books.

What does going this route accomplish? It allows Ethel to avoid the dividend income of $15,000 that she would have realized had the stock been bought directly from her by LGA and she then contributed the proceeds to Roosevelt.

Caution. The IRS can still spoil the fun if Roosevelt is legally bound, or can be compelled by LGA, to surrender the shares for redemption. In this event, warns an IRS ruling, the agency will treat the contribution-redemption as a dividend to Ethel anyway (Rev. Rul. 78–197).

Not to worry. Actually, there need not be any kind of promise, wink, wink. After all, what else is Roosevelt going to do with 150 shares of LGA? Ordinarily, it makes sense for the university to convert the shares into cash by selling them, and the most logical buyer is LGA itself, which gets to liquidate a potentially bothersome minority interest.

Note, though, that approval of the contribution-redemption device by the IRS does not bar it from trying to cut the amount of Ethel's charitable deduction by valuing the shares of LGA at a figure lower than the $15,000 that she claimed.

Caution. LGA must be a regular corporation, which is taxed on its profits and losses. LGA cannot be an S corporation, which passes profits and losses through to its shareholders, who report them on their own returns. That is because there are restrictions on who can be a shareholder of an S corporation. A nonprofit organization engaged in religious, educational, or other philanthropic activities, such as Roosevelt, cannot be one of the shareholders. Were Roosevelt to become a shareholder, LGA would cease to qualify as an S corporation. (For more on S corporations, see "Section 1244 Stock" in Chapter 10.)

Tip. The law requires you to obtain an appraisal for a more-than-$10,000 donation of stock in a closely held company. See the discussion in the next section of this chapter.

APPRAISAL RULES FOR SIZABLE DONATIONS OF PROPERTY

Congress has made it easier for the tax collectors to uncover phony charitable deductions for inflated property values. The law now imposes stricter substantiation rules for sizable donations to charities of art, real estate, closely held stocks, and other hard-to-value assets.

You must obtain an independent valuation from a qualified appraiser when you claim a charitable deduction of over $5,000 for any gift of property or over $10,000 in the case of stock in a closely held company. There is no appraisal requirement for donations of stock of publicly traded companies, as the value of such shares can be easily ascertained.

At filing time, you must submit the required information on Form 8283 (Noncash Charitable Contributions), a form that includes an appraisal summary. You should retain a signed copy of the appraisal itself for further use in case the IRS questions the deduction.

Unless you submit Form 8283 with your tax return, the IRS will disallow the deduction, as a general rule. But it is not necessarily fatal if you file Form 1040 without the appraisal summary. The IRS will accept a late-filed Form 8283 if you submit one within 90 days after the agency asks for it, provided your failure to file it in a timely manner was a "good faith omission."

Appraisal Requirements

To avoid loss of a deduction, the appraisal has to be "qualified," that is, pass certain tests. A key requirement is that the appraisal be made within the 60-day period that precedes the date on which the appraised item is contributed and is prepared, signed, and dated by a "qualified appraiser," a term that is explained below.

Appraisal Fees

Usually, an appraisal fails to pass muster with the IRS when the fee arrangement is based on a percentage of the appraised value. The IRS, however, makes an exception for fees paid to a generally recognized nonprofit association that regulates appraisers. The exception applies when the appraiser receives no compensation from the association, and the fee is not based on the value of the property allowed as a charitable deduction after an IRS audit.

Caution. Appraisal fees are deductible only as miscellaneous expenses, not as charitable contributions. Most miscellaneous itemized deductions are allowable only to the extent that their total in any one year exceeds 2 percent of your adjusted gross income. (For the rules on miscellaneous deductions, see Chapter 9.)

Qualified Appraiser

This term, as defined by the IRS, means someone who holds himself or herself out to the public as an appraiser and who has the necessary qualifications to value the property in question. Understandably, the IRS refuses to accept an appraisal made by, among others, the donor, the charitable organization that receives the gift, and someone who is a party to the transaction in which the donor acquired the property (for instance, the art dealer who originally sold a painting to the person donating it).

Sale of Property by Donee

The law imposes a "tattletale" reporting requirement on a charitable organization when, within two years of the receipt by the organization of property (other than stock of a publicly traded company) valued at more than $5,000, it sells, exchanges, or otherwise disposes of the gift. After the charity sells the item, it has 90 days to file Form 8282 with the IRS (and give a copy to the donor). Form 8282 identifies the donee and the donor, describes the gift, and lists the dates of contribution and sale and how much the property fetched when sold.

Tip. The IRS has at least three years from the filing deadline for a return to begin an audit. (See "How Long to Keep Tax Records" in Chapter 11.) Therefore, the donor's return is still open for examination at the time the IRS receives a report from the charity of the sale. Odds are that the feds will ask the donor for an explanation if there is a sizable difference between the donor's deduction and the sales price.

Penalty for Overvaluation of Donation

If the IRS determines that a donor overstated the value of his or her gift by more than 200 percent, the agency is empowered to assess a penalty. The nondeductible penalty can be as much as 40 percent of the tax underpayment due to the overvaluation; that's in addition to the back taxes and interest.

Help from the IRS

For more information on how to value donated property, see IRS Publication 561, *Determining the Value of Donated Property.* For a free copy, call 1-800-TAX-FORM (allow at least 10 work days for mailing) or stop by the IRS office serving your area to pick one up immediately. Many libraries also have copies of this and other IRS tax guides. IRS Publication 910, *Guide to Free Tax Services,* provides a complete list of booklets and explains what each one covers. (For a discussion of IRS publications, see "Get the Right Help at Tax Time" in Chapter 13.)

Questions and Answers

Q. *My church agreed to sponsor a Cambodian refugee, and a group of us has been collecting food, clothing, and money for the refugee's support. Is any of what we give tax deductible?*

A. Because your church is sponsoring the refugee, donations are considered contributions to the church in carrying out its charitable purpose. You can take an itemized deduction for what you give, including the fair market value of donated goods.

Q. *Can I deduct magazine subscriptions if they are donated to a church?*

A. Magazine subscriptions may be deducted if they are made to a church, school, hospital, or other qualified organization. A receipt given to the contributor by the organization will normally suffice as proof of the gift.

Q. *I just came from a meeting where I was told how easy it would be to almost wipe out my income taxes. They said that for a fee*

I would be able to purchase a church charter, be ordained as a minister, and then qualify for the tax benefits available to churches. Is this true?

A. Don't bet the farm on it. The Internal Revenue Code does include a provision, Section 170, that allows contributors to deduct donations to churches. But what those hucksters failed to mention is that Section 170 also requires recipient organizations to operate exclusively for religious purposes, not for the private interests of their founders or other individuals.

Q. *Does the fact that an organization claims to be a church mean that I get to deduct a contribution to it?*

A. Just because some outfit passes itself off as a church does not guarantee that a charitable deduction will go unchallenged by the IRS. Similarly, the receipt by the organization of a church charter from an existing organization does not guarantee deductibility. What ultimately controls is whether the organization to which the contribution is made *itself* meets the Section 170 standard—it is organized and operated exclusively to further its expressed religious purposes, not the private interests of the founder or other persons.

Q. *How can I find out if an organization is legitimate?*

A. Most organizations that are eligible to receive tax-deductible contributions are listed in IRS Publication 78, *Cumulative List of Organizations.* To find out if an organization is listed, telephone or stop by your local IRS office.

Caution. Be wary of a sales pitch that implies that a church can be operated solely to provide benefits to the individuals creating it, that it need not have a creed, dogma, or moral code, and that the individual need undertake no specific duties or responsibilities as a minister.

Q. *Suppose an organization is able to establish that it qualifies as a church. Then can funds I transfer to it count as contributions?*

A. The IRS remains free to challenge a transfer, termed a "contribution," whether by you or the organization receiving it. Forget about the transfer justifying a deduction if you expect a return benefit—for example, the payment by the "church" of such personal items as your food and rent.

Q. *What if I take a vow of poverty? Will the vow make it possible for me to transfer my income to another organization to avoid paying income taxes?*

A. You are not off the hook for taxes just because you assign your future earnings to another individual or organization. It makes no difference what motivates you to make the assignment—an IRS reading of the law that has been backed up by the Supreme Court.

Q. *What happens if the tax collectors disallow my contribution to the church or ministry?*

A. The feds will demand full payment of the taxes and interest and might assess penalties. Even worse, the government might bring criminal charges against a "minister" whose only earthly mission is to evade taxes.

Q. *A foreign student who attends our high school is living with us this year. The school says we are entitled to a modest deduction for some of our expenses. How much of a charitable deduction can we claim?*

A. As long as the student is not a relative or dependent, you can deduct as much as $50 of what you spend for each full calendar month he or she lives in your home and attends grade

12 or lower. Count anything over 14 days as a full calendar month. Qualifying expenses include outlays for food (that alone should bring you up to the ceilings of $50 monthly and $600 yearly), clothing, medical and dental care, entertainment, books, and tuition.

Understandably, there is some paperwork. The student must be in your home under a written agreement between you and the exchange organization; the reason for the exchange must be to provide educational opportunities for the student.

For more information, including a list of what you must file with your return if you deduct expenses for a student living with you, see IRS Publication 526, *Charitable Contributions*. To obtain a free copy, call 1-800-TAX-FORM (allow 10 days for mailing) or contact the IRS office for your area to pick up one immediately.

Q. *I made a donation to a Danish charity. Can I deduct it?*

A. The law generally bars deductions for gifts made directly to foreign organizations, such as schools, museums, and religious institutions. However, you are allowed to deduct contributions to a U.S. organization that forwards the money to a foreign group and meets certain requirements, as when the U.S. organization controls the use of the funds or the foreign organization is only an administrative arm of the U.S. organization.

Q. *My hobby is painting. I donated one of my works to a church bazaar where it sold for $100. Can I deduct that as a contribution?*

A. No. Your deduction is limited to your unreimbursed out-of-pocket expenses for materials—the canvas, paints, and brushes. The entire $100 is deductible only if you sell the painting yourself and donate the pro-

ceeds to the church. But this maneuver does not help because the bigger deduction is completely offset by an increase in your reportable income of $100.

Q. *Is an estate entitled to a charitable deduction for a bequest of scholarships when religion or sex enters into selection of the recipients?*

A. Yes, according to IRS rulings. One will established a fund for deserving Jewish students with high academic ability. Another favored male Protestant graduates of a specified high school. Still, the IRS allowed the deduction in both cases.

Q. *Is a charitable-contribution deduction available to a speaker who declines an honorarium and asks that the money be donated to a charity he or she picks?*

A. Yes. But the good deed generates no tax saving; the speaker has to declare the honorarium as income.

Q. *My company allows employees to turn over part of their accumulated sick leave to help ailing co-workers who have used up their own paid leave and face a substantial loss of income during prolonged medical emergencies affecting themselves or members of their families. Does the sizable amount of leave that I gave up entitle me to a charitable deduction?*

A. As is true of many other good deeds, your reward will be in the life yet to come, not on April 15. According to an IRS ruling on the tax effects of leave-sharing arrangements, you get no deduction. Worse yet, the IRS taxes persons who receive donated sick time on their added leave pay because it amounts to extra compensation for their services (Rev. Rul. 90–29).

9 OTHER DEDUCTIONS AND CREDITS

CASUALTY AND THEFT LOSSES

Relatively recent law changes drastically tightened the rules on deductions for casualty and theft losses. It is now much more difficult to qualify for tax relief when you suffer property damage. The damage must be the result of an auto accident, fire, flood, vandalism, storm, theft, or some other event that is sudden, unexpected, or unusual in nature. Here is a rundown of the limitations that currently apply.

Both the past and present rules allow write-offs for uninsured losses on property used for personal purposes only if you itemize your deductions. Another restriction imposed by the old and current rules is that you cannot deduct the first $100 of loss from each casualty or theft incident.

Under current law, the key curtailment is that you are able to deduct unreimbursed losses only to the extent that the total amount in any one year (reduced by $100 per incident) exceeds 10 percent of your adjusted gross income (AGI), the amount you show at the bottom of page 1 of Form 1040 after listing salaries, interest, dividends, and other sources of income and deducting such items as funds placed in Individual Retirement Accounts and alimony payments, but before itemizing for outlays such as medical expenses and charitable contributions.

Previously, your itemized deductibles included all but the first $100 of each uninsured loss. Then Congress enacted the 10 percent of AGI limitation, which effectively eliminates any deduction unless you have modest income, suffer a loss that is catastrophic, or endure a string of lesser disasters.

To illustrate the curtailment, assume you have an AGI of $40,000 and a loss of $4,500, after subtracting $100 and any insurance proceeds that you may recover. You once could deduct $4,500. Now, $4,000 (10 percent of $40,000) is nondeductible; you can take a deduction of only $500. With an AGI above $45,000, you cannot write off any of that $4,500 loss.

Partial disallowance of certain deductions for persons with AGIs above a specified amount—$111,800 for tax year 1994. On the plus side, casualty and theft losses are not subject to this partial disallowance. (See "Curtailment of Most Itemized Deductions for Individuals with AGIs above a Specified Amount" in Chapter 14.)

Proposed legislation. As this book goes to press in the summer of 1994, Congress is considering a proposal to further tighten deductions for losses. There would be an increase in the threshold deduction for each loss from

$100 (plus 10 percent of AGI) to $500 (plus 10 percent of AGI). Moreover, the $500 amount would be indexed, that is, adjusted upward to reflect inflation, as measured by changes in the Consumer Price Index.

Measure of the Loss

Yet another hurdle is the way the IRS calculates your loss. Contrary to what many people mistakenly assume, the allowable loss is not the property's replacement value. Actually, cautions the IRS, the measure of your loss is the *lesser* of the following two amounts: (1) the difference in value of the property just before and after the event (in the case of a theft, the value afterward is, of course, zero, since you no longer have the property) or (2) the "adjusted basis" for the property.

Often, your adjusted basis is simply what you originally paid, in the case of property that you use solely for personal purposes—for instance, a family automobile or furniture. Then the amount of the loss is subject to the 10 percent of AGI rule and the $100 floor.

Homes. You may be in for a good deal of pencil pushing if you need to compute the basis for your home. First, you have to revise the original cost upward for subsequent improvements (backed up by bills and canceled checks) that add to its value. Then, you have to revise downward for amounts claimed in previous tax years as deductions for casualty losses or credits for installation of energy-saving devices, as well as for depreciation write-offs if you use part of your dwelling as a business office, etc. (For more on home improvements, see "Keeping Good Records" in Chapter 3.)

To see just how harsh the casualty- and

theft-loss rules are, consider this example. A thief steals fur coats and other clothing that originally cost $15,000, but were worth only $5,100 at the time of the theft; there is no insurance recovery. With that set of facts, the measure of your loss is only $5,000 (the lesser of $15,000 or $5,100, minus the $100 floor). *Result:* No tax deduction if your AGI surpasses $50,000.

Suppose, instead, that the thief filches uninsured antiques that originally cost you $5,100 but had been appraised for $15,000 just before the theft. Here, too, the measure of your loss is $5,000 (still the lower of the two valuations, minus the $100 floor). To reap any deduction for the loss, AGI must be below $50,000.

Tip. Ordinarily, you get to claim the entire loss for the year in which the casualty or theft takes place. But a special rule applies if you reasonably expect to recover your loss in a later year. Your deduction for the year in which the event occurs is limited to the part of your loss for which you do *not* expect recovery. If your later recovery turns out to be less than you expect, you get to deduct the difference for the year in which you determine that it's no longer reasonable to expect an additional recovery.

When a casualty or theft loss cannot be deducted because the amount is in dispute, it may pay to settle the matter in the year your income will be lower. That way, more of the loss will exceed the 10 percent of AGI floor and thus be deductible.

The IRS acknowledges that there is only *one* casualty and only one $100 reduction has to be made when, for instance, the *same* flood damages your home and detached garage or your year-round home and your summer cottage, or a hurricane damages your cottage, first by winds and then by high waves.

Caution. Because the old rules allowed almost complete deductibility for casualty and theft losses, many individuals (particularly those in tax brackets that were much higher than the current brackets) carried only a limited amount of casualty insurance coverage on their homes, automobiles, and other property. In some instances, they may have selected insurance with a high deductible (the amount that a policyholder has to absorb before he or she becomes entitled to recover from the insurer); in others, no insurance at all. These persons reasoned that their losses would be cushioned by tax deductions. They should reevaluate their insurance coverage, especially the size of the deductible, to make sure it continues to be adequate in the light of the 10 percent of AGI limit on deductions for uninsured casualty and theft losses, notes Maxine Caselbore of the Maxx Agency, Somers, New York.

Another Tightening

Several court cases held that a person who has insurance coverage, but chooses not to file a claim with the insurer, can still deduct a casualty or theft loss, subject to the $100 threshold and the 10 percent of AGI restriction. The Tax Reform Act of 1986, however, bars a deduction to the extent that the loss is covered by insurance and no claim is filed. It matters not that you fail to submit a claim for fear that the insurer will cancel coverage or hike the premiums.

IRS Audits

No theft-loss deduction is allowed for property that is merely lost or misplaced. That is why write-offs for thefts make it more likely that your return will be picked for audit and why it's prudent to document a substantial loss as best you can; you need proof that the theft actually happened and records to substantiate the amount. To be on the safe side, gather that proof as soon as possible after the theft occurs and information is still available; don't wait until you start to fill out your return, since that could turn out to be too late. (For a discussion of audits, see Chapter 11.)

When the IRS questions a theft loss, it routinely asks for proof that you were in fact burglarized or robbed of the particular items that are missing. That is one reason for promptly providing the police with a theft report that is as complete and accurate as possible. Your report should state what items were taken, their description, value, etc. Ask the police for a copy of their report, if available—particularly if the facts do not clearly show that the loss was due to a theft, rather than some other cause. You have nothing to lose by doing so, even if you think there is no chance of recovering your property; making a report to the police may strengthen your deduction against an attack by the IRS.

More than one burglary victim has discovered to his sorrow that it pays to make a report. Earl Jefferson deducted a theft loss for clothing that was missing from a closet in his apartment. But the Tax Court held that he failed to prove there had been a theft. For one thing, Earl made no attempt to show that someone had broken into his apartment or to indicate who might have had access to it. His case was further weakened by his testimony that he made no report to the police because he did not think it would help recover his property.

True, Earl might have lost his deduction even if he *had* reported the theft. But his chances would have been better if he made a report.

Also, as explained previously, you must show what the missing property originally cost you and what it was worth when taken from you. Unless you keep adequate records, you can at best rely only on estimates; and when an IRS agent runs into unsupported estimates that help cut taxes, the agent's usual reaction is to disallow or reduce them.

Tip. Since the tax collectors are so insistent on proof of value, it's a good idea to sit down and prepare an inventory of your personal property, with bills, if possible, for valuable jewelry, silver, coin and stamp collections, and the like, which are prime targets for burglars. (Such an inventory is discussed later in this chapter.) Then you can back up your tax deduction in case your property is stolen or damaged or destroyed by a flood, fire, or other mishap.

What Is a Theft?

As defined by the IRS, it "is the unlawful taking of money or property with the intent to deprive you of it." Consequently, the feds are understandably wary where the victim and the "thief" are acquainted or related and the facts fail to establish that there was a taking without consent. Here's a case in point.

It seems that while Jim Wilson was at work, his mother called to report that she had witnessed the removal of furniture and other belongings from his home by a woman with whom Jim had shared quarters for several years. Jim told the police that the missing items included a necklace that was worth $10,000. He never brought any civil action to recover the necklace, although he apparently knew the out-of-state address to which his girlfriend moved following the theft.

The IRS contended that Jim was not entitled to a theft-loss deduction because his failure to sue meant that he acquiesced in the taking of the necklace. The Tax Court noted that he took this course on the advice of his lawyer, and others he trusted, and that recovery costs would exceed the value of the property, given the departure of the woman to another state. "The mere fact that probably fruitless or economically ill-advised steps were not taken does not necessarily indicate any acquiescence in the actual taking."

But Herman Schonhoff was not allowed a theft-loss deduction of $3,900 for unused dance lessons with a St. Louis dance studio that, as Herman belatedly discovered, refused to allow its instructors to date customers. An unsympathetic Tax Court ruled he had not been victimized by the dance studio. Merely because the studio had pretty dance instructors available did not imply that they would date customers.

The Tax Court refused to allow a theft-loss deduction for costs incurred by a father trying to find a daughter who had been abducted by a former wife. The deduction is allowed only for a loss of property. Moreover, as discussed previously, the item stolen must have an adjusted cost basis and a fair market value at the time of the theft. The daughter cannot be considered property, noted the court, as "the ownership, purchase, and sale of human beings, commonly known as slavery, has been barred since the adoption in 1865 of the Thirteenth Amendment to the Constitution."

No theft-loss deduction is available to a

shareholder of a corporation for funds embezzled from his corporation. The loss was suffered by the corporation, not the shareholder.

What Is a Casualty?

As a general rule, a casualty is "the complete or partial destruction or loss of property from an identifiable event that causes actual damage to property and is sudden, unexpected, or unusual in nature." Under this definition, qualifying events include damage or loss caused by a hurricane, tornado, volcanic eruption, fire, earthquake, flood, storm, shipwreck, sonic boom from jet aircraft, auto accident, and vandalism. There's a long list of possibilities.

Nonqualifying events include damage or loss that stems from natural action, such as termite damage or gradual deterioration of property caused by normal weather conditions.

For instance, an IRS ruling barred a casualty-loss deduction for squirrel damage. Holes in a roof caused by squirrels were not "unexpected" and "unusual" events, according to the ruling, which also noted "it is common knowledge that squirrels are destructive (Ruling 8133097).

But the Tax Court approved a deduction for damages to shorefront property buffeted by a storm. The washing away of land was not caused by gradual erosion, but by the storm's waves. Consequently, the damage was due to a "sudden and unexpected event," the requisite for a casualty write-off, rather than "progressive deterioration through a steadily operating cause," which is not a casualty.

Cars.   You are entitled to take a deduction for damage from, say, a wreck caused by an icy road or a collision caused by faulty driving on the part of yourself (or someone else operating your car) or the other driver, so long as the damage did not result from your willful act or willful negligence. "Willfulness" includes drunken driving.

Casualty losses have been denied for tire blowouts caused by overloading and motor damage caused by an oil-line leak, but they have been allowed for damage resulting from a child pressing a starter button and freezing of a motor following an accident.

The Tax Court agrees with the IRS that no casualty-loss deduction should be allowed for damages to a person's life style due to suspension of his driving license.

Was your car a "lemon" from the day the dealer handed you the key? That, say the courts, does not entitle you to a casualty-loss deduction when you trade it in.

Nevertheless, a bona fide casualty loss is allowable even under odd circumstances. Take the case of Abraham Hananel, who returned from a visit to friends to discover that the auto he had parked in a tow-away zone had been towed away. Even worse, the city failed to identify the owner and, as authorized by law, crushed the car.

According to the IRS, no deduction should be allowed because Abraham ought to have forseen the consequences of selecting the particular parking space that he did. Like the Vichy French police chief played by Claude Rains in "Casablanca," the IRS was shocked, shocked to find that its peevish reasoning failed to convince the Tax Court, which responded that Abraham could have anticipated that the city might move the car, but *not* that it would become scrap metal.

Forced demolitions of homes in disaster areas.   There is a special break on casualty-loss deductions for owners of unsafe homes in disaster areas that, by government order, must be demolished or moved.

The usual rule is that a loss is deductible only when there is actual physical damage to property because of a sudden, unexpected, or unusual event, such as an earthquake. Prior law barred a deduction for a decline in the value of property merely because it is in or near an area that suffered, say, a mudslide or that might again be subject to a similar event.

But the law now allows casualty-loss deductions for persons whose residences are in locations declared by the president to be disaster areas eligible for federal assistance, and who satisfy certain requirements. The tax relief is restricted to individuals who demolish or relocate their residences under orders of a state or local government because their dwellings "have been rendered unsafe for use as a residence by reason of the disaster." Also, there is a deadline for the state or local agency to issue its order—120 days after the presidential declaration.

Example. A deductible loss occurs when a government agency determines that a dwelling in a storm disaster area has become unsafe because of nearby mudslides. No deduction, though, when the dwelling's decline in value is due to preexisting dangerous conditions, such as the home's location in an area prone to storms. Here, it makes no difference that a government agency condemns the house.

When deductible. A forced-demolition loss is deductible under the special provisions for disaster losses, which are discussed in the next section of this chapter. Consequently, you have the option of a deduction for the loss on the Form 1040 for the year in which the govern-

ment orders you to demolish or relocate, which means waiting until filing time rolls around, or on the return for the immediately preceding year, which means a speedy refund now, when you may be hard pressed for cash to cover the cost of property replacement.

Mislaid or lost property. An accidental loss or disappearance of money or property can qualify as a casualty loss. The usual tests apply; an identifiable event causes the loss, and it is sudden, unexpected, or unusual. An IRS-approved example: A husband accidentally slammed the car door on his wife's hand, causing the diamond in her ring to fly out of its broken setting, never to be seen again.

Of course, no deduction is allowed for routine household accidents—for instance, breakage of china or glassware through normal handling or damage done by a family pet.

William Clem persuaded the Tax Court that lost goods are deductible. His household belongings were lost after they were mistakenly shipped to the wrong country when he took an overseas assignment. The IRS' justification for disallowance of the write-off was the absence of evidence that an unexpected casualty had caused the loss. But the Tax Court pointed out that there had been civil unrest in the country where his possessions were mistakenly sent. It was likely that they had been pilfered, vandalized, or destroyed.

Incidental expenses. There is no deduction for expenses incident to a casualty, such as the care of personal injuries (though this may qualify as a medical expense; for more on medical expenses, see Chapter 7) and the cost of temporary lights, fuel, moving, and rental of temporary quarters.

In calculating your allowable casualty loss for a personal car, do not include these items:

towing charges, the cost of renting a replacement car, damages to a car registered in your child's name even though you provided the funds for the purchase of the car, or legal fees to defend against a suit for negligent operation of your car.

Prevention of casualty loss. A long-standing rule bars a casualty-loss deduction for preventive measures taken to avoid damage to property by a flood, storm, or other casualty. An example would be the cost of a dike to prevent flooding. The expenditure is considered a permanent improvement that is added to the cost of the property for purposes of determining gain or loss on a later sale.

Similarly, no deduction is allowed for the value of trees that are removed from residential property for fear that they will be brought down by the next storm, though a deduction is allowed if they are felled by a storm.

At Cade Austin's residence, some of the pine trees had grown until they interfered with power lines to his dwelling. With Cade's consent, the utility company had tree surgeons remove all the branches from the side of each tree close to the power lines. Since the absence of branches on one side of the trees might cause them to break or uproot during an ice storm and damage his residence, he had the utility company remove the trees completely.

The way Cade read the law, he was entitled to a casualty-loss deduction for the resulting reduction in value of his property. But the Tax Court thought otherwise. There was "no sudden and unexpected occurrence"—the usual requisite for the deduction. Moreover, noted the court, if Cade could claim a casualty loss, so could someone who installs a burglary alarm or smoke detector in a residence.

Records. To the extent possible, the deduction should be supported with proof based on appraisals, photographs, etc., of the difference in value of the property just before and after the casualty. Photos showing the condition of the property after it has been repaired, replaced, or restored may also be helpful, says the IRS.

Tip. Better gather that proof while the damage is fresh in your mind and information remains available. Don't wait until you start to fill out your return because that could turn out to be too late.

Keep good records of repair or replacement and clean-up expenses. True, the repair and replacement costs don't count as part of the deductible casualty loss, but the drop in value can be measured by your actual outlays for reasonable repairs, provided they meet the following requirements: They must do nothing more than restore the property to its precasualty condition, can only take care of the damage suffered, and cannot increase the property's value to more than its precasualty value.

Appraisals. When a sizable deduction is at stake, it's wise to support your claim with a written opinion from a competent appraiser as soon after the casualty as possible. The appraisal report should pinpoint the amount, cause, and time the loss was incurred. If a disputed casualty loss winds up in court, the IRS can bring in its own appraisers; but because of the time lag, usually their appraisals are less persuasive.

Tip. You do not have to count those appraisal fees under the 10 percent rule that trims your casualty deductions. Instead you can include them in full on Schedule A of

Form 1040 with your other itemized deductibles under "miscellaneous deductions," just the same as payments for preparation of returns or publications that help you with your tax planning, such as this book. But most miscellaneous itemized deductions are allowable only to the extent that their total in any one year exceeds 2 percent of your adjusted gross income. (For the rules on miscellaneous deductions, see the discussion later in this chapter.)

Free Household Inventory Handbook

The IRS offers a tax deduction to ease the pain if your home suffers property damage or destruction because of a fire, flood, or some other disaster or if you are the victim of a burglary or robbery. But, as discussed previously, if the IRS questions your casualty- or theft-loss deduction, you must be able to prove (1) what the damaged or missing items originally cost you and (2) what they were worth just before and after the casualty or theft.

Chances are, you do not have adequate records to back up your deductions and can at best rely only on estimates. That's assuming you can even recall, for instance, all those valuable and not-so-valuable belongings stored in your closets. Unfortunately, when the IRS uncovers unsupported estimates that help reduce taxes, the agency's usual response is to throw out or trim them. But the IRS is well aware of this problem and has some valuable help to offer.

Your local IRS office has available a free booklet, *Nonbusiness Disaster, Casualty and Theft Loss Workbook* (Publication 584), that is designed to help determine the amount of a casualty- or theft-loss deduction for house-

hold goods and personal property. You can use this handy booklet to list your possessions on a room-by-room basis. It has separate sheets for the entrance hall, living room, kitchen, and other rooms, and it lists belongings generally found in each area. For instance, the listing for the entrance hall sheet starts with chairs and ends with umbrella stands. Alongside each item are spaces in which you can record the number, date acquired, cost, value at time of loss, and amount of loss.

Tip. Even if you never need to figure a casualty or theft loss, this booklet will help you inventory your household goods and personal property. It can turn out to be invaluable when, for example, you want to reconsider the amount of your insurance coverage, file an insurance claim, or if you simply plan to move.

It's not a simple project to list all your possessions, their cost, and other details. But it's easier than trying to remember all those details after a theft or fire. When you make out an inventory or bring one up to date, just make sure to keep it in a safe place, such as a safe deposit box.

Quick Relief for Disaster Losses

Buried in the tax code is a provision that can provide immediate relief to individuals whose property is damaged or destroyed by natural disasters, such as droughts, hurricanes, and heavy snows, to cite some of the disasters that regularly hit many sections of this country.

The usual rule is that casualty-loss deductions can be claimed only on the tax return for the year in which they take place. But thanks to a special rule that comes into play when the losses occur in places declared by the president to be disaster areas eligible for federal assistance, you qualify for quick tax help, as well as other types of aid.

You can choose between a deduction for the disaster area loss on the Form 1040 for the current year when you file in April of next year or by amending the return for the previous year that you have already submitted, whichever offers the greater tax benefit. Going the previous-year route means a speedy refund now, when you may be in need of cash to take care of property repairs or replacements. If you opt to deduct the disaster loss in the earlier year, you must use the earlier year's adjusted gross income (AGI) in calculating the 10 percent of income limitation for casualty deductions, which is discussed previously in this chapter.

Example.   Your county is declared a disaster area because of severe storms and flooding in 1995. The flooding causes $5,000 in uninsured damage to your dwelling. Your AGI is $40,000 for 1995 and $35,000 for 1994. For 1995, the allowable deduction is $900 ($5,000 reduced by the $100-per-occurrence rule to $4,900, then reduced by $4,000 or 10 percent of your AGI). But for 1994, the deduction is $1,400 ($5,000 reduced by $100 to $4,900, then reduced by $3,500 or 10 percent of your 1994 AGI).

Tip.   A couple who decides to claim the deduction on an original (not amended) return for the year in which the loss takes place should consider whether the damaged property is owned jointly or separately and whether one of them has more income than the other. These circumstances might determine whether they should file joint or separate returns.

Refund Claims

You can amend your previous-year return without complicated red tape by using Form 1040X (for individuals) or Form 1120X (for corporations). These forms merely ask you to explain the disaster area loss and compute the refund due. To help speed up the processing of your refund, write "disaster area claim" at the top of the form.

Caution.   Before you elect to take advantage of this optional provision, take the time to compare your tax bracket for the previous year with what you expect it to be for the current year to see when the deduction would do you the most good. (For information on how to determine your tax bracket, see "What Is Your Real Tax Bracket?" in Chapter 14.) The entire deduction must be taken in a single year; splitting the deduction between two years is not permissible. Remember, too, that when you amend your return for any reason, it may prompt the IRS to question other items or, worse yet, other returns. Note also that approval of a refund claim does not bar a later audit of your return. (For a discussion of refund claims, see Chapter 14.)

Help from Others

Your deductible loss is cut down by cash or property you receive from your employer or from disaster relief agencies specifically for the purpose of restoring your property, but not by cash gifts that aren't so designated, even though you use the money to pay for rehabilitating your property.

Any food, medical supplies, and other forms of subsistence you receive that are not for replacement of your property, do not reduce your loss, and do not count as taxable income.

To find out if your neck of the woods has been declared a "disaster area," contact the regional office or the Washington office of the Federal Emergency Management Agency.

Interest on Home Equity Loans

In this time of constant change, two things remain the same: The tax collectors want more of your hard-earned money, and you want to keep more of it for the things you need. So it pays to consider the tax consequences beforehand as you make those everyday financial decisions, whether it be to go ahead with that much-needed face-lift for your kitchen or how to pay for your youngster's college education.

Be particularly mindful of how to use the tax rules to your best advantage if you are a homeowner who has sizable outstanding loans. Because of restrictions introduced by tax reform, it could make sense to consolidate your debts and thereby reap a double benefit—be able to borrow at a lower rate and gain a tax deduction, too. In fact, your home, whether a house, condo, or co-op apartment, could open the door to one of your smartest money moves right now.

For starters, let's look at how the 1986 Tax Reform Act overhauled the rules. Previously, you could deduct all interest payments on "consumer" loans. Now, though, you get

no deduction for consumer interest, a category that includes revolving charge accounts, auto loans, college loans, and other personal debts, such as overdue federal and state income taxes.

Fortunately, the interest-deduction restrictions introduced by tax reform left most homeowners unscathed. Under the rules applicable to tax year 1994 (the most recent year for which information is available as this book goes to press), you still are able to deduct 100 percent of the interest charges on as much as $1,000,000 of mortgage loans incurred to buy, build, or improve your year-round residence and one other home, such as a vacation retreat.

Moreover, you can deduct 100 percent of the interest on up to an additional $100,000 of loans secured by your home, without any restrictions (other than the purchase of tax-exempt obligations) on your use of the loan proceeds. These borrowings are known as home equity or tax-advantaged loans. The home-mortgage–interest rules create a unique double benefit, should you tap the equity built up in your home. First, deducting the interest saves federal, as well as state and city income taxes, depending on where you live or work. Second, you borrow for less. How come? Because lenders furnish home equity loans at much lower interest rates than for comparable unsecured consumer loans.

Bottom line: Getting the things you need today needn't mean you're saddled with high interest rates. Instead, it can mean trimming taxes considerably, courtesy of a tax-advantaged loan.

How, then, does going this route help you? Many financial planners and tax advisers counsel clients to convert nondeductible consumer loans into less expensive, fully deductible home equity loans. As long as the mortgage-interest rules remain unchanged, this strategy keeps more money in your pocket for this and later years.

Note, too, that debt consolidation is not the only reason to use tax-advantaged loans. Other borrowing needs might include such "big ticket" items as autos or your children's educations.

Caution. Home equity loans are not without some risk, however. Because there is a lien on your home, the lender has the option to foreclose on your property if circumstances prevent you from repaying the loan. So it's important to calculate accurately your ability to repay any loan for which your home is collateral. If you feel uncomfortable with this type of risk, take a look at other borrowing alternatives.

Partial disallowance of certain deductions for persons with AGIs above a specified amount, which is adjusted annually to reflect inflation. You suffer a partial disallowance of your allowable write-off for most itemized deductibles, including interest on home mortgages. The disallowance is 3 percent of the amount by which your AGI surpasses a specified amount—$111,800 for 1994. (See "Curtailment of Most Itemized Deductions for Individuals with AGIs above a Specified Amount" in Chapter 14.)

Proposed legislation. As this book goes to press in the summer of 1994, Congress is studying proposals to curtail deductions for interest on home mortgages.

"Points" for Home Mortgages: When and How Quickly You Get to Deduct Them

Do you plan to buy a home or to refinance a mortgage to obtain a more favorable interest rate? Be aware that the IRS lays down some tricky deduction rules if you have to pay "points" to obtain a loan or to refinance one.

What are points? They are additional, upfront fees, instead of higher interest rates. When money is scarce, lenders charge points, also known as "loan origination fees" or "premium charges"; 1 point equals 1 percent of the amount borrowed.

The key to points being 100 percent deductible in the year of payment, along with your other home-mortgage interest, is that you pay the points to obtain a specific type of loan. It must be a loan to buy, build, or improve (as when you add or remodel a room) your "principal residence," legalese for a year-round home, as opposed to a vacation retreat or property for which you charge rent. (For timing payments of interest expenses to your best advantage, see "Timing Payments of Deductible Expenses" in Chapter 1.)

There are several other requirements that have to be satisfied for the full amount of points to count in the year of payment as a deduction for interest on a home mortgage, as opposed to a gradual write-off over the life of the loan.

- The loan is secured by your year-round home.
- At loan closings, most buyers receive a Uniform Settlement Statement. The statement must clearly identify the amount that the lender charges as points

and can do so with designations such as "loan origination fees," "loan discount," "discount points," or "points."

- The points must be calculated as a percentage of the amount borrowed. *Translation:* They represent an identifiable percentage—say, 2 percent—of the loan, not just a flat fee.

- The charging of points has to conform to an established business practice in your area.

- The deduction cannot exceed the number of points generally charged in your area. Under this limitation, the amount charged as points cannot be in lieu of fees that are ordinarily separately stated in the settlement statement—for instance, appraisal fees, inspection fees, title fees, attorney fees, property taxes, and mortgage insurance premiums.

No Longer Necessary to Write Your Own Check

Things are seldom straightforward when it comes to taxes. At one time, whether you were entitled to deduct points when paid or bit by bit over the loan's life sometimes depended on *how* you paid them.

Previously, the IRS prohibited a full, immediate deduction for points if they were merely withheld by the lender from the loan. The feds insisted that you had to pay for the points with a separate check. Otherwise, the points were deductible only as you repaid the loan.

This stipulation deep-sixed deductions for many borrowers. For example, Roger Schubel pledged his home as security for a $55,000 loan from a bank, which subtracted

$2,000 for points and put $53,000 at his disposal. But the Tax Court agreed with the IRS that Roger's receipt of the discounted loan proceeds did not entitle him to a $2,000 year-of-payment deduction. Interest withheld from a note cannot be deducted until the loan is repaid, reasoned the court, a ruling that agreed with how the IRS then interpreted the law.

Now, however, your own check is no longer necessary to establish that you did not simply borrow the money from the lender. All you have to do is come up with enough cash at closing to cover the amount deducted for points.

Caution. A recent rules tightening makes it easier for the IRS to check on whether a homeowner properly deducts points. The law now requires a lender to report to the IRS the amount of points, other than refinancing points, paid directly by a borrower. The amount must be listed on Form 1098. Like 1099 forms from banks and brokerage firms that report dividend and interest information, 1098 forms are sent to the IRS for use by its computers, which compare 1098 figures with amounts listed as deductions for points on Schedule A of Form 1040.

Refinancing an Existing Mortgage

Here is how the IRS reads the law: "Points you pay to refinance a mortgage, regardless of how you arrange to pay them, are not deductible in full in the year you pay them unless they are paid in connection with the purchase or improvement of a home. This is true even if the new mortgage is secured by your main home." However, as explained below, the way the IRS reads the law is not binding on the courts.

Example. In September, you refinance an existing mortgage with a new 15-year (180 monthly payments) home loan of $100,000, of which you use $60,000 to pay off the balance on the old mortgage and the remaining $40,000 for home improvements. You pay $3,000 in points.

Because you use some of the loan proceeds for improvements, you have to allocate the points for deduction purposes. For the year of refinancing, you can immediately deduct $1,200, which is 40 percent ($100,000 divided by $40,000) of $3,000.

As for the $1,800 remainder ($3,000 minus $1,200) of the points payment, you get only a gradual write-off over the life of the loan. The IRS authorizes two ways to calculate just how much you can deduct each year.

The first way is the easier method. All you need to do is divide the points ($1,800) by the number of months of the loan (180). With these numbers, you wind up with a monthly deduction of $10 and a year-of-refinancing deduction of $40 (the four mortgage payments for the months of September through December times $10).

For the year of refinancing, your total deduction for points is $1,240 (the sum of $1,200 plus $40); you add that figure to the other home-mortgage interest that you are allowed to claim. For the following year, your points deduction is $120 ($1,800 divided by 180 and multiplied by 12 monthly payments).

Note, though, that the first method of equal monthly deductions can shortchange you because the interest charges are not spread in equal amounts over the mortgage term. You incur the bulk of the charges in the earlier years, when the unpaid balance is larger.

But you have the option to skip the first method and use another one. The second method authorized by the IRS is more complicated and requires use of a mortgage amortization table. The payoff for number crunching is a greater deduction in the early years.

Under the second method, you make a two-step calculation: (1) Divide the amount of regular interest paid during the year in question by the total amount of regular interest to be paid over the mortgage term (disregarding the points fee). (2) Multiply the fraction in (1) by the amount of the total points payment. The result is a points deduction for that year equal to the portion of the regular interest charge you pay for that year.

Tip. Whether you use the first or second method, remember to claim your yearly write-off for yet-to-be-deducted points. These points are deductible in full if you pay off the mortgage early, whether you sell your home or refinance again.

Caution. Be mindful of a tax trap if you refinance again through the *same* lender. There is no immediate deduction for the remainder of the previous points unless, as discussed earlier, you pay enough cash to cover those points. Otherwise, you have to write them off over the life of the new loan.

Strategy. As mentioned previously, not all courts go along with the IRS view that points paid to refinance a mortgage must be written off over the life of the loan. In 1990, the Eighth Circuit Court of Appeals allowed James and Zenith Huntsman of Stillwater, Minnesota, an immediate full deduction of

$4,400 for points paid to obtain a $148,000, 30-year mortgage. The Huntsmans had used the proceeds to pay off a $122,000 three-year mortgage with a balloon payment and a home-improvement loan secured by a $22,000 second mortgage.

The appeals court concluded that the couple intended to refinance at the time they bought their home. The 30-year loan was sufficiently "in connection with" their original purchase and not just an attempt to refinance at a lower rate. *Translation:* Some, though not all, refinancers should get up-front deductions.

In 1991, an unyielding IRS announced its disagreement with the Eighth Circuit and reminded its auditors that they should continue to disallow current deductions for points paid on refinancing.

Some yet-to-be-answered questions: Will the IRS pursue this issue in other courts? In that event, will those courts agree with the Eighth Circuit's pro-taxpayer position on short-term loans with balloon payments? Stay tuned.

Points Paid by Seller

The IRS retroactively reversed its position on the payment of points by the seller to induce the lender to arrange financing for the buyer. Previously, the IRS treated the payment as a selling expense that reduces the amount realized on the sale and is not deductible by the buyer.

But a 1994 announcement changed the rules for homes purchased after 1990 (Rev. Proc. 94-27). The payment continues to be a downward adjustment of the sales price, but paid by the seller on behalf of the buyer and deductible by the buyer.

Caution. The buyer has to subtract the amount paid from the purchase price in computing the home's basis—the figure used to determine gain or loss on the sale of an asset. (For a discussion of adjustments to basis, see "Keeping Good Records" in Chapter 3.)

Mortgage Prepayment Penalty

If you prepay the mortgage on a principal residence, you may be hit with a hefty penalty (a percentage of the unpaid balance) for the privilege of paying it ahead of time. No matter what the lender calls it, that extra charge is fully deductible home-mortgage interest.

Help from the IRS

An IRS booklet, *Home Mortgage Interest Deduction* (Publication 936), provides detailed information on deductions for points. For a free copy, telephone 1-800-TAX-FORM (allow at least 10 work days for delivery) or stop by the IRS office that serves your area to obtain one immediately.

Many libraries also have copies of this and other IRS tax guides. IRS Publication 910, *Guide to Free Tax Services,* provides a complete list of booklets and explains what each one covers. (For a discussion of IRS publications, see "Get the Right Help at Tax Time" in Chapter 13.)

Tip. Don't rely absolutely on IRS advice, whether it is information that employees give to telephone or walk-in inquiries or instructions that the agency prints in its publications. Mistakes in instructions or advice are inevitable, and the IRS is not bound by them.

LENDING MONEY TO A RELATIVE OR FRIEND

These being the times they are, you may be tapped for a loan by a relative or friend who is unable to come up with the down payment for a home or wants to start a business. If the loan goes sour, as so often happens, the tax rules on deductions for bad debts can be more bad news for you. So if you find yourself in the position of staking someone, it's prudent to know beforehand how the Internal Revenue Service looks on worthless loans.

The IRS says you can deduct a worthless loan if there is no likelihood of recovery in the future. But you cannot take a deduction for an outright gift. That's why the agency looks closely at bad-debt deductions where the lender and borrower are related and why it may insist on proof that the transaction was actually a loan, rather than a gift.

Advance Planning

Before making a loan, there are steps you can take that will help in case a revenue agent questions your write-off. The key is to set up the transaction with the same care that you would a business loan.

To begin with, you should ask the borrower to sign a note or agreement. Moreover, make sure the note spells out the amount borrowed and the dates and amounts of repayments. Charge a realistic rate of interest —say, the rate your money would earn in a savings account if it were not out on loan. Arrange for a witness to sign the note if the law in your state requires it.

If keeping the deal as businesslike as you can sounds like a rough way to deal with a friend or relative, remember that it is the only way if you want to deduct a bad debt later. The tax collectors routinely throw out deductions for handshake deals.

Tip. It's not widely known, but the IRS will not quibble about a bad-debt deduction if you make a deposit or advance payment and the seller fails to deliver the promised product. For example, you put a deposit on a new house, and the builder goes bankrupt before the house is finished.

When to Deduct

You can take a deduction for the loan only in the year that it becomes worthless. You need not, however, wait until the loan is past due to determine whether or not it is worthless; a loan becomes worthless when there is no longer any chance of being paid what you are owed.

Tip. Be mindful that the IRS will want good evidence that the loan is actually worthless and will remain so in the future. That means you must take reasonable steps to collect it. On the other hand, the IRS does not require you to hound a debtor into court, provided you can show that a judgment, if obtained, would be uncollectible; but you should at least send a letter asking for repayment. Generally, the debtor's bankruptcy is a good indication that the debt is at least partially worthless.

Example. You loan money to your uncle for another of his "can't miss" deals but do not try to collect it; several years later, he becomes bankrupt. The IRS will refuse to allow a bad-debt deduction. You could have collected the money at an earlier date while your uncle was financially solvent, yet made no effort to do so. This, reasons the IRS, "is strong evidence that you did not intend a creditor-debtor relationship to exist between you and your uncle."

Nonbusiness Bad Debt Treated as Short-Term Capital Loss

Another point to keep in mind is that the law authorizes more advantageous treatment for business-related bad debts than for nonbusiness bad debts, such as a personal loan to a relative. Unlike a business bad debt, which is deducted directly from income, a nonbusiness bad debt comes under the rules that limit a deduction for a short-term capital loss. Consequently, for the year the personal loan becomes uncollectible, you first use the loss to offset any capital gains and then use up to $3,000 of the remaining loss to offset "ordinary" income from, say, your salary.

Special rules apply if the loss exceeds $3,000. Any unused loss can be carried forward and claimed in the same way on your return for the following year and beyond until the loss is used up. (For more on capital losses, see "Capital Gains and Losses" in Chapter 10.)

Example. For 1994, you had no capital gains, but suffered short-term capital losses of $8,000, including uncollectible nonbusiness bad debts. You subtracted $3,000 of your capital loss from ordinary income. That left you with $5,000 to carry forward into 1995, when the remaining loss (unless offset against capital gains) may be used to again reduce ordinary income by $3,000. Your unused loss is now down to $2,000 and is carried forward to 1996 when (unless offset against capital gains) it is finally used up as a subtraction from ordinary income.

Paperwork

The IRS requires a detailed explanation for a bad-debt deduction. Your return must be accompanied by a statement that includes the following information:

1. The nature of the debt.
2. The name of the debtor and any business or family relationship to you.
3. The date the debt became due.
4. What efforts you made to collect the debt.
5. The reason you determined the debt to be worthless.

Help from the IRS

Need more information? For a helpful, plain-language explanation, see IRS Publication 550, *Investment Income and Expenses.* To obtain a free copy, call 1-800-TAX-FORM (allow at least 10 work days for mailing) or stop by the IRS office serving your area to obtain one immediately. Many libraries also have copies of this and other IRS tax guides. IRS Publication 910, *Guide to Free Tax Services,* provides a complete list of booklets and explains what each one covers. (For a discussion of IRS publications, see "Get the Right Help at Tax Time" in Chapter 13.)

WORK CLOTHES AND UNIFORMS

Paying the shirt off your back at tax time? Don't count on a deduction for what you wear to work from what you make at work.

Generally, it makes no difference that your work requires you to be fashionably or expensively dressed. You reap no write-off for what you spend on clothing that is adaptable to *general* wear off the job. However, a long-standing rule authorizes a deduction for the cost and upkeep of *special* work clothes or equipment that satisfy a two-step test. The first stipulation is that they must be required as a condition of employment. The second one is that they are not suitable for everyday use. Some examples of items that readily pass IRS muster are uniforms worn by ballplayers, firefighters, police officers, letter carriers, nurses, and jockeys, as well as clothing that protects workers from injuries, a category that includes safety shoes and glasses, hardhats, and work gloves.

An often-overlooked point is that the deduction is allowable only if *both* conditions are met, cautions the IRS. It is not enough that your employer requires you to wear special clothing.

Usually, the IRS prevails in disputes over clothing deductions. For example, the feds eventually emerged triumphant in a case involving Sandra J. Pevsner, who managed the Sakowitz Yves St. Laurent Rive Gauche Boutique in Dallas, a store that sold only St. Laurent–designed clothing and accessories for women. The high-fashion boutique required Sandra to buy and wear only its designer clothes while working.

The boutique manager claimed a business-expense deduction for the cost, plus cleaning expenses, of the apparel she was expected to purchase and wear at work. She was backed up by the Tax Court, which used a subjective test to justify the write-off. The test, reasoned the Tax Court, of whether the garb in issue is suitable off the job must be determined by a worker's particular lifestyle.

What clinched the case for Sandra was her unchallenged testimony that she was on a lower social and economic level than the women who patronized her boutique. She could not easily afford St. Laurent creations, even with her discount, and never wore them away from work, except to commute. The chic clothes were inappropriate for the "very limited and informal" outside-of-work socializing by Sandra and her husband, who was partially disabled as a result of a severe heart attack.

But the IRS persevered, just like the Little Engine That Could, imaginatively described by the *New York Times* as "that stalwart mechanical hero of childhood lore that defied the odds of physics and huffed and puffed to the top of a very steep hill."

The unsympathetic tax collectors told an appeals court that her way of life made no difference. Sandra should not be entitled to take the expensive outfits off her taxes just because she took them off after work. The clothes suited lots of other women who wore these outfits outside of work; that made them unsuitable personal expenses that are never deductible.

Unfortunately for Sandra, the Tax Court's subjective-test approach was overruled by an appeals court, which held that an objective standard should be used. Under an objective test, the cost is never deductible as long as the clothing is suitable off the job. Objective rules, the appeals court noted, are easier for IRS examiners to apply than subjective rules, which require the feds to figure out when either price or style causes clothing to become inappropriate to a worker's lifestyle; price and style are personal choices, governed by taste and fashion.

Another drawback is that the Tax Court's approach could cause unfair results. The tax tab, said the appeals court, might vary for two boutique managers with identical wardrobes, but differing "lifestyles and socio-economic levels."

Nationally ranked Chicago tennis pro Cecil Mella lost his match with the IRS on the issue of business write-offs for tennis clothes and shoes. Cecil worked for two private tennis clubs, both of whom barred players, including instructors, from playing on the courts unless they wore proper attire.

On the return for the year in issue, he claimed deductions for clothes, including warm-up jackets and pants, shirts with a collar, and shorts that were brief to give maximum freedom of movement and had pockets for tennis balls, as well as shoes, each pair of which lasted only 2 or 3 weeks and were designed, according to Cecil, to decrease the chances of injuries.

Cecil said he wore the items only when playing or teaching. But the Tax Court, in its unsought role as official interpreter of fashion correctness, noted: "It is relatively commonplace for Americans in all walks of life to wear warm-up clothes, shirts, and shoes of the type purchased by [Cecil] while engaged in a wide variety of casual or athletic activities." As for the shoes' safety functions, the court was unpersuaded by his "uncorroborated and vague statements."

The Tax Court threw out deductions for business suits bought by Edward J. Kosmal, a Los Angeles deputy district attorney who was planning to leave government service and decided that the right way to impress his future employers and colleagues was to upgrade his wardrobe to a sartorial standard appropriate to that of a "big-time Beverly Hills P.I. [personal injury] attorney." But the Tax Court denied the write-offs because, unquestionably, the clothes were suited to ordinary wear.

Makeup or hair styling. Hair dressing outlays are nondeductible personal expenses, says the IRS, even for someone like Mary McFadden, a big-name, New York fashion designer who is in the public eye and is "noted professionally for her distinctive hair style."

Vivian Thomas worked as a private secretary for an attorney who required her to be perfectly coiffed at all times while in the office. So she deducted the cost of twice-weekly trips to the beauty parlor. Sorry, said the Tax Court, but a secretary's coiffure-maintenance costs are nondeductible, even in her case.

But the Tax Court sided with Margot Sider, who wrote off the cost of 45 extra beauty parlor visits that were made, she argued, only because her hairstyle was an integral part of her job demonstrating and selling "a high-priced line" of cosmetics in a department store to a "sophisticated clientele." When she quit selling cosmetics, she went back to a simpler style.

At her trial, Margot cited a 1963 Supreme Court decision written by Justice John Marshall Harlan: "For income tax purposes Congress has seen fit to regard an individual as having two personalities: one is a seeker after profit who can deduct the expenses incurred in that search; the other is a creature satisfying his needs as a human and those of his family but who cannot deduct such consumption and related expenditures."

Margot asserted she had spent the amount

in issue as a "seeker after profit," not as "a creature satisfying her own needs." That satisfied the judge, who ruled she was entitled to fully deduct the outlay beyond "the ordinary expenses of general personal grooming."

Back in 1979, notes *Money* magazine, actress September Thorp offered an unassailable not-adaptable-for-general-wear defense —and won—when the IRS challenged her deduction for makeup: "I'm in *Oh! Calcutta!* and I have to appear nude onstage every night, so I cover myself with body makeup. I go through a tube every two weeks, and it's very expensive."

More bad news. Recent law changes drastically curtail write-offs for work clothes even if they are employment-required and unsuitable for general wear. The tougher rules require you to satisfy two stipulations.

First, as under the old rules, you have to be an itemizer. You forfeit any deduction if you claim the standard deduction, the no-questions-asked amount that you automatically get without having to itemize.

Second, the law now lumps outlays for work clothes together with most other miscellaneous itemized deductions. This grouping includes such expenses as dues payments to unions, rentals of safe deposit boxes, and return-preparer fees. Miscellaneous deductibles can be claimed only to the extent that their total in any one year is more than 2 percent of your AGI, short for adjusted gross income. Anything below the 2 percent of AGI floor is not deductible. (For the rules on miscellaneous deductions, see the discussion later in this chapter; for timing payments of miscellaneous expenses to your best advantage, see "Timing Payments of Deductible Expenses" in Chapter 1.)

AGI is the amount you show at the bottom of page 1 of Form 1040 after listing salaries, interest, and other sources of income and claiming certain deductions like money channeled into IRAs. The AGI figure is before itemizing for things like charitable contributions and real estate taxes and listing exemptions for yourself and your dependents.

Example. You have an AGI of $45,000 and itemize. Your work clothes and other miscellaneous expenditures total $1,600. Before tax reform, the full $1,600 was deductible. Now, however, the 2 percent threshold shrinks your deduction to just $700—what is left after the $1,600 is offset by $900, which is 2 percent of $45,000.

Partial disallowance of certain deductions for persons with AGIs above a specified amount, which is adjusted annually to reflect inflation. You suffer a partial disallowance of your allowable write-off for most itemized deductibles, including miscellaneous deductions. The disallowance is 3 percent of the amount by which your AGI surpasses a specified amount—$111,800 for 1994. (See "Curtailment of Most Itemized Deductions for Individuals with AGIs above a Specified Amount" in Chapter 14.)

Alternative minimum tax. For AMT purposes (see Chapter 14), no miscellaneous deductions are allowed.

JOB-HUNTING EXPENSES

There are long-standing limitations imposed on the deductions allowed for job search expenses. These expenses are deductible only if, among other things, they are incurred to find a new job in the same line of work.

Besides the existing restrictions, recent law changes further curtail job-search deductions. What follows is a detailed look at how the revamped rules affect job hunters.

Under prior law, job hunters had two kinds of expenses. Unreimbursed travel costs and away-from-home-overnight meals and lodgings were one of those "above-the-line" adjustments; that is IRS jargon for deductions that are subtracted from gross income to arrive at adjusted gross income. The result was that you got to claim those job-search expenditures whether you itemized your deductions for charitable contributions and the like or used the standard deduction for nonitemizers.

But there was a different rule for all other job-search expenses, such as fees charged by employment agencies and career counselors, as well as the cost of want ads, telephone calls, and typing, printing, and mailing of resumes to prospective employers. Under the old law, you had to itemize to deduct those expenses. They were nondeductible if you used the standard deduction.

Now, though, job hunters have to satisfy a tougher, two-step requirement. First, no longer is there a special break for travel, meals, and lodgings. *All* job-search expenses are allowable only if you itemize.

Second, the revised rules lump job-search expenses together with most other miscellaneous itemized deductions. This category includes, among other kinds of spending, return-preparer fees, rentals of safe deposit boxes, and union and professional dues, as well as employment-related expenses for education, provided the courses neither qualify you for a new job nor enable you to meet the minimum entry-level requirements for your present employment. (For education deductions, see "Educational Travel Not Deductible" in Chapter 5.)

There is a nondeductible floor for expenses gathered under the miscellaneous grouping. They are allowable only to the extent that their total in any one year exceeds 2 percent of your AGI (adjusted gross income). Anything below the 2 percent of AGI threshold is nondeductible. (For the rules on miscellaneous deductions, see the discussion later in this chapter.)

Yet another tightening applies to meals and entertaining. The 50 percent ceiling on the deduction for most business meals and entertainment also applies to spending for meals and entertainment in the course of a job search.

To illustrate just how stringent the revised rules are, consider this example. You declare an AGI of $40,000 and itemize. Your job-search, including only 50 percent of spending for meals and entertaining, and other miscellaneous expenses aggregate $1,200. Formerly, the amount deductible was the entire $1,200. But now the amount allowable drops to just $400 (what is left after the $1,200 is reduced by 2 percent of your AGI). With an AGI above $60,000, the $1,200 ceases to be deductible at all.

Partial disallowance of certain deductions for persons with AGIs above a specified amount, which is adjusted annually to reflect inflation. You suffer a partial disallowance of your allowable write-off for most itemized deductibles, including miscellaneous deductions. The disallowance is 3 percent of the amount by which your AGI surpasses a specified amount—$111,800 for 1994. (See "Curtailment of Most Itemized Deductions for Individuals with AGIs above a Specified Amount" in Chapter 14.)

Win some, lose some. Assuming you expect to incur sufficient miscellaneous deductibles to surpass the 2 percent benchmark, you need to familiarize yourself with the deductions that become available when you search for another job. Here are some reminders of the numerous possibilities. Note, however, that while some readily pass muster, others are subject to often-misunderstood limitations.

Under both the former and the current rules, the key requirement is that all expenses be directly connected with looking around for a new job in the same line of work. Pass that test and you can count on a deduction, notwithstanding that you fail to find another position or decide not to leave your present one.

The Internal Revenue Service, however, is unyielding in its refusal to allow any deduction for search expenses when you look for new employment in a different line of work. It makes no difference that your quest is successful.

Example. A computer programmer for a Chicago department store interviews for an identical position with a Boston bank. The Internal Revenue Service concedes a job-hunt deduction, whether or not the programmer actually switches jobs. Suppose, instead, that this Chicagoan wants to change careers and is able to find work selling real estate in Houston. The feds say no deduction for the search expenses, though the job hunt succeeds.

Special rules apply if you are unemployed when looking for work. Among other things, your occupation is what you did for your last employer.

Also, to satisfy the same-occupation requirement, there must not be a "substantial break" between your previous job and your present hunt for work. The IRS, however, provides no specific guidelines on how much time must elapse before a spell of unemployment becomes sufficiently lengthy to justify disallowance of a job-search deduction. Nevertheless, the current IRS position is that the deduction is unavailable, even though you secure employment, when there is a substantial break between your last job and your present search or when you enter the job market for the first time because, for example, you are just out of college.

Tip. Suppose, though, that a jobless person previously worked at different jobs. Presumably, that person can cite any of those previous positions, provided it was recent, to establish that he or she seeks a new job in the same line of work.

Caution. But tax relief is unavailable when, say, a teacher switches to selling for a few years and now wants to resume teaching or a woman leaves work to raise a family and resumes her career after several jobless years. Under the IRS guidelines, both fail the same-line-of-work test.

An IRS ruling illustrates the agency's willingness to take a liberal view of a deduction for career counseling. The attorney who sought the ruling worked full-time as a lawyer and part-time as an instructor at a law school. He went to a career counselor for advice on how to improve his resume and sharpen his interview techniques. Through his own efforts, the lawyer landed a position as a full-time teacher at another law school. The ruling said okay to a deduction for counseling to obtain a full-time post in his part-time field. True, the lawyer got the teaching job on his own; but the help he got with his resume and interview skills "directly assisted" him in his efforts to obtain new employment in the same type of work.

But the agency takes a dim view of a job-search deduction for a Renaissance man like Robert Evans, a career military officer. His last assignment before retirement was a four-year stint as "special assistant" to a base commander. This position, as Robert told the Tax Court, required him to perform a "potpourri of duties." Among other chores, he relocated base families during housing renovations, reviewed recreation areas, established an aircraft museum, dealt with juvenile delinquency problems, and managed the base's Bicentennial ceremonies. The catch-22 for Evans turned out to be the uniqueness of his military duties. Any employment in the private sector, reasoned the Tax Court, would be so substantially different as to be a new job, therefore no deduction for any of his job-hunt expenses.

The IRS also balks at a break for someone who is an employee and wants to become self-employed. Someone who switches from employee to self-employed goes into a different business, says the IRS; the Tax Court, though, thinks that the tax collector wants to "draw his line too fine."

The court sided with Howard Cornut, a CPA who explored the possibilities of quitting his position as an employee with the Portland, Oregon, office of a national accounting firm to become his own boss. To test the waters, Howard huddled with clients of his employer to see how many of them would shift their business from the firm to him. The response was encouraging enough to convince the CPA to leave his employer and set up shop with another ex-employee of the firm.

When Howard filled out his Form 1040, he took a write-off for the trips to his former employer's clients. No deduction, argued the IRS, as the disputed outlays were incurred to establish a business that was new, rather than continuing. But the Tax Court ruled for the CPA as he simply sought "to improve his employment opportunities in his profession."

The IRS scrutinizes write-offs for travel, including 50 percent of meals, to find a new job in the same line of work, disallowing deductions unless the main reason for the trip is to find employment. A key element in determining the main reason is how much time you devoted to job hunting, as opposed to personal pleasures. But even when a trip is primarily personal and you are ineligible to deduct some travel outlays, you nonetheless remain entitled to claim other expenses specifically linked to finding employment.

Example. A Detroit architect on vacation in San Francisco goes on a side trip to Los Angeles for job interviews. The architect is entitled to deduct her transportation between San Francisco and Los Angeles, as well as her lodgings and 50 percent of her meals while in Los Angeles.

Some job seekers try to push things too far. Predictably, the IRS nixed a deduction by a Manhattan-based model for trips from her home to modeling agencies in the Big Apple, where she auditioned for assignments. Those trips, ruled the IRS, were nondeductible commuting (Ruling 7948002). (For more on commuting expenses, see the discussion in Chapter 5.)

However, the IRS does not always have its way on travel expenditures. The Tax Court ruled that unemployed persons can deduct their travel costs to job interviews.

Back in 1984, Elizabeth Campana, an administrative assistant with Toyota in San Francisco, quit work when the company relocated and her daily round-trip commute became a stressful 100 miles. In the 10-month period following her resignation, Elizabeth searched unsuccessfully for new employment as an administrative secretary. During that search, she drove her Cadillac El Dorado over 4,600 miles.

The IRS contended that the unemployed secretary's driving expenses were nondeductible because Elizabeth was not currently employed. But the court decided she still could be considered in the business of being a secretary and okayed a deduction for the expenses—a write-off that now is subject to the nondeductible 2 percent floor.

Alternative minimum tax. For AMT purposes (see Chapter 14), no miscellaneous deductions are allowed.

MISCELLANEOUS ITEMIZED DEDUCTIONS

Revised rules make it much harder for itemizers to deduct miscellaneous expenses like return-preparation fees and employee business expenses. Most miscellaneous expenses are deductible only to the extent that their total in any one year exceeds 2 percent of AGI. (Adjusted gross income, or AGI, is the amount you show at the bottom of page 1 of Form 1040 after reporting salaries, dividends, and other income sources and deducting such items as funds placed in Individual Retirement Accounts and pay-

ments of alimony. The AGI figure is before itemizing for outlays such as charitable contributions and listing exemptions for yourself and your dependents.)

Example. You have an AGI of $35,000 and itemize. Your miscellaneous expenses aggregate $900. Previously, the amount deductible was the entire $900. Now, though, the 2 percent floor wipes out any deduction for the first $700 (2 percent of $35,000) of the expenses, which leaves you with a write-off of only $200. With an AGI above $45,000, forget about any deduction for the $900.

Partial disallowance of certain deductions for persons with AGIs above a specified amount, which is adjusted annually to reflect inflation. You suffer a partial disallowance of your allowable write-off for most itemized deductibles, including miscellaneous deductions. The disallowance is 3 percent of the amount by which your AGI surpasses a specified amount—$111,800 for 1994. (See "Curtailment of Most Itemized Deductions for Individuals with AGIs above a Specified Amount" in Chapter 14.)

Three Kinds of Miscellaneous Expenses

Miscellaneous expenses encompass *unreimbursed* outlays for a hodgepodge of items. Moreover, miscellaneous expenses include *reimbursed* employee business expenses if your employer does not require you to substantiate the actual expenses. (For timing payments of miscellaneous expenses to your best advantage, see "Timing Payments of Deductible Expenses" in Chapter 1.)

Many money-saving possibilities are often

missed because of confusing rules. Here is a rundown of three categories of expenses.

Employee business expenses.   For the first category, count things such as:

- travel, meals, after applying the 50 percent ceiling, and lodging while away from home
- local transportation, such as job-to-job travel, as opposed to commuting from home to job and back (see "Commuting Deductions" in Chapter 5 for more on job-to-job travel)
- entertainment, after applying the 50 percent ceiling (note that the entertaining must precede or follow a business-related discussion, except that the entertaining can be the day before or after the discussion when the business guest is from out of town; for more on deductions for entertaining, see the discussion later in this chapter)
- subscriptions to business publications
- a briefcase to carry business papers to and from work, even if you occasionally use it for surreptitious brown bagging
- business gifts, such as a birthday present or flowers for your secretary, though there is a $25 limit on how much you can give to any one person in one year
- use of home telephones to make business calls, but not the standard monthly base charge for the first telephone line into your home
- education (to the extent the courses neither qualify you for a new job nor enable you to meet the minimum entry-level requirements for your present employment; see "Educational Travel Not Deductible" in

Chapter 5 for more on deductibility of courses and other expenses)
- searching for a new job in the same line of work (for more on job-hunting expenses, see the discussion earlier in this chapter)
- union and professional dues
- work clothes and uniforms that are required as a condition of employment and are unsuitable for everyday use (for more on deductions for work clothes and uniforms, see the discussion earlier in this chapter), and
- qualifying home-office costs.

Exemption for "statutory employees." There is an exemption from the 2 percent floor for business expenses of employees who come within the definition of "statutory employees." Because this part of the tax law treats these individuals as though they were self-employed, they do not have to list their business expenses on Schedule A and deduct just the part above 2 percent of their AGI. Instead, they get to deduct their expenses in full on Schedule C.

Which employees qualify for this break? There are four categories: (1) full-time life insurance agents; (2) full-time sales representatives seeking orders from retailers, wholesalers, contractors, or operators of hotels, restaurants, or other businesses dealing with food or lodging, for goods they resell or use in their own businesses; (3) agent or commission drivers who deliver laundry, dry cleaning, or food or beverage items, other than milk; and (4) individuals paid to do work at home under guidelines set by the person for whom the work is done, with materials that person furnishes, and to whom the products are returned.

Investment expenses. Among the second category's qualifying outlays are rentals of safe deposit boxes, investment counsel fees, and subscriptions to investment advisory publications. (For more on investment expenses, see Chapter 10.)

Other miscellaneous deductions. For the third category, include items such as fees for return preparation or tax advice in connection with such matters as a divorce (see "Legal Fees for a Divorce" in Chapter 4), estate planning (see "What the Lawyer Will Charge" in "Making Out a Will Is Not Enough" in Chapter 16), or the negotiation of an employment contract, as well as tax books and videotapes and appraisals to determine the amount of a casualty loss (see the discussion earlier in this chapter of casualty losses) or a charitable contribution of property (for more on contributions, see Chapter 8).

Some taxpayers try to push things a tad too far. The Tax Court threw out a deduction taken by James P. and Yvonne H. Stuart of Santa Rosa, California, for $1,430 of lost vacation time that she used to pursue their dispute with the IRS.

Exception for Schedule C, E, or F preparation or tax advice. The IRS authorizes a significant break for the part of your return-preparation fees that are allocable to Schedule C (business income from self-employment), Schedule E (rental income from stores, vacation homes, or other properties; royalties; and partnerships) or Schedule F (farm income). Make sure to treat such fees as "above-the-line" adjustments that you subtract from gross income to arrive at AGI. *Result:* You get a *full* deduction for them on Schedule C, E, or F, instead of a miscella-

neous deduction subject to the 2 percent floor. Also fully deductible are fees for advice on planning or to fight audits of Schedule C, E, or F activities.

Tip. Remind your preparers or advisers to furnish bills that show the charges allocable to Schedules C, E, or F.

Example. You do not have sufficient miscellaneous expenses to surpass the 2 percent floor. The charge for filling out your return is $800, of which $400 is attributable to Schedule C. If you are in a 35 percent federal and state bracket, that means a savings of $140. (For instructions on how to determine your tax bracket, see "What Is Your Real Tax Bracket?" in Chapter 14.)

Tip. Moving the deduction from Schedule A to Schedule C also lowers the amount of earnings subject to self-employment taxes. (See Chapter 15.)

Alternative minimum tax. For AMT purposes (see Chapter 14), no miscellaneous deductions are allowed.

Help from the IRS

For more-detailed information, see IRS Publication 529, *Miscellaneous Deductions.* For a free copy, call 1-800-TAX-FORM (allow at least 10 work days for mailing) or stop by the IRS office serving your area to obtain one immediately. Many libraries also have copies of this and other IRS tax guides. IRS Publication 910, *Guide to Free Tax Services,* provides a complete list of booklets and explains what each one covers. (For a discussion of IRS publications, see "Get the Right Help at Tax Time" in Chapter 13.)

BUSINESS LOSSES

Do you expect your business to operate at a loss for this year? Then you need to know how to take advantage of a special tax break for red-ink years. This frequently overlooked relief provision allows you to use a loss from the *active* operation of a business to recover or lower taxes paid in other years. (Special restrictions introduced by tax reform apply to a loss that is classified as passive, as opposed to active. For more on passive losses, see "Section 1244 Stock" in Chapter 10.)

The key to this opportunity is Internal Revenue Code Section 172. It permits a business that suffers a NOL (short for net operating loss, which is tax jargon for when expenses exceed income) to carry that loss back to earlier years or forward to later years.

Two Choices

One option for an ailing business is to use the NOL to first offset business profits or other kinds of income in the three previous years, thereby generating a refund of taxes paid on income for those years. This strategy is particularly advantageous when cash is tight.

What happens when the NOL is greater than three years' income? Then the carry-forward rules come into play. Under those rules, you apply the unused part of any NOL not employed as an income offset, until used

up, against profits or other kinds of income in the following 15 years.

The second option is to skip the entire carry-back and simply carry forward the NOL for the year in question, provided it is advantageous to do so. This tactic might be preferable when, for instance, your income was taxed at low rates for the previous three years and you expect to be in higher brackets in future years.

Example.   The bottom line is not going to be black for 1994, and 1991, 1992, and 1993 were low-income years. With that scenario, you should come out ahead by electing to forgo a carry-back of the NOL for 1994; this assumes that you are able to use up the NOL during the carry-forward years that begin in 1995.

Lots of Leeway

You have ample time to assess your tax situation for 1994 and decide whether to carry forward a NOL. The deadline is not until the due date, including extensions, for filing your 1994 Form 1040. (For information on filing extensions, see "More Time to File Your Return" in Chapter 13.) Once made, however, the election generally is irrevocable.

Going the Carry-Back Route

The law mandates a strict chronological sequence. You must first carry back and deduct your 1994 NOL on your 1991 return to obtain a refund of part or all of your 1991 taxes. Only if the NOL surpasses your 1991 income can the unused part then be carried to your 1992 return. If the remaining part exceeds your 1992 income, it can then be carried back to your 1993 return. If there is still a part of the 1994 NOL left, it can then be carried over to your 1995 return, and so forth.

Tip. Does it pay to build up the loss for 1994 and thereby increase the amount of the carry-back to 1991? In that event, where possible, delay the receipt of income until 1995 and accelerate the payment of deductions from 1995 into 1994. (See Chapter 1.)

Audit Odds

Before you decide to claim a NOL, check to see whether there are any items on your returns for the three prior years that might be challenged by the IRS. Filing for a carry-back refund does not mean that your return for the loss year will be automatically flagged for an examination. Nevertheless, be aware a refund claim might prompt the feds to question not only your return for the loss year but also returns for earlier years. (For more information, see "Refund Claims" in Chapter 14.)

Help from the IRS

For additional information on the complex carry-back/carry-forward regulations, consult IRS Publication 536, *Net Operating Losses.* To obtain a free copy, telephone 1-800-TAX-FORM (allow at least 10 days for delivery) or you can pick one up immediately at the IRS office that serves your area.

Protecting Your Business Reputation

Ordinarily, deductible business expenses include payments to settle disputes, whether the payments are made to satisfy judgments or as out-of-court settlements. But an outlay is allowable only if the argument arose from a business-related activity, as opposed to a personal matter.

This seemingly straightforward general rule sometimes proves difficult to apply when a reputation-protection dispute has to be classified as "business" and deductible or as "personal" and nondeductible. What controls the outcome are the particular circumstances.

For example, a federal appeals court refused to allow a write-off for the cost of settling a will contest, notwithstanding that the taxpayer settled to protect his reputation as a lawyer. Apparently because of a close friendship, attorney William McDonald was named the major beneficiary in the will of a client, an elderly widow. The New York lawyer had not prepared the original will, but did draft a later codicil that modified the will by including him among the beneficiaries. That circumstance prompted some of the widow's relatives to contest the will on the basis that he had exerted undue influence. McDonald agreed to an out-of-court settlement of $121,000, which was embodied in a written agreement, noting, among other things, that "it appears the litigation of the issues would engender much publicity and would endanger the reputation of McDonald as an attorney."

The court barred a business expense for the $121,000. The proper standard for deductibility here, said the court, is the "origin-of-the-claim" test. The *origin* of McDonald's rights under the will was his personal relationship with the client, not his law practice. Consequently, it made no difference that his primary purpose in agreeing to the settlement was to protect his reputation as a lawyer.

Then there was William Harper, who owned rental property and taught high school science. He paid damages and legal expenses to settle an invasion of privacy suit brought against him by a tenant. The tenant asserted that Harper installed a listening device in her apartment and connected it to his office so he could hear what was said and done in the apartment. The suit, noted the Tax Court, might make it more difficult for Harper to do business in his West Virginia community, but the payments were not deductible because they were made for his own personal protection.

J. C. McCaa, an Arkansas auto dealer who disapproved of divorce, settled a claim for personal injuries resulting from his having struck a girlfriend of his married son. A skeptical Tax Court concluded that the payment was made to shield McCaa and his family from potential scandal, not to avoid cancelation of his dealer's franchise.

But John Clark emerged a winner in the ongoing tussle between taxpayers and the IRS. Clark's duties as branch manager of a Georgia magazine publishing firm included interviewing prospective saleswomen; if an applicant happened to be married, Clark interviewed her husband as well, to find out if he approved of this line of work for his wife. (This was in 1954, at a time when, if you should need a reminder, attitudes differed significantly.)

For one of these interviews, the obliging manager paid an 8 A.M. call at the residence of a married applicant to speak with her husband. The early visit was to accommodate the husband because his working schedule made it difficult to come to the manager's office. The husband was not home and, according to Clark's testimony in the Tax Court, he remained only a few minutes, leaving without agreeing to hire the wife. Later that same day, the wife swore out a warrant charging Clark with assault with intent to rape her during the visit.

The Tax Court approved a deduction for payments to obtain dismissal of criminal charges and to settle civil claims. It held that the manager "placed himself in jeopardy by pursuing a proper business objective" when he conducted such interviews.

Tip.   Under tax reform, Clark's deduction is subject to the 2 percent floor for miscellaneous itemized deductions, which is discussed earlier in this chapter.

BUSINESS EXPENSES MUST BE "ORDINARY AND NECESSARY"

Just because you incur expenses for business reasons does not mean that they automatically qualify as deductible. The Internal Revenue Code includes a provision, Section 162, which stipulates that these outlays must be "ordinary and necessary" in relation to your business.

Both the IRS and the courts have defined an "ordinary" expense as one that is customary or usual, though it need not be customary or usual for you, as long as it is customary or usual for your particular trade, industry, or community. The Supreme Court held that even a one-time-only expenditure falls within the definition. Similarly, "necessary," reasoned the Second Circuit Court of Appeals in New York, should be defined as "appropriate" and "helpful," rather than necessarily essential to a taxpayer's business.

Despite these pro-taxpayer decisions, whether the expense is allowable hinges upon the particular circumstances. To illustrate, consider the unusual case of the supervisor who wanted to share a portion of his bonus with his subordinates. His employment contract entitled him to additional compensation if the bottom line was black. Although under no obligation to do so, he opted to redistribute part of the bonus to his subordinates. But the IRS ruled that the redistribution was nondeductible.

What prompted this hard-nosed approach? An IRS finding that no employer-employee relationship existed between the supervisor and his subordinates.

The IRS concedes that an employee who in turn employs others to assist him can deduct payments to them. There is, however, another hurdle as tax reform limits write-offs for such payments. Unreimbursed employee business expenses, along with most other miscellaneous itemized deductions, are allowable only if their total is greater than 2 percent of adjusted gross income. (For the rules on miscellaneous deductions, see the discussion earlier in this chapter.)

In the following administrative rulings or court decisions, the taxpayers prevailed on the ordinary and necessary issue:

A hockey player gets to deduct the cost of answering fan mail. It is immaterial, reasoned the Tax Court, that his contract does not require him to answer letters.

An executive who leaves his commuter train without an attaché case stuffed with important business documents is entitled to write off a reward for its return, as well as the cost of a newspaper ad offering the reward.

"Publish or perish" outlays pass muster. The Tax Court sustained a deduction by a research scientist who paid for publication of a paper on his research. In his field of work, published papers were considered a prerequisite to job advancement.

Is it ordinary and necessary for a closely held company to pay a shareholder-director to stay away from the business? Yes, said the Tax Court.

Jim and John Shea were brothers and co-owners of Fairmont Homes. As Jim saw things, John's participation in the business adversely affected Fairmont and its reputation. Moreover, Jim feared a threatened lawsuit by John would create additional problems.

The IRS saw things much differently. It argued that Fairmont's payments to John were nondeductible outlays to acquire a capital asset, that is, Fairmont stock. That contention was rejected by the Tax Court, which noted that payments to ward off the threat of litigation are deductible, as are payments made to induce a partner or employee to take a course of action favorable to the business. Here, though John agreed to limit his participation in management, he retained his rights in the corporation.

In these rulings or decisions, deductions were deep-sixed:

The Tax Court agreed with the IRS that an author's payments to a "vanity" publisher to get a book published fail to qualify as an allowable business expense.

A remodeling firm's president asked the IRS about the deductibility of his payment for a transcendental meditation seminar. His contention was that the practice of TM made him more creative on the job.

Unfortunately for him, the karma was wrong. Although the agency agreed that the seminar "may have been of some benefit to the business," that was insufficient reason to go along with the deduction; "TM by its very nature generates benefits which are primarily personal."

J. Michael Springmann, ex-commercial attaché at the U.S. Embassy in New Delhi, ought not to deduct pay to servants, reasoned the Tax Court, regardless of his need to maintain his social standing in caste-conscious India.

A lawyer-CPA could not deduct the cost of operating a boat flying a red, white, and blue pennant bearing the number "1040." He contended that the write-off was justified because this gimmick generated some tax clients, but the Tax Court was unimpressed.

A Tax Court judge's remark that "hope springs eternal in the heart of the American taxpayer" might have been the inspiration for a Los Angeles physician to deduct payments to his children for answering the telephone at home. Predictably, the court saw nothing special in his situation and reminded him that "children normally answer the family home telephone."

Weddings, funerals, and other family events are more personal than business in nature. Is it possible to justify a business-expense deduction for a trip to a funeral? A man flew to Europe to attend his wife's rites, at which he met many business contacts, and also visited others during the balance of his stay abroad. The Tax Court's response: "We cannot believe that the funeral was incidental, and business was the primary motive for the trip."

A skeptical Tax Court took a similar tack with Arnold H. Feldman, a Philadelphia rabbi, who invited his entire congregation to his son's bar mitzvah reception. About 700 attended, of whom 100 were friends and relatives. A bar mitzvah reception, the rabbi urged the court, "may to the lawyer be a personal or social event, to the rabbi serving in a congregation it is an integral part of his professional activities."

The court disagreed and denied the deduction. It said the rabbi "stands in no better a tax position than anyone else who invites a large number of people to a family celebration and has in mind the idea that the invitations might enhance either an existing business relationship or a hoped-for business relationship."

Tip. This decision does not mean that the court is unwilling to ever allow a family celebration to qualify as a business expense. But the court's unsympathetic approach underscores just how hard it can be to justify a deduction for a gathering that by its very nature is primarily personal, not business.

Dear Abby, this one's for you. Is it ever possible to hire your live-in companion and take a business deduction for the wages you pay him or her? Sometimes. But expect the IRS to try to scuttle your deduction, though the Tax Court might be a tad more sympathetic, which is what Douglas Bruce experienced.

Douglas, a Los Angeles district attorney, paid Elissa Elliott, his girlfriend, $9,000 to cover her living expenses and those of her son and dog. In return, she agreed to run his household and assume major responsibility for the management of his extensive rental properties, chores that included finding furniture and overseeing repairs.

Douglas deducted the entire $9,000 as compensation to Elissa for property mangement. The IRS disallowed all of it, asserting that her services were personal and that he was unable to establish any measurable business expense.

But an understanding Tax Court allowed a reduced write-off. It was indisputable that he had to have a property manager and clearly she acted as one. Still, noted the court, "it would be naive at best to conclude that every penny of the support" that he furnished was "solely for purposes related to his investment properties."

By the court's reckoning, "the significant number of properties which were actually rented or were held out for rental during the period" justified a deduction of $2,500 for the compensation paid by Douglas to Elissa for managing his real estate.

What is extravagant for one taxpayer might be an ordinary and necessary expense for another. Rebuffing the IRS' pinched view of what is "extravagant," the court allowed Mr. Denison, an investment adviser, to deduct the cost of transporting potential customers in chauffeur-driven Cadillacs. What helped persuade the Tax Court was the nature of Denison's business, testimony that many of his clients were wealthy Europeans and the court's awareness of "the generally obnoxious traffic situation in midtown and lower Manhattan."

Legal fees. The IRS is ever on the prowl for improper deductions for payments to attorneys. The agency has repeatedly received the backing of the courts.

A drug-trafficking probe of the Phoenix Fire Department resulted in the conviction on possession charges of firefighter Frank Zielezinski of Scottsdale, Arizona. Personal conduct, not firefighting duties, caused him to shell out for defense fees, which is why the Tax Court threw out his deduction.

A carpenter's union member fought a suit charging union officials with misappropriating funds. The suit was unrelated to his work as a carpenter; hence, the Tax Court ruled he was not entitled to deduct them.

Ditto for an airline passenger's outlays to defend against criminal charges of threatening an airline crew and assaulting passengers. That the events occurred during a business trip was irrelevant.

A driver's license was lifted because the police spotted the driver weaving while on the way home from a cocktail party and he balked at taking a sobriety test. His lawyer's fees to fight the license suspension were nondeductible personal expenses, said a federal district court, notwithstanding his inability to work without a license.

The Tax Court refused to go along with a New York husband whose justification for deducting the cost of defending his wife on shoplifting charges was that she would have lost her job if jailed.

Nor would the court allow a man to write off what he spent to successfully defend himself against a charge of murdering his sister-in-law. The court was indifferent to the argument that the man's business "would have been destroyed" had he been found guilty and sent to prison.

The court was unwilling to okay a deduction by a company for legal expenses paid on behalf of its principal shareholder in a divorce action in which his wife sought to acquire an interest in his stock. The company's unpersuasive argument: The wife suffered from mental problems and her intrusion in its affairs would have jeopardized its continued success.

Voluntary repayment of a moral obligation. As a general rule, you flunk the "ordinary and necessary" tests and lose out on a deduction when you voluntarily pay someone else's obligation. One exception allows you to deduct the repayment of a "moral obligation" when you do so "to protect or promote your own ongoing business."

The Tax Court applied the exception in favor of Harold Jenkins, better known as country-music singer Conway Twitty. It approved a business-expense deduction of $97,000 for Twitty, who felt honor-bound to repay investors and creditors of a corporation involved in a failed franchising business known as Twitty Burger Fast Food Restaurants.

The IRS characterized his reimbursement of the investors as "very nice," but nondeductible since he failed to link his payments of the corporation's debts with his business as a performer. Twitty, though, struck a far more responsive chord with the Tax Court. It was convinced that he made the payments primarily to safeguard his personal reputation with his fans and his business reputation in the country-music industry.

Some of the investors were themselves country and western stars, such as Merle Haggard. Several had threatened to sue. As Twitty's lawyer pointed out: "Imagine trying to keep a band together where somebody (meaning Twitty) has stiffed the drummer's mother."

The court closed with a composition of its own, "Ode to Conway Twitty," that included these stanzas:

Twitty Burger went belly up
But Conway remained true.
He repaid his investors, one and all,
It was the moral thing to do.
Had Conway not repaid the investors
His career would have been under cloud,
Under the unique facts of this case
Held: The deductions are allowed.

Cost of staying healthy not deductible. You get no business-expense deduction for a health club membership. That expenditure is a purely personal expense. It makes no difference that your employer requires you to stay in excellent physical condition, according to an IRS ruling that denied deductions for police officers (Rev. Rul. 78–128).

Similarly, the Tax Court threw out a write-off for exercise equipment claimed by David A. Kelly of Worthington, Ohio, a certified public accountant with a heavy workload. The court was unimpressed with David's argument that he was better able to maintain his stamina with regular workouts.

Daily dining and birthday bashes are nondeductible. When it comes to slipping through deductions for personal expenses, lawyers fare no better than CPAs with the Tax Court. For instance, making sure to talk about business at luncheons fails to transform routine noshing into deductible conclaves—a legal lesson learned by, of all persons, John Moss, a partner in a firm that regularly argued cases in the courts.

John deducted his share of the partnership's daily business lunches attended by the firm's partners and associates. The diners discussed such matters as settlement of cases and scheduling of afternoon court hearings.

He argued that these meetings were considered part of the regular work day and were the most convenient time to meet. The participants did not feel free to make alternate plans or eat elsewhere. Therefore, the disputed dining should be deductible.

This contention got exactly nowhere with the court, which concluded that the discussions, the convenience, and the benefit to the firm did not make the lunches deductible when they took place five days a week, 52 weeks a year, any more than riding to work together each morning to discuss partnership affairs would make commuting costs deductible. (For commuting deductions, see Chapter 5.)

Then there was Joe Flaig, a Los Angeles attorney who handles personal injury cases and celebrated his birthdays by hosting lavish parties. He sent about 1,000 invitations to past and present clients and their families and friends. The guests ate buffet dinners and sipped champagne while orchestras provided dance music; their partying was reported by L.A. papers and TV.

Not much business was transacted at these parties. Clients sometimes asked about the status of their cases or introduced potential clients, and Joe would make a few comments and, when necessary, suggest an office appointment. Also, he occasionally asked clients to sign wills or other documents; but the lawyer himself conceded that signing documents was not the main reason for the shindigs.

Joe wrote off his outlays as "promotion and public relations" expenses. The court, though, threw out the entire deduction because the entertaining was not "directly related" to the "active conduct" of his law practice. The brief chitchats with clients and the signing of a few documents over a period of many years were, at best, incidental to the parties.

Professional blood donor gets to deduct some unusual costs.   For the year in issue, Margaret Green, whose blood type is a rare AB negative, earned most of her income by selling her blood to a laboratory. When filing time rolled around, she staunched the hemorrhaging to the IRS with hefty business-expense deductions for travel, medical insurance, special drugs, and high-protein diet

foods and a depletion write-off for the loss of her blood's mineral content.

The tax collectors argued that the deductions should all be disallowed, as she did not carry on a business. For the most part, however, the Tax Court sided with Margaret. It was precisely for business reasons, that is, the sale of her plasma, that she maintained a special diet and regularly traveled to the lab.

For starters, the court approved Margaret's outlays for high-protein foods and diet supplements to maintain the quality of her plasma. Moreover, she prevailed on the issue of deductions for home-to-lab travel (see Chapter 5).

No business write-off, though, for the full cost of what she spent on medical-insurance premiums. They are personal in nature and deductible only under the usual rules for medical expenses (see Chapter 7). Her medical insurance is not comparable to insurance maintained by a business to protect against loss or damage to machinery.

Nor was Margaret entitled to a depletion deduction for the loss of her blood's mineral content and the loss of her blood's ability to regenerate. The stopper is that Congress enacted the tax code provisions on depletion to promote the exploration and development of our nation's geological mineral resources. The court noted that "bodies and skills of taxpayers are not among the 'natural deposits' contemplated by Congress in those depletion provisions."

HONORARY DIRECTOR GETS NO TAX BREAK

If some friends ask you to serve as a director of their corporation, be aware that becoming a director can have its perils. Whether you take a director's seat for money, power, prestige, or just to be obliging, you assume certain responsibilities when you accept the position.

Let's suppose that you agree to do a favor for a friend and serve as an "honorary" director without pay. Suppose, though, that you later have to come up with the cash to cover the company's losses. What you might belatedly discover is that the IRS refuses to allow you to deduct your payments.

Consider what happened to Angus De-Pinto, an Arizona physician. DePinto agreed to accommodate his longtime friend, James Kelly, the president and majority shareholder of an outfit with the impressive title of United Security Life Insurance Co., and joined its board of directors.

DePinto was not very active during his two-year stint on the board. For one thing, he never bothered to ask about United's financial condition. Nor was he aware that it was losing money. He readily signed minutes of directors' meetings without reading them— even though some of them said he was present when, in fact, he was not. Moreover, for 15 months he was not even aware of Kelly's resignation as president of the company.

When Kelly eventually decided to sell his United stock, he suggested that DePinto resign as director. The ever-obliging doctor did that, just days before a new board of directors got control. Kelly proceeded to swap United assets for worthless stock in another company that the new directors had just organized; they then used the assets to pay off Kelly.

The net result was a loss to United of several hundred thousand dollars. Unfortunately for DePinto, but fortunately for the remaining shareholders, they were able to immediately recover the entire amount by bringing suit against him, the only one still

around worth suing. DePinto had to pay the shareholders because of his negligence in failing to keep himself informed about the company's affairs and for resigning just before the looting, instead of trying to thwart it.

To ease the financial hurt, DePinto took a business-loss deduction for his payment, as well as for some substantial legal fees. But the disallowance of the deduction by the IRS was upheld by the Ninth Circuit Court of Appeals.

The snag was that the losses were not incurred in a profit-motivated transaction. As proof, the court cited DePinto's "total lack of interest in the financial affairs of the company" and the fact that he did not expect to receive fees for his director's chores.

Tip.   A point worth noting is that the IRS would not have disputed the deduction had DePinto served as a *paid* director. In one of its administrative rulings, the IRS authorized a deduction for the very type of expenses that the doctor incurred (Ruling 8127085).

Caution.   For wannabe directors who are waiting for a call from Central Casting, the moral of this case should be clear: Sit on a board of directors only if you mean business. Even then, you should get the protection afforded you by a directors' and officers' liability insurance policy.

PROFIT VERSUS PLEASURE: STRICT RULES FOR LOSSES

Those obliging folks at the IRS allow write-offs to ease the pain for losses you suffer in transactions entered into to make "profits." (See "Business Losses" earlier in this chapter.) But a long-standing rule disallows deductions for losses incurred in pursuing "hobbies." Because of that distinction, the feds program their computers to bounce returns that show full-time salaries and other sources of income offset by losses from sideline ventures that turn out to be hobbies— writing, photography, and painting, to cite some of the activities that are likely to draw the attention of the tax collectors.

How does the law determine whether your intention is to turn a business profit from, say, your writing or just to have fun? There are no all-purpose guidelines. The answer depends upon the particular circumstances.

For instance, a string of yearly losses usually indicates that your enterprise is nothing more than a hobby. However, bad luck is not necessarily fatal. This point was underscored in a Tax Court decision that allowed losses sustained by Gloria Churchman, a painter who operated in the red for 20 straight years.

The IRS had disallowed the art losses, claiming that Gloria's lack of a profit motive for her artistic endeavors barred an offset of those losses against her husband's income.

But an understanding Tax Court sided with Gloria because she devoted a substantial part of her time to her art activities and acted in a businesslike manner. Among other things, she kept good records of what was sold to whom and tried continually to sell her pictures by exhibiting them and promoting them in other ways, such as by writing books that featured her artworks; when sales faltered, Gloria altered her style. Her testimony persuaded the court that Gloria was a dedicated artist who craved recognition as an artist and believed she would attain that recognition by deriving a profit from her painting.

The Tax Court approved the disputed deductions because she showed the required intention to make a profit. Conceivably, the court noted, "she may someday sell enough of her paintings to enable her to recoup the losses which have been sustained in the intervening years."

The Tax Court also allowed losses sustained by a sailing enthusiast who let his yacht out for charter, despite the puritanical contention by the IRS that the enterprise was actually a hobby and that the owner enjoyed sailing. Anyone who faces a similar attack should find reassurance in the court's response: "A 'business' will not be turned into a 'hobby' merely because the owner finds it pleasurable; suffering has never been made a prerequisite to deductibility."

Help from the IRS

For more information, consult IRS Publication 535, *Business Expenses.* For a free copy, call 1-800-TAX-FORM (allow at least 10 work days for mailing) or, to obtain one immediately, stop by the IRS office serving your area. Many libraries also have copies of this and other IRS tax guides. IRS Publication 910, *Guide to Free Tax Services,* provides a complete list of booklets and explains what each one covers.

DEDUCTIONS FOR ENTERTAINING AT HOME

Winers and diners take a big hit under the 1993 tax act. There is a cap on deductions for business meals and entertainment. They are only 50 percent deductible, down from the previous 80 percent ceiling introduced by the Tax Reform Act of 1986. The curtailment takes effect starting with returns for 1994 to be filed in 1995.

Expenses included and excluded from 50 percent ceiling.   Besides meal and entertainment charges, expenses subject to the ceiling include meal- or entertainment-related taxes and tips, cover charges for night club admissions, room rentals for dinners or cocktail parties, and parking at sports arenas, but not transportation to and from business meals, such as cab fares to restaurants or theaters.

Example.   The charge for a business meal comes to $80, which includes $65 for food and beverages, $5 for sales taxes, and $10 for tips. The limit on the deduction is $40, which is 50 percent of $80. However, cab fare to the restaurant of $6, including tip, is 100 percent deductible.

Deductions for entertaining at home.   Do you use your home to entertain clients, customers, or other business associates? Whether you have at-home gatherings to keep clients or woo new ones, you should be up to date on tightened rules for business-entertainment deductions.

To qualify for that 50 percent write-off, the home entertaining has to satisfy either of two requirements. It must be "directly related to" (there is a business discussion during the entertaining) or "associated with" (the entertainment directly precedes or follows a substantial and bona fide business discussion) the active conduct of business.

Tip.   There is a noteworthy exception when you are host to business guests from out of town. You get to deduct entertaining that takes place the day before or after the business discussion.

Deductible partying.   The entertainment write-off is not limited to a modest meal for yourself and your business guests. Despite the restrictions, it remains possible to host a catered affair at your home before or after a business discussion, invite a few friends, and deduct 50 percent of your qualifying expenditures.

Example.   You are involved in a business venture with Ennui Enterprises. Four Ennui executives come to your office for an afternoon business meeting. Afterward, you invite them and their spouses to a gathering at your home. Also on the guest list are five other couples, who are your personal friends. So, counting yourself and your spouse, a total of 20 people attend the affair.

Because the party directly follows a business discussion, it passes muster as deductible entertainment. And just how much do you get to deduct for the party? No deduction for expenses attributable to those five couples who are not business guests, with a cap of 50 percent on the remaining expenditures.

Assume that the party's total cost runs to $1,000. That means an allowable deduction of $250, which is 50 percent of $500 (the amount left after the total cost of $1,000 is reduced by the $500 allocated to those five couples who are social, as opposed to business acquaintances).

Caution.   As in the past, the law directs the IRS to disallow deductions for entertaining deemed "lavish or extravagant" under the circumstances. Still, an understanding IRS realizes that hosting a first-class bash is not necessarily lavish or extravagant.

Example. The feds might be a tad skeptical when your explanation for uncorking a $400 bottle of wine is that it enabled you to sell $1,000 worth of equipment, but nod agreeably if it helped you to land a megabucks account.

Exceptions to the 50 percent rule. Tax reform retains a 100 percent deduction for some kinds of home entertaining. There is no 50 percent cap when, for example, you use your home to host social gatherings for employees—Christmas parties or summer picnics are some of the standard get-togethers. At that kind of socializing, business does not have to be discussed before, during, or after the event. Note, though, that there is a full deduction only for an affair that is open to employees generally—the rank and file, not just the top executives or other higher-ups.

Employee expenses. There is another hurdle if you are an employee and are not reimbursed for your entertainment expenditures. The law requires you to include those unreimbursed outlays with other miscellaneous itemized deductions, such as fees for preparing returns, on Schedule A of Form 1040. Most miscellaneous expenses are allowable only to the extent that they, in the aggregate, exceed 2 percent of your adjusted gross income. The 2 percent floor is discussed earlier in this chapter.

Alternative minimum tax. For AMT purposes (see Chapter 14), no miscellaneous deductions are allowed.

Help from the IRS

Need additional information? Consult IRS Publication 463, *Travel, Entertainment, and Gift Expenses.* For a free copy, call 1-800-TAX-FORM (allow at least 10 work days for mailing) or stop by the IRS office serving your area to obtain one immediately. Many libraries also have copies of this and other IRS tax guides. IRS Publication 910, *Guide to Free Tax Services,* provides a complete list of booklets and explains what each one covers. (For a discussion of IRS publications, see "Get the Right Help at Tax Time" in Chapter 13.)

10 INVESTMENTS

INVESTMENT EXPENSES

The United States got along without an income tax for over a century and a quarter. Not until 1913 did we amend the Constitution to permit one. And not until World War II did the tax become democratized, when tax withholding was introduced and the term "take-home pay" entered the language. (See "Is Your Withholding Out of Whack?" in Chapter 14.)

Since then, harkening to the voice of the homefolks, all American Presidents have committed themselves to tax reform. I think you will enjoy what Russell Baker's *New York Times* column of September 4, 1976, had to say about how we have benefited from that commitment:

> The words "tax reform" send chills down the spine of every sentient American because each new reform deepens the nightmare of income tax law. Just when you have got a purchase on this monster, Congress reforms it and everybody has to start all over again. It has become a complexity to confound a Dickens lawyer, a maze to make King Minos' labyrinth look like a playpen. The conscientious citizen would have to devote every waking hour to its study if he wanted to make a reasonably close guess at what he owes his government each April.

> Even then, he would probably be wrong. Last year a test of Internal Revenue's workers—the people who help the desperate fill out their forms—showed that the majority even of these "experts" didn't know what the law means. So now, unless supernatural providence intervenes, it is all going to be changed again.

Before I discuss investment expenses, I thought to comfort those readers who, like me, are vocabulary challenged. As someone described by his mother-in-law as incapable of being embarrassed, it is in no way discomforting to divulge my need to peek in Webster's Dictionary to find out that it defines "sentient" as "finely sensitive in perception or feeling."

Russell Baker's invitation to supernatural providence to intervene went unheeded, perhaps because it would be inherently unfair to deprive Americans of the opportunity to show just what sensitive souls they actually are. Whatever the reason for divine forbearance, his column was right on the money about further change.

Segue to a decade later, when President Ronald Regan and a complaisant Congress cut a deal that spawned the Tax Reform Act of 1986. Tucked into that overhaul of the Internal Revenue Code was a provision that scaled back the write-offs allowed investors who itemize their deductions on Schedule A of Form 1040.

The tightened rules apply to miscellaneous itemized deductions for such investment-related expenses as subscriptions to publications that track the ups and downs of the stock market, rentals of safe deposit boxes, and fees charged by financial planners and other advisers. Besides investor outlays, the miscellaneous category includes deductions such as dues payments to unions and professional associations.

Formerly, the law allowed itemizers to deduct 100 percent of their miscellaneous expenses. Now, however, most of these expenses are allowable only to the extent that their total in any one year exceeds 2 percent of AGI. Anything below the 2 percent of AGI floor is no longer deductible. (AGI, or adjusted gross income, is the amount you list on the last line of the front of Form 1040 after all reportable income is offset by certain deductions such as payments of alimony and funds placed in an IRA.)

Partial disallowance of certain deductions for persons with AGIs above a specified amount, which is adjusted annually to reflect inflation. You suffer a partial disallowance of your allowable write-off for most itemized deductibles, including miscellaneous deductions. The disallowance is 3 percent of the amount by which your AGI surpasses a specified amount—$111,800 for 1994. (See "Curtailment of Most Itemized Deductions for Individuals with AGIs above a Specified Amount" in Chapter 14.)

Alternative minimum tax. For AMT purposes (see Chapter 14), no miscellaneous deductions are allowed.

Example. You declare an AGI of $30,000 and itemize. Your investment and other miscellaneous expenses aggregate $800. Previously, the amount deductible was the entire $800. Now the allowable amount is just $200 (what is left after the $800 is reduced by $600, which is 2 percent of $30,000). With an AGI above $40,000, the $800 ceases to be deductible at all under the revised rules. (For more information on the rules for miscellaneous deductions, see Chapter 9; for timing payments of miscellaneous expenses to your best advantage, see Chapter 1.)

Assuming you incur sufficient miscellaneous deductions to surpass the 2 percent of AGI floor, you should familiarize yourself with the array of deductions available to investors. Allowable expenses include many more items than just those obvious outlays for investment counseling, subscriptions to advisory services, telephone calls, and postage. Often, though, it is difficult to know just where the Internal Revenue Service and the courts draw the line on what you can deduct.

For instance, your deductibles include the cost of a safe deposit box that holds stocks, bonds, or other investment assets but not one that contains only personal papers or tax-exempt securities. Similarly, you can write off fees paid to a bank or broker for collection of dividends or interest, but not brokerage commissions that must be added to the cost of the securities purchased.

Gray areas abound because revenue agents and judges take their cues from guidelines set by Internal Revenue Code Section 212, a loosely worded statute that authorizes investors to write off their expenses "for the production or collection of income" or "for the management, conservation, or maintenance" of income-producing property. What follows is a detailed look at some IRS rulings and court decisions to help you decide whether your expenses pass muster.

Travel

One frequently overlooked deduction is for the cost of travel, though not all trips are deductible. For example, the Tax Court allowed Martha Henderson and other investors to deduct what they spent on trips to their brokers to discuss specific stock transactions. On the other hand, the court refused to approve travel deductions for someone like Stanley Walters who regularly spent his lunch hours in brokers' offices where he merely watched the ticker tape to "get a feel for the market."

When your investments require travel by bus, train, plane, or taxi, simply keep a record of your fares. Include them on Schedule A of Form 1040 with your other itemized deductions under "miscellaneous deductions," just the same as payments to return preparers or for publications that help you with your tax planning, like this book.

As for travel by auto, you have the usual options in figuring deductions:

1. Claim your allowable operating expenses (gas, repairs, depreciation) attributable to use of the car.

2. Simplify the record keeping by using a standard mileage rate. Under the rules applicable to tax year 1994 (the most recent year for which information is available as this book goes to press), the standard rate is 29 cents a mile.

Whether you claim operating expenses or a flat allowance, don't forget to deduct for parking fees and bridge or highway tolls. You should back up your donations for invest-ment travel with a glove-compartment diary in which you record why and how far you went, along with the cost of parking and tolls. A typical diary entry might read: 7/8/94; travel expenses to Shearson Lehman Hutton; re purchase of common stocks; round trip of 20 miles at 29 cents per mile equals $5.80, plus $2.00 for bridge tolls, for a total of $7.80. (For more information, see "Business-Car Deductions" in Chapter 5.)

Back in 1956, the IRS issued a ruling that spelled out its guidelines for persons who attend stockholders' meetings of companies in which they own stock but have no other interest. The ruling bars any deduction for travel expenses when such stockholders attend merely to get information that would help in making future investments. It makes no difference that their major sources of income are dividends and profits on stock transactions (Rev. Rul. 56–511).

Subsequently, however, the IRS yielded on a deduction for expenses incurred by the leader of a stockholders' revolt. It seems that John Hickey owned a substantial number of shares in Icarus Airlines. His shares had dropped in value because the company had issued new shares to the public at prices below book value. To stop such sales, an irate John hied himself to Icarus's annual meetings and persuaded the concern to poll its shareholders about joining an association. Assuming sufficient support for his proposal, there would be an organizational meeting at which John expected to be a mover and a shaker.

An obliging IRS linked the travel to protection of his investment. It ruled that John was entitled to deduct what he spent for travel, including lodging and 50 percent of meal expenses, to the annual and organizational meetings, provided two requirements were satisfied. First, he must be "one of the main organizers of the association, so that his presence at the meeting would be required." Second, the primary purpose of the trips must be to "form the association to prevent or reduce the dilution of his stock" (Ruling 8042071).

Protection of an investment also justified a deduction for Robert Montesi, who traveled to an annual shareholders' meeting of Procrustes Furniture. Robert introduced and maneuvered to pass a resolution requiring the company to halt its practice of issuing shares at below-book value through dividend reinvestment and stock-purchase plans. The IRS distinguished his case from its 1956 ruling, which disallowed deductions for shareholders who attend annual gatherings mainly to pick up information for future investment moves. Here, Robert's pilgrimage was prompted primarily by his desire to safeguard his sizable stake in Procrustes (Ruling 8220084).

Frequently, the courts interpret the law far more liberally than the IRS. Consider, as an example, some observations made by the Tax Court. It rejected travel expenses claimed by William Kinney, who frequently bought and sold substantial blocks of stock in several listed companies. He based his investment decisions, in part, on on-site investigations of factories and retail outlets of these companies. The court sided with the feds because of the large amount of time William spent with relatives on some 15 trips for the year in issue and his failure to link the disputed trips with his investment activities. But William might have prevailed, the court noted, had he produced evidence to satisfy these four requirements:

1. The trip is part of a rationally planned, systematic investigation of investment opportunities.

2. The costs are reasonable in relation to the size of the investment and value of the information the investor expects to derive from the trip.

3. Personal benefits are secondary—that is, the trip is not a disguised vacation.

4. The information gained on the trip is used in investment decisions.

Investment Seminars

Tax reform also abolished deductions for costs incurred by investors to attend conventions, seminars, or similar meetings at which they obtain information that helps them plot strategies. Disallowed expenses include travel to the meeting site, attendance fees, meals, lodging, and local travel while attending.

What prompted Congress to enact this absolute prohibition? A key factor was the unhappiness of the IRS with the pro-taxpayer position taken by the Tax Court in a dispute involving Lorraine Gustin of Brown Deer, Wisconsin, a serious student of the stock market.

Lorraine's pursuit of profits took her to investment club conferences in Amsterdam, Cleveland, and San Diego during the year selected for audit by the IRS. She devoted a considerable amount of time to managing her portfolio and held posts in the National Association of Investment Clubs, an organization that holds conventions where members can discuss investment strategies with stock market analysts and other experts and listen to presentations from executives about their companies.

Lorraine took a write-off for her expenses of attending the three meetings, but not those of her husband or the cost of their post-convention side trips to places like the Greek islands and San Francisco. The IRS argued that her expenditures of $2,400 for air fares, meals, and hotel rooms were nondeductible personal expenses because the main aim of her conventioneering was not to collect investment information.

But Lorraine convinced the court that "her attendance at the convention was part of a rationally organized investigation into investment opportunities and strategies. It was reasonable to spend $2,400 to protect and enhance a portfolio worth $98,000. Any personal benefits of the trip were secondary to the investment benefits." Moreover, the information that she obtained at the conventions from analysts and company representatives directly influenced her later decisions on what stocks to add to or remove from her portfolio.

Predictably, the IRS persuaded an accommodating Congress that Lorraine's victory should not be repeated. That is why the long list of scaled back or repealed deductions features a provision that wipes out any tax breaks for investment seminars, a move guaranteed to cause those gatherings to be less alluring to investors.

Tip. The disallowance is aimed solely at expenses incurred for *investment* reasons (such as an investor seeking to obtain information about whether to buy or sell particular stocks), not those incurred for business reasons (such as a financial adviser meeting with prospective clients).

Example. International Investors holds a convention at which stock market investors pay for the opportunity to discuss strategies with representatives of brokerage firms and listen to presentations from executives about their companies. *Result:* The seminar

measure bars deductions of expenses by investors, but leaves unchanged the rules governing deductions of expenses by stockbrokers and others who are at the convention for business reasons.

Proxy Fights

Usually, the IRS goes along with a deduction for the cost of carrying on a proxy fight, except where a shareholder engages in the fight for personal reasons rather than to protect income. Moreover, the Tax Court has held that this rule applies to legal fees paid in anticipation of a proxy fight that never took place because the dispute was compromised. Here's a case in point.

Jean Nidetch was president and director of Weight Watchers International, as well as a major shareholder. A dispute arose among Weight Watchers shareholders, and a proxy battle was foreseen. Jean had earlier placed a substantial block of Weight Watchers stock in two trusts for the benefit of her children. The trusts were managed by trustees who were friendly with the opposing group in the upcoming proxy contest. To bolster her position, Jean brought legal proceedings to replace those trustees with individuals who were friendly to her. Ultimately, the dispute was settled without the necessity of a proxy contest.

The Tax Court held that the legal fees paid by Jean to replace the trustees did qualify as expenses incurred to protect her divided income from the corporation and to safeguard her job. It made no difference that the proxy contest never came to pass.

"The preliminary steps taken in anticipation of a proxy fight preempted by settlement are incurred for the same purposes as those incurred in the initial stages of a dispute culminating in any actual proxy battle. To deny deductibility of the former, while according deductibility to the latter, would penalize those parties who are able to amicably settle their disputes," said the court.

Investment Clubs

A club cannot simply offset its income with expenses for advice, bank charges, accounting, etc. and then let each of the partner members report his or her share of the net income. Instead, the club must segregate each member's share of income and expenses. A member can then include his share of expenses with other itemized deductions under "miscellaneous deductions," subject to the 2 percent of AGI floor, as noted previously. But a member forfeits a write-off for his share if he forgoes itemizing and uses the standard deduction (Rev. Rul. 75–523).

CAPITAL GAINS AND LOSSES

As Plato foresaw in *The Republic* nearly 2,500 years ago, "When there is an income tax, the just man will pay more and the unjust less on the same amount of income."

The Tax Reform Act of 1986 sought to end preferential treatment for income from long-term capital gains, a special break that had been embedded in the Internal Revenue Code since 1921. Under the rules that applied just before tax reform took effect, there was an exemption from taxes for 60 percent of gains on sales of stocks and other investments owned more than six months. Because of the 60 percent exemption, the top tax rate

on long-term capital gains was effectively limited to 20 percent.

For the years 1987 through 1990, capital gains were taxed at the same rates as "ordinary income," which is IRS jargon for income from sources such as salaries, business profits, dividends, and interest. So it made no difference how long you owned your investment.

Then, in 1991, preferential treatment was reintroduced. Under the rules applicable to tax year 1994 (the most recent year for which information is available as this book goes to press), there is a top rate of 28 percent on long-term capital gains from assets owned more than 12 months, versus a top rate of 39.6 percent for ordinary income. (See "What Is Your Real Tax Bracket?" in Chapter 14.) However, the actual effective rate can be higher if your adjusted gross income exceeds the phaseout thresholds for exemptions (see Chapter 2) and itemized deductions (see Chapter 14).

Tip. Someone who is in an above-28-percent bracket has to do a special calculation on Schedule D of Form 1040 to gain the benefit of the 28 percent cap on long-term capital gains.

Caution. Be mindful of a time-tested admonition: Base your decision on when to sell stocks or other investments on how much you expect them to appreciate in the future, not just on the basis of tax advantages.

Tip. Plan to make sizable donations to charities? Consider contributions of appreciated stocks or other investments that you have owned for more than one year. You avoid the tax that otherwise falls due on a sale of the stock and get a charitable deduction for the full value of the property. (See

"Contribution of Appreciated Property" in Chapter 8.)

Lower capital gains rate for investors in original issue stock of certain small companies. The 1993 tax legislation includes a provision that allows these investors to escape taxes on 50 percent of their gains, provided they hold their stock for five years. (See "Lower Capital Gains Rate for Investors in Stock of Certain Small Companies" later in this chapter.)

Losses

Tax reform also revised the rules for capital losses. To ease their pain, you are still able to deduct capital losses, within limits, or to fully offset them against capital gains on your other investments.

But tax reform retained a ceiling on the deduction allowed if you have a "net capital loss," that is, when your total losses exceed your total gains. The amount of your ordinary income (salary, for instance) that can be offset each year by a net loss is limited—$3,000 for joint and single filers and $1,500 each for marrieds filing separately. (Special, more favorable, rules apply to losses on Section 1244 stock, which is discussed later in this chapter.)

On the plus side, the law no longer requires you to reduce long-term losses by half before you are able to use them as an offset against ordinary income. Now, both long- and short-term capital losses offset ordinary income on a dollar-for-dollar basis. For instance, $2,000 of long-term losses can offset an equal amount of salary. Previously, that $2,000 loss could offset only $1,000 of salary.

What if total losses exceed $3,000? The law allows you to "carry forward" any unused net loss over $3,000 into the following year and beyond, should that be necessary.

Example. For 1994, you had long-term capital losses of $15,000 and long-term capital gains of $8,000, resulting in a net long-term capital loss of $7,000. You subtracted $3,000 of your capital loss from ordinary income. That left you with $4,000 to carry forward into 1995, which may be used (unless offset against capital gains) to reduce ordinary income by $3,000. Any unused loss ($1,000, with this set of numbers) then can be carried forward to 1996.

Caution. There is no time limit to the carrying forward of losses, but you must use carry-forwards as soon as possible. You cannot opt to forgo a deduction for a carryforward in a low-income year and save it for a high-income year.

Tip. When calculating your total losses, remember to include stocks or bonds that became worthless, perhaps because of corporate bankruptcy, during the year. (Worthless stocks are discussed later in this chapter.)

Wash sales. When you sell shares for a tax loss and want to keep a position in the same company, the loss is currently deductible only if the repurchase takes place more than 30 days after the sale of the original stock. (See "Wash Sale Rule" later in this chapter.)

Tip. Losses cannot be claimed on the sale of assets held primarily for personal use, such as a year-round home (see Chapter 3 for the rules on home sales), an automobile, or furniture.

Investment loss must be bona fide. You are not entitled to a write-off for a loss on the sale of an investment unless you suffer a bona fide economic loss. This long-standing tax rule was underscored in a decision by a federal appeals court.

David Fender was trustee for two trusts that he had set up for his youngsters. During the year in issue, the trusts had realized hefty capital gains. To offset these gains, Fender arranged for the trusts to sell tax-free municipals that had dropped in value. The trusts sold them to a bank in which Fender owned the largest single block of stock. The trusts repurchased the bonds 42 days later.

The appeals court held the loss on the sale should be disallowed; the transaction merely shuffled the bonds back and forth. The trusts had, therefore, not incurred a real economic loss. Fender, reasoned the court, "had sufficient influence over the bank to remove any substantial risk that the trusts would be unable to repurchase the bonds and thus eliminate the apparent loss on the sale to the bank."

Among other things, noted a skeptical court, the bank did not normally purchase the type of bonds that it acquired from the trust. Another bank, where Fender lacked similar clout, refused to buy the bonds. Nor was his case bolstered by the disclosure that the trusts allowed the sale proceeds to remain with the bank until the bonds were repurchased. The clincher was testimony by the bank's president that the transaction was an accommodation to Fender and a repurchase agreement existed, although no time and price for the repurchase of the bonds were fixed.

LOWER CAPITAL GAINS RATE FOR INVESTORS IN STOCK OF CERTAIN SMALL COMPANIES

As discussed in the previous section, the 1993 tax act retained the top rate of 28 percent for long-term gains from sales of stocks and other investments owned more than 12 months. But the act includes a provision that authorizes a lower capital gains rate for investors (individuals or partners, not corporations) in newly issued stock of certain small companies.

The provision is supposed to generate more venture capital for the growing companies that are most likely to create jobs. Under this break, investors are taxed at just 14 percent, or half the regular capital gains rate of 28 percent.

They can exclude, meaning they pay no taxes, 50 percent of their gains. The other 50 percent is subject to the maximum 28 percent rate. To reap the exclusion, investors must hold their stock (only original issue shares qualify) for five years.

This incentive of a 14-percent rate for people to buy into small businesses is subject to a lengthy list of restrictions. Hence, as of now, it is unlikely to greatly appeal to investors. Furthermore, the tax laws are likely to change during the five years that investors have to hold their stock.

What companies qualify. The key limitations on companies that seek to qualify for the break are on the amount of their assets and the way they can use the assets. There are other significant restrictions.

Note, too, that there is no exclusion for gains from investments in S corporations, the ones named after the section of the Internal Revenue Code that authorizes them and generally taxed under rules similar to those for partnerships. Unlike C, that is, regular corporations, which are taxed on their profits and losses, S corporations pass profits and losses through to their shareholders, who report them on their own returns. (For a discussion of S companies, see "Section 1244 Stock" later in this chapter.)

A qualifying company's assets cannot exceed $50 million as of the stock issuing date, which must be after August 10, 1993, the date President Clinton signed the 1993 tax act. Also, it must use at least 80 percent of these assets in the "active conduct" of a business, such as manufacturing. Forget about excluding gains from investing in companies that, for example, provide personal services, such as accounting or law, or are in the finance, insurance, leasing, farming, mineral extraction, hotel, or restaurant business.

There is another cap on the amount of capital gains eligible for the break. The jackpot cannot exceed the greater of (1) 10 times the original investment or (2) $10 million. The gain cannot be reduced by any capital losses. Still, that is not chopped liver.

Alternative minimum tax.   Other complexities kick in when an investor is subject to the AMT (see Chapter 14). The amount of gain excluded is reduced by 50 percent. Put another way, 25 percent of the gain is thrown back into income in calculating the AMT.

The AMT's purpose is to exact a minimum tax from certain high-incomers involved in ventures that allow them to properly use deductions and other breaks to greatly lower, or even escape, their regular income tax.

To make payment of a minimum tax likely, the AMT permits fewer deductions and counts more items as reportable income than the regular method used to determine your tax liability. The result is you have to figure your tax both ways—regular and AMT—and pay the higher of the two taxes.

When Tax-Exempt Investments Make Sense

A top tax rate of 39.6 percent for tax year 1994, the latest year for which information is available as this book goes to press in the summer of 1994, prompts many investors to ask this question: When does it make sense for them to move money into municipal bond funds? Specifically, their question is how can they determine whether municipal bond funds and other tax-exempt investments provide a higher yield than fully taxable investments.

The answer depends upon a person's federal and state tax brackets. (For how to determine your bracket, see "What Is Your Real Tax Bracket?" in Chapter 14.) The higher your bracket, the higher the taxable yield that is equivalent to the yield on your tax-exempt investment.

To illustrate, assume you are in the 28 percent federal bracket, which kicks in at modest levels. For tax year 1994, this means taxable income between $38,000 and $91,850 for a joint filer and between $22,750 and $55,100 for a single person. A tax-free return of 6 percent is equivalent to a taxable return of about 8.33 percent in the 28 percent bracket, 8.69 in the 31 percent bracket, 9.30 in the 36 percent bracket, and 9.83 in the 39.6 percent bracket.

Caution. Tax-exempts are even more attractive for people in high-tax areas, such as New York City and the District of Columbia. But they might prove to be less attractive for those in the 28 percent bracket in the event increased demand from above-28-percent-bracket individuals causes prices to rise and yields to decrease.

Tip. Even though the interest you receive from state and municipal bonds is exempt from federal taxes, you remain liable for taxes on any capital gains from sales of these bonds. (For capital gains, see the preceding section of this chapter.) Also, income from "private activity" municipal bonds may be subject to the alternative minimum tax (Chapter 14), which is imposed on taxpayers who use certain deductions and other tax preferences to reduce or eliminate their regular income tax liability.

How to determine what the taxable equivalent yield is at your tax bracket. To find the equivalent of a tax-exempt investment, subtract your tax rate (say, 28 percent) from 100 percent. Divide the tax-exempt yield (say, 5 percent) by the remainder. With those numbers, the taxable equivalent is 6.94 percent (100 minus 28 equals 72; 5 divided by 72 equals 6.94). So if your option is a taxable yield of 7 percent or a tax-exempt yield of 5 percent, the taxable investment generates a slightly better after-tax return for people who fall into the 28 percent bracket.

Tip. The calculations become more complicated for middle- and upper-income retirees and other investors who also receive Social Security benefits. The snag is that these taxpayers are indirectly taxed on the municipal bond interest that they receive.

Starting with returns for 1994 filed in 1995, they are liable for income taxes on up to 50 percent of their benefits when their pensions and other sources of income, *including* tax-exempt interest, is between $25,001 and $34,000 for single persons or between $32,001 and $44,000 for couples filing jointly. They are taxed on up to 85 percent of their benefits when such income exceeds $34,000 for singles and $44,000 for joint filers.

For 1993 and previous years, they were taxed on up to 50 percent of their benefits when such income exceeded the $25,000/32,000 thresholds. (For taxation of Social Security benefits, see Chapter 15.)

State income taxes. Things become slightly more complicated when you need to figure in your state tax bracket for investments that are exempt from both federal and state taxes.

Nonitemizers. If you forgo itemizing and use the no-questions-asked standard deduction that is available without having to itemize (see "Itemizing versus Standard Deduction" in Chapter 1), all you need to do is add your state tax bracket to your federal bracket and complete the calculation described above. Assume you are in the 28 percent bracket and your state tax rate is 6 percent. Use a 34 percent rate to calculate the equivalent yield.

Itemizers. If you itemize your deductions, your actual state tax rate is reduced by the amount of your federal deduction for state income taxes. Thus if you are in the 28 percent federal bracket, your actual state tax rate drops from 6 percent to about 4 percent (28 percent multiplied by 6 percent equals almost 2 percent; 6 percent minus 2 percent equals 4 percent). In this case, you would use a combined federal and state rate of about 32 percent to calculate the taxable equivalent yield.

SALE OF INHERITED PROPERTY

The tax laws provide an important advantage for people who sell inherited stocks, real estate, or other investments that have appreciated in value. Here is a rundown of how this break works.

Suppose that Uncle Fred writes a will that says you inherit appreciated stocks or other property. When you sell the stock, you qualify for special treatment—a "step up" in basis (the figure from which gain or loss is measured) for the property from its original cost (revised upward in the case of, say, rental property, for the amount spent for any subsequent improvements and revised downward for depreciation) to its date-of-death value. (In certain cases, instead of date-of-death, it is the property's value six months thereafter, if an executor chooses an alternative valuation date.) Put another way, you escape paying any capital gains taxes on the amount the stocks appreciated while Uncle Fred owned them. You are taxed—if and when you sell—only on post-inheritance appreciation.

Example.   Fred paid $10,000 for stock that was worth $150,000 at his death when he left it to you. You later sell it for $200,000. Because your basis for the property is considered to be $150,000, your taxable profit is only $50,000—the increase in value between the time your benefactor died and the time you unload the stock. You are off the hook for any income taxes on the $140,000 increase in value between the time Fred bought

the stock and the time he died. The amount he paid for the stock is irrelevant.

A less favorable rule may apply if you sell property left by someone who is a missing person. Here, you qualify for a step up to date-of-death value only if your benefactor is considered to have died before the sale takes place. For a missing person to be declared dead, says the IRS, either a court has to have ruled that he is dead or the assets (pursuant to a state statute) are, in effect, disposed of as though they were the property of a decedent. If his last residence was in a state without a law that specifies the time when a missing person is presumed dead, he is considered dead after seven years of continuous absence, unless death is established earlier.

An IRS ruling illustrates how these rules operate. The scenario is that Amelia von Crater disappears while on a flight over the Atlantic in the early part of this year. The search party fails to find Amelia or the plane. Her husband, Klaus, is appointed conservator of her estate. As conservator, he is authorized to sell real estate owned by Amelia that had cost her $40,000 several years ago and was valued at $300,000 when she disappeared. Klaus sells the property before the close of this year and files their final joint return.

According to the law of the state in which the von Craters resided, a person is presumed dead if the individual is absent from the last known place of domicile continuously for five years and the absence is not satisfactorily explained after diligent search and inquiry. Death is presumed to occur at the end of the five-year period unless there is evidence establishing that death occurred earlier.

Verdict: State law does not presume Amelia to be dead at the time of the sale. Therefore, no step up for Klaus. In figuring his tax on the transaction, his sales price must be measured against her cost of $40,000 (Rev. Rul. 82–189).

Tip. To sidestep the problem and gain the benefit of the step up, Klaus must wait to sell the property until the presumption of death takes effect. (More information on estate planning is found in Chapter 16.)

Proposed legislation. As this book goes to press in the summer of 1994, proposals are being studied that would curtail or end the step up in the continuing effort to attack the bulging budget deficit. Under one proposal, capital gains would be taxed at death, with exceptions for, among others, assets inherited directly by a spouse or donated to charity. Another proposal would carry over the deceased person's basis for the asset and then tax the gain when the asset is sold by the heirs. If any such proposal is enacted, whether your planning needs to be revised depends on what the effective date is and what kind of transitional relief is provided.

Section 1244 Stock

Are you planning to operate a new business as a corporation or to issue new stock in an existing venture that needs to raise more capital? If you are like most entrepreneurs, you look forward to substantial profits right from the start. Still, these being the troubled times they are, it is prudent to plan for the worst because all too many new or refinanced enterprises experience losses, especially in the early years of operation, or, even worse, wind up belly up.

Before you actually move any money into the company, a vital element of your plan-

ning should be to familiarize yourself with an important break that becomes available when the newly issued shares are designated as "Section 1244" stock—named for a provision long embedded in the Internal Revenue Code. Unfortunately, in my experience, many attorneys, accountants, and other advisers neglect to advise owners of small companies that Section 1244 stock helps to ease their financial hurt if things fail to pan out.

In effect, Congress designed Section 1244 to provide no-cost "tax insurance" for investors in case of undertakings that go sour; that, in turn, reasoned Congress, makes it easier for small companies to attract investment capital. How does Section 1244 help shareholders who suffer losses on the sale or worthlessness of their shares? By allowing them to deduct their losses more quickly than usual, provided the shares meet the requirements for 1244 stock.

You are well aware that the 1986 Tax Reform Act curtails or cancels many long-cherished breaks for investors. But the legislation left intact the key benefit bestowed by Section 1244 on individuals who start or expand their own businesses or invest in someone else's company. If the investors incur losses when they sell their shares or the shares become worthless because the firm ceases operations, they get special treatment: Ordinary-loss deductions of up to $100,000 per year for joint filers and $50,000 for single filers, rather than capital-loss deductions of no more than $3,000 per year (see the discussion earlier in this chapter of the rules for capital losses). The faster-than-usual deductions for 1244 stock cover not only shares bought from a company that is just starting out, but also shares later bought from an outfit in need of additional capital.

Old Rules

Under prior law, the tax rules could be summed up simply: Heads, the investor wins, and tails, the IRS loses. Profits from sales of 1244 stock were lesser taxed, long-term capital gains, just like other stock sales.

But Section 1244 stacked the deck in your favor if things failed to pan out. Usually, any loss on the sale, exchange, or worthlessness of stock comes under the rules for capital losses. Consequently, the loss may be of limited value if you have no capital gains from other business or personal investments. In fact, it can take years to use up a sizable capital loss.

The snag is the $3,000 ceiling in any one year on the amount of net capital losses that can be deducted from "ordinary income," such as salaries or other compensation. Any unused loss for that year can then be carried forward and claimed in the same way on your return for later years until the loss is used up.

Another drawback was that net long-term losses offset ordinary income on a two-for-one basis. Thus, it took $6,000 of long-term losses to erase the taxes on $3,000 of ordinary income.

But the usual $3,000 cap for capital losses did not apply to a loss on 1244 stock. Instead, more liberal rules allowed you to claim a deduction in any one year for a loss on 1244 stock as an offset against ordinary income of up to $100,000 on a joint return or up to $50,000 on a single return.

New Rules

Tax reform abolished preferential treatment for long-term capital gains. For the years 1987–1990, capital gains and ordinary income were taxed at the same rates.

But preferential treatment was reintroduced after 1990. There is a top rate of 28 percent on long-term capital gains from assets owned more than 12 months, versus a top rate of 39.6 percent for ordinary income.

Tax reform preserves the special protection authorized by Section 1244. Both the old and the new rules clamp a lid on the amount of net capital loss that can be subtracted from ordinary income each year. The ceiling continues to be $3,000, though long-term losses now are deductible on a one-for-one basis, instead of a two-for-one basis. But take heart. The annual ordinary-loss limit for 1244 stock remains $100,000 for joint returns and $50,000 for separate returns.

Some fine print that rates a mention is a relief provision for married couples who do not put their holdings in joint ownership. The 1244 stock need not be held jointly by you and your spouse to qualify for the top deduction of $100,000.

What if you are a partner in a partnership that sustains the loss? The $100,000 (or $50,000) limit is determined separately for each partner.

To the extent the loss is below the $100,000 (or $50,000) limit, it is considered a business loss. Consequently, the excess of any qualifying loss that cannot be offset against other income in the year incurred comes under the net operating loss rules and can be used to recover or reduce taxes paid in other years. (For more on net operating losses, see "Business Losses" in Chapter 9.) The carry-back and carry-forward procedures for a net operating loss allow a current loss to be taken as an additional deduction for the three prior years and the 15 following taxable years. Any loss over the $100,000 (or

$50,000) limit comes under the rules for capital losses discussed earlier.

Assuming your loss runs to less than the $100,000 (or $50,000) limit, you get the same tax protection provided a partner or sole proprietor who suffers a loss on the sale or worthlessness of his or her business. Thus, you avoid the need to operate as a partner or proprietor, even though incorporation might have been better for such nontax reasons as freedom from liability.

Tip.   It can pay to unload your shares gradually if your loss surpasses the $100,000 (or $50,000) cap. The limit is a *yearly* limit and not a limit on total losses from 1244 stock. If the losses can be spread over more than one year, more than $100,000 (or $50,000) can qualify for ordinary-loss treatment.

Example.   Ruth Stone, who is married, invests $220,000 in a business. It proves unsuccessful and she can unload her stock for $20,000. Assuming Ruth sells 50 percent of her stock for $10,000 this year and does the same next year, she can take an ordinary write-off of $100,000 each year—a total of $200,000.

What if your dreams do pan out and you sell your 1244 stock for a nifty gain? Then, assuming you have capital losses from sales of other businesses or personal investments, you can use them to offset a gain from 1244 stock. Otherwise, your long-term capital gain is taxed at a top rate of 28 percent under the rules applicable to tax year 1994, the latest year for which information is available as this book goes to press in the summer of 1994.

Qualifying for the Advantages of Section 1244

There is no burdensome paperwork for a corporation that wants to ensure Section 1244 treatment for its shareholders. The company does not have to file any notification with the IRS or adopt a formal plan.

IRS regulations spell out what needs to be done before you invest. Make sure that the company specifically designates in its records that all of your stock is 1244 stock. There is a deadline for the designation. It must be made by the fifteenth day of the third month following the end of the corporation's tax year—by March 15 for a calendar-year corporation. Other record-keeping rules require the company to list the serial numbers of the qualifying share certificates. No serial numbers? Then the corporation must use an alternative designation in writing at the time it issues the shares.

IRS regulations also explain what to do when you claim an ordinary-loss deduction. Your return must be accompanied by a statement that includes the following information: the company's address; the manner in which you acquired the 1244 stock and the nature and amount of the consideration you paid; and, if you acquired the stock in exchange for property other than cash, the type of property, its fair market value on the date of transfer to the corporation, and its adjusted basis on that date.

An ordinary-loss deduction increases the chances of your return drawing the attention of the IRS. (See "Red Flags for an Audit" in Chapter 11.) If challenged, expect the revenue agent to insist on substantiation from the corporation. So it should keep records that show the persons to whom the 1244 stock was issued; dates of issue; amount and type of consideration paid (with basis and fair market value of payments other than in cash); amount of money (and corporation's basis in property other than cash) received for stock as contributions to capital and as paid-in surplus; and company financial statements for the last five years.

Qualification under Section 1244 is not automatic. There are, understandably, some restrictions.

For starters, the stock must be common or preferred stock of a U.S. corporation that is issued in exchange for money or property other than stock or securities. That stipulation disqualifies any stock issued to you in payment for services rendered or to be rendered.

Another limitation is that the aggregate amount of money or other property received by the corporation for the 1244 stock and previously issued stock cannot exceed $1 million. There are no ceilings, however, on the number of shareholders, size of profits, and so on.

The law also requires a company to engage in business, rather than investment, activities. Generally, it cannot derive its income primarily from what the law dubs "passive sources"—specifically, royalties, rents, dividends, interest, annuities, and gains from sales or exchanges of stock or securities.

Finally, the stock must be held continuously by the same individual or partnership from the time of issuance to the time of loss. The requirement that the stock be newly issued bars an ordinary-loss deduction for, say, someone who acquires 1244 stock by purchase, gift, or inheritance. It makes no difference that a previous shareholder qualified for ordinary-loss treatment. *Result:* You cannot pass the 1244 break on to someone else by, say, a gift of stock to that person. You alone are allowed the ordinary-loss write-off.

Purchase of an already existing corporation. To satisfy the newly issued requirement, follow this sequence: Purchase all of the company's assets, transfer them to a new company, and have it issue 1244 stock.

Tip. Failure to pass muster under Section 1244 merely means that should you later incur a loss, it will be capital, not ordinary. That, though, is just the same as what will happen if your company opts not to issue 1244 stock when it sets up a business or issues new stock for a going venture that needs additional capital. *Result:* There are no drawbacks to issuing 1244 stock.

Combining Section 1244 Stock with an S Corporation

Many investors with 1244 stock have their businesses operate as S corporations (named after the section of the Internal Revenue Code that authorizes them). Unlike regular corporations, which are taxed on their profits and losses, S corporations pass profits and losses through to their shareholders, who report them on their own returns.

A company that issues 1244 stock and elects to be an S corporation gives its shareholders the best of both possible worlds from a tax standpoint. They get current deductions for operating losses and Section 1244 treatment for losses from stock sales.

As for the operating losses, S corporations pass them through to the shareholders in proportion to their ownership interest. The shareholders offset the loss passthroughs against their other sources of income. This break, though, ceases to be available when the passthroughs are to shareholders who are passive investors and, therefore, subject to the restrictions imposed by the Tax Reform Act on passive-loss deductions.

Passive losses.   Under the rules applicable to tax year 1994 (the most recent year for which information is available as this book goes to press), special rules apply to individuals who put money in tax shelter investments—the kind designed to generate large paper losses, at least in the short term, to offset income from salaries, investments, and other sources. These persons face strict limitations on current deductions for passive losses ever since the Tax Reform Act became effective on October 22, 1986.

These broadly defined curbs on shelter investors apply to losses that are suffered by, among other individuals, shareholders of S corporations who are classified as passive investors. The passive-loss restrictions target investors who do not "materially participate" in their company's operations.

Note, though, that these restrictions are not applicable to shareholders who *do* materially participate, that is, are actively involved in business operations. How actively involved must the shareholders be to free themselves from the passive-loss limitations? There must be year-round, active involvement on a "regular, continuous, and substantial basis."

What happens to operating losses that are passed through to shareholders who assume only a passive role in operations? These losses cannot be used by passive shareholders to offset their earnings from other sources, whether "active income" (salaries and other earnings) or "portfolio income" (dividends and interest, as well as profits from sales of stocks and other investments). Generally, they are able to offset passive operating losses only against their earnings from other shelters.

Unused losses.   Eventually, relief rolls around for S corporation shareholders and others with disallowed losses from passive investments. These unused losses can be carried forward indefinitely to later years until the investors are able to apply them against income from the same or other passive sources. Lastly, the remaining unused losses serve as offsets against income from other *nonpassive* sources, as under prior law, when the investors sell their 1244 stock or otherwise dispose of their interests in the passive activities.

Exception to passive loss rules for real estate losses incurred after 1993 by people in the real estate business.   Starting with returns for 1994 filed in 1995, liberalized rules for passive losses authorize special relief for persons who "materially participate" in the operation of real estate enterprises, whether as developers, builders, landlords, managers, brokers, or the like.

Who qualifies? Someone who passes a two-step test. First, he or she must devote more than 50 percent of his personal services to real estate businesses. Second, that person must work more than 750 hours in the businesses in which that person materially participates.

There is a further requirement for someone who performs these services as an *employee,* as opposed to someone who performs them as a self-employed. He or she has to own at least a 5-percent share of the employer's business. Thus, someone who works for a real estate development corporation and owns none of its stock remains subject to the passive loss rules on his or her personal real estate investments.

The reward for qualifying individuals who actually spend most of their time in real estate: They can offset their real estate losses against other kinds of income, such as wages, bonuses, profits from unrelated businesses, dividends, interest, and so forth.

Caution. The revised rules provide no relief for individuals with losses from other kinds of real estate tax shelter deals, such as limited partnerships. The passive loss rules already on the books allow these individuals to offset their losses only against income derived from similar shelter arrangements.

Special rules for rental property owners who qulify as "active managers." When the Tax Reform Act of 1986 introduced restrictions on passive losses, it carved out an important exception. Under that exception, there is limited relief for individuals who come within the definition of "active managers" —legalese for those helping to make decisions on such things as OK'ing tenants, setting rents, and approving capital improvements. Active managers can deduct up to $25,000 in rental losses against other types of income, such as salaries and dividends. Note, though, that this break begins to phase out when adjusted gross income exceeds $100,000 and vanishes when it tops $150,000. (See "Losses on Rental Properties" later in this chapter.)

Help from the IRS

Need more-detailed information on the rules for passive losses? See IRS Publication 925, *Passive Activity and At-Risk Rules.* For a free copy, call 1-800-TAX-FORM (allow at least 10 work days for mailing) or stop by the IRS office serving your area to obtain one immediately. Many libraries also have copies of this and other IRS tax guides. IRS Publication 910, *Guide to Free Tax Services,* provides a complete list of booklets and explains what each one covers. (For a discussion of IRS publications, see "Get the Right Help at Tax Time" in Chapter 13.)

Tip. Don't rely absolutely on IRS advice, whether it is information that employees give to telephone or walk-in inquiries or instructions that the agency prints in its publications. Mistakes in instructions or advice are inevitable, and the IRS is not bound by them.

WASH SALE RULE

It's a routine maneuver to sell a stock to establish a tax loss. But don't ignore the calendar if you then buy it back because you feel your depressed stock will eventually recover. Unless at least 31 days elapse between the sale and the repurchase, you will run afoul of something called the "wash sale" rule and forgo your loss for the time being.

An often-misunderstood point is that the wash sale restriction does not apply to a *profit* on the sale of shares of stock. You are free to take your profit and immediately reinvest.

The wash sale rule comes into play only when you suffer a loss on the sale of shares of stock (including shares of a mutual fund) or securities and then purchase, or buy an option to purchase, "substantially identical" stock or securities. If you do so within 30 calendar days (not trading days when the market is open) before or after the sale date, a total period of 61 days, you will not be able to use that loss to offset other capital gains until you sell the newly acquired investment. The wash sale rule also applies to an option to sell stock or securities.

To illustrate, assume you sell stock at a loss on October 28. The proscribed 61-day period is September 28 through November 27.

Why is there a wash sale rule? Because without such a restriction, savvy investors could keep their portfolios intact, yet time the recognition of capital losses to offset gains just by unloading losers and buying them right back (the rules for capital losses are discussed earlier in this chapter).

Caution. The wash sale rule also bars a loss when you sell stock and then your spouse or some other "related person," such as a corporation controlled by you, buys substantially identical stock.

Example. You buy 100 shares of Worldwide Widgets for $5,000, which you later sell for $3,750. Within 30 days of the sale, you acquire another 100 shares for $4,000. In effect, your $1,250 loss is *postponed,* rather than disallowed permanently. This is because the basis of the new stock for purposes of figuring gain or loss becomes $5,250, which is the sum of the $4,000 cost and the $1,250 disallowed loss.

Note also that you cannot use a wash sale loss on one block of stock to offset gain on other blocks of the same stock sold that same day. Take this situation. On three different occasions, you bought 100 shares of Consolidated Uranium. Your price per share was $150 for the first block of 100, $100 for the next block, and $95 for the last one. At the start of the month, you sell your entire investment for $120 per share. Before the month ends, you re-buy 250 shares. The wash sale re-

striction not only denies a deduction for the loss of $30 per share on the first block, but also bars an offset of the loss against the gain on the sale of the other two blocks.

Avoiding Wash Sales

Here is a rundown on the pros and cons of some IRS-blessed, uncomplicated ways to get around the wash sale rule and turn stock losses into tax deductions, but still keep your position in an investment that you think is a sound one for the long haul.

Sell, then buy. The easiest way to nail down a tax loss for this year and retain the stock is simply to sell and then wait more than 30 days before you repurchase. The loss-registering sale can take place as late as the close of trading on the last business day of the year.

The benefit from this maneuver is that it allows you to get your tax deduction without channeling more money into the market at that point. But there can be drawbacks. Your tax saving will be trimmed by the amount of any increase in the price of the stock during the waiting period, and you may forfeit some dividend income as well. But if the stock declines, you can replace it at a lower cost, and your tax saving stays the same.

Buy, then sell. Another maneuver can provide an identical tax break. Buy the same amount you already hold, wait at least 31 days, and then sell the original holding. To qualify the loss as a deduction on this year's return, the doubling up must take place by the end of November, so you can sell by the end of the year.

Your gamble is that, besides tying up more

money, your loss doubles if the stock falls even more during the 30-day period. But if the stock goes up during that time, you make double what you would have otherwise, and you suffer no loss of dividends. Assuming you have the necessary cash or credit, doubling up on your investment makes sense only if you feel confident that the price will move upward.

Switching.   Yet another tactic allows you to bypass the wash sale problem and remain an investor in the same industry, but not the same company. Sell your stock and buy similar shares of a comparable outfit. For instance, you might unload a steel stock and immediately buy the shares of another steel company. (At year end, investment advisers provide long lists of suitable switches.)

While the switching need not take place on the same day, the deadline to establish a loss for this year is the final trading day. Here, the hitch is that the original investment may outperform the replacement—and dividend income may not be comparable.

Tip.   Before you unload a stock, check with a broker to make sure that the costs you must incur for trading commissions will not cancel out your potential tax savings.

Short sales.   The wash sale rule applies to short sales, including a sale "against the box" where you hold stock that is identical to the stock that you sell short. A loss on a short sale is deferred if you sell the stock or enter into a second short sale of the stock within the period beginning 30 days before and ending 30 days after the closing of the short sale. (For more on short sales, see "Timing Receipt of Income" in Chapter 1.)

Help from the IRS

For additional information on the wash sale rule, see IRS Publication 550, *Investment Income and Expenses.* To obtain a free copy, call 1-800-TAX-FORM (allow at least 10 work days for mailing) or stop by the IRS office serving your area to obtain one immediately. Many libraries also have copies of this and other IRS tax guides. IRS Publication 910, *Guide to Free Tax Services,* provides a complete list of booklets. (For a discussion of IRS publications, see "Get the Right Help at Tax Time" in Chapter 13.)

RELATED-PARTY SALES

Your investment holdings could well include an asset that has dropped in value since you bought it. Maybe you want to sell it, claim a capital loss, and start over with something else. Or maybe you have great hopes for this investment and, though you would like to take the loss, you would really hate to part with your old friend. Should you sell your property to your spouse or your child?

In most cases, you can claim losses on your investments when you sell them. But the law generally disallows deductions for losses on sales to certain family members and other related parties. Under the loss-disallowance rules, related parties include close relatives, such as a spouse, child, grandchild, parent, brother, or sister, or a company in which you own more than 50 percent of the stock.

The law authorizes the IRS to invoke the related-party rules even if you make the sale in "good faith," that is, without intending to avoid taxes, or involuntarily, as when a family member forecloses a mortgage on your property. The loss-disallowance rules also snag an indirect transaction—for instance, when you sell stock through a public stock exchange and a related party purchases stock in the same company.

Why are there restrictions on losses for sales between family members? To stop tax avoidance through transactions that merely shuffle property back and forth within the same family or group.

Example. You buy 100 shares of DEF Company for $10,000, which you later sell to your sister for $8,000. You cannot deduct your $2,000 loss. This holds true even though you make the sale in good faith.

Pass the loss on. Sometimes a disallowed loss can be salvaged. Your disallowed loss becomes available to your sister in the event that she realizes a profit on the sale of her DEF shares. Her profit escapes taxes up to the amount of your disallowed loss.

Her basis for the DEF shares is the $8,000 that she paid you. If she eventually sells them for $9,000, her gain of $1,000 sidesteps taxes because it is offset by $1,000 of your disallowed loss. If the sales price is $11,000, making her gain $3,000, then she is liable for taxes on only $1,000 of the gain ($3,000 gain minus the $2,000 disallowed loss).

Sell to a "nonrelated" relative. The related-party rules apply only to losses on sales of property to related parties such as your sister or son. Those restrictions do not bar a deduction by you for a loss on the sale of the DEF shares to an *in-law,* such as a son-in-law or daughter-in-law.

This is an often-overlooked strategy worth noting if, say, your DEF shares have declined drastically and you wish to realize some of your paper loss without being out of the

stock for more than 30 days. Under yet another set of restrictions, known as the "wash sale" rules, your loss on a sale of the DEF shares is currently deductible only if the repurchase takes place more than 30 days before or after the sale. (See "Wash Sale Rule" earlier in this chapter.)

To maneuver around the related-party rules legitimately and get the loss deduction, yet keep the DEF shares in the family, just make a bona fide sale to an *in-law.* Instead of selling the stock on the open market, get a current quote and sell the stock at the market price to any in-law with whom you enjoy a good relationship. This will keep the benefit of a future upturn within the family, while you will have had your deduction.

Caution. If the IRS questions the transaction, be prepared to back up the sale with evidence of a fair market payment from the in-law, followed by delivery of the stock into his or her name or brokerage account, etc.

Let's say you sell the stock to your daughter-in-law and she later transfers the shares to her husband or children. In that event, the IRS can disallow your loss deduction if the agency is able to establish that the second transfer was what you had in mind all along.

No break for family feuds. The related-party rules remain applicable despite a family fight. This was underscored in a decision by the Tax Court, which disallowed a loss deduction for a brother-to-brother sale. It mattered not that the brothers disliked and distrusted each other and that the sale was bona fide and involuntary.

The sale in question was ordered as a result of binding arbitration to separate the stock and real estate holdings of the brothers. The Tax Court held that the hostility was irrelevant. The law makes no exception to the absolute prohibition of deductions for such transactions merely because family members have a falling out.

Sometimes, the IRS does not insist on a literal interpretation of the law. For example, an IRS ruling approved a loss deduction for an estate on the sale of real property to the decedent's daughter, who was co-executor of the estate.

It all began when Mr. Webb wrote a will that established a trust to hold property for several grandchildren until they became adults. The will designated his daughter and brother as trustees of the property and executors of his estate. On Webb's death, the assets placed in the trust included some rental property valued at $100,000. The executors attempted to sell the property through an agent who represented that she could find a buyer willing to pay $106,000. But the agent's allegedly unceasing efforts produced no offers at that price. Later, she recommended that the estate accept an offer for $60,000, if one was made. Eventually, an offer of $70,000 was made by one executor and accepted on behalf of the estate by the other executor.

The ban on loss deductions applies to a sale of trust property to a trust beneficiary. But the ruling noted that, unlike a trust that can be set up at an appropriate time and readily used to achieve such tax ends as artificial losses, the creation of Webb's estate was not the result of his "forethought." Therefore, the estate was allowed to deduct its loss on the sale to the coexecutor (Ruling 7737025).

Caution. Even when the related-party rules are inapplicable, the transaction must be bona fide. A loss can still be disallowed if the IRS determines that the primary motive was tax avoidance.

Beware of multiasset sales. Related-party sales can cause other complications. When the property sold in one transaction consists of a number of blocks of stock or pieces of property, the IRS measures gain or loss separately for *each* asset sold—not by the *overall* result of the sale. Thus, even if a lump-sum sale results in a net loss for you, the feds can create a taxable gain simply by disallowing losses that were sustained on some of the assets involved. *Result:* The *taxable* gain may far exceed the net dollar gain from the sale.

Consider, for example, what happened to Klaus Netter, the owner of over 50 percent of the stock of Geneva Enterprises. To satisfy part of a debt to Geneva, he gave it $65,000 worth of stock he owned in a publicly held corporation. The net result of the transfer was that Klaus reaped a loss of $1,000.

But by figuring the profit or loss separately on *each* block of stock Klaus had purchased at different times and at different prices, the IRS computed total losses of $10,000 and total gains of $9,000. Because the sale was between related parties, the $10,000 loss was disallowed, and he wound up with a taxable gain of $9,000 (Rev. Rul. 76–377).

Tip. To avoid this unfavorable tax result, Klaus should have sold his loss stock on the market and given the proceeds to Geneva. That way, he would have wound up with a $10,000 deductible capital loss to offset his $9,000 gain.

LOSSES ON
WORTHLESS STOCKS

You are entitled to claim a tax loss for stock that becomes worthless during this year, but be aware that the IRS insists that it must be *entirely* worthless. The loss deduction is not available merely because the stock is no longer traded on a market and is practically worthless for all intents and purposes.

If the IRS questions your loss, be prepared to establish that there is no current liquidating value, as well as no potential value. The lack of a ready market or the decision of a company to file for bankruptcy doesn't mean that stock is worthless.

Assuming that you've passed these hurdles, your next worry is *timing*. A loss on worthless stock is always deemed to have been sustained on the last day of the calendar year, regardless of when it became wholly worthless during the year.

You can write off worthless stock only in the year it becomes worthless. If you are uncertain about the year of worthlessness, nail down your deduction by claiming it for the first year in which you believe the stock becomes entirely worthless. If the IRS disallows the loss and contends that worthlessness did not actually occur until a later year, you still have time to claim the loss in that year. But if you hold off claiming the loss until a later year and the IRS says worthlessness occurred in an earlier year, it may be too late to file a refund claim. (For a discussion of refund claims, see Chapter 14.)

The Second Circuit Court of Appeals in New York offered this advice: "The taxpayer is at times in a very difficult position in determining in what year to claim a loss. The only safe practice, we think, is to claim a loss for the earliest year when it may possibly be allowed and to review the claim in subsequent years if there is any reasonable chance of its being applicable for those years."

KEEP GOOD RECORDS
OF STOCK PURCHASES

It can be important for investors to keep track of what they paid for which stock certificate when they buy shares of one company at different times and at different prices. Usually, there is no problem in determining your cost basis when you sell all the shares in one transaction. But there can be some complications when you dispose of only part of your holdings.

The hitch is that the tax laws do not permit you to use an average price per share to calculate gain or loss on a sale. What counts is which certificate you unload.

You get the most favorable gain or loss only if you are able to identify which certificate you sold. If the shares you want to sell do not match the certificates you deliver, the IRS treats the first shares bought as the first shares sold—in tax lingo, "the first-in-first-out" (FIFO) rule. This requirement affects the basis used in determining the gain or loss.

Example. Your portfolio includes 600 shares of JKL stock, 200 of which were acquired two years ago at $10 a share, a second block of 200 acquired 11 months ago at $30 a share, and a third block of 200 acquired in this year at $45 a share. Now JKL is trading at $20 and you want to sell 200 shares. Unless you are able to identify the second or the third lot as the one sold, the IRS automatically assumes that you sold the first lot. *Result:* Instead of a short-term loss of $2,000 on the second lot or $5,000 on the third lot that can be used to offset some investment gain or other income, you have a long-term gain of $2,000—a sequence that probably differs from the order in which you intended to establish your cost.

However, it is easy to steer clear of the FIFO rule and achieve the tax result you want. You can do so even when shares bought in different lots and on different dates are held by your broker in "street name" (that is, registered in the brokerage firm's name and intermingled with shares held for other customers) or held by you but represented by a single stock certificate. If you just make sure to meet these three requirements imposed by the feds, you are deemed to have adequately identified the shares you want to sell:

1. Specify to your broker (this can be done orally) the sequence in which you want the shares to be sold.

2. Identify the particular shares to be sold, either by their purchase date, cost, or both.

3. Be sure the broker confirms the sale in writing within a reasonable time.

Your instructions govern the sale, and the shares so specified are considered sold. This holds true, says the IRS, even though the broker delivers the wrong certificate. Remember, though, that the FIFO rule remains applicable if you merely intended to sell particular shares but failed to inform your broker adequately.

Tip.   There is a special rule for investors in mutual funds. They can use an average price per share to figure their gain or loss on the sale of mutual funds.

EASEMENT PAYMENTS

The tax rules can be confusing when a land owner receives a payment for granting an easement—the right for something or someone to have access to or use of a portion of the property. The tax result depends upon whether the easement affects all of the property or only a specific part of it.

If only a specific part is affected, the owner's gain is measured by the difference between the payment received for the sale of an easement and the basis (usually, cost) of the property allocated to that part. But if no allocation is necessary because the entire property is affected or if it is impossible or impractical to make an allocation due to the nature of the easement or of the property, the sales proceeds simply reduce the total basis of the property. Thus, the owner has to count the gain as reportable income only if the proceeds run to more than the full cost of what he paid for his property.

The courts often have to resolve the factual issue of whether an easement affects all or part of the property. Consider, for example, what happened when David Fasken, the owner of a 165,000 acre ranch, received $18,000 for granting easements for pipelines, towers, etc. on his land, plus rights of ingress and egress.

According to David's calculations, he owed no taxes on the $18,000 because it merely reduced the total basis of the ranch. The IRS, however, contended that only 32 acres were affected, not the entire ranch. Because the basis for these 32 acres was $300, he realized a capital gain of $17,700. The IRS was backed up by the Tax Court. It refused to offset the $18,000 by the entire cost of the ranch.

Tip. The gain may qualify for deferral under the Code Section 1033 rules for involuntary conversions, where the proceeds are used to acquire similar property.

INDIVIDUAL RETIREMENT ACCOUNTS

Tax reform restricts deductions allowed individuals for money placed in Individual Retirement Accounts. Under the revised rules, the allowable deduction of up to $2,000 of earnings depends on whether you or your spouse "actively participate" in (are covered by) a pension plan and the amount of your adjusted gross income. (There is no ceiling on the amount that can be set aside in a rollover IRA, which is discussed in the next section of this chapter.)

Tip. Deductible IRA contributions are one of those "above-the-line" adjustments, that is, a subtraction from gross income to arrive at adjusted gross income. So you can write off amounts put in IRAs, whether you itemize or use the standard deduction.

Caution. As this book goes to press in the summer of 1994, Congress is considering changes in the rules for IRAs. The proposed legislation includes a provision that would allow more people to deduct contributions to their IRAs. Another provision would authorize penalty-free withdrawals before age 59½ for certain purposes—for example, to buy a first home or pay educational expenses.

Individuals Not Covered by Pension Plans

Under the law now applicable to tax year 1994, the pre–tax-reform rules continue to apply if you are employed and neither you nor your spouse is covered by a pension plan at work. You get to deduct contributions to an IRA of up to $2,000 a year ($2,250 for a spousal IRA; $4,000 if each spouse makes a maximum contribution of $2,000). It makes no difference how sizable your income is.

Individuals Covered by Pension Plans

The limitations introduced by tax reform apply if you file jointly and either of you is covered by a pension plan. You get a full deduction of up to $2,000 if your adjusted gross income (before a reduction for deductible IRA contributions) is less than $40,000 for a married couple filing jointly and $25,000 for a single person.

Only a partial deduction is allowed when AGI is between $40,000 and $50,000 for a couple filing jointly and between $25,000 and $35,000 for a single person. Forget about any IRA deduction for someone covered by a pension plan when AGI exceeds $50,000 for joint filers and $35,000 for a single person.

Adjusted gross income, AGI for short, is the term the IRS uses to designate the amount you show at the bottom of page 1 of your Form 1040 after listing salaries, dividends, and other kinds of income and deducting items like money put in IRAs and alimony payments. The AGI figure is before you itemize for outlays like contributions, mortgage interest, and real estate taxes.

Tip. The law considers a person to be "covered by" a pension plan as soon as he or she qualifies to participate in it, which may be immediately after starting work. This is so even though an employee is not yet *vested,* which means the right that a person acquires when he or she works at a place long enough to become entitled to receive a specified pension upon retirement.

Nondeductible Contributions

All is not lost if tax reform restricts or abolishes your deduction for funds stashed in an IRA. Under the rules that now apply, you have the annual option to make nondeductible contributions of as much as $2,000 (or, as explained above, $2,250 or $4,000). Like earnings on deductible funds in an IRA, earnings on nondeductible funds continue to accumulate untaxed until withdrawals start. To escape being taxed twice, after-tax, nondeductible contributions to an IRA are not again taxed upon withdrawal. Only deductible contributions and earnings are taxed when you make a withdrawal.

Caution. Suppose you have made both deductible and nondeductible contributions. In that case, any withdrawal is treated as having come proportionately from each kind. This holds true whether you establish separate deductible and nondeductible accounts or use a single account to hold both deductible and nondeductible contributions. Also, whatever you withdraw includes a proportionate part of the earnings on deductible and nondeductible funds.

Example. You have $70,000 in two IRAs, with $50,000 (composed of $30,000 deductible contributions and $20,000 earnings) in the first one and $20,000 (composed of $14,000 nondeductible contributions and $6,000 earnings) in the second one. You withdraw $10,000. With those numbers, $2,000 is nontaxable ($14,000 nondeductible contributions divided by $70,000 total balance in the two accounts) and $8,000 is taxable. It makes no difference that the $10,000 comes entirely from the second IRA.

Setting up a nondeductible IRA means added paperwork at tax time. For each year in which you make a nondeductible contribution or a withdrawal, you must complete Form 8606 and attach it to your Form 1040.

Caution. The record keeping doubles if you and your spouse each make nondeductible contributions or withdrawals. The law requires each of you to fill out and submit a separate Form 8606. There is a nondeductible $50 penalty for each failure to file Form 8606.

Help from the IRS

For detailed information on the rules for IRAs, get IRS Publication 590, *Individual Retirement Arrangements (IRAs).* To obtain a free copy, call 1-800-TAX-FORM (allow at least 10 work days for mailing) or stop by the IRS office serving your area to obtain one immediately. Many libraries also have copies of this and other IRS tax guides. IRS Publication 910, *Guide to Free Tax Services,* provides a complete list of booklets and explains what each one covers. (For a discussion of IRS publications, see "Get the Right Help at Tax Time" in Chapter 13.)

401(k) PLANS: HOW A PAY CUT CAN HELP YOUR RETIREMENT PLANNING

In these uncertain times, it becomes more important than ever for everyone to assume greater responsibility for his or her financial future. That is why almost one out of four American workers voluntarily agree to pay cuts to get valuable tax breaks that enable them to easily accumulate funds for their retirement. You, too, should go that route if your company's fringe benefits package includes a 401(k) plan.

Most major corporations offer 401(k)s, named after the section of the Internal Revenue Code that authorizes these tax-deferred, company-sponsored retirement savings programs. Yet fewer than 60 percent of the employees eligible to set aside some of their earnings in 401(k)s actually decide to use such plans—inaction that many of them will rue, should they become victims of corporate cutbacks and find themselves without sufficient funds for their retirement years.

How 401(k)s Save Taxes

The 401(k) break is available just for persons covered by one of these plans at work. Unlike an IRA, which is discussed in the preceding section of this chapter, you cannot set one up on your own. But if you are covered, stash as many dollars as you can afford into the 401(k) and then keep adding to it, a savvy tactic that provides a triple benefit.

First, every before-tax dollar you channel through payroll deductions into the 401(k) reduces your reportable income by a dollar. This is especially attractive if you are ineligible for a deductible IRA because of restrictions resulting from the restructuring of the Internal Revenue Code by the Tax Reform Act of 1986.

A 401(k) also helps when your adjusted gross income is greater than a specified amount that is adjusted annually to reflect inflation—$111,800 for tax year 1994. In that event, you are subject to a partial disallowance of most itemized deductions. (See "Curtailment of Most Itemized Deductions for Individuals with AGIs above a Specified Amount" in Chapter 14.)

Just how much pay you are able to move into a 401(k) changes each year. The maximum 401(k) deferral rises annually for inflation. For 1994, it is $9,240, up from $8,994 for 1993. Depending on how much you earn and other factors, however, chances are that your plan imposes a lower limit. Still, that limit is well above the $2,000 deduction ceiling for an IRA contribution.

Second, you also defer taxes on the interest, dividends, capital gains, or other earnings that accumulate on the funds while they remain in the plan. Not until you begin withdrawals do you have to reckon with the IRS.

Third, to get people to participate, many employers match part of an employee's contribution up to a certain percentage of salary. So if your company chips in half of what you contribute, up to 6 percent of your pay, you actually get 9 percent. That immediate return of 50 percent on your contribution should be an irresistible incentive for you to put aside the maximum.

Example. Here is how sheltering salary in a 401(k) can magnify your contributions well beyond your out-of-pocket cost. Assume you are in a 30 percent federal and state bracket. (For information on how to determine your tax bracket, see "What Is Your Real Tax Bracket?" in Chapter 14.) If your plan permits you to put in $4,000, you defer taxes of $1,200 ($4,000 times 30 percent). What if you keep the $4,000 to spend, rather than socking it away in the 401(k)? You lose $1,200 to the tax gatherers. *Result:* You really wind up with an after-tax $2,800. So moving $4,000 into the savings plan means that your current out-of-pocket outlay is only $2,800. Also, more often than not, your $4,000 is boosted by a tax-deferred employer matching.

Investment Choices

Most of the time, the one who decides how to invest your contributions is not your employer, but you. The wider your range of choices within a company-sponsored retirement plan, the better.

Selecting among investments is as difficult as it is vital; how well your 401(k) does can have a lot to do with how enjoyable your retirement turns out to be. Your goal is to achieve the appropriate balances for your contributions between short-term risks and long-term rewards, whether you are at early- or mid-career, approaching retirement, or already there. Usually, you are allowed to divide your 401(k) money among at least three options—stock funds, your own employer's stock, and GICs, short for guaranteed investment contracts.

GICs. Individuals who are a long way from retirement and need to keep ahead of persistent inflation should not rely exclusively on GICs. Moreover, few employees bothered to read the fine print in their contracts when they signed up for GICs. So they were unaware of an important difference between GICs, which are issued and backed by insurance companies, and bank certificates of deposit (CDs). Unlike the protection of federal insurance for CDs, there is no federal insurance for GICs.

Still, you don't have to be a money maven to figure out why GICs have been the most popular choice—attracting about two out of every three dollars that employees place in 401(k)s. In contrast to the uncertainties of the stock market, GICs provide an attractive, predictable yield, and, until fairly recently, they were considered safe.

Not anymore. Back in 1991, state regulators seized several of the nation's largest life insurance companies, and private rating services downgraded their ratings on many life insurers.

Tip. Understandably, those seizures have caused many of you to become concerned about the shakiness of the life insurance industry. And you frequently ask this question: Suppose my insurer becomes insolvent and I cannot recover all of my 401(k) money. What kind, and how much, of a tax deduction can I claim to alleviate the loss?

Unfortunately, the answer is that most of you are ineligible for any relief under the Internal Revenue Code. You get no tax deduction if insolvency occurs and you are unable to recover before-tax—that is deductible—dollars that went into a 401(k). [Before-tax money means salary put into a 401(k), not listed on your W-2, and on which you previously paid no taxes.] The hitch: In tax jargon, you have a zero "basis" for deductible contributions.

There is limited relief only to the extent that a 401(k) is a receptacle for after-tax money, that is, nondeductible, voluntary contributions, assuming you have a 401(k) that accepts such contributions. (After-tax money means salary put into a 401(k), listed on your W-2, and on which you previously paid taxes.) Presumably, your basis is the amount of those after-tax deposits.

Why am I hedging? Because a gun-shy IRS has yet to spell out its position on the amount and type of deduction you get. Stay tuned.

Stock funds. Do you want to go for growth with stock funds? Chances are that your 401(k) lets you select from among several equity portfolios that range from conservative balanced funds, consisting of a mix of stocks and bonds, to more aggressive funds that venture largely into growth stocks.

Your own employer's stock. Still another option is to put 401(k) money into the stock of your own company. Note, though, that investment advisers warn against tying up a large part of your nest egg in that basket, no matter how well your company appears to be doing. In the event corporate profits shrivel, its share price could suddenly head south and stay there for a long while.

Withdrawing 401(k) Money

These tax-deferred plans are supposed to be for retirement only. Therefore, the general rule is that you cannot tap the 401(k) money, unless you leave the company. However, the general rule is subject to an important exception. Typically, within limits, you can obtain a tax-free loan from your plan.

Caution. Be mindful of what the law authorizes if you decide to leave and take the money at a time when you have yet to attain the age of 59½. In that case, the IRS might exact a stiff penalty.

Tip. There is no penalty for after-age-59½ withdrawals. Nor is there a penalty for tapping the 401(k) before you turn 59½ if you can qualify under any one of a number of exceptions. The IRS does not get to assess the penalty if, among other things, one of the following occurs:

- You are at least age 55 in the year you retire or leave the company.
- You become permanently disabled or die (they're all heart at the IRS).
- You part ways with the company and take out substantially equal payments (at least annually) based on your life expectancy or the joint life expectancy of you and your beneficiary and (1) you receive those payments for at least five years or (2) you attain age 59½, whichever is later.

Example. Your 401(k) accumulation is $150,000. When you are under age 55, you leave your company and decide to take the $150,000 in a lump sum, of which you have $100,000 directly rolled over into an IRA [401(k)-to-IRA transfer; none of the $100,000 comes into your hands] and channel the remaining $50,000 (minus withholding of 20 percent for federal taxes; see the discussion in the next section of this chapter) into a business venture. *Result:* Besides collecting taxes on the

$50,000, the IRS sticks you with a penalty of $5,000 (10 percent of $50,000). The $100,000 directly moved into an IRA continues to collect tax-deferred income.

Proposed legislation. As this book goes to press in the summer of 1994, Congress is considering several revisions for 401(k)s. One change is to reduce the age requirement for penalty-free withdrawals from 59½ to 59. Another is to end the use of five-year special averaging, which is discussed below.

Rollover versus Special Averaging for a Lump-Sum Withdrawal

When you withdraw your money in a lump sum, you must decide whether to pay tax on it immediately or put it in a rollover IRA and postpone the tax. You might be able to delay the tax if you move to another job and can put the money in your new employer's retirement plan.

If you need the money right now and decide against a rollover, see whether you are eligible to substantially lower the tax on your distribution by using ten- or five-year averaging (available only for those born before 1936; only five-year averaging is available for those born after 1935 and then only after they reach age 59½). Under these special averaging methods, the lump sum is taxed *separately,* as though you had received it in equal amounts over a five- or ten-year period, without regard to any other taxable income in the year of receipt.

Contrary to what many people would prefer to believe, the use of five- or ten-year averaging does not give you more time to pay the tax on the lump sum. You must pay the entire tax (plus, perhaps, an early-withdrawal penalty for funds taken out before 59½) with the return for the year in which you receive the money.

An IRA rollover within 60 days after you receive the payout puts off the tax (and any penalty) tab on the money, as well as the earnings on it, until you start to take out funds from the account. Withdrawals, though, are taxed as "ordinary income," that is, at regular income tax rates, just like salaries. You cannot use special averaging for withdrawals, even though the IRA holds money rolled over from a 401(k).

Strategy. Generally, says Paul Westbrook, a nationally recognized retirement planner in Watchung, N.J., it is preferable to do the rollover when you receive a substantial sum and have a long way to go to retirement. But the better bet usually is five- or ten-year averaging and investing the after-tax proceeds when you have a small distribution and are close to retirement. You might have no choice other than averaging when you end your employment and have an immediate need for the cash—to set up a new business, for example, or to buy a retirement home.

WAYS TO SAVE TAXES WHEN RETIREMENT NEST EGGS HATCH

Are you among the millions who will retire, resign, or get fired from a job this year? If so, does your company have a 401(k) plan (discussed in the preceding section of this chapter), profit-sharing plan, or some other kind of retirement plan that gives departing employees the option to take what they have coming in a lump sum, rather than in monthly installments? Retirement advisers report that a steadily growing number of workers opt for one-shot settlements and depart with checks representing the largest single amounts they are ever likely to see in their lives, aside from home-sale proceeds. In fact, nest eggs well up into the six-digit range are not uncommon.

Let's say that you retire, become disabled, voluntarily quit, or, for some other reason, leave your job and receive a one-time payment, known in IRS lingo as a lump-sum distribution. You need no reminder that Uncle Sam will get his share of that money sooner or later. But just how quickly the IRS becomes entitled to its share and exactly how much winds up with the agency depends on what you do with the distribution. Before you make a decision that can have major tax consequences, consider carefully what options become available when you receive in a lump sum whatever is due you from a company-sponsored pension, profit-sharing or savings plan, or from a Keogh plan for self-employed persons.

Caution. Be aware that there is a deadline for your decision, says Herbert Behrens, a pension specialist in Las Vegas. Unless you decide what to do *before* the distribution check is issued, the entire amount could become subject to income taxes, and perhaps a 10 percent penalty as well.

Tip. To minimize what could be a huge tax bill on your settlement at a time when you can least afford it, your first step probably should be to seek the advice of an attorney, accountant, or other specialist in retirement financial planning (deductible, within limits, at filing time; see "Miscellaneous Item-ized Deductions" in Chapter 9). It takes someone familiar with the labyrinths of the Internal Revenue Code to figure out which is the better of two ways to handle your particular situation.

One way is to pay an immediate tax on the money and use the remaining, after-tax cash as you see fit. The other is to delay the tax by, among other options, a direct rollover of the entire sum into an IRA (retirement-account-to-IRA, with none of the funds coming into your possession, thereby avoiding withholding requirements, as discussed below). Going the direct rollover route allows the full distribution to grow tax-free until you begin withdrawals.

Caution. Whether it is more advantageous for you to pay taxes now or to use a rollover depends on many variables, besides the size of the settlement: You have to make some assumptions about how long you can afford (or how long the tax code will permit you) to delay the start of withdrawals, your anticipated tax bracket at the time withdrawals begin, and the rate of return obtainable from different investments. So it is vital to evaluate your options.

There are four choices that you should know about: (1) leave the distribution in the plan; (2) reinvest in an annuity; (3) take a lump-sum distribution; and (4) open a rollover IRA. What follows is a close look at the four choices and strategies to help you sidestep a tax ordeal.

Leave the Distribution in the Plan

Your company's retirement plan might allow you to leave the distribution in the plan, rather than take it. Staying put permits you to defer taxes until you start withdrawals from the plan.

Reinvest in an Annuity

Another deferral option is to reinvest your distribution in an annuity that is arranged either through your company's retirement plan or by yourself. An annuity is an insurance contract that guarantees to provide you a series of income payments at regular intervals. The advantage: The distribution will grow on a tax-deferred basis over the years.

Take a Lump-Sum Distribution

Forget about any postponement option if you take direct possession of your distribution. In that event, you are liable for income taxes on the entire amount, as well as a 10 percent penalty, in most cases, if you are under age 55.

But take heart. You might be eligible to use either ten- or five-year averaging (authorized only for those born before 1936; only five-year averaging is available for those born after 1935 and then only after they reach age 59½) to calculate the tax on your distribution. The averaging computation can reduce your tax liability significantly. Do the tax figuring on IRS Form 4972, which is submitted with your Form 1040. If you decide to take direct possession of your distribution, your tax adviser can help you determine how best to handle it to minimize taxes.

Proposed legislation. As this book goes to press in the summer of 1994, Congress is considering a proposal to end the use of five-year averaging.

Withholding rules for lump-sum distributions: Yet another tax trap, this one is for the unaware and the inattentive. Before 1993, it was easy to postpone all taxes on a lump-sum distribution received from a pension, profit sharing, 401(k) plan, or similar arrangement. As explained below, all you had to do was roll over the amount withdrawn into an IRA within 60 days from when the plan mailed the check to you. It made no difference that the funds first came into your hands during those 60 days; you nonetheless qualified for the postponement option.

Now, though, it does make a big difference if you get your mitts, however briefly, on the check. The retirement plan must withhold taxes at a 20 percent rate on a withdrawal that you do not *directly* roll over (old-retirement-account-to-new-retirement-account) into an IRA or another qualified plan. Put another way, you must not handle the distribution, though it is permissible for you to receive a check payable to an IRA.

The much misunderstood withholding requirements *do not* impose higher taxes. They do, though, require payment *now,* not when filing time rolls around.

Example. You plan to withdraw $100,000 from a 401(k) plan with your employer. What you will actually receive is just $80,000—80 percent of what you ask to take out. The retirement account has to withhold $20,000 for federal taxes against taxes due on the payout. When you prepare your Form 1040, you report the entire $100,000 as income. You show the $20,000 as tax withheld, and it is credited against any income tax you owe.

Suppose, though, that you do roll over the $80,000 before 60 days elapse. That tactic defers taxes on the $80,000, but fails to provide complete relief.

The snag is that the withheld $20,000 *it-self* is considered a withdrawal that counts as reportable income and is taxed. Assuming you are in a total tax bracket (federal, state, and, perhaps, city) of 40 percent, the tax comes to $8,000. (For how to determine your tax bracket, see "What Is Your Real Tax Bracket?" in Chapter 14.) Moreover, in most cases, there is a 10 percent penalty if you are under age 55—$2,000 on a $20,000 withdrawal. *Result:* After you file your return, all you recover as a refund is $10,000—what remains after the $20,000 withholding/withdrawal is offset by the $8,000 tax and $2,000 penalty.

Tip. All is not necessarily lost. You still can avoid the tax and penalty and recover a refund of the $20,000 withheld by the retirement plan. But to do so, you will have to come up with another $20,000 from other sources (your own funds, a home equity or other kind of loan, etc.) and put $100,000 into an IRA. And there might not be many days left in the 60-day rollover period to get ahold of that money.

Caution. There is no way around the requirement that the retirement plan withhold $20,000 for federal taxes. The plan must do so even if no tax is due because you roll over the entire $100,000 within the 60-day deadline.

Exceptions to withholding requirement. There are several exceptions for distributions that cannot be rolled over. They include annuity-like payments scheduled for at least 10 years and minimum distributions that are required after attaining age 70½.

As under prior law, there is no withholding requirement for what you receive as regular, usually monthly, payments from pension plans. You retain the option to have a pension plan withhold nothing from the payments.

Strategies. There are several easy, completely legal ways to avoid up-front, 20 percent withholding. (To help acquaint you with them, you are supposed to receive a written explanation of the rollover and withholding rules from your employer.) Here are four options to carefully consider *before* your retirement plan cuts the distribution check.

- The first option is the one that most people are going to use. It is a maneuver available to everyone who wants to postpone taxes on the distribution. Just make sure that none of the money withdrawn from your retirement account comes into your possession during the 60 days. Instead, arrange beforehand for your retirement plan to make a *direct rollover* of all the funds into an IRA. Rollover IRAs are discussed below.

Tip. IRS regulations spell out how to handle a direct rollover. Make it with a check payable to the IRA. It is okay for your retirement plan to give you a check payable to the IRA, which you deliver yourself. What is verboten is for that check to be payable to you.

Are you under time pressure? You need not find the perfect IRA immediately. Just open up an IRA to hold the retirement-plan withdrawal. Then research the best IRA investment opportunity and transfer the funds there later.

The likelihood is that you will not have the immediate option to put the money into several IRAs. That is because IRS regulations expressly authorize your retirement plan to restrict the direct rollover to just one IRA.

Nyet probleney. After you accomplish the direct rollover, it is easy to then diversify your holdings. All you need to do is make tax-free direct transfers from your rollover IRA to other IRAs.

Caution. Avoid commingling that retirement-plan withdrawal with other existing IRAs that hold previous annual contributions. Instead, house it in a newly established, separate IRA, known as a conduit IRA.

There is a reward for your forethought, assuming you become employed elsewhere. Use of a conduit enables you to preserve your option to roll over the distribution into the plan of another employer, thereby remaining eligible for ten- or five-year averaging (remember, both are authorized for those born before 1936; but only five-year averaging is available for those born after 1935 and then only after they reach age 59½). There is *no averaging* for money removed from an IRA.

- The second option is to let the funds remain in your present employer's plan, assuming it allows you to do so. In that event, you hold on to your options to roll over the distribution into an IRA, or the plan of another employer, and qualify for ten- or five-year averaging.
- The third option is to let the funds remain in your employer's plan and annuitize your withdrawals. This is IRS jargon for when you start to take out substantially equal amounts (at least annually) based on your life expectancy or the joint life expectancy of you and your beneficiary and declare those payments as income.

Caution. The annuitizing maneuver has several drawbacks. To qualify, you must receive the periodic payments for (1) at least five years or (2) until you attain age 59½,

whichever happens later. After that, you have the option to speed up or slow down your withdrawals. Also, annuitizing disqualifies you for ten- or five-year averaging. On the plus side, you escape that 10 percent penalty.

Tip. IRS guidelines authorize three methods to calculate the amount of the annual withdrawal, resulting in substantially different payouts. These methods give you a good deal of latitude in deciding how much cash to take out and how much to leave within the shelter of your employer's plan.

- The fourth option is the one least likely to be used by you. It is to have your old employer's retirement account transfer the funds directly to your new employer's plan. This assumes your new employer provides a plan that imposes no waiting period and will immediately accept a distribution from your old plan. Many plans stipulate a one-year waiting period for new hires.

Open a Rollover IRA

Let's go back to the first of the previously discussed options to avoid withholding, which is to roll over your distribution within 60 days after receiving it. Unlike the $2,000 cap on the annual amount that can be set aside in a regular IRA, which is discussed earlier in this chapter, there is no ceiling on the amount placed in a rollover IRA. With a rollover IRA, you postpone taxes on your distribution; you do not become liable for taxes until withdrawals begin.

Excess contributions. The law allows you to put only the taxable portion of a distribution (pre-tax contributions and earnings on pre-tax or after-tax contributions) into an IRA —a stipulation that many persons have learned about the expensive way. What if you mistakenly roll over after-tax voluntary contributions, assuming your plan permitted them? The IRS exacts a penalty for an excess contribution to the IRA. The penalty is a 6 percent excise tax on the excess contribution. To avoid the penalty, you must withdraw the excess contribution before the filing deadline, including extensions, for your Form 1040.

Deadlines. The IRS strictly enforces the requirements for deposit of a distribution into a rollover IRA and subsequent withdrawals from an IRA. So you need to be aware of exactly how to proceed.

To qualify for the tax postponement, you have to open and fund your rollover IRA within 60 days after you receive your distribution. The earlier date on the check is not controlling. (As mentioned earlier, the 20 percent withholding rules do not apply when you receive a check payable to the IRA and turn it over to the IRA within 60 days.) Because the IRS is unyielding on the deadline, it's prudent to choose your IRA investments in advance.

Also, later on, there is a deadline for withdrawals from IRAs. You must start withdrawing by April 1 of the year following the year you attain the age of 70½. However, there is no early-withdrawal penalty for a withdrawal after you reach age 59½.

Proposed legislation. As this book goes to press in the summer of 1994, Congress is considering a simplification measure that would reduce the age 59½ and 70½ requirements to 59 and 70.

Tip. Withdrawals at any age are taxed at the same rate as ordinary income, the IRS term for income from sources such as salaries, dividends, and interest. Under the rules applicable to tax year 1994 (the most recent year for which information is available as this book goes to press), the top rate is 39.6 percent. (See "What Is Your Real Tax Bracket?" in Chapter 14.) There is no special five- or ten-year averaging. It makes no difference that the money was rolled over from a company plan. Consult your tax adviser about the tax consequences of withdrawal options.

Help from the IRS

For detailed information on lump-sum distributions and IRA rollovers, get IRS Publications 575, *Pension and Annuity Income,* and 590, *Individual Retirement Arrangements.* To obtain free copies, call 1-800-TAX-FORM (allow at least 10 work days for mailing) or stop by the IRS office serving your area to obtain them immediately. Many libraries also have copies of these and other IRS tax guides. IRS Publication 910, *Guide to Free Tax Services,* provides a complete list of booklets and explains what each one covers. (For a discussion of IRS publications, see "Get the Right Help at Tax Time" in Chapter 13.)

THE KIDDIE TAX

Capitol Steps, a group of performers who satirize Washington politics, offer this parody of the song that begins "Teach Your Children

Well": "Tax/ Our children well/ To pay for swell/ Old age adventures./ It's you/ We're living off/ So we can golf/ And buy our dentures."

The Tax Reform Act of 1986 overhauled the rules for taxing children on their wages and investment earnings. One of the more significant changes severely curtailed the advantages of many maneuvers employed for decades by higher-bracket parents to shift investment income from themselves to their lower-bracket children by making gifts to them of money, stocks, and other income-producing assets.

Under the law that now applies, there are two distinct sets of rules for taxing children who receive dividends, interest, rents, royalties, capital gains, and other kinds of investment earnings. These rules became effective at the start of 1987.

One set covers children over the age of 14. The over-14 rules are similar to the old-law rules that applied before 1987.

The second set of rules, the so-called kiddie tax, are less favorable and apply to children under the age of 14. The kiddie-tax rules generally tax investment income received by an under-age-14 child at the parent's top rate when that kind of income is above a specified amount that is adjusted annually to reflect inflation. For tax year 1994 (the most recent year for which information is available as this book goes to press in the summer of 1994), the amount is $1,200.

Children over the Age of 14

The under-14 rules, the so-called kiddie tax, are *not* applicable for the year in which the child attains the age of 14. Instead, an over-14 child continues to be taxed at the child's, not the parent's, rate on investment income.

Also, as under prior law, the child is taxed at his or her rate on wages or other compensation from jobs. For a child with modest investment and wage income, taxes begin to bite at a 15 percent rate (under the rules applicable to tax year 1994, as this book goes to press in the summer of 1994; that compares with 11 percent before the Tax Reform Act of 1986 became effective).

Children under the Age of 14

The kiddie tax applies until the year in which a child becomes 14. Investment earnings above $1,200 (this figure is adjusted yearly to reflect inflation) received by an under-14 child usually are taxed at the parent's, not the child's, top rate. That is, the child is taxed as if the parent were the one who received the income.

It makes no difference whether the earnings are generated by investing money or other assets received by the child from parents or from persons other than parents—grandparents, for instance. Nor does it matter that such gifts were received before the start of 1987, which is when the new rules took effect. Whatever the source, the earnings are taxed at the parent's rate.

As the law now stands, the top rate is 39.6 percent (under the rules applicable to tax year 1994, the most recent year for which information is available. For information on how to determine your tax bracket, see "What Is Your Real Tax Bracket?" in Chapter 14.)

Yet another, less stringent, set of rules comes into play when an under-14 child has investment earnings below $1,200 for tax year 1994. The law allows the child to shelter some investment earnings by using up to

$600 of his or her standard deduction, which is $3,800 for 1994 and is scheduled to go up in later years. The next $600 is taxed at the child's rate. In most cases, that is 15 percent (under the rules for tax year 1994, as this book goes to press in the summer of 1994). Consequently, the parent's rate applies only to earnings above $1,200.

Paperwork

The kiddie tax can mean more paperwork at filing time for parents with an under-14 child whose investment income exceeds $1,200. But the law relieves most parents of the need to fill out Form 8615 and attach it to a child's return.

Instead of a separate return for the child, the parents have another option. They can include the child's investment earnings on their return. If they invoke that option, they must fill out Form 8814 and attach it to their return.

Parents who want to use Form 8814 have to meet these requirements. The child's investment income must be only from interest and dividends (no capital gains or earnings from a job) and be under $5,000. The child must not make separate payments of estimated taxes or be subject to the 20 percent backup withholding tax for incorrect reporting of a Social Security number. Also, the parents have to pay a 15 percent tax rate on the child's investment earnings between $600 and $1,200. That 15 percent rate is the same rate, as explained earlier, that the child pays.

Special rules apply to divorced parents. Include the child's investment earnings in the return of the custodial parent.

What happens when married parents choose to file separate returns? Not to worry, says the IRS. Include the child's investment earnings on the return of the parent with the greater taxable income.

Caution. For many parents, combined returns are inadvisable. Including a child's investment earnings on the return of a parent increases the parent's AGI (adjusted gross income). *Result:* That raises the nondeductible floors for several categories of itemized deductions that are based on AGI—10 percent for casualty and theft losses (see Chapter 9), 7.5 percent for medical expenses (see Chapter 7), and 2 percent for most miscellaneous expenses (see Chapter 9).

Moreover, you suffer a partial disallowance of certain itemized deductions to the extent of 3 percent of the amount by which AGI is above a specified amount that is adjusted annually to reflect inflation—$111,800 for tax year 1994. (See "Curtailment of Most Itemized Deductions for Individuals with AGIs above a Specified Amount" in Chapter 14.)

As for dependency exemptions, they start to phase out when AGI surpasses certain levels that are adjusted upward each year for inflation. For tax year 1994, exemptions phase out when AGI is above $111,800 for singles, $167,700 for joint filers, $139,750 for heads of households, and $83,850 for marrieds filing separately. (See Chapter 2.)

There are other drawbacks for parents who make investments. Combining the income of the child and the parent can curtail or cancel otherwise allowable deductions by the parent for contributions to IRAs (discussed earlier in this chapter) and for losses on rental properties (discussed later in this chapter).

Parents should also be mindful of state income taxes. A combined Form 1040 may require a parent to file a combined state return in certain states, which means higher state income taxes.

Separate returns for child and parent. For parents who are stuck with filing Form 8615, calculating kiddie taxes may be so daunting that they will seek professional help. The law requires parents to make "as if" calculations on Form 8615 to figure their child's tax liability for investment earnings. They must determine the difference between the tax that would have been due had their income included the earnings received by each under-14 child and their actual tax liability. The difference is the kiddie tax.

There are additional complications when parents have more than one under-14 child who receives investment earnings. First, the parents must combine the children's investment income and figure the tax the couple would have paid on all of it. Then the parents apportion the kiddie taxes among their children's returns.

Sidestepping the Kiddie Tax

Using your child as a tax shelter may sound Dickensian, but there is nothing wrong or illegal about it.

—U.S. News & World Report,
January 23, 1984

The top-to-bottom revamping of the rules on income shifting does not end all maneuvers. There remain ways to lower the taxes on investment earnings of under-14 children. The idea is to give them assets that defer taxable income until the child reaches 14 and is taxed at his or her own rate.

For instance, you could make gifts now to a child of stock in growth-oriented compa-

nies or mutual funds that pay low or no dividends now, but are expected to appreciate substantially. After the child becomes 14, you could sell the shares; the profit is then taxed at the child's rate, not yours.

Another, less risky, tax-deferral option is to buy U.S. Savings Bonds, Series EE. The interest that accumulates does not count as reportable income until the bonds are cashed in; so the strategy here might be to make the redemption after the child turns 14.

But the Treasury Department's Savings Bonds Division has this advice: For most average-income families, it is much more advantageous to declare the interest as it builds up each year and take the standard deduction of $600 each year than to defer the redemption until after the child becomes 14, avoid tax at the parent's rate on interest above $1,200, but get to use the standard deduction of $600 only once.

Caution. Buy the bonds in your youngster's name as sole owner. (It's all right to name yourself or someone else as beneficiary in case of the child's death.) There is no income shifting if you name yourself as co-owner. Why? Because you are still liable for taxes on the earnings from co-owned bonds acquired with your funds. This holds true even if your youngster gets to keep the money when those bonds are cashed in.

New Rules for EE-Bond Interest Spent on Education

Under a law change that became effective at the start of 1990, middle- and lower-income families who need to set aside funds for the future education of their children get a tax shelter for interest from Series EE bonds.

The revised rules allow these families to exclude interest from certain EE bonds, (meaning they completely escape federal taxes) instead of the usual deferral of taxes until they collect their interest.

These are the key requirements for tax-free treatment of bonds used to cover educational expenses. The tax break applies only to bonds bought in 1990 and later years, which means absolutely no exclusion for bonds bought in 1989 or earlier years. The bonds have to be owned by individuals who are 24 or older at the time of issuance and cashed in by them during a year when they pay tuition and fees at colleges and universities for themselves or for children or others for whom they can claim dependency exemption. (For the rules on dependency exemptions, see Chapter 2.) Also qualifying are nursing schools and some vocational schools.

There are other restrictions. The tax break for EEs does not apply to expenses for room and board. Forget about any exclusion for EEs bought in a child's name.

Child-must-be-a-dependent requirement. Because of this stipulation, there is no escape from taxes when, say, a generous grandparent redeems bonds to pay tuition costs of a grandchild who is not a dependent of the grandparent.

Tip. To preserve the EE exclusion, it is not necessary for the grandparent to engage in a charade and give or lend the money to the parents and let them buy the bonds. The IRS says it is okay for the grandparent to buy bonds in the name of the child's parents.

Be mindful of another rule that prohibits an exemption for a child age 24 or older who is a full-time student and has reportable income in excess of the dependency exemption amount (which is $2,450 for tax year 1994 and is scheduled to be adjusted annually to provide relief from inflation, as measured by increases in the Consumer Price Index). Without an exemption for a child older than 23, the IRS remains entitled to tax interest on EEs cashed in to pay educational costs.

Scholarships. There are more numbers to crunch in the case of children who receive scholarships, fellowships, or other tuition reductions. The law requires qualifying educational costs to be reduced by scholarship amounts and the like. Put another way, the exclusion is only for the payment actually made.

Phaseout of exclusion. The full exemption from taxes is available only for families with adjusted gross incomes below certain levels in the year that the bonds are *redeemed,* not the year that they are bought. Starting with tax year 1991, the income caps are adjusted annually to reflect inflation.

For 1994 (the most recent year for which information is available as this book goes to press), the exemption begins to phase out when adjusted gross income is above $61,850 for joint filers and $41,200 for singles and heads of households. There is no relief from the phasing out for marrieds who file separate returns. No exemption at all is allowed for interest received by marrieds filing separately.

Proposed legislation. As this book goes to press in the summer of 1994, Congress is considering a proposal to end the phaseout of the exclusion.

Help from the IRS. To claim the exclusion, use IRS Form 8815, which must accompany your Form 1040. To keep track of redeemed EEs, use IRS Form 8818, which you should retain and not submit with your Form 1040. For additional information on the exclusion, consult IRS Publication 550, *Investment Income and Expenses.* To obtain them, call 1-800-TAX-FORM (allow at least 10 work days for mailing) or stop by an IRS office. (For more on EEs, see Chapter 1.)

Tax-Exempts

Other options available to parents are to put a child's funds in tax-free municipal bonds, muni bond funds, or discounted zero-coupon municipal bonds. Remember, though, that municipal bonds rise and fall in value in accordance with market interest rates. Should interest rates rise dramatically, bond holders could suffer economic losses. Brokers also charge commissions on bond purchases and sales. Those commissions, of course, reduce bond yields.

Wages

All children, whether under or over 14, continue to be taxed at their own rate on wages from jobs. But the rules are tricky when an under-14 child invests his wages. Whereas the wages are taxed at the child's rate, interest or other earnings in excess of $1,200 (for tax year 1994) that are generated by the invested wages are taxed at the parent's rate.

Tax Breaks for Hiring Your Youngsters

Another maneuver still works if you have a family business. Put your youngsters on the payroll and let the business pay them compensation that it deducts and which they report on their returns. Hiring your children continues to provide a way to keep income in the family, but shift some out of your higher bracket and into their lower bracket.

The often-overlooked point is that the crackdown on *investment* income does not apply to the *wages* a child earns. This holds true whether those wages come from babysitting, delivering newspapers, or even from a job with a business owned by a parent. The wages remain deductible by the business and taxed to the child at his or her rate. Consequently, it now can make more sense to pay wages to an under-14 child than to bestow properties on him or her that generate an identical amount in income.

The overhauled law also allows a child to use the standard deduction as an offset against income, within limits. For tax year 1994, the standard deduction offsets investment income to the extent of no more than $600, but wages to the extent of $3,800 (those $600 and $3,800 figures are scheduled to increase in later years). *Result:* The more income that the child receives as wages, the more that escapes taxes, thanks to the standard deduction.

Example. During 1994, you pay $3,800 to a teenage son to make deliveries or do clerical work for your family business, which operates as a sole proprietorship. You fall into a 35 percent federal and state bracket. *Result:* Your child sidesteps taxes on his wages. They are sheltered by a standard deduction of $3,800. Your tax savings is $1,330 (35 percent of $3,800). However, your savings will be less if, as explained below, the wages are subject to Social Security and other payroll taxes.

Tip. Your son is liable for taxes on above-$3,800 earnings. Typically, though, he is in the bottom bracket of 15 percent. Also, you still get to take an exemption for him, regardless of how much he receives from earnings and other sources, so long as you furnish more than half of his total support for the year. (For dependency exemptions, see Chapter 2.)

IRS audits.   For this income-shifting device to survive an IRS audit, you must be able to establish that your children *actually* render services. Moreover, the wages that you pay them must be "reasonable," that is, not more than the going rate for unrelated employees who perform comparable tasks. That does not mean you have to be a stingy paymaster. You do, however, have to treat your children the same as any other employees and keep the usual records showing amounts paid and hours worked. Otherwise, the tax collectors may claim that you paid more than the going rate or there was no bona fide employment relationship, just some token services that children are usually expected to perform.

Tip.   The chores that responsible students can handle include answering the telephone, receptionist, bookkeeping, secretarial and other clerical work, and making deliveries.

Caution.   More than one person has found out the hard way that it pays to keep supporting records. For instance, the Tax Court threw out deductions for payments over a two-year period by a surveyor to his children, ages nine and eleven, for sweeping out his office and helping him with surveys.

For one thing, he kept no records of the time they worked. And his case went down the drain when the judge examined the children's paychecks and found all of them had been redeposited in the father's account.

In another case, the Tax Court concluded that the payment in issue, which had been turned over by a doctor to his college-student daughter, was merely an allowance, rather than wages paid for secretarial services at his office and for answering calls from patients at his home. Among other things, a skeptical judge noted that children normally answer the family phone. Nor was the doctor's case helped by his admission that he made the entire payment to her in advance and paid nothing to his son for answering calls. The clincher was his failure to keep any records showing when she worked for him, at the office or at home, or to withhold taxes on the payment.

Payroll taxes on wages paid to children. There is a special exemption from payroll taxes for family businesses that are run as sole proprietorships or husband-wife partnerships.

Wages paid by owners to children under the age of 18 are not subject to Social Security taxes (Internal Revenue Code Section 3121(b)(3)(A). But forget about any payroll-tax exemptions for family businesses that are incorporated and employ a shareholder's children.

Previously, the rules were more advantageous. Before 1988, the cutoff was 21 for children and there was an exemption for wages paid to husbands or wives who worked for their spouses.

Losses on Rental Properties

There are strict limitations on losses from investments in tax shelter deals, such as limited partnerships. Generally, tax shelter losses can be offset only against income from similar investments. No longer can shelter losses shield from taxation non-shelter income, such as wages and stock market profits. (For more on passive losses, see the discussion of Section 1244 stock earlier in this chapter.) However, the tough anti-shelter restrictions are subject to several exceptions for investors.

Tax reform authorizes limited relief for losses of up to $25,000 suffered by relatively small-scale investors in rental properties, be they multiple-family homes, condominiums, cooperative apartments, or stores. To qualify, property owners must be "active" managers.

Active Management Test

This requirement is not especially demanding. All that the landlords have to do is help make decisions on such essentials as approving new tenants, deciding rental terms, and okaying capital or repair expenditures. They need not personally mow lawns, make repairs, or answer middle-of-the-night calls from tenants. So long as the owners actively participate, they can delegate day-to-day operations to managing agents or others hired to collect rents and run the properties.

Deduction Ceiling

Under this special exception, lower- and middle-income landlords still get an annual offset of as much as $25,000 of their losses against other income. Note, though, that the ceiling drops from $25,000 to $12,500 for married persons filing separate returns and living apart at all times during the year. The law bars any offset for married couples who live together and file separate returns.

Phaseout of Deduction

The full deduction of up to $25,000 is available only for individuals with adjusted gross incomes (AGIs) below $100,000, disregarding any shelter losses. The offset shrinks by one dollar for each two dollars of AGI beyond $100,000 and vanishes completely when AGI surpasses $150,000. For someone with, say, an AGI of $110,000, there is a $20,000 cap on the write-off for a rental loss. Anyone with an AGI above $150,000 is ineligible for this tax trimmer. (For married persons filing separate returns, the $100,000 and $150,000 figures become $50,000 and $75,000.)

Caution. Some other fine print worth noting is that the break is authorized solely for an investor who owns at least a 10 percent interest in the property. But this, of course, includes "mom and pop" investors who acquire one- or two-family homes and other small properties.

Example. Ed Holland, a retiree in South Carolina, owns a small apartment building in New York and retains an agent to run it. Ed can use up to $25,000 of tax loss from the property to shelter other taxable income, as long as his AGI is under $100,000, and claim at least a partial deduction if AGI is under $150,000.

IRS Audits

Claiming rental losses increases the likelihood of your return drawing the attention of the tax enforcers. The IRS suspects that many investors are incorrectly deducting losses because of the complexities created by tax reform. If you are audited, expect the examiner to require proof of your active participation in management decisions, ownership of an at-least-10-percent interest, and correct computation of the deduction under the AGI test. (See "Red Flags for an Audit" in Chapter 11.)

Paperwork

As in the past, you continue to use Schedule E of Form 1040 to report rental income and expenses. You also may need to complete Form 8582 to determine how much, if any, of the $25,000 deduction is allowable, as well as how to handle an above-$25,000 loss.

Help from the IRS

For more information, consult IRS Publications 527, *Residential Rental Property,* and 925, *Passive Activity and At-Risk Rules.* For free copies of these and other IRS publica-

tions, call 1-800-TAX-FORM (allow at least 10 work days for mailing) or contact the IRS office serving your area to obtain them immediately. Many libraries also have copies of these and other IRS tax guides. IRS Publication 910, *Guide to Free Tax Services,* provides a complete list of booklets and explains what each one covers. (For a discussion of IRS publications, see "Get the Right Help at Tax Time" in Chapter 13.)

INVESTORS' QUESTIONS

Q. *Can I take an immediate deduction for the sales commission paid for a mutual fund investment?*

A. No. But the commission does count as part of the cost of your investment for purposes of figuring gain or loss on a later sale.

Q. *I know that the tax rules stop me from claiming a loss on the sale of stocks, collectibles, or other investments to my spouse or my children, brothers, sisters, or parents. Is there some legitimate way to claim a loss and still keep the property in the family?*

A. The rules do not apply in the case of sales to in-laws. Thus, you can deduct the loss incurred on a bona fide sale made, say, to your son-in-law instead of your daughter. (See "Related-Party Sales" earlier in this chapter.)

Q. *A company in which I own stock declared a 50 percent stock split, an action increasing the number of my shares from 200 to 300. I plan to keep 150 of the post-split shares and sell the other 150. The original investment cost me $3,000. How do I figure my cost for the shares I sell?*

A. The split makes it necessary to recalculate your cost basis. First, divide the amount invested ($3,000) by the total number of shares (300) to determine the adjusted cost per share ($10). Then multiply the adjusted cost by the number of shares sold ($10 times 150 equals $1,500). To determine your gain or loss, offset the $1,500 against the sales price.

Q. *I placed money in a mutual fund that is part of a family of funds. There is no charge if I shift from one fund to another. What if I choose to switch and show a capital gain? Is the tax deferred to the time I sell the new shares?*

A. No. The gain is taxable as of the date you switched. It makes no difference that the funds are under one management. The law treats any switch as a separate sale and purchase, a ruling that means you have to report your gain or loss each time you switch. However, you are excused from this reporting requirement when the fund holds money stashed in a tax-deferred retirement plan, such as an IRA or a Keogh; nothing need be reported in the event a switch occurs.

Q. *Several months ago, I opened an account with a stockbroker who frequently buys and sells stocks for me. I have yet to withdraw any funds from the brokerage account, although there have been profits. Are those profits considered income; am I liable for taxes on them?*

A. Merely because you make no withdrawals from the account does not postpone taxes. Those profits are taxed in the year the sales take place. It is immaterial that the profits might be offset, or even surpassed, by losses suffered in later years. Each year stands on its own.

Q. *I own some paintings and other collectibles that have substantially increased in value since I purchased them. If I give them to my daughters, do I have to declare the profits?*

A. Neither gains nor losses have to be reported when you dispose of assets by gifts.

Result: You escape being taxed on your capital gains when you give away assets now worth more than their original cost.

Caution.   This rule cuts two ways. You forfeit a deduction for the decline in value when you make a gift of property worth less than it cost you.

Q.   *Does making gifts of appreciated property to my daughters mean that the capital-gains taxes are completely avoided on sales by them?*

A.   No. There is a special rule for figuring a donee's gain. Her sales price must be measured against your cost, plus any gift tax attributable to the difference between the value of the property when gifted and your cost. Therefore, what you actually accomplish is not an avoidance of the capital gain, but a shifting of it from yourself to your daughter—a maneuver that can still be advantageous, provided her tax bracket is substantially below yours.

Caution.   This strategy is inadvisable if you have a daughter who has yet to attain the age of 14 by the close of the year in which she sells the property. Under the kiddie-tax rules as they apply to 1994, investment earnings above $1,200 from dividends, interest, capital gains, and the like that are received by a child under the age of 14 are taxed to the child at the parent's top rate—not, as before, at the child's typically lower rate. (For more on the kiddie tax, see the discussion earlier in this chapter.)

Q.   *Suppose I do not make lifetime gifts to my children. Instead, the paintings pass to them as part of my estate. How much of a difference does that make?*

A.   In that case, what you paid for the

paintings is irrelevant. Your daughters qualify for an important advantage when they sell inherited assets that have appreciated in value—a "step up" in basis (the figure from which gain or loss is measured) for the paintings from their original costs to their date-of-death values. Stated differently, your children sidestep paying any capital gains taxes on the amount the assets appreciated while you owned them. Your daughters are taxed—if and when they sell —just on post-inheritance appreciation. However, any *estate* taxes (Chapter 16) due from your estate are figured on date-of-death values, not original costs. (See "Sale of Inherited Property" earlier in this chapter.)

Q. *My parents gave me 100 shares of stock 12 years ago, and six years ago I bought another 50 shares. This year I sold them because we bought a house. How do I figure how much gain I have to pay tax on? I do not have exact figures, but I can look them up.*

A. The usual rules apply for the shares you bought. Gain or loss is the difference between your basis, that is, what you paid for them, and your net selling price.

Different rules determine your basis for the shares that your parents gave you. If you sold at a gain, your basis is the sum of (1) what the stock cost your parents and (2) any gift tax attributable to the excess of the market value of the stock at the time your parents gave it to you over what they paid for it. In most cases, your basis is what they paid. If it turns out that you have a loss, your basis is the *lower* of either (1) the market value of the stock at the time of the gift or (2) what they paid.

Q. *Recently, I realized a sizable profit on the sale of some coins from my collection. Does the law allow me to defer payment of the capital gains taxes on the profit if I reinvest*

the proceeds in more coins or other collectibles, such as stamps or ceramics?

A. No postponement is permitted. The profit counts as reportable income on your return for the year that the coins are sold, whether you reinvest the proceeds or not. A profit from the sale of collectibles or stock is not eligible for the tax-deferral break for a profit on the sale of a personal residence when you reinvest the proceeds in a replacement dwelling that costs at least as much as the sales price of your old home.

Q. *Suppose I swap some collectibles for stock in a listed company, with no cash involved in the deal. Does that entitle me to postpone being taxed on my capital gain?*

A. No. You are, however, entitled to defer the tax on a gain from the swap (in tax jargon, a "like kind" exchange) of collectibles you hold for investment for similar property —say, an exchange of one stamp collection for another. If you intend to go the like-kind route, it's prudent to check beforehand with a tax pro to make sure that your deal meets the requirements.

Q. *Last year, my husband had sizable losses on sales of stock held in his name only. He didn't have any capital gains, so he planned to carry forward his unused capital losses and claim them on our future joint returns. But he died this year. After filing our final joint return, can I carry forward his capital losses that remain unused and claim them on my own returns in subsequent years?*

A. No. Ordinarily, unused capital losses can be carried forward indefinitely (see "Capital Gains and Losses," earlier in this chapter). But the IRS says the carry-forward ends with the individual's death. This rule still holds true even if you subsequently qualify for the special break that allows a surviving spouse with dependent children the benefit of joint return rates for two years after the spouse's death (Rev. Rul. 74–175; for information on surviving spouses, see "Joint-Return Rates for Surviving Spouses" in Chapter 4.)

Q. *While vacationing abroad, I bought more foreign currency than I actually used. Some of the unused foreign currency dropped in value before I could convert it back into U.S. dollars. Do I get any tax break for my conversion loss?*

A. You can claim a capital loss, just the same as when an investment goes sour. Of course, the reverse is also true if the foreign currency goes up in value and you wind up with more dollars when you convert back. You are required to report this transaction as a capital gain.

Q. *Several years ago, I made a sizable loan to my daughter so she could open a shop. While we merely shook hands and put nothing in writing, she did promise to repay the loan in monthly installments. However, she ran into some unexpected problems, and I did not press her for repayment. Now the loan is uncollectible because my daughter closed out her business through bankruptcy. Will the IRS go along with a bad-debt deduction?*

A. No. The fact that you made no effort to collect while she was still solvent may be deemed evidence that the "loan" was actually a parent-to-child gift for which, of course, you cannot take a deduction. (See "Lending Money to a Relative or Friend" in Chapter 9.)

Q. *To make good on a charitable pledge of $5,000, I can donate recently acquired stock that has declined from $7,000 to $5,000 or sell it and contribute the sales proceeds. Which way is better?*

A. You are better off selling stock that has dropped in price, donating the sales proceeds, and claiming both the $5,000 charitable contribution and the $2,000 short-term capital loss. You forfeit the loss deduction if you donate the stock. (See "Contribution of Appreciated Property" in Chapter 8.)

Q. *Am I excused from declaring the interest earned on Treasury bills if I roll over the proceeds into similar bills?*

A. No. You must report the interest on your return for the year the bills become due. A rollover does not defer taxes on the interest.

Q. *Some rental property that I acquired 10 years ago for $50,000 is now worth $100,000. If I use the property as collateral for a loan of more than $50,000, does that entitle me to base my depreciation deductions on the current value of $100,000?*

A. No. You cannot step up your write-off merely because an asset appreciates. Your annual deduction remains tied to the original cost, less, of course, the value of the land, which is not depreciable.

Q. *I recently purchased some bonds that give me the option to exchange them for common stock of the same corporation. How do the tax rules work in the event I exercise my conversion option?*

A. You do not have to report any gain or loss on the conversion from bonds to stocks. To figure gain or loss on a *later* sale of the stock, use your cost basis for the bonds—which includes any payment you made to exercise your conversion right. To determine whether your gain (or loss) is long-term or short-term, include the time you held the bonds in your holding period.

Q. *If I buy a condominium or a coopera-*

tive apartment, do I get the same tax breaks as a homeowner?

A.   Yes. Your itemized deductibles still include real estate taxes and mortgage interest. You can also deduct depreciation if you use your property for business or rent part or all of it to someone else.

Q.   *Can I deduct premiums on my life insurance?*

A.   No. They are nondeductible personal expenses.

Q.   *I recently cashed in a life insurance policy. Can I take a capital-loss deduction for the* difference between the premium payments and the cash value?

A.   No. Your "loss" reflects what you paid for insurance protection.

Q.   *Am I allowed a deduction for travel expense to check on rental property?*

A.   You can claim expenses (under tax reform, meals are only 50 percent deductible) on a trip to check maintenance, upkeep, etc. But the IRS will take a close look at trips to resort area property. And no deduction is allowed for family members who accompany you on the trip just to see the sights.

11   AUDITS

AND THE TRUTH SHALL SET MOST OF YOU FREE

Those of you who are of a certain age or are familiar with the Twentieth Amendment to the constitution know that presidential inaugurations did not always take place on January 20. Presidents used to take their oaths of office on March 4.

That happened for the last time in 1933 at noon on a cold and gray Saturday in Washington, when Franklin Delano Roosevelt was inaugurated for the first time. Heavy winter clouds hung over the Capitol as FDR spoke these memorable words: "Let me assert my firm belief that the only thing we have to fear is fear itself—nameless, unreasoning, unjustified terror which paralyzes needed efforts to convert retreat into advance."

But was FDR right when it comes to the IRS? Was he ever audited? Regrettably, I have to tell you that his words evoked snickers at an agency that knows and never forgets that nothing else causes Americans to experience plain old, garden variety, stomach-churning fear like receiving an audit notice.

I am no exception, though my entire adult working life has been in the tax field, including ten years with IRS in its Chicago, Washington, D.C., and New York City offices.

I started out in Chicago as a revenue officer; that's agency lingo for staffers who collect overdue taxes. Some of my more memorable moments were at stores and restaurants, where I opened cash registers and scooped out the contents—a drastic tactic that I employed only after I first dropped by to casually chat and thereby minimize the chances of being fatally mistaken for a robber.

Next, while attending law school at night, I became one of the IRS' special agents. These sleuths, popularly known as T-Men (T-Persons, eventually, perhaps), investigate criminal violations of the tax laws. (See "Criminal Investigations" later in this chapter.) Finally, I was an attorney in the Washington and New York offices. Both paper-generating places religiously adhere to Parkinson's Law—an English historian's observation about office organization: Work expands so as to fill the time available for its completion.

Then I became a convert. As a member in good standing on the other side, I wear several hats: syndicated columnist, author of this annual tax guide and other books, attorney in private practice who strives to help the afflicted render less unto Caesar, and tax expert for the Prodigy on-line service, which means I answer queries from subscribers about audits and other tax troubles.

I need to wear all of them to report these IRS statistics: Most audits take about two to four hours and are completed in just one session. Typically, an inquiry covers just a few items the agency wants to question, such as deductions for contributions and exemptions for dependents, and is soon over, provided you are able to furnish adequate verification in the form of receipts and the like.

Those comforting statistics leave unanswered the question of whether most auditors are reasonable about what is acceptable as proof. I can say that the answer is affirmative, in my experience.

Still, my general experience is no comfort to you if your auditor is a zealot—a problem so pervasive that the IRS acknowledges it ought to increase the sensitivity of employees who deal directly with taxpayers. In fact, in the words of a former IRS Commissioner, some staffers "need more training on how to be courteous."

That candid assessment is right on the money, as I can personally affirm. Consider my stint as a special agent. One of my supervisors held me captive for chats during which his eyes misted when he expounded his revisionist theories on how the West, in general, and the United States, in particular, misunderstood the Fuehrer. In retrospect, my boss was eerily evocative of the "Springtime for Hitler" playwright in Mel Brooks' "The Producers."

My post-IRS anecdotes are equally encouraging. Like other tax pros who go to the mat with the agency, I can recount audit war stories of encounters with IRS personnel who went out of their way to resolve any doubts about whether they are "mentally moribund, seriously incompetent, and, on frequent occasion, offensively arrogant," which is how some government employees are characterized by John Kenneth Galbraith in *The Culture of Contentment* (Houghton Mifflin, 1992).

Fortunately, most persons singled out for audits soon see a light at the end of their tun-

nel. For an unfortunate few, though, this light signals oncoming trains.

For an egregious example of bureaucratic imperiousness, reflect on what a three-judge panel of the United States Court of Appeals for the Second Circuit in New York had to say about the ordeal of Leona Weiner. All she sought, said the judges, was "a prompt and courteous remedy from the IRS" for three erroneous seizures of money in her pension fund and bank accounts. Those boners, Ms. Weiner testified, caused her to be denied credit, lose income from the accounts, suffer embarrassment at work, and become ill. So she sued the IRS to recover her money, as well as for damages and an apology. What follows are excerpts from the Second Circuit's opinion.

"Her efforts to resolve the situation resulted in repeated but unfulfilled verbal assurances from IRS staff that the errors would be corrected. Her correspondence to the IRS seemed to have been disregarded, and her personal visits to the office were similarly unhelpful . . . . Illustrative of her experience was a letter telling her that writing the IRS within the next three months, while the agency underwent a computer-system conversion, would be futile and would, in fact, delay processing requests concerning her account."

What did the unrepentant federales have to say? They did not dispute that "computer error" caused them to mistakenly grab her money three times. In fact, those friendly folks entered into an agreement to return the funds filched from the pension, though, as the court emphasized, not "until two and one-half-years after Weiner filed her lawsuit."

Having summarized the undisputed facts, the judges then addressed themselves to "Weiner's principal concern . . . .Not money damages, but what seems like a reasonable request under the circumstances that the IRS provide a letter acknowledging its multiple errors and why her return was handled in an unauthorized manner." Also, she wants the IRS to be "courteous and acknowledge and respond to communications. Finally, in a plea that evokes almost Orwellian imagery, she asks this court 'Is there something in the IRS record that I should know about?'"

Unfortunately, concluded the court, she is not entitled to damages for computer errors. Federal statutes immunize the IRS and its employees from liability for those kinds of damages.

Three frustrated federal judges ended their opinion with these words: "We are often expected to live with governmental actions that resist characterization as rational. And while modern urban life may bring to all its share of petty insults or injuries, we certainly sympathize with the plight of one like Weiner, who, using all methods at her disposal, was still unable to secure a speedy resolution of such obvious govenmental error. The reason she cannot obtain the apology that she so clearly deserves is no doubt due, regrettably, to the fact that probably not one individual in the entire IRS bureaucracy believes that he or she did wrong. While this court cannot speak for the IRS, it may be some comfort to Weiner that she has convinced us that while she is entitled to no legal remedy, fair dealing and simple courtesy should have impelled the IRS to have corrected its error more expeditiously, to have apologized for having erred in the first place, and to have provided her with sufficient documentation of its error to enable her to undo some of the harm done to her."

HOW LONG TO KEEP TAX RECORDS

Dear Mr. President, Internal Revenue regulations will turn us into a nation of bookkeepers. The life of every citizen is becoming a business. This, it seems to me, is one of the worst interpretations of the meaning of human life history has ever seen. Man's life is not a business.
—Saul Bellow, *Herzog*, 1964

You need no reminder to hold on to your tax records in case your returns are questioned by the Internal Revenue Service. But just how long do you need to save those old records that clutter up your closets and desk drawers? Unfortunately, there is no flat cutoff. The IRS says the answer depends on what information the records contain and the kind of transaction involved.

It supplements this vague guideline with a cryptic warning: Keep supporting records for "as long as they are important for any federal tax law." Translated from governmentalese, this means you should save receipts, canceled checks, and whatever else might help support income, deductions, exemptions, credits, exclusions, deferrals, and other items on your returns, at least until the expiration of the statute of limitations for an audit or for you to file a refund claim, should you discover a mistake after filing. The statute of limitations is the limited period of time after which the tax gatherers are no longer able to come knocking and you cannot recover an overpayment. (For a discussion of refund claims, see Chapter 14.)

Three-Year Limit

In most cases, the IRS has only three years to audit your return after you file it. For instance, the deadline is April 1998 for the government to start an examination of a return for tax year 1994, with a filing due date, for most persons, of April 1995.

Caution. Contrary to what many people prefer to believe, you cannot game the system by filing early. In calculating when the three years start, the IRS treats a Form 1040 filed in advance of its due date as though it had been filed on that date.

Example. In the case of a Form 1040 for 1994 that arrived at the IRS in early January 1995, the return remains open to IRS scrutiny until April 1998, the same as the deadline for one that arrived in April 1995.

What if you were excused from the usual April 15 filing deadline because you obtained an automatic four-month filing extension to August 15? Not to worry, an ever-vigilant IRS says. It calculates the three years from August 15. (For a discussion of filing extensions, see "More Time to File Your Return" in Chapter 13.)

Exceptions to the Three-Year Limit

As soon as three years elapse, you could toss out supporting records. Candidates for the garbage pail include W-2s, canceled checks for alimony payments, charitable contributions, medical expenses, and the like.

Predictably enough, nothing is absolutely straightforward when it comes to taxes. There are two exceptions to the three-year

test, though they do not apply to most persons. Those exceptions aside, there are other situations in which it is advisable to keep documentation for far longer than three years—proof of when you bought and sold investments, to cite a common example. More on that in a moment.

Six-year rule. The first exception authorizes the IRS to double the audit deadline from three to six years if the amount of income a person fails to report on his or her return is greater than 25 percent of the amount shown on it. Using the six-year test, the deadline expires in April 1996 for returns for tax year 1989 that were submitted in 1990.

Fraudulent returns. Under the second exception, there is no time limit on when the IRS can come after someone who fails to file a return or files one that is deemed false or fraudulent. The audit, admonishes the IRS, can begin "at any time."

Amending a Fraudulent Return

Like most other tax deadlines, the ones for audits are spelled out precisely. Real-life situations, however, do not always fall conveniently into place.

Consider these circumstances. A taxpayer files a fraudulent return, but later files a non-fraudulent amended return. Does the later submission of a corrected return (which alerts the IRS to the wrongdoing) purge the initial fraud and start the running of the three-year period, or does the statute of limitations remain open indefinitely? The answer, says a pro-IRS decision by the Supreme Court, is that the amended return has no effect; therefore, the feds have an unlimited time to assess the tax and exact a fraud penalty. It makes no difference that more than three years have elapsed since the filing of the amended return.

But the IRS does not always have its way. A different rule applies when a taxpayer originally files no return at all and then files a delinquent, nonfraudulent return. The later submission triggers the three-year period, even though the taxpayer's failure to file a timely return was due to fraud. This does not "elevate one form of tax fraud over another," the Supreme Court concluded, as Congress intended that different limitations should apply in this situation.

Three-Year Deadline Extended by Third-Party Records Dispute

The law authorizes the IRS to obtain records from third parties, such as banks and brokerage firms, that do business with taxpayers whose returns are being audited. But the three-year statute of limitations continues to run even when disputes arise between the tax collectors and third parties over access to those records. *Problem:* The statute of limitations could, and often does, expire before there is a final determination by a court on whether the IRS is entitled to the records in issue, though the statute is suspended when the taxpayer intervenes in such a dispute.

To sidestep this problem, the IRS persuaded Congress to change the law. Buried in the Tax Reform Act of 1986 is a provision that authorizes a suspension whether or not the taxpayer intervenes. *Result:* When the IRS issues a summons to a third party to turn certain records over to the IRS and six months elapse with an IRS-versus-third-

party dispute still unresolved, the statute is suspended until the dispute is resolved.

Some other legislative fine print may require a third-party record keeper to provide notification of the statute suspension to the taxpayer targeted for audit. The third party becomes obligated to perform that chore when the IRS issues what is known as a "John Doe" summons; that is, a summons that demands certain records, but does not identify the taxpayer by name. Note, though, that the third party's failure to notify the taxpayer does not stop a statute suspension.

Records to Keep Till the Cows Come Home

Copies of returns. You should retain them indefinitely. They take up little space and are always helpful as guides for future returns or for amending previously filed returns. Also, copies of tax forms may prove helpful in case the IRS claimed you failed to file them.

Concerned about whether your return will actually reach the IRS? To really nail things down at filing time, all you need to do is hand deliver it to your local IRS office, which will stamp the receipt date on both the filed return and the copy you keep. That way, there ought not to be any question that you filed.

If you failed to copy your returns and now need them, here is what to do. The fastest way, provided you paid someone to complete your returns, is to ask the preparer for copies. The law, in most cases, requires preparers to keep copies of returns for at least three years after the filing deadline. Going this route, notes the IRS itself, may save you both time and money, as the agency imposes a charge for each return requested.

Understandably, there is some paperwork

involved when you ask the IRS to provide copies of returns and all attachments. You have to use IRS Form 4506 (Request for Copy of Tax Form), easily available by calling 1-800-TAX-FORM (allow at least 10 work days for mailing) or stopping by the IRS office that serves your area to get it immediately.

Have you moved? After you complete Form 4506, send it to the IRS Service Center where the returns were filed, not to the service center for your current address. Allow at least 45 days for delivery of copies. (For more information on Form 4506, see "Paperwork" in "Coping with the IRS after April 15" in Chapter 14.)

Win some, lose some. In the course of the ongoing tussle between taxpayers and the IRS, many persons have learned the hard way that they should have saved copies of their returns and canceled checks for tax payments. For instance, the IRS charged that returns had not been filed by Clem Block, a Michigan attorney (no kin to the author of this book). Clem contended that he had filed, but was unable to produce copies of the returns, canceled checks, or any other records to back up his claims. The Tax Court refused to believe him; he was nailed for additional taxes, interest, and late-filing penalties.

On the other hand, a federal district court held that just because the IRS failed to find any records of a particular return didn't necessarily mean the taxpayer had failed to file it. The court found that Aaron Harzvi had been a regular filer before and after and refused to impose any penalties. Moreover, the judge noted that IRS "faith in the perfection of their system is commendable, but the court is not persuaded that IRS index records are the only man-made records free from error."

Property records. Besides copies of returns, which ought to be kept for at least three years, there are other tax-related records that must be kept until they can no longer affect future returns, which can prove to be much longer than three years.

Tip. Be particularly mindful of the need to retain records, for as long as they are needed, that establish the cost basis of stocks and other assets that you own (see Chapter 10). The possibilities include statements for stocks, mutual funds, and bonds that show the dates of purchases and sales, number of shares, and prices, including commissions, as well as stock splits, stock dividends, and dividends reinvested.

For tax purposes, the basis is the figure used to determine any gain or loss on a sale of the property that may not take place until many years later—say, more than three or six. Assume you purchase XYZ stock in 1984 and sell it in 1995; you should keep the buy-and-sell records at least until 1999. Without those records, you might lose more to taxes than necessary.

Home sales. Did you sell your home and postpone taxes on the profit because you acquired a costlier dwelling? The regulations require you to subtract the postponed profit from the replacement's cost when determining its basis on a subsequent sale. That is why you should keep indefinitely IRS Form 2119 (Sale of Your Home), which reports the details of the sale of one home and the purchase of another, including the amount of postponed gain. (For the rules on home sales and what records to save, see Chapter 3.)

Individual Retirement Accounts. Did tax reform completely abolish your deduction for money set aside in an IRA because you are covered by some other kind of pension plan and your adjusted gross income exceeds $35,000 if single or $50,000 if filing jointly? (As this book goes to press in the summer of 1994, Congress is considering legislation that would liberalize the rules for IRA deductions.) You might still seek shelter through nondeductible contributions. Like earnings on deductible dollars in an IRA, earnings on nondeductible dollars continue to grow untaxed until withdrawals begin. To avoid being taxed twice, nondeductible contributions of already-taxed wages to an IRA are not taxed when you make a withdrawal. Only deductible contributions and earnings are taxed when withdrawn. So retain indefinitely, too, the IRS Forms 8606 that you fill out for each of the years in which you make any nondeductible contributions or (even if you make no nondeductible contributions) those in which you make any withdrawals. Keep the 8606 forms until you completely withdraw the money in all of your IRAs. (IRAs are discussed in Chapter 10.)

Tip. Those forms are your protection against a hefty tax bill on money that has already been taxed—only one of the many ways a well-maintained set of records helps you to avoid confrontations with the IRS.

Net operating losses. The law confers a break on losses from the active operation of a business. Those losses can be carried back three years and carried forward 15 years. (See "Business Losses" in Chapter 9.) So it is important to retain records evidencing how you calculated your loss.

Help from the IRS

For detailed information, consult IRS Publication 552, *Recordkeeping for Individuals.* To obtain a free copy, call 1-800-TAX-FORM (allow at least 10 work days for delivery) or pick it up at a local IRS office.

RECONSTRUCTION OF LOST RECORDS

Generally, the IRS allows deductions for business travel and entertainment expenses only if you are able to substantiate those outlays with diaries or other "adequate records." The tax collectors, though, authorize some exceptions to the general rule.

Among other things, the feds will waive the record-keeping requirements and accept a "reasonable reconstruction" of your records when, according to the agency's administrative regulations, the loss of your records was "due to circumstances beyond the taxpayer's control, such as destruction by fire, flood, earthquake, or other casualty." Understandably, those regulations include a cautionary reminder that whether an event was beyond a person's control depends on the particular circumstances.

Consider, for instance, what happened in a dispute over write-offs for travel and entertainment that pitted the IRS against Joe Gizzi, who acted as his own attorney before the Tax Court. According to Joe, the government acted unreasonably when the examining agent refused to excuse him from the usual substantiation requirements. It seems that Joe had stored records of entertainment expenditures in his home and they somehow vanished after he voluntarily moved out because of marital problems.

Unfortunately for Joe, that explanation got exactly nowhere with the Tax Court, which refused to treat the loss as caused by a casualty beyond his control. "Marital difficulties and their consequences, no matter how seemingly independent of the taxpayer's will, do not sufficiently resemble floods or fire to be considered a casualty," the ruling stated. Moreover, noted the court, even if marital problems provided a good excuse, Joe failed to furnish an adequate reconstruction of his records.

Subsequently, however, the Tax Court had some second thoughts. It ruled that marital problems caused the loss to be beyond the control of Matthew Canfield, who also represented himself before the court, but did so with more success than Joe Gizzi.

Here, the circumstances differed considerably. Unlike Joe, Matthew did not voluntarily move out of his home and leave his records; he departed because his wife obtained a court order requiring him to stay away from their dwelling. The wife destroyed his records during the time the couple was separated, and Matthew was unable to enter his home because of the court order.

Note, though, that the Tax Court has no second thoughts where records disappear while a person moves his or her belongings to a new residence. It flatly refuses to allow reconstruction of such records.

Still, sometimes the tax takers try to press things too far. To the surprise of no one but the IRS, the Tax Court relieved Raymond Jackson of the need to produce records that disappeared after he handed them over to a revenue agent during an audit. *Result:* Raymond was allowed to reconstruct what he spent on entertainment and managed to

convince the judge that the disputed deductions were backed up by the lost records.

AUDIT ODDS

The IRS audit program has been a disaster in its very limited coverage. People are playing the audit lottery in the expectation of not being examined.

—A former Internal Revenue Service Commissioner

Few readers of this book will be disheartened by the news that, like most government agencies nowadays, the Internal Revenue Service is obliged to operate under severe budget and personnel limitations. Those constraints should mean that fewer tax returns will be selected for audit, and the generally downward trend over the past few years will continue.

Even if the Revenue Service edges out other agencies in the scramble for operating funds, the odds against any return being chosen for audit are reassuringly long—better than 100 to 1. Put another way, the IRS is scheduled to audit about 1 percent of the individual filers. Of course, those odds can shorten considerably, depending on such factors as the amount and type of income you declare and what you do for a living.

Overall odds may not mean that much anyway. Some years, the tax enforcers zero in on certain occupations—doctors, dentists, attorneys, and accountants, to cite some of the high-visibility groups that are routinely favored for examinations. The reason: These folks file returns that show high incomes, hefty personal deductions in relation to their incomes, and sizable gray-area write-offs for business, as well as losses on investments in questionable tax shelters or in sideline ventures that turn out to be hobbies. Moreover, the IRS learned long ago that many of them are persistently poor record keepers.

Strangely enough, where you file affects the odds. For example, latest available statistics disclose that a Los Angeles filer stands better than four times as much chance of audit as a Philadelphia filer. How come? Only the inscrutable IRS knows, and it's invoking the Fifth Amendment. In any event, if you report high income, it won't make much difference where you file.

Nor will it help to complain about how the odds vary. An Illinois taxpayer charged the IRS with violating his civil rights by picking his return for audit, thus requiring more supporting data from him than from the millions who escaped audit. The Tax Court was cold to his complaint.

Caution. There is a myth that makes the rounds every filing season about how to lessen the likelihood of an audit. According to that fable, the IRS programs its computers to go after late filers, not early filers. Why does it pay less attention to early returns? Supposedly, the agency expects people whose Form 1040s cannot stand a close look to delay submission of their forms until the last minute. The companion myth is to go the reverse route. The computers are less likely to kick out the 1040s of late filers because the IRS is overwhelmed with all kind of returns around April 15.

Actually, says the IRS, and knowledgeable tax professionals agree, it makes absolutely no difference whether returns reach the agency early, in between, or barely make the due date. That is because it is not until much later in the year that all returns go through computers that look them over for arithmetic errors and also single out those

most ripe for audit on the basis of top-secret computations that assign scores to various items—charitable contributions and interest expenses, for instance. High-scoring returns, along with some chosen purely at random, are then closely scrutinized by IRS agents to determine which ones should actually be examined.

Each year, the IRS submits an annual report to the Secretary of the Treasury. Among other things, the report explains how the agency's watchdogs whiled away the hours during the fiscal year. Like earlier reports, the latest available version (for fiscal year 1992) reveals that audit odds vary considerably, depending on the type of return, income level, and even (as explained above) where the taxpayer filed.

Total Positive Income

At one time, the IRS classified returns filed by individuals on the basis of adjusted gross income (AGI). The agency used the classification system to group taxpayers of like economic circumstances together. It then assigned revenue agents to the various groupings to provide audit coverage in the most cost-effective manner.

However, the IRS eventually discovered that a classification system based on AGI was often inappropriate. For example, a corporate executive or a self-employed person with $200,000 income and $191,000 in tax shelter deductions (a scenario that was possible before the Tax Reform Act of 1986 drastically curtailed shelter write-offs) might have been placed by the IRS in the under-$10,000 AGI class—a category that received relatively little audit coverage.

Yet another disadvantage was that some persons primarily derive their income from wages, but also report small amounts of income on Schedule C (business) or Schedule F (farming) of Form 1040. Under the AGI system, such returns were classified as business returns and competed with other returns that were predominantly business. Because the audit selection formulas for business returns used items on Schedules C and F, these returns often received relatively lower scores and thus avoided being selected for audit.

To overcome these problems, the IRS switched from classification on the basis of AGI to a selection based on *total positive income* (TPI). This is the sum of all positive income items on the return, unreduced by losses. Negative items are treated as zero.

In the case of persons filing returns classified as nonbusiness (no income reported on Schedules C or F), the IRS grouped individuals according to their TPI.

For persons reporting TPI between $25,000 and $50,000, there has been a steady decline in the audit percentages for the past eight years—0.59 for 1992, 0.64 for 1991, 0.74 for 1990, 1.00 for 1989, 1.21 for 1988, 1.40 for 1987, 1.66 for 1986, and 2.02 for 1985. For persons reporting TPI between $50,000 and $100,000, the audit percentages for these years also declined—1.01 for 1992, 1.11 for 1991, 1.09 for 1990, 1.81 for 1989, 2.32 for 1988, 2.24 for 1987, 2.96 for 1986, and 3.53 for 1985.

As for returns classified as business, the IRS grouped individuals according to TGR (total gross receipts, the sum of all receipts that appear on Schedules C and F). For persons with TGR between $25,000 and $100,000, the audit percentages for the past eight years have gone down—1.99 for 1992, 1.85 for 1991, 1.86 for 1990, 1.92 for 1989,

2.12 for 1988, 2.01 for 1987, 2.27 for 1986, and 2.55 for 1985.

For those with TGR over $100,000, the audit percentages for these years similarly dropped—3.95 for 1992, 3.63 for 1991, 3.38 for 1990, 3.79 for 1989, 4.20 for 1988, 3.86 for 1987, 4.74 for 1986, and 5.40 for 1985.

Under the previous AGI system, a return that included *any* income reported on Schedules C or F was classed as a business return. On the other hand, the TPI/TGR system makes certain comparisons between TGR and nonbusiness TPI to determine whether a return should be classed as business or nonbusiness. As a general rule, the *predominant* income on the return determines whether it is classified as business or nonbusiness.

Caution. Federal and state revenuers now cooperate more closely on audits. Chances are greater of your returns being examined twice and assessment for extra taxes from one triggering assessment from the other.

The law allows the IRS to disclose your tax returns and audit results to your state tax agency. This does not violate your privacy rights.

AVERAGE DEDUCTIONS

Whether the Internal Revenue Service computers will pounce on your return can depend on how your itemized deductions compare with the average amounts claimed by other persons in your income category. Take a look on the following page to see how your deductions stack up against the averages based on AGI. (Adjusted gross income, or AGI, is the amount you show at the bottom of page 1 of Form 1040 after listing sources of income and deducting such items

AGI (Thousands of Dollars)	Medical	Taxes	Contributions	Interest
$ 25–30	$ 4,247	$ 2,216	$ 1,273	$ 5,422
30–40	2,991	2,627	1,401	5,435
40–50	3,641	3,263	1,450	5,811
50–75	4,588	4,379	1,734	6,856
75–100	5,239	6,214	2,368	8,867
100–200	6,088	9,854	3,776	12,174
Over 200	15,600	37,679	9,906	22,114

as money put in Individual Retirement Accounts, but before claiming itemized deductions for outlays such as charitable contributions or taking the standard deduction.) The figures are based on returns filed in 1993 for the 1992 tax year, the latest one for which information is available.

Tip. Changes introduced by tax reform eliminate or curtail deductions. Previously, medical expenses were allowable only for amounts in excess of 5 percent of AGI. Now, however, the nondeductible floor is 7.5 percent. Sales taxes ceased to be deductible after 1986. For 1986, interest payments on consumer loans, such as car payments and school loans, were 100 percent deductible. For 1987, only 65 percent of such interest was allowable, falling to 40 percent in 1988, 20 percent in 1989, and 10 percent in 1990. After that, the deduction vanished.

Caution. The IRS releases its statistics with a standard warning to forget the averages. You are entitled to claim only your actual payments for, say, contributions; the tax collectors can insist on proof in the form of canceled checks, receipts, and the like.

Despite that warning, these averages may provide an important clue for your chances of examination. Your risk is greater if your deductions stand out as unusually high compared to amounts being claimed by other taxpayers in your income class. It is immaterial that you have actually spent and are able to substantiate every dollar claimed. Even worse, above-average deductions might prompt the IRS not only to challenge other items on your return but also to scrutinize your returns for earlier years.

On a personal note, my work with the IRS included several years in the agency's Chicago office as a special agent. (See the discussion of criminal investigations later in this chapter.) One of my assignments was the return of a man of modest means who claimed charitable contributions way out of line with the averages. It turned out to be a quickly concluded case, as he was a Seventh Day Adventist whose unusually generous practice was to tithe 10 percent of his gross salary before any subtraction for taxes—a pattern of giving that was corroborated by church records.

Going in the opposite direction, what if you discover that your itemized write-offs fall significantly below the averages? Perhaps you neglected to claim some perfectly legal, but often missed, deductions like transportation to obtain medical treatment (see Chapter 7) or unreimbursed, out-of-pocket expenses incurred to do volunteer work on behalf of charitable organizations (see Chapter 8). There are many possibilities. These averages should prompt you to take a closer look at filing time.

Tip.   Just because you claim average deductions does not mean you can forget about an audit. There can be trouble ahead unless you hang on to receipts, checks, etc. that support deductions and other items on your return, at least until the expiration of the statute of limitations for an audit. (How long you need to retain records is discussed earlier in this chapter.)

WHAT IRS AGENTS LOOK FOR

There are simply not a sufficient number of people available to work for the IRS who have the sophistication and the intellect necessary to handle many of the problems that the service must face.
> —Jerome Kurtz, a Washington attorney
> and former IRS commissioner,
> as quoted in *U.S. News &
> World Report,* April 18, 1983

As explained under "Audit Odds," most Form 1040s are selected for examination on the basis of a top-secret scoring system fed into the IRS's computers. But even a high scorer may escape audit because explanations or attachments (something brief, not a blow-by-blow account) to the return indicate that an audit is not warranted. For instance, someone with a sizable medical-expense deduction for plastic surgery may head off an audit by attaching a note explaining that insurance did not cover the entire cost, along with copies of the bills. That is why returns bounced by the computers are then screened manually to eliminate those that are unlikely to justify the cost of an audit.

Here are some of the questions that the IRS tells its screeners to ask themselves before passing over a return that seems to lack audit potential:

- Is the income sufficient to support the exemptions claimed?
- Does the refund appear to be out of line with the gross income and exemptions?
- Is there a possibility that income may be underreported?
- Could the taxpayer be neglecting to report moonlighting, tips, or other types of income not subject to withholding tax?
- Is the taxpayer engaged in the type of business or profession normally considered to be more profitable than reflected by the return?
- Is the taxpayer's yield (net profit) on an investment (equity in assets) less than what could have been realized by depositing the same amount in a savings account?
- Does the taxpayer show a high gross business income, low net profit, and claim only the standard deduction? "Experience has shown that the incidence of fraud is greater on low business returns when the return reflects large receipts ($100,000 or more), a sizable investment, and the standard deduction is

used." Put less elegantly, the feds frequently find fraud in that combination.

According to IRS audit-selection guidelines, revenue agents are also supposed to focus on "significant items." The scope of an audit "should be limited to or expanded to the point that the significant items necessary for a correct determination of tax liability have been considered."

How should agents decide what is significant? That, the guidelines say, depends on their "perception of the return as a whole and the separate items that comprise the return." Agents, however, must consider these factors.

- *Comparative size:* A questionable expense item of $6,000 is significant with total expenses of $30,000, but ordinarily not if total expenses are $300,000.
- *Absolute size:* Despite the comparability factor, size by itself may be significant. For example, a $50,000 item may be deemed significant even though it represents a small percentage of taxable income.
- *Character:* Although the amount may be insignificant, the nature may be significant, such as airplane expenses used to offset business income reported by a plumber, to cite an obvious red flag.
- *Evidence of intent to mislead:* This may be evidenced by missing, misleading, or incomplete schedules or by items shown incorrectly on the return.
- *Beneficial effect of the manner of reporting:* The benefit may be significant when, for example, outlays that are allowable only as itemized deductions (real estate taxes on a home) are claimed as business expenses by a person who

does not have enough itemized deductions to itemize.

- *Relationship to/with other items on a return:* No deduction for interest expense when real estate taxes are claimed may be significant (though easily explainable if the mortgage has been paid off), as may be the absence of dividend income when sales of stock are listed (similarly explainable if the stock paid no cash dividends or paid only stock dividends).

Tip. Agents are also told to consider "items that are not shown on the return, but would normally appear on returns of the same examination class. This applies not only to unreported income items, but also for deductions, credits, etc. that would result in tax changes favorable to the taxpayer."

RED FLAGS FOR AN AUDIT

The legal right of a taxpayer to decrease his taxes or to altogether avoid them by means which the law permits cannot be doubted.
—Supreme Court Justice
George Sutherland (1842–1942)

Even the IRS agrees with Justice Sutherland's view that you should use every legal means available to reduce taxes. Nevertheless, there are certain kinds of deductions and other items which, though legal, might trigger the agency's interest in your 1040. If these are breaks to which you are legally entitled, my view is that you ought to take advantage of them and thereby lessen the amount siphoned off for taxes.

However, if you know ahead of time that they might increase the chances that your return will be bounced by the IRS computers for an audit, be sure to keep sufficient backup information and documentation in your files. Here are some of the items that increase the likelihood of your return drawing the attention of the tax collectors.

Annual income in excess of $50,000. If your income is above the $50,000 threshhold, you are four times more likely to be audited than someone whose income is between $10,000 and $25,000 and takes the standard deduction, according to latest available IRS statistics.

Rental losses. Because of complex rules introduced by the Tax Reform Act of 1986, the IRS may demand proof that you actively participated in the rental activity. Satisfy that requirement and you can offset up to $25,000 of a rental loss against nonpassive income, such as salary or investment income. But if you were a passive participant, generally, you get to offset the loss only against passive income from, say, a limited partnership. (Losses on rental properties are discussed in Chapter 10.)

Office-at-home deductions. A perennial target, these write-offs are sure to get additional scrutiny because tax reform further complicated the already confusing rules.

Travel and entertainment. The IRS knows that most taxpayers write off more than the law allows. Make sure your records documenting these expenses are able to pass muster under the tougher standards mandated by tax reform.

Personal interest. The Tax Reform Act curbed itemized deductions on Schedule A of Form 1040 for interest payments on personal or "consumer" loans, a category that includes credit card and charge account debts, college fees, auto loans, and overdue income taxes. Although home-mortgage interest continues to be 100 percent deductible for most persons, tax reform introduced a phaseout of personal-interest deductions, starting with tax year 1987. The allowable percentages were only 65 for 1987, 40 for 1988, 20 for 1989, and 10 for 1990. Starting in 1991, the deduction became zero. (For year-end strategies for interest deductions, see Chapter 1.)

Understandably, the IRS suspects that many taxpayers misclassified their interest deductions, either because they were confused or wanted to fudge write-offs. Consequently, the agency will check returns to see, for example, whether individuals improperly sidestepped Schedule A's percentage caps for personal-interest payments by listing them as fully deductible business interest on Schedules C (for self-employeds) or F (for farmers).

Miscellaneous itemized deductions. Another revision curtails the deductions that itemizers are allowed to claim for most miscellaneous expenses. This category encompasses write-offs such as return-preparation fees, safe deposit box rentals, subscriptions to investment advisory publications, and unreimbursed employee business expenses, such as union and professional dues, educational outlays, and job-hunting costs.

These kinds of miscellaneous expenditures are allowable only to the extent that their total in any one year exceeds 2 percent of your adjusted gross income. As in the case of personal interest, IRS examiners will look to see whether itemizers, intentionally or otherwise, circumvented the 2 percent floor on Schedule A for miscellaneous expenses by listing them elsewhere—Schedule C, to cite a likely suspect. (For a detailed discussion of miscellaneous deductions, see Chapter 9. For year-end strategies, see Chapter 1.)

How to Win in a Tax Audit

Most persons pale at the prospect of an audit. (See "And the Truth Shall Set Most of You Free" earlier in this chapter.) However, there are ways to lessen the trauma and expense of an encounter with the feds. What follows are detailed tips on how to prepare for an audit, how to deal with a revenue agent, what records you need, when you should seek someone to represent you, whether to go to court over a tax dispute, and which court to use.

Keep Good Records

Be aware that you can get a refund and still be called in for an audit. In fact, it happens every day. So hang on to receipts and other records that support deductions or other items on your return until the statute of limitations runs out for an audit. Generally, that's three years from the filing due date, which is April for most individuals. For example, the deadline is April 1998 for the IRS to begin an audit of a 1040 for tax year 1994, with a due date of April 1995. (How long to keep records is discussed earlier in this chapter.)

Prepare for the Audit

The audit usually begins with a letter from the IRS notifying you of the audit. What you

have to do after that depends on the type of audit you must undergo and the records you need to assemble. The three types of audits are correspondence, office, and field.

Correspondence audit.   This is the simplest type of inquiry. The IRS will want more information to justify one or two relatively simple items on your return. Send an explanation of your position by return mail, along with any records needed to support it.

Do not, though, send originals; send copies. Records can be mismailed, misfiled, or mishandled by either the post office or the IRS and may not be available when you need them. In case your records are too extensive or bulky to photocopy and mail conveniently or if you feel it would be difficult to explain your position in writing, you can ask the IRS for an in-person appointment.

Caution.   Be sure to comply with the deadline set in your audit notice or arrange for an extension. Otherwise, the IRS has no choice but to rule against you and send a bill for additional taxes.

Office audit.   This is the most common type of audit. The audit notice will list a specified time for a face-to-face meeting at the nearest IRS office. But you can phone or write the agent and reschedule the appointment for another time if that is more convenient.

Tip.   Pick your time carefully. The IRS examiner might be more harried right before lunch or more distracted on Friday or the day before a holiday.

The audit letter will list a number of items —contributions, medical expenses, exemptions for dependents, and the like. There are also blank spaces to fill in other items not listed. Next to each item is a box. Those that are checked will tell which items are up for audit. Thus, you know in advance that this is what you are going to be asked about. If the items checked can be readily documented by checks and receipts, it may be possible to have the inquiry handled as a correspondence audit.

Before you appear for an office audit, organize your records and go over your explanation. If the IRS questions an item for which you have no substantiating records, at least you'll have some explanation ready. It's also a good idea to make your own audit and see whether you can uncover some deductions or anything else in your favor that you overlooked when you filed. Then you may be able to reduce any added taxes that the IRS wants to impose. You are entitled to argue new points in your favor, as well as to defend your return as filed.

Tip. Whether you should be accompanied to the audit by an attorney, accountant, or other tax professional depends on what kinds of deductions are being scrutinized and how much is at stake. Perhaps the examination involves nothing more than routine substantiation of expenses; either you can come up with the required records or you cannot. It might be possible for you to handle the audit without the assistance of a pro.

To illustrate, suppose the questioned deductions include medical expenses or interest payments, the types of outlays that usually pass muster if they are documented. If that is the scenario, it often proves possible to get through the audit on your own.

Tip. Be aware that the law always authorizes you to go in yourself at first to find out just what is at stake. Think of that tactic as comparable to chicken soup: It can't hurt and it might help.

Let's say you do go in on your own and discover that the IRS is willing to settle for another $250, plus a few dollars of interest. Odds are that you are going to decide against hiring someone to contest that amount.

Assume, instead, that the feds want to exact several thousand dollars, as well as a hefty charge for interest and penalties. All is not lost. The law specifically allows you to request a delay in which to seek assistance.

Caution. Are there issues that involve questions of interpretation of the frequently fuzzy language in the Internal Revenue Code? If so, it might be wise to have an expert on your side.

An example: The dispute could be whether uncollectible funds that you advanced to a family member or friend ought to be designated as a loan—deductible as a bad debt under the rules for short-term capital losses on Schedule D of Form 1040—or as merely a gift—a nice gesture that should ensure you of a preferred place in the life yet to come, but no deduction anywhere on Form 1040 because of the absence of a creditor-debtor relationship (see "Lending Money to a Relative or Friend" in Chapter 9).

Tip. Fees paid for tax advice are usually included with your other itemized deductibles under "miscellaneous deductions" on Schedule A of your next Form 1040. Most miscellaneous itemized deductions are allowable only to the extent that their total in any one year exceeds 2 percent of your adjusted gross income. However, be aware that the IRS is more generous when it comes to the part of your fees allocable to advice on planning or to fight audits of Schedule C (business income from self-employment), Schedule E (rental income from stores, vacation homes, or other properties; royalties; and partnerships) or Schedule F (farm income) activities. The IRS itself concedes that those fees are "above-the-line" adjustments that you subtract from gross income to arrive at adjusted gross income. *Result:* You get a *full* deduction for them on Schedule C, E, or F, instead of a miscellaneous deduction subject to the 2 percent floor. (For the rules on miscellaneous deductions, see the discussion in Chapter 9.)

Field audit. This type of examination is conducted at your home or place of business or at the office of your attorney, accountant, or other representative. It can involve an extensive examination of your entire return and is usually reserved for someone with a more complex return that shows business or professional income.

Tip. If an IRS agent is conducting a field audit at your place of business, don't think the civil servant uncivil just because he or she turns down your offer to pick up the tab for lunch. The agent is merely following instructions spelled out in the official IRS manual for its employees, a multivolume work with thousands of pages of indecipherable and ever-changing bureaucratese that is sometimes described by IRS staffers themselves as "the world's most confusing publication."

Tucked away in the manual are some tough guidelines that tell the law enforcers to decline an invitation from John Q. Taxpayer for a free lunch. Predictably, because the IRS is responsible for the enforcement of legislation that, depending on one's view, is riddled with countless loopholes or contains some appropriate distinctions, the publication makes a few cautious exceptions to the flat prohibition on breaking bread with a taxpayer unless it's Dutch treat.

The manual allows agents to ignore the guidelines and dine for free when "the invitation occurs during the course of an on-site official assignment; the lunch takes place at a company facility where checks are not issued; and there are no public dining facilities in the area where the agent could go for lunch and return within the time normally allotted for lunch periods." Nevertheless, presumably to keep things kosher, an agent who forgoes brown bagging and accepts lunch under these circumstances must explain the purpose and need for accepting the invitation to the powers that be.

As part of this uncharacteristic concession, those swingers at the IRS also say that where circumstances would otherwise make it uncomfortable to refuse, employees may occasionally accept a soft drink, a cup of coffee, or equivalent nonalcoholic beverage.

How to Deal with a Revenue Agent

An audit is basically an adversarial proceeding. But unlike a criminal trial, where you are presumed to be innocent until the government proves you guilty, the burden of proof in a tax dispute is on you, not the IRS, as a general rule.

In the case of deductions, for example, the burden is on you to show that you incurred and paid the expenses. If you refuse to do so, the IRS will simply disallow the expense. You need evidence (1) that you had the expenses (bills can take care of that); (2) that you paid them (usually, canceled checks are sufficient); and (3) that the items in question were business related or deductible for other reasons. For your deductions to pass muster, you have to satisfy all three requirements. Two out of three is not a passing grade.

Example. Canceled checks may not be enough by themselves to substantiate deductions for contributions to churches and other organizations. The auditor may also ask for letters or receipts from the charities. Why? Because some taxpayers have been known to cash checks at church bazaars and list them as acts of charity. Also, you may have received something valuable in return for your donation—for instance, theater tickets (see "Virtue Is Its Own Reward" in Chapter 8).

Tip. The auditor has some leeway to let you get by with incomplete verification where you have a reasonable explanation for how you came up with the figures that are being questioned. That's why it pays to be cooperative and to answer questions politely.

Caution. Bring with you only those checks, receipts, and whatever else is necessary to substantiate your position, and confine your answers to the questions raised. Otherwise, you may wind up with more auditing than you bargained for.

At the audit, either you or your spouse (if the two of you signed a joint return) or both of you can attend. You can also be represented by an adviser, such as an attorney, a CPA, or a person enrolled to practice before the IRS (someone who is not an attorney or CPA, but who is a former IRS employee or

has passed a stiff IRS examination on taxes; for more information on representation by an enrolled agent, see "Get the Right Help at Tax Time" in Chapter 13).

You do not have to appear with your representative if you have granted him or her a power of attorney (Form 2848) to negotiate on your behalf. Be sure to decide in advance just how much leeway you want your adviser to have in settling the case without first checking with you. That will avoid unpleasant surprises later.

Second audit.   Generally, once the IRS completes an audit of your return, it cannot reexamine that return. There are two exceptions, though they do not apply to most people.

The first exception authorizes the government to conduct another audit should you conclude that you have overpaid your taxes and opt to apply for a refund. (See "Refund Claims" in Chapter 14.) Assuming you accept the revenue agent's findings, you need not be concerned about the possibility of an encore examination.

Under the second exception, the IRS is empowered to conduct a second examination provided it complies with Internal Revenue Code Section 7605(b) and notifies you in writing that a second examination is necessary. In most cases, however, the longstanding policy of the IRS is not to undertake another audit.

Tip. Sometimes written notice is unnecessary. The law relieves the IRS of the need to send written notification when evidence of fraud is uncovered during a routine audit and a revenue agent with the Examination Division reassigns the case to a special agent with the Criminal Investigation Division. (Special agents mainly determine whether taxpayers have engaged in conduct that constitutes criminal violations of the Internal Revenue Code; see "Criminal Investigations" later in this chapter.) This type of reassignment, according to several pro-government court decisions, is merely an ongoing examination, as opposed to a second audit.

Your Appeal Rights

Whether it makes sense in your particular case to appeal the examining agent's findings depends on the issues and amounts involved and on IRS policy in settling similar disputes. But the IRS's own statistics reveal that it settles many appeals for far less than the examining agent demanded.

If your case is reassessed by the agent's superiors, and you and the IRS fail to reach an agreement, or if you skipped the agency's appeals systems, you can then take the dispute to court.

Most persons who choose to battle the IRS do so in the Tax Court. Going that route allows you to have your case heard without having to first pay the taxes in issue. If you lose, you then pay the taxes plus interest.

Tip. Tax reform phased out deductions for payments of interest on personal debts, a category that includes interest on overdue federal or state income taxes. Starting with tax year 1991, the deduction vanished. (For more information, see the discussion of interest deductions in "Timing Payments of Deductible Expenses" in Chapter 1.)

Other options to the Tax Court. You can bypass the Tax Court and battle the IRS in one of the federal district courts (which are located in most principal cities and, unlike

the Tax Court, allow you to have a jury trial) or in the Claims Court (which hears cases in Washington, D.C., only), should you conclude that either court is more likely to rule in your favor than the Tax Court. But to do so, you must pay the taxes, file a refund claim (see "Refund Claims" in Chapter 14), and bring suit after the refund is rejected.

Appeals to a higher court. What if you lose? You can appeal a loss, whether in the Tax Court (unless the case is heard by its Small Tax Case Division, which is discussed in the next section of this chapter), a district court, or the Claims Court, to the appeals court for your judicial circuit, then from the appeals court to the Supreme Court. Don't count, though, on spending some time at the Supreme Court. Usually, it allows appeals from lower courts only for disputes over important legal issues.

IRS statistics reveal that taxpayers fare poorly when they go beyond the IRS itself and try their luck with the courts.

How not to do battle with the IRS. The feds successfully prosecuted Dean M. Hicks, a Costa Mesa, California, engineer, on charges that he fired 13 mortar shells at an IRS Service Center in Fresno, and placed a truck bomb—discovered before it exploded—at the agency's West Los Angeles office. His motive? Dean told of a telephone conversation, during which IRS staffers made rude remarks and joked about the disallowance of a contribution deduction.

Help from the IRS

For detailed information, see IRS Publications 1, *Your Rights as a Taxpayer,* and 556,

Examination of Returns, Appeal Rights, and Claims for Refund. There are several ways to obtain free copies of these and other IRS publications. You can call 1-800-TAX-FORM (allow at least 10 work days for mailing) or stop by the IRS office serving your area to obtain them immediately. Many libraries also have copies of IRS tax guides. IRS Publication 910, *Guide to Free Tax Services,* provides a complete list of booklets and explains what each one covers. (For a discussion of IRS publications, see "Get the Right Help at Tax Time" in Chapter 13.)

Tip. Don't rely absolutely on IRS advice, whether it is information that employees give to telephone or walk-in inquiries or instructions that the agency prints in its publications. Mistakes in instructions or advice are inevitable, and the IRS is not bound by them.

SPECIAL COURT FOR SMALL TAXPAYERS

Let's suppose your Form 1040 is bounced by those relentless Internal Revenue Service computers. Worse yet, as you fear, things fail to go smoothly, and you become embroiled in a dispute with the tax takers.

It all begins with a form letter from the Internal Revenue that announces your return has been flagged for examination and summons you to a face-to-face meeting with an auditor, who proves to be pleasant and efficient, but also tough. Though most of your deductions pass muster, the examiner disallows some and asserts Uncle Sam is entitled to exact an additional $1,000 in back taxes, plus interest, and maybe even a penalty to boot. Your appeals within the IRS get you nowhere.

You still feel that the examiner incorrectly interpreted the often-fuzzy language in the Internal Revenue Code or unreasonably refused to accept the checks, receipts, and other documentation you submitted to support deductions and other questioned items. Yet you also are aware that it is not worthwhile to hire an attorney to contest the assessment.

What next? Is there nothing to do but fork over the $1,000? Fortunately, you have several options. The one used most often by a taxpayer who wants to fight an IRS finding that extra taxes are due is to take the dispute to the United States Tax Court, which is entirely independent of the IRS.

Why does the Tax Court hear the great majority of tax cases? Because the Tax Court is the only forum where you can contest additional taxes, interest, and penalties without first paying the disputed amounts. You need not pay unless the Tax Court sides with the IRS. (In other federal courts, you pay and then sue for a refund; see the discussion of your appeal rights in the preceding section of this chapter.)

Special Break for Small Cases

It is even easier to go to the Tax Court when your case involves no more than $10,000 in disputed income, gift, or estate taxes for any one year. The Tax Court has a Small Tax Case Division that settles cases with as little formality, expense, or delay as possible.

This choice of action is particularly worthwhile when you decide that it is inadvisable to hire an attorney (though you remain free to do so) to be on your side because the stakes are too small, but you nevertheless want a hearing. Your suit will be considered by a judge who has no ties to the IRS and will make every effort to bring out facts that support your position, which is especially helpful when the controversy involves borderline factual issues, such as whether you have sufficient documentation to back up claims for charitable contributions and other itemized deductions or for dependency exemptions.

Tip. An often-overlooked point is that the $10,000 ceiling is not an absolute barrier. To illustrate, assume that the IRS insists on an additional $13,000, and you concede more than $3,000 of that amount. *Result:* You become eligible to challenge the balance under the special rules for small cases.

Caution. Be mindful, though, that you should not jump rashly into the Tax Court. Tucked into the Internal Revenue Code is a provision that entitles Uncle Sam to a damages award of up to $25,000 from someone who brings a suit that the Tax Court finds is frivolous or merely a delaying tactic.

Paperwork

To have your case heard by the Tax Court, you must ask the IRS to send you a "statutory notice of deficiency." This notice is a formal letter assessing additional taxes, which is your ticket to the Tax Court, and is often referred to as a "90-day letter." It gives you a maximum of 90 days from the date when it is mailed to you (*not* 90 days from the date when you receive it) to file a form, known in legal lingo as a "petition," with the Tax Court. (A special rule lengthens the usual 90-day deadline to 150 days if the notice is mailed to you when you are outside the United States.)

Miss that strict deadline by so much as a day and you forfeit your opportunity to appeal to the Tax Court. All is not lost; you can still bring a refund suit (as explained in the discussion of your appeal rights in the preceding section of this chapter) in a federal district court or the Claims Court, but not without first shelling out the disputed amount. Also, you'll probably need a lawyer to guide you through the more formal proceedings in a district court or the Claims Court.

The Tax Court is unyielding on the deadline requirement, as many thousands of taxpayers have learned when their petitions were tossed out. Consider, for example, what happened to Bradley Fawcett, whose dunning notice was mailed by the IRS on September 14, 1984. His petition bore a postmark of December 5, 1984, which was well within the 90-day deadline; unfortunately for Bradley, it was sent back to him marked "insufficient postage." Bradley's remailed petition bore a postmark of January 8, 1985, which was after the deadline passed. That, said the IRS, meant the Tax Court should dismiss Bradley's suit. The Tax Court agreed that it should refuse to make an exception for a petition that "was clearly not timely filed," despite the circumstances. *Translation:* All that's left to Bradley is a refund suit, a maneuver that is available to him only if he first settles the bill.

Gary A. and Alene C. Adkison, who lived on an Alaskan island reachable only by plane or boat, missed the 90-day deadline and contended they qualified for the 150 days authorized individuals who live outside the

United States. Sorry, said the Tax Court, "no special rule for persons living on islands."

Another way to flunk the filing deadline is to send a "telegram, cablegram, radiogram, telephone call or similar communication." They are all unacceptable as substitutes for petitions.

Nor will the Tax Court bend its rules for electronically transmitted documents. That's what the Court told Lois Blum. Lois was represented by an attorney who waited until the 90th day to send a petition from St. Paul, Minnesota, via Federal Express's satellite-relay Zapmail, for delivery that same day to the Tax Court in Washington, D.C. Not until the next day did the original petition reach the court. Unsurprisingly, an unsympathetic court was unwilling to stretch things for Zapmail or any other kind of electronic transmission; it zapped a petition received on the 91st day as untimely.

To avoid having your suit dismissed, make sure to comply with the "timely mailed, timely filed" rule. A petition passes the timely filed test, provided it is properly addressed and bears a United States post office postmark dated before the due date.

To really nail things down, get and keep proof that you mailed the petition. What tax pros recommend is that you send it certified mail, return receipt requested, and retain the receipt. The registration or postmark date is counted as the filing date, legalese for saying that if the petition reaches the Tax Court after the last day to file, the IRS cannot claim that you failed to beat it.

As for filling out the petition, you should be able to handle that chore yourself. The petition merely asks that you provide a short and simple explanation of what errors were made by the IRS and what facts support your position.

For the convenience of petitioners, the Tax Court hears small cases in over 100 cities around the country; so ask to present your arguments in a location at or near where you live.

How expensive is it to go before the Tax Court? The filing fee is only $60. Moreover, the Tax Court can waive the $60 fee in cases where taxpayers establish hardship.

Publicity

Court records are generally open to the public, which can cause embarrassment, not to mention a dent in the wallet; the facts and figures in Uncle Sam's 90-day letter and your petition, along with other documents and testimony, may prove newsworthy and eventually be relayed by reporters and broadcasters to the entire country.

To avoid unfavorable publicity, can you ask the Tax Court to seal its records? It's unlikely that the court will go along with your request. Take, for instance, a 1985 confrontation that pitted country-music singer Willie Nelson and his wife, Connie, against the tax gatherers. Willie and Connie sought to keep their Tax Court proceedings from public view when they challenged attention-attracting assessments of over $1,500,000 in taxes, plus negligence and fraud penalties of over $750,000. The Nelsons asked that the court seal all of its records until the time of trial and prohibit any disclosure of information in those records to the media.

The couple contended that "intense and continual" scrutiny by the media of their tax tribulations had caused them "undue embarrassment and considerable emotional distress." Then there was the slowdown of their cash flow. Because of the publicity, they had been "unable to negotiate large up front payments in long-term, product endorsement contracts."

The court, though, would not buy those arguments; it refused to stop the presses. True, the Nelsons correctly argued that the law does authorize the court to seal records to protect a party from embarrassment or harassment. Nevertheless, their argument was unpersuasive because the facts were against them. Generally, the press coverage was fair; most of the newspaper articles mentioned their denials of fraud. The clincher was that the publicity had not hurt their bookings for performances. "If anything," observed the court, "Willie Nelson's popularity and desirability as a performer has remained intact, if not increased."

Settlement

Within a short time after submitting your petition, you will receive a notice of when your case is scheduled for trial. Don't be surprised if the IRS contacts you at that point to work out a pretrial settlement; the great majority of taxpayers do just that, whether they hire professional help or not. In fact, IRS statistics reveal that most taxpayers compromise their disputes for less than the assessments asked for; a good percentage escape without paying any additional taxes. But those statistics also reveal that when small tax cases actually go to trial, the IRS usually triumphs. (See the discussion of your appeal rights earlier in this chapter.)

At the Trial

If you decide to go the trial route, here are some points to keep in mind.

1. You do not have to bring a lawyer or file a written brief, although you can do either or both if you prefer.
2. Bring with you to court all records needed to support your arguments, including any records you turned over to the IRS.
3. Base your arguments on what the law actually allows, not on what you believe it should allow. The rules of evidence have been considerably relaxed for small tax cases and any information that bears on your case will be admissible. Nonetheless, steer clear of issues that do not bear directly on your case.
4. Listen carefully to questions. Answer them simply and directly.

Within a short time after the trial ends, you will find out whether you won or lost. Either way, the decision is binding. Neither the IRS nor you can appeal a small case decision to a higher court. This means that the IRS cannot later take away a decision for you and that you cannot later change a decision against you. For most persons, the inability to appeal is not a drawback.

More Information

For a booklet explaining the procedures of the Tax Court in understandable language and for the necessary forms, write to the Clerk of the Court, 400 Second Street, N.W., Washington, D.C. 20217. It's free for the asking.

REPETITIVE AUDITS

Speak up if you receive a letter from the Internal Revenue notifying you that an appointment has been scheduled to audit the identical items that the agency examined in either of the two preceding years. Actually, you'll be helping the IRS, which wants to stop repetitive audits that waste time and money for all concerned and to cut down on complaints from taxpayers about being hauled in for an examination on the same issue year after year.

But you have to alert the examining agent to the proposed encore. At that point, he or she is supposed to suspend the examination until the IRS has had time to review those returns for prior years and decide whether to go ahead with a fresh audit.

If it turns out that the items now targeted for questioning were examined for either of the two previous years and there were no changes (the return was accepted as filed) or the assessment attributable to the issue was small (usually, under $50), the agent is authorized to end the audit and send a no-change letter, or if no records were examined, send a closing letter. You are also entitled to raise this objection at the actual audit.

Understandably, this relief procedure is subject to several exceptions. The policy against repetitive audits does not stop an agent from delving into issues of a *nonrecurring nature* that were previously audited and left unchanged.

For instance, allowance of a casualty-loss deduction for flood damage to a basement claimed on a return for one year does not preclude the IRS from questioning another casualty loss for storm damage to a roof claimed on a return for the following year. Other nonrecurring issues are capital gains

and losses, moving expenses, and "any situation where facts and circumstances point to the high probability of change in the present audit."

Tip. When you receive a no-change or small-change audit report from the IRS after an examination of your return, make sure to hold that letter. This will help the IRS verify your claim. As a matter of fact, attaching a copy to your returns for the next two years may help ward off an audit.

Caution. The IRS is free to decide whether to adhere to its self-imposed ban on repetitive audits, according to a Tax Court decision that gave short shrift to Robert Chapman, who improperly claimed deductions for the daily commute by automobile from his suburban home to his job as a New York City police officer. When his income tax return for 1975 was audited, the revenue agent disallowed some expenses, but overlooked Chapman's car commuting outlays, which should have been thrown out. On a subsequent audit of his return for 1977, however, the commuting expenses were challenged.

Chapman contended that the tax collectors should terminate the examination for 1977 because the disputed deduction went unchallenged for 1975. But the IRS was backed up by the Tax Court, which refused to disturb the disallowance for 1977.

Two snags, said the court. First, the decision on whether to discontinue the examination of a particular issue because it was covered in a prior audit is completely within IRS discretion. Second, even assuming the court had the authority to invoke the no-repetitive-audits policy, all that Chapman managed to show was that he did write off commuting costs on his return for

1975. He failed to show that the earlier audit actually approved of those expenses.

TCMP—THE ULTIMATE AUDIT

If Patrick Henry thought taxation without representation was bad, he should see how bad it is with representation.
—The Old Farmer's Almanac

The IRS operating budget back in 1798: "For compensation to the Commissioner of the Revenue, clerks and persons employed in his office, five thousand five hundred and twenty-five dollars. For expenses of stationery, printing and all other contingent expenses in the office of the Commissioner of the Revenue, four hundred dollars."

Most persons experience only a momentary feeling of dread when notified that their returns have been singled out for scrutiny by the IRS. After all, audits are usually routine. The typical inquiry covers just a few items, such as deductions for contributions and exemptions for dependents, and is quickly completed, provided the feds are furnished verification in the form of receipts and the like. But a comparative handful of unlucky taxpayers face ordeals that are time-consuming and costly because their examinations come under the Taxpayer Compliance Measurement Program, TCMP for short, and, unofficially, "the ultimate audit."

Every three years, the IRS randomly selects about 50,000 Form 1040s—without any indication of error or fraud—and subjects these returns to exhaustive examina-

tions. Why do the T-Men conduct these TCMP grillings? Because ultimate audits provide data that helps the IRS to determine where, how, and to what extent taxpayers purposefully fail to comply with or fudge the rules on their returns.

Unlike routine examinations, which generally are limited to those items that triggered selection of the 1040s, TCMP examinations seek line-by-line documentation for all items—not just deductions—on the returns. Among other things, the chosen few may be asked to show birth certificates for children claimed as dependents, produce marriage licenses if they are joint filers, collect checks or receipts to substantiate all contributions, interest payments, and other deductions, establish the cost of investments sold, and explain the sources of all deposits to their checking accounts.

Predictably, taxpayers have sought to forgo the honor. But the IRS has been backed up by the courts, which say taxpayers cannot refuse to be guinea pigs.

Take the case of George Flagg. George's return was selected for a TCMP examination, but he declined to produce his books and records, a decision that led the IRS to issue a summons and ask a federal district court to order him to comply. The court refused, saying the IRS cannot use its summons authority solely to do research, and the agency was unable to show that the return was pulled for any other reason.

Under Section 7601 of the Internal Revenue Code, said the court, the tax collectors "can request voluntary cooperation for any legitimate purpose concerned with the payment of federal income tax. That is not a compulsory section of the code. The IRS can look, they can question, they can do whatever else they want, but they cannot force that information to be given by summons. Section 7602 says that if they are conducting an investigation and there is some reason to believe they need more information for investigative purposes, as specifically set out in that section, then the IRS has subpoena power. The subpoena power does not extend to Section 7601. TCMP clearly fits within Section 7601 and certainly does not fit within Section 7602."

Unfortunately for George, the lower court's decision was reversed by the Eighth Circuit Court of Appeals. It held he must undergo a TCMP audit. The canvassing power granted under Section 7601, the appeals court reasoned, "would be frustrated if the Section 7602 summons authority were construed to be subject to a limitation against such examination in cases where the primary purpose was to gain research data."

The *Wall Street Journal* notes that rewards have been suggested, but never adopted, for taxpayers who emerge from the full-scale rigors of TCMP audits without owing additional taxes.

CRIMINAL INVESTIGATIONS

How to Deal with a Special Agent

The power to tax involves the power to destroy.
—Supreme Court Chief
Justice John Marshall,
McCulloch v. *Maryland, 1819*

The power to tax is not the power to destroy while this Court sits.
—Supreme Court Justice
Oliver Wendell Holmes, Jr.,
Panhandle Oil Co. v.
Mississippi ex rel. Knox, 1928

Usually, an audit of your tax return is fairly routine. The Internal Revenue will ask you to produce receipts, canceled checks, and the like to verify deductions, exemptions, and other facts and figures. Come up with the required substantiation and the examiner sends your return back to the files. In fact, the feds frequently close cases without exacting extra taxes, and in many others they even authorize refunds.

But you are probably in hot water when an Internal Revenue investigator walks in unannounced at your home or office and asks to see your records. Odds are that a surprise audit means the Revenue Service suspects you filed a return that is fraudulent. So if you are targeted for what looks like an out-of-the-ordinary audit, make sure to find out whether the person with whom you are suddenly chatting is a revenue agent with the Examination Division or a special agent with the Criminal Investigation Division.

The difference is not academic. Revenue agents conduct routine examinations of business expenses, dependency exemptions, and similar items; ordinarily, special agents are assigned exclusively to investigate suspected criminal violations of the tax laws.

Also be on guard when you receive advance notice of an audit and two examiners show up to scrutinize your returns. Both may be revenue agents—one a veteran and the other a rookie who's along merely to get some on-the-job experience.

But the appearance of two examiners often means that a special agent and a revenue agent are teamed together on a "joint investigation." This is the bureaucratic euphemism that the IRS uses to describe what goes on when the agency accumulates evidence for a criminal prosecution that can culminate in a stay in the slammer of as much as five years, as well as a fine of as much as $100,000, for each fraudulent return. Those sentences and fines, by the way, are in addition to the sizable civil penalties for fraud, plus back taxes and interest, that the T-Men routinely exact from cheaters who are spared criminal prosecution.

The IRS sets strict guidelines for its special agents on what to do when they drop in, with or without notice. They are supposed to identify themselves as special agents and to advise individuals of their constitutional rights. The ones that most concern you are the right to remain silent and to be advised by an attorney.

When you become aware that you have been singled out for a criminal investigation, your options immediately dwindle to one: Get the advice of an attorney knowledgeable about criminal investigations before you hand over any records or make any statement to special agents. Such disclosures can come back to haunt you when they are pieced together and repeated on the witness stand by government sleuths.

Consider what happened when an Illinois dentist tried to pull one on the IRS and was targeted for a joint investigation. He arrived at his office one morning and was met in the parking lot by two agents. The T-Men had not called for an appointment, and he was scheduled to play golf. But he had read a dental magazine article on how to handle IRS agents without a lawyer present. So he saw no harm in agreeing to meet with them for an hour after treating several patients. As things turned out, he never kept his golf date. The conversation stretched well beyond one hour because the sleuths spotted payments from patients that somehow never found their way into the dentist's records, and they refused to accept his explanation. After several hours,

he realized the agents had him dead to rights and confessed to not reporting many thousands in payments. He wound up receiving a three-year sentence and a sizable fine for tax fraud.

Tip. If you are under investigation by the IRS, it can compel third parties to furnish information about their business dealings with you. In fact, the IRS can obtain information for a year later than the one in issue.

There is no violation of your constitutional rights when an IRS summons forces the disclosure by, among others, a bank of records of your deposits and the dates you entered safe deposit boxes, or an employer of your personnel records.

Nor are you entitled to damages for harassment and humiliation by IRS agents just because they try to collect overdue taxes. That, predictably, was what a judge told an aggrieved taxpayer.

For more on your constitutional rights, see "Family Trusts and Other Tax Scams" later in this chapter.

Voluntary Disclosures

Suppose you filed false returns (or no returns at all) and would like to make amends. If you make a voluntary disclosure, will the government settle for civil penalties, taxes, and interest and forgo a criminal prosecution?

The IRS says it will not bring criminal charges against "any taxpayer who comes forward, makes a true voluntary disclosure, and files an accurate tax return." Understandably, the IRS does not consider a disclosure to be voluntary when a taxpayer files an amended return after being notified that his return has been selected for examination.

Caution. It might be advisable to check first with a lawyer experienced in tax-fraud investigations on whether, when, and how to make a voluntary disclosure.

The Conscience Fund

From time to time, the IRS receives anonymous payments from remorseful taxpayers who want to atone for their past oversights or cheating. The money goes into what the agency calls its "conscience fund."

One such payment of $300 was accompanied by a letter from a guilt-ridden individual who explained that he was unable to sleep at night for worrying about his tax evasion. His letter ended: "P.S., if I can't sleep, I will send more later."

Some years back, there was the surprise ending case of the retired businessman who anonymously sent five new $1,000 bills. IRS sleuths quickly traced the payment through the serial numbers. When the agents called on him, he explained that he came to the United States as an immigrant and built a flourishing business. Out of gratitude to the country, he sent in the money just in case he might have made an unintentional error on his tax returns. But when his books were examined by the agents, they discovered that he had actually overpaid by $11,000 and sent him a Treasury Check for $16,000, plus interest. Presumably, the IRS later checked to see if he declared the interest as income.

Fear of Filing

The law empowers and encourages the IRS to make life decidedly disagreeable for people who intentionally fail to file their returns at tax time. The key federal statute is the Internal Revenue Code, which authorizes the imposition of severe sanctions, both criminal and civil, on those who fail to comply with our "voluntary" system.

First, consider the provisions for criminal offenses. The one most frequently invoked, Code Section 7203, makes willful failure to file a misdemeanor punishable by a fine of as much as $25,000 and a jail sentence of up to one year, or both, plus the costs of prosecution.

For instance, the feds successfully targeted a CPA on failure-to-file charges. An appeals court rejected the CPA's contention that his records were too sloppy for him to file proper returns.

An airline pilot's conviction was upheld by an appeals court, which held that the pilot was not entitled to have the jury hear psychiatric testimony about the pilot's obsession with the idea that payment of taxes is voluntary.

For more serious situations, the feds have the option to bring charges under Section 7201 for willful evasion. This offense is a felony, the punishment for which is a maximum fine of $100,000 and five years in prison, or both, plus prosecution costs.

Because of budget constraints and crowded court dockets, Uncle Sam subjects relatively few taxpayers to criminal prosecutions. So let's look at what the IRS routinely does: slap nonfilers with civil penalties. Those severe, nondeductible penalties are in addition to nondeductible interest charges.

Under Section 6651, the IRS can exact a late-filing penalty—generally, 5 percent of the balance due for each month, or part of a month, that a Form 1040 is overdue. The maximum penalty is 25 percent of the balance due (the amount that remains unpaid after subtractions for taxes previously paid through withholdings from wages and quarterly payments of estimated taxes).

Example. A balance due of $10,000 means a penalty of $500 a month and as much as $2,500 for a more-than-four-months-tardy return.

The severity of the penalty escalates considerably when the IRS accumulates sufficient evidence to establish that the late filing is due to fraud, in which event, the Section 6651 penalty jumps from 25 to 75 percent. (For additional information on the late-filing penalty, see "More Time to File Your Return" in Chapter 13.)

To escape responsibility for civil fraud penalties, taxpayers frequently contend that the first failure to file caused their later failures to file. How come? Because submitting returns for subsequent years would reveal their initial nonfiling to the IRS, which then would press criminal charges—an argument that leaves the courts unmoved.

For instance, the Ninth Circuit Court of Appeals refused to attach any significance to the underlying fear of a criminal prosecution. To do so, observed the court, would "open a Pandora's box of illusory defenses to the fraud penalty."

Tip. Besides the late-filing penalty, the IRS can assess a late-payment penalty, which, as a general rule, is one-half of 1 percent of the unpaid amount for each month, or part of a month, up to a maximum of 25 percent. However, when the IRS assesses penalties for both late filing and late payment, one partly offsets the other.

On top of penalties for late filing and payment, you are liable for interest from April 15 on the balance due. Even worse, forget about any deduction for interest on overdue taxes. To further twist the knife, the IRS charges interest on the penalty for late filing, but not the one for late payment.

FAMILY TRUSTS AND OTHER TAX SCAMS

A tax-protester case became so irksome for U.S. District Judge Patrick Conmy of Bismarck, North Dakota, that he was reminded of Count Dracula, "the legendary vampire who would not die and gained in strength and evil with each new transgression." Added the judge: "This file is beginning to acquire the status of immortality, and apparently no sharpened stakes are on hand."

The IRS is relentless in its pursuit of persons who try to trim their tax tab with "family trusts." These devices, also known as "pure" or "educational" trusts, are often advertised as "IRS-approved" by the promoters, who charge hefty fees based on the size of a person's income and assets. But the tax collectors caution that such trusts are merely sham arrangements.

According to the typical promotion pitch, all you need to do is assign your assets and future earnings to a trust. In return, the trust not only will pay a fee for your services as an officer, trustee, or director, but also provide you with a long list of tax-free fringes. These goodies include "pension rights," use of a residence and car assigned to the trust, and "educational endowments" for your youngsters. Since you are no longer the taxpayer on your earnings or other income, you fall into a much lower bracket and that cuts your tax on any fees or other payments you receive from the trust.

Moreover, you will be assured that the IRS

can exact little or no taxes from the trust because it is entitled to deduct as a business expense its payments for your services, as well as for such personal items as your food, clothing, and rent. Some of the more imaginative promoters even claim that the IRS also loses out on estate taxes as long as you are survived by the trust. (For information on estate taxes, see Chapter 16.)

As part of their search-and-destroy mission, the tax collectors announced that channeling compensation into a trust does not excuse the earner from reporting the income on his or her own return. Predictably, the courts readily side with the IRS. They invoked the long-standing rules on assignment of income that tax compensation to the person who earns it.

Subsequently, with the support of the Tax Court, the IRS decreed that it will not allow any deduction for the cost of setting up a family trust. The feds also warned that they will move against a similar kind of tax scam involving people who form their own "churches" because they want to render less unto the tax takers. Here, too, the IRS has been backed up by the courts, which consider these churches to be shams.

The warning took the form of a ruling that barred a charitable write-off by a self-ordained minister who founded his own church. Its only congregants were himself, his wife, his children, and a few friends. The founder, a full-time civil servant, donated his salary checks to the church. It used most of the money to take care of earthly expenses, such as his housing, food, and clothing. Not surprisingly, the IRS was unwilling to bless this type of tithing. It held that the church was merely a tool to serve his personal needs.

Equally predictable was the refusal of the Tax Court to allow charitable contributions claimed by, of all people, an accountant for donations of cash and the furniture in his rented apartment to his six-member church. The church dispensed these alms to, among others, his landlord and the electric company. (For more on charitable contributions, see Chapter 8.)

Taking the Fifth on Form 1040.   Tax protesters contend that there is a constitutional basis for not filing a Form 1040 or for not paying taxes. One of the dodges relied on by protesters is to claim that an individual's Fifth Amendment right not to be forced to testify against himself justifies his failure to file.

Does that sound too good to be true? Absolutely, says the IRS, which has been backed on this issue by the courts in scores of cases.

On a personal note, I remember my appearance not that many years ago on an evening radio talk show in New York City, hosted by the late Candy Jones. Candy paired me with Irwin Schiff, a leading guru in the protest movement who refused to pay federal income taxes and traveled about the country to tell other Americans that they can refuse, too, as he did during our broadcast. Not unexpectedly, the IRS noticed that broadcast, as well as his other efforts, including authorship of "How Anyone Can Stop Paying Taxes" and "The Federal Mafia—How It Illegally Imposes and Unlawfully Collects Income Taxes." Eventually, Irwin was twice convicted on criminal charges involving his own returns and served time in prison.

Strange to say, Irwin continues to be confrontational, though not so heedless of the rules as to again wind up at Club Fed. The *Wall Street Journal* of April 8, 1992, reported that he "lost another civil case. The Tax Court ordered him to pay tax for 1979, civil-fraud and other penalties, and $25,000 for taking a frivolous case to court." The *Journal* made no mention of an additional inconvenience for Irwin: On top of the penalties, the interest that already accrued on his Form 1040 for 1979 exceeded the tax.

Caution. Contrary to what protesters and other self-proclaimed experts in constitutional law assert, the IRS is not powerless to take any action against someone who files a 1040 on which he completes only the lines for his name and address and invokes the Fifth as his reason for not filling in the other lines that apply to him. The courts routinely uphold the collection by the IRS of a nondeductible civil penalty for each failure to file. (See "More Time to File Your Return" in Chapter 13.) That penalty is in addition to other penalties for negligence and not making estimated payments, as well as the back taxes and interest.

Moreover, these *civil sanctions* are not the only weapons that the Internal Revenue Code empowers the tax enforcers to unleash against far-out protest scams. It is longstanding law that claiming the Fifth does not prevent the feds from bringing *criminal charges.* A conviction can mean a jail term of up to a year and/or a fine of up to $25,000 for each failure to file. (See the earlier discussion in this chapter under criminal investigations.)

As Supreme Court Justice Holmes noted back in 1927, a taxpayer cannot "draw a conjurer's circle around the whole matter by his own declaration that to write any word upon the government's blank would bring him into danger of the law."

This point was driven home to Donald Johnson, who unsuccessfully argued that he was excused from filing a return because he would incriminate himself if he reported his income from illegal dealings in gold. His conviction by a jury was upheld by the Fifth Circuit Court of Appeals. Although Johnson or anyone else faced with a similar problem can refuse to answer specific incriminating questions on a return, he cannot refuse to file. The proper way for a person to comply with the tax laws and still exercise constitutional rights, the court noted, is to record illegal income in the space provided on Form 1040 for "other income." The *amount* of income is not shielded by the Fifth, only the source.

12 Gambling and Taxes

The United States has a system of taxation by confession. That a people so numerous, scattered and individualistic annually assesses itself with a tax liability is a reassuring sign of the stability and vitality of our system of self government. It will be a sad day for the revenues if the good will of the people toward their taxing system is frittered away in efforts to accomplish by taxation moral reforms that cannot be accomplished by direct legislation.

—Supreme Court Justice
Robert H. Jackson (1892-1954)

The tax rules for gamblers can be summed up simply: "Heads, the Internal Revenue Service wins; tails, you lose." Your reportable income includes all of your *winnings* from cards, horses, lotteries, and other games of chance, whereas your *losses* are deductible only to the extent of your winnings.

Even worse, those spoilsports at Internal Revenue like to stack the deck against gamblers who strike it rich. The feds routinely nail them for taxes on their winnings, yet disallow their losses unless they have records to back up losing bets, just as they need records to substantiate other kinds of deductions. The tax moral is clear: Keep track of your successes and failures if you do much wagering.

Proposed legislation. As this book goes to press in the summer of 1994, Congress is considering a proposal to allow you to de-duct only 80 percent of the losses otherwise deductible. Hence, for every $100 of winnings you list, write off just $80, though losses aggregate at least $100.

Here, let us pause to reflect on whether the national purpose would be properly advanced by the enactment of legislation that authorizes draconian treatment for gamblers. What could have possessed Congress to consider such a loopy law? One is reminded of the worst excesses of the French Revolution, as was the imperious Lady Bracknell of Oscar Wilde's *The Importance of Being Earnest.*

Unsubstantiated Losses

More than one big bettor who neglected to save records later learned the expensive way just how difficult it can be to persuade the IRS that he had offsetting losses or that his actual winnings did not run to more than the figure shown on his return. Consider the case of the late bridge expert Oswald Jacoby, who suffered from an uncontrollable urge to gamble. The IRS dropped by to chat when it learned that Jacoby and his wife, Mary, had winnings and losses that in one year alone ran to more than $100,000. Eventually, the agency insisted that the couple ante up the taxes on $270,000 from unreported winning bets on cards, dice, and sports over a five-year period, plus hefty charges for interest and penalties.

The Jacobys decided to try their luck with the Tax Court, where they argued that Oswald lost at least $270,000 over the five years in question. Mary testified that "Mr. Jacoby is a compulsive gambler. If he would only follow what he writes in his books on gambling," she lamented, "he would be as winning a player at anything he performs in, as he is in bridge tournaments."

The court was readily convinced that Oswald actually suffered substantial losses because he "gambled frequently, compulsively, and unwisely," but basically sided with the IRS and trimmed his loss deduction to about $140,000 because of his failure to document the losses completely. Luckily for Oswald, his modest standard of living indicated heavy losses. He enjoyed "few of the luxuries that would normally flow from such activities as his writings, his individual genius, and his gross gambling receipts," observed the court.

Losing Tickets

Then there was Carol Manzo, a Miami cocktail waitress and frequent visitor to the tracks, who won a spectacular $46,306 at the harness races, but got clobbered by the IRS. Manzo filed a return on which she erased almost all of the taxes on her gains with a write-off of about $40,000 for losses that were documented solely by losing tickets from various tracks. Predictably, her Form 1040 never made it past the computers, and the IRS assigned Manzo's questioning to none other than James Bond—the agent's real name.

Unfortunately for Manzo, a number of inconsistencies cropped up between what she told Bond and her later testimony in court about the role played during her track excursions by William Lawton—referred to by the court as a professional gambler and "very probably her boyfriend." Manzo told Bond she made all her bets personally, but told the court that Lawton selected all her bets. A skeptical judge refused to believe the losing wagers were hers. Among other things, the judge cited Manzo's "convenient ability to forget all relevant matters" and concluded that her failure to call Lawton as a witness meant that his testimony might have been more harmful than helpful to her case.

There is, of course, something else that causes IRS agents, as well as judges, to distrust deductions for gambling losses that are substantiated by losing tickets. Any track fan who wants to supplement his loss records can do so by collecting the worthless tickets that other players throw away after every race. That's what the Tax Court commented in a case involving William Green, a cab driver who collected $21,854 on a twin double ticket. Green tried to wipe out the taxes on his windfall with $23,680 in losing tickets, all dated within a few weeks after the winning race and many on several starters in the same race, but was thwarted by a dubious judge who scrutinized the tickets and discovered that several displayed "unmistakable heel marks." Unsurprisingly, his honor was unimpressed with the cabbie's explanation for the heel prints and allowed only $2,000 of the claimed losses.

Equally predictable was the close look that the Tax Court took at the losing tickets when Tony Saitta won $174,000 on two bets and made the ritual claim that his losses were at least that amount. Saitta's case wasn't helped when he displayed tickets for the same race that were bought from widely separated betting windows. His case was tossed out when he showed a stack of other tickets that were purchased at the same window, but not numbered consecutively. To have bought such tickets, he would have repeatedly gotten in line at the same window to play the same horse, rather than purchasing all the tickets in one visit to the window.

Yet another dispute over losing tickets involved James Rogers, an inveterate gambler, who was called on the carpet by the IRS to explain reports from a number of tracks that his winnings for the year in issue ran to $56,000. Rogers conceded the $56,000 figure and even admitted that he had cashed in many other tickets that he failed to declare. He also told the IRS that his winnings were more than offset by his losses. But the only proof he had to back up his claim was 1,151 losing tickets totaling $11,654. The IRS demanded better evidence than losing tickets and refused to allow a deduction for more than $11,654. That prompted Rogers to take his case to the Tax Court, where he wound up before a judge who was cold to his claim. In fact, the judge chided the IRS for being "extremely generous" in allowing *any* deduction based on losing tickets. "It's common knowledge," he said, "that disgruntled bettors discard thousands of losing tickets immediately following each race."

IRS Loses on the Witness Stand

Some horseplayers nose out the tax takers in contests over betting losses. For example, the IRS didn't get away from the starting line when it tried to nail Bernard Colletti for failing to report $54,000 in twin double winnings at Yonkers Raceway. Colletti testified that he only bet small amounts and actually wound up a loser for the season. Fortunately for Colletti, the only witness that the IRS could muster was Lawrence Strauss, who testified that he made his living by cashing in big winning tickets for a fee for other gamblers who wanted to conceal their winnings from the IRS. The way Strauss remembered things, he turned over at least $50,000 to Colletti. But Colletti owed nothing, decided the judge, who was unwilling to accept the testimony of Strauss, a felon whose unsavory record included convictions for robbery, cashing bum checks, and possession of stolen government property. Nor was the government's case bolstered by Strauss's admission that he filed no tax returns for six years in a row, "had lied during a previous trial and would lie again to stay out of jail or to keep from paying taxes." Moreover, noted the judge, Colletti's modest spending habits were inconsistent with his having hefty winnings, and the IRS was unable to show he stashed away sizable sums.

Nondeductible Expenses

Several imaginative taxpayers have tried to sidestep restrictions on loss deductions by claiming write-offs for their spending on trips to local tracks or longer jaunts to places like Las Vegas. For instance, James Shiosaki made regular pilgrimages from California to shoot craps at the Sands Hotel and other establishments in Las Vegas. James's losses at the crap tables ran to $50,000 over a 10-year period, despite dedicated efforts by him to improve his skill.

For the year in issue, his score was $1,300 won and $10,000 lost. In addition to claiming losses of $1,300 to match his winnings,

Shiosaki decided to reduce his tax bite by writing off $1,230 spent traveling to Las Vegas and staying in hotels there as an expense "for the production of income." But the law says such expenses are deductible only if an activity is profit motivated. (See "Profit versus Pleasure: Strict Rules for Losses" in Chapter 9.) Consequently, the judge, though sympathetic, concluded that James flunked this test and threw out the entire $1,230. He reasoned that the main motivation for any crapshooter with an abysmal record like James's was not profit but pleasure.

Miracle in Mexico

Some pilgrimages are a good deal more rewarding, as Jose Diaz discovered. Down in Jaurez, Mexico, life was hard for Jose, who suffered from poor vision, walked with a limp, and had to make do running errands for $12 a week. Despite his problems, Jose remained a pious person who attended church daily and made annual pilgrimages to pay homage to the Virgin of Guadalupe, patron saint of Mexicans.

The payoff came one summer night when, as Jose later testified in the Tax Court, he had a wondrous dream in which the Virgin told him to buy Mexican National Lottery ticket number 37281. An inspired Jose scraped together $300 and turned for advice to his nephew, Alfonso Diaz, who lived in Texas and worked for a bank. Using money that belonged to Jose, Alfonso bought the entire sheet of 75 tickets numbered 37281. The Virgin had steered Jose right. Number 37281 copped the grand prize of 32 million pre-devaluation pesos, which then translated into 3 million pre-inflation dollars.

After he collected his winnings, Jose asked Alfonso to invest the 3 million; most of it went into a bank account that Alfonso opened in both of their names—a step that came back to haunt them. Somehow, the IRS got wind of the news and decided to cut itself in for $1,621,000 of the winnings. The long reach of the IRS usually doesn't extend south of the border. But it claimed the real winner was Alfonso, a U.S. citizen.

The Tax Court rated the case a toss-up; nevertheless, it decided to buy Jose's story that he was the real winner and that Alfonso owed nothing. The clincher was convincing corroboration furnished by Alfonso's "86-year-old grandmother, obviously closer than most to her Maker and face-to-face with her priest in the courtroom."

STAYING OUT OF TAX TROUBLE

If you do hit a jackpot, there are steps you can take to avoid getting caught in a tax trap, like Oswald Jacoby or Carol Manzo. Here are some tips on ways to trim taxes and steer clear of trouble with the IRS.

At filing time, the IRS expects you to count as reportable income all of your gambling winnings, whether from horses, lotteries, cards, or other games of chance. The agency insists that you report the entire amount of winnings on the line for "other income" on page 1 of Form 1040 and list the source as gambling. This requirement remains applicable even if winnings are less than losses. (See "How to Avoid a Hassle with the IRS" in Chapter 13.)

As for losses, tax reform left intact the previously discussed cap on your allowable deduction. The amount cannot exceed the total reported as winnings for the year. The law absolutely bars any use of losses to offset wages and other kinds of income.

Another stipulation is that you get to write off losses only if you itemize on Schedule A of Form 1040. The loss deduction is unavailable if you pass up itemizing and take the standard deduction, which is the amount that you automatically get without having to itemize. Include your allowable losses with your "other miscellaneous deductions" at the bottom of Schedule A.

Tip. Tax reform authorizes a break of sorts for itemizers who deduct gambling losses. They are not subject to the 2 percent nondeductible floor that applies to most miscellaneous expenses—for instance, payments for tax advice and safe deposit box rentals. You can continue to offset the full amount of losses up to the amount of winnings, provided you itemize. (For information on miscellaneous itemized deductions, see Chapter 9.)

Tip. The law allows you to offset losses from one kind of wagering against winnings from other kinds of wagering.

Example. You declare lottery winnings, in which case your itemized deductibles are not limited to the cost of losing lottery tickets. They also include your gambling losses from horse racing, cards, and the like.

Another plus is that an illegal bet is just as deductible as a legal one. Assuming the IRS decides to question your return and your proof is acceptable, an agent will not quibble because you deducted those off-track losers placed with bookies from winning bets made legally at the track or in Atlantic City.

Be mindful, too, that each year stands on its own. Suppose your losses exceeded your winnings for last year and the reverse is true for this year. Your unused gambling losses for one year cannot be carried back or carried forward and deducted from gambling winnings for another year.

Partial disallowance of certain deductions for persons with AGIs above a specified amount, which is adjusted annually to reflect inflation. You suffer a partial disallowance of your allowable write-off for most itemized deductibles, including gambling losses. The disallowance is 3 percent of the amount by which your AGI surpasses a specified amount—$111,800 for 1994. (See "Curtailment of Most Itemized Deductions for Individuals with AGIs above a Specified Amount" in Chapter 14.)

Constructive receipt rule for reporting income. Under this long-standing rule, there is no leeway on when you become obligated to report gambling winnings. You have to declare winnings that come under your control before the year ends. For instance, you cannot postpone reporting track winnings on this year's return merely by waiting until next year to cash the tickets. (For more on constructive receipt, see "When Income Is Reportable" in Chapter 13.)

Special rule for joint filers. There is some leeway for married couples. On a joint return, they can pool their gambling losses and winnings for the year so that his losses are deductible from her winnings, or vice versa.

Example. For the year in question, you win $4,000 and lose $8,000 and your mate wins $3,000. As joint filers, your combined winnings of $7,000 are offset by an itemized deduction of $7,000. It makes no difference that your losses surpass your winnings.

Social Security. Even the IRS has a heart when it comes to senior citizens. Their Social Security benefits won't be cut, regardless of how much they ran up in winnings.

Tip. When a person buys a sweepstakes or lottery ticket and makes a valid assignment of part or all of it before it becomes a winning ticket, that shifts the taxes on the winnings to the assignee to the extent of the percentage assigned. (See "Assigning a Lottery Ticket: The Right Way to Shift Income" later in this chapter.)

KEEPING AN IRS DIARY

An understanding IRS wants to avoid record-keeping hassles with gamblers that it targets for audit. To help them, the IRS has issued guidelines that spell out what sort of records and other substantiation it will accept. The IRS recommends that they record their winnings and losses in "an accurate diary or similar record"—the same method that the agency allows businesspeople to use to keep tabs on their travel expenses.

Keeping a diary, however, can turn out to be a waste of time and effort if your entries fail to show the information called for by the guidelines.

To be on the safe side, make certain that your diary contains at least the date and type of specific wager or wagering activity, the name and address or location of the gambling establishment, the names of other persons, if any, present with you at the gambling place, and amounts won or lost.

The best way to keep a diary is to develop the habit of recording bets when you make them. It's tough to try to compile a diary when filing time rolls around. And one that's not prepared until just before an audit is bound to be unacceptable.

Gamblers are also warned to keep what the IRS dubs "verifiable documentation." This term includes betting tickets, canceled checks, and credit records. Whenever possible, the IRS would prefer the diary and backup documentation to be supported by other proof of a person's wagering activities or visits to a gambling site. The guidelines specify such items as hotel bills, airline tickets, gasoline credit cards, bank deposits and withdrawals, and affidavits or testimony from "responsible gambling officials"—a term that the IRS conveniently opted to leave unexplained.

As for frequenters of horse and dog races, the tax collectors ask them to list the races, entries, how much was collected on winners and lost on losers, *and* to keep unredeemed tickets and any payment records from the racetrack.

The guidelines recommend that slot machine players record their winnings by time, as well as date; that gamblers at table games, such as blackjack or roulette, note the number of the table at which they were playing; and that bingo players record the number of games played, cost of tickets purchased, and amounts collected on winning tickets, along with supplemental records, such as any receipts from casinos and parlors.

The IRS discreetly describes its guidelines as "suggestions" and says that most bettors will satisfy the record-keeping requirements if they follow them. Nevertheless, it cautions that its guidelines are not intended to cover all possible situations and that whether a bettor will be liable for extra taxes will depend on the facts and circumstances in a particular situation. This implies that gamblers who comply will generally avoid a dispute with the IRS, while a failure to comply is not necessarily fatal.

Just how important a diary can be was underscored in a dispute that pitted the IRS against Leon Faulkner, a disability retiree who spent much of his time at racetracks.

On his Form 1040 for the year in issue, he reported winnings of $38,000 and losses of $34,000. The $38,000 figure reflected only amounts listed on 1099 forms received by him from tracks at which he had placed winning bets. As required by law, those tracks also had sent copies of the 1099 information forms to the IRS for use by its computers, which compare 1099 figures with amounts listed on returns.

Leon must have experienced some discomfort during the audit, particularly when he admitted to winnings in excess of $38,000. His explanation: He understood that the law entitled the IRS to share only those wins recorded on 1099 forms. Another snag was that Leon neglected to save losing tickets, though he kept a monthly diary in which he noted amounts bet for the month and net wins or losses.

The revenue agent assigned to the examination must have been in a generous mood. For whatever the reason, the IRS accepted the $38,000 figure as Leon's winnings. But in what has now become a ritual response, the government refused to allow any deduction whatever for losses.

The Tax Court, however, held that Leon's diary accurately reflected winnings and losses. It concluded that "the amounts recorded 'as wagers' are in complete accord with the amounts listed each month on the sheet attached to his income tax return filed several years previously. Furthermore, the amounts recorded as winnings reflect not only his 1099 winnings but the additional sums he won from gambling."

CANCELED GAMBLING DEBT IS NOT TAXABLE INCOME

The tax laws routinely spell out in excruciating detail just what you do or do not have to count as reportable income, whether the source of that income is wages, investments, or what have you. Moreover, to resolve most disputes about whether a particular item should be classified as reportable, the law authorizes the IRS to collect its share of "all income from whatever source derived," unless something is specifically exempt from taxation, such as property received as a gift or an inheritance. (For more on what must be reported, see "Adding Up Your Taxable Income" in Chapter 13.)

With that background out of the way, consider something called the "canceled debt" rule—a provision known to few people, aside from lawyers and others like me who get paid to demystify the tax code. Under that rule, you even can have reportable income when a debt that you owe is canceled, reduced, or paid by someone else. The amount that you no longer owe must be listed on Form 1040, just the same as wages or interest from savings accounts.

The IRS unsuccessfully attempted to invoke the rule against David Zarin, an engineer and a compulsive gambler, who had a credit line at Resorts International Casino Hotel in Atlantic City, where he routinely bet the house maximum at his favorite game, craps.

David's huge bets attracted crowds to his table; because of the excitement that he generated, other gamblers wagered more than they might otherwise have. So an understandably appreciative Resorts designated him a "valued gaming patron" and, starting in 1978, conferred complimentary perks, such as the use of a luxury three-room suite. The casino steadily increased the roster of perks to include free meals, entertainment, and round-the-clock access to a limo. By late 1979, Resorts also made the comps available to David's guests.

Between June 1978 and July 1979, David lost about $2,500,000 at the casino's craps tables. New Jersey's Casino Control Commission issued an order that prohibited Resorts from allowing him to gamble on credit. However, the casino ignored the order and authorized more credit for him.

By the start of 1980, he was betting 16 hours a day and had lost another $3,500,000. Unable to recoup, Resorts sued in 1980 and settled in 1981, when David paid $500,000 and the casino forgave the balance of $3,000,000.

Not long thereafter, the IRS assessed taxes for 1981 on the forgiven debt of $3,000,000. With interest accruing over the years on the back taxes, the total bill exceeded $5,200,000.

David took the dispute to the Tax Court, a decision that meant he could have his dispute heard without having to first pay the amount in issue. He lost in the Tax Court but won on an appeal to the Third Circuit Court of Appeals, which held that the initial debt failed to meet either of two tests—that the debt be legally enforceable or be secured by property.

The Third Circuit quickly disposed of the first issue. Under New Jersey law, Resorts was unable to collect the debt because it had violated state gambling regulations designed to protect compulsive gamblers.

As for the second issue, David had no debt that, in legalese, was "subject to which he held property." Although he received gambling chips, they were not property. Rather, reasoned the appeals court, they were "merely an accounting mechanism to evidence debt." David could not do as he pleased with the chips, which were unusable outside the casino. Because the debt David owed Resorts always exceeded the chips he held, redemption would have left him with "no chips, no cash, and certainly nothing that could have been characterized as 'property.'"

In a newspaper interview, an attorney for David provided a postscript for his client's tax triumph: "He gave up gambling and now speaks regularly at gatherings of Gamblers Anonymous."

ASSIGNING A LOTTERY TICKET: THE RIGHT WAY TO SHIFT INCOME

There is a basic rule that you cannot escape tax on income that you have a right to receive simply by assigning it to someone else without first paying the tax on it. The IRS labels this restriction the "fruit of the tree" principle. It evolved out of a case in which a father tried to transfer some income to his son without first having paid tax on it. The strategy seemed a good idea because the father was taxed at a much higher rate than the son.

But the Supreme Court ruled that "the fruit of the tree cannot fall far from the tree on which it was grown." This was the Court's way of saying that once income has been earned you cannot avoid tax on it by transferring it to another person.

For example, you cannot shift tax on a winning lottery ticket or sweepstakes ticket by giving all or part of it to another person after the winning draw. To shift tax, you must be able to show that you made a valid assignment of all or part of it before it became a winning ticket.

An IRS ruling shows how a winner successfully shifted income. It seems that Rudolph and Flavia were longtime, unmarried acquaintances who lived with her parents. Rudolph's income came from occasional manual labor; Flavia's from AFDC payments for two children of a prior marriage. The two of them pooled all of their meager cash by keeping it in her purse, and she disbursed funds as needed.

On their lucky day, they shopped at a convenience store. Flavia gave Rudolph some money from her purse to buy food and an additional $2 to buy a lottery ticket. He bought the groceries and a ticket, which he put in his coat pocket. Later, upon becoming aware that he held a winning ticket, he gave it to Flavia, who put it in her purse for safekeeping.

Then things got complicated. To collect the prize, the back of the ticket had to be signed and sent to the State Lottery Commission. Flavia signed it and asked for the first installment to be split equally between her and Rudolph. But the couple was told that the Commission's regulations allowed the winnings to be paid to only one person.

To get around that stipulation, they signed an equal-ownership agreement, and designated a manager to receive and disburse the payment to each of them. That arrangement prompted the IRS to consider an arcane question: Had Rudolph, the ticket's purchaser, become liable for gift taxes because he made a gift to Flavia either by (1) giving the winning ticket to her to keep in her purse or (2) signing the agreement?

No, concluded the IRS, given the particular scenario. The couple had always pooled their funds to buy necessities and occasionally tickets. They saw themselves as the owners of equal interests in the winning ticket from the time Flavia gave Rudolph the $2 to buy it.

When they signed the agreement, all they did was formalize their previous understanding, and they made it because of the Commission's regulations permitting payment to only one person. *Result:* No gift tax liability, and Rudolph shifted half of the tax from himself to Flavia (Ruling 9217004).

OTB CLERK'S HORSES DIDN'T WIN, AND IRS SHOWED HIM HIS PLACE

Mark D. Collins worked as a ticket seller at an Off-Track Betting parlor in Auburn, New York. Back in 1988, Mark, a compulsive gambler, began to work a scam on OTB.

Mark's embezzlement scheme was low-tech. Without shelling out money for the privilege, the ticket seller entered bets for himself simply by punching them into his computer terminal. His system was always to bet on the favorite and increase the amount wagered until he finally hit a winning wager, thereby enabling him to recoup prior losses and also to reap a slight profit.

The first few times, Mark usually netted a modest amount on his stolen bets, or lost just a small sum, which he would place in his cash drawer after the last race.

Inevitably, one July day it all hit the fan. By the end of the tenth and last race, Mark had lost so frequently that he wound up short for the day by about $38,000—total unpaid bets of $80,000 minus winning tickets of $42,000 from the final two races.

Unable to replace the $38,000 that should have been in his cash drawer, Mark confessed to his supervisor what he had done and surrendered the $42,000 in winning tickets to OTB. Subsequently, he was prosecuted for grand larceny.

This being a tax book, the story does not end with Mark's punishment. Enter the IRS, which billed him for back taxes and interest charges on unreported gambling income of $80,000.

Mark challenged the assessment in the Tax Court, which meant that he could have the case resolved without having to first pay the amount in issue. He contended nothing extra was due the IRS because the tickets were worthless.

The Tax Court easily rejected that argument and concluded that he had additional income of $80,000. Betting tickets, reasoned the court, have an economic value; they represent "opportunities to gamble" that horseplayers are willing to purchase at face value. As a betting clerk, Mark assumed sufficient control over the tickets to realize that value. Previously, he had sidestepped detection; had he won on that July day, Mark would have put the winnings in his cash drawer to cover the amount bet and kept the excess.

Strip away the legalese, and Mark had stolen opportunities to gamble. However, he gained a partial victory. The court permitted him to offset the $80,000 with the $42,000 in winning

tickets that he had given back to OTB, reducing his unreported income to $38,000.

But what about those losing tickets of $38,000? After all, the long-standing rule is that gamblers can deduct losses to the extent that they have winnings.

The Tax Court refused to authorize that subtraction. Instead, it characterized the $80,000 as income attributable to *theft*, not gambling.

Why did the court do that? Because the law says gain from a wagering transaction is the excess of the amount won over the amount bet. Hence, no gain can result without a prior wager.

Here, there was no prior wager. The court said that what Mark did was wagering "only in the sense that he gambled that he would not be caught."

The Tax Court's decision was affirmed by the United States Court of Appeals for the Second Circuit in New York.

Appeals Court Says the Tax Court Can Split the Difference

There is a laundry list of well-settled rules that help the IRS discharge its mission to collect taxes. For example, when the IRS bills a taxpayer for additional taxes, the agency's assessment is presumed to be accurate until the taxpayer is able to establish that it is erroneous.

Another helpful precept is that the law empowers the IRS to pursue more than one taxpayer for the same assessment. This approach makes it possible for the tax collectors to ensure that somebody is held responsible for payment of the tab.

Both rules were made expensively clear to

a pair of Texas gamblers, Idus P. Ash and Ralph Cannon. IRS sleuths somehow discovered that an unidentified individual wagered about $65,000 on a college football game with Idus, who laid off some part of that with Ralph.

That unusual set of facts left the IRS with the chore of figuring out whether to exact the taxes on gambling income of $65,000 from Idus or Ralph. The feds took the easy way out, hitting each Texan for the total tax tab.

Idus and Ralph thought they could best the IRS. The pair decided to take their tax predicament to the Tax Court, where a taxpayer can contest additional taxes, interest, and penalties without first paying the contested amounts. They asked the court to decide who actually owed the taxes.

The two gamblers did not make things easy for the court. Arriving at a decision proved to be particularly difficult because neither of them had kept records of their operations. Moreover, neither could offer other evidence that was believable. To the surprise of no one but Idus and Ralph, their litigating approach failed to endear them to the court.

The right thing to do, concluded an unsympathetic Tax Court, was to take a cue from the Bible and hold each gambler liable for half of the taxes. As a basis for appealing the finding to a higher court, both of them contended that the Tax Court had arbitrarily arrived at a "Solomon-like decision."

Unfortunately for them, the Tax Court's ruling was narrowly upheld by an appeals court panel comprised of three judges. Because both Idus and Ralph failed to rebut the IRS's presumptively correct assessments, each man could have been taxed on the entire $65,000. Therefore, tersely reasoned two of the judges, getting stuck with payment of

half "is certainly not a matter which either can complain of."

That sort of analysis got exactly nowhere with the third judge, who thought the appeals court ought to have reversed the Tax Court. His reading of the law was that the presumption favoring the government "clearly becomes irrational the moment it is extended to both taxpayers simultaneously"—a thought that probably comforted Idus and Ralph, but did not relieve them of their tax obligations.

Big Sweepstakes Winner Is Big Loser in Tax Evasion Case

McNulty would never forget the day he read the names of the holders of the winning tickets for that year's Irish Sweepstakes. He was one of the big winners, the holder of a ticket good for several hundred thousand dollars.

However, he was discomforted by the thought of what would happen next April 15, the deadline for the annual reckoning with the IRS. He was going to have to file a Form 1040 that listed the winnings as income.

Soon, though, McNulty perked up, for he had figured out a way to sidestep that disagreeable chore—just forget about filing. When tax time rolled around, he implemented his tax-saving strategy and did not submit a 1040 and thus paid no tax on his winnings.

As someone who made no bones about what he thought of the IRS, McNulty did not hesitate to tell several completely trustworthy friends of his intention not to file. Those statements came back to haunt him when they were repeated on the witness stand at his trial on charges that he evaded income taxes.

There was other evidence that helped the government make its case against him. On three separate occasions, McNulty went so far as to ask the IRS to calculate just how much would be due in taxes on his winnings. Obliging IRS staffers advised him of the amount of taxes.

Then there was the matter of his efforts to better familiarize himself with the workings of the Internal Revenue Code. In response to another of his inquiries, the IRS explained that, contrary to what he understandably preferred to believe, he would remain liable for the taxes even if the money was left in Ireland.

More on the trial in a moment. First, a bit of background. As I have previously pointed out, what counts is whether a gambler is subject to the reach of the IRS, not where he chooses to deposit his winnings. That snag arises because Uncle Sam taxes his citizens on a worldwide basis; it matters not that the funds in question never find their way into the United States.

The government's case was bolstered by testimony establishing that McNulty had journeyed to Ireland to personally pick up the money. The next step in his itinerary, before returning to the United States, was a stop in the Channel Islands, where he put nearly all of the winnings in a bank.

Why, rhetorically asked the government, did McNulty choose to do his banking outside the United States? The government-provided answer: He was aware that the Channel Islands have strict laws that bar the disclosure of bank deposits.

Unsurprisingly, the trial judge found him guilty of tax evasion. McNulty was similarly unsuccessful when he appealed his conviction. Said the appeals court: "McNulty set for himself and successfully navigated a firm course leading to the shoals and rocks of a guilty verdict."

FOREIGN GAMBLERS

Q. *I am a Canadian citizen and live in our capital, Ottawa. Last month I went on my first visit to the United States, a ten-day stay, part of which was in Las Vegas, where I won $10,000 at a casino.*

To my dismay, I left the casino without all of my winnings, the $10,000 having shrunk to $7,000 after the casino withheld $3,000 for U.S. income taxes.

I contacted the U.S. Embassy in Ottawa. It said the way to recover the $3,000 is to contact some agency known as the Internal Revenue Service, which, I was assured, is renowned for its prompt, understandable, and helpful responses to inquiries.

According to some of my American friends, that might not always be so, which is why I thought it prudent to get advice from someone like you, who has no connection with the IRS. How do you rate my recovery prospects?

A. Unfortunately, less than zero. With your scenario, you get nothing back.

As someone from outside of the U.S. who briefly vacations here, you come under a special set of tax rules for a nonresident alien—an individual who is not a U.S. citizen or an alien who resides in the U.S.

IRS regulations specify how much to withhold for income taxes on various kinds of income, including gambling winnings, received by a nonresident alien. Generally, those regulations require a casino, such as the one you visited, to withhold at a rate of 30 percent of your winnings.

There is a limited exception to this requirement that provides no relief for you. For that exception to apply, the U.S.-Canada income tax treaty has to permit withholding of income taxes at a less-than-30-percent rate or, as might be the case, no withholding at all, that is, a complete exemption from taxes. Nowhere does that treaty authorize an exception to the usual rule that compels 30 percent withholding by a U.S. casino on the full amount of gambling winnings received by a Canadian.

Nor would my advice differ had you suffered any gambling losses during your visit to the U.S. According to IRS guidelines: "You must report the full amount of your winnings. You cannot offset losses against winnings and report the difference." *Result:* No recovery of the $3,000, if your losses are sufficient to offset your winnings of $10,000.

As it happens, there is a different, more favorable, set of rules for someone who is a U.S. citizen or a resident alien. Those rules similarly tax gambling winnings; however, gambling *losses* are deductible up to the amount of winnings, a relief provision that, as I explained, is unavailable to someone like you.

Understandably, odds are that you are unlikely to appreciate the appropriateness of that distinction. Moreover, you might even be inclined to view the rules for foreign tourists as an example of governmental rapacity on the part of the U.S.

13 FILING TIPS

GET THE RIGHT HELP AT TAX TIME

Form 1040 simplicity: the quintessential oxymoron. You have lots of company if you think continuous changes in the tax laws make your 1040 too complicated to handle with just the filing instructions that accompany your return. The Internal Revenue Service estimates that nearly half of all taxpayers (more than two-thirds of those who file the 1040 form, the more complicated long form) think the answer to the annual filing chore is to hire someone to decipher dozens of pages of mind-boggling instructions that are revised each year and then to select, from among the steadily growing list of different supplementary forms, schedules, and worksheets, the ones that should be used to detail income, claim deductions, credits, exemptions, exclusions, and deferrals, and calculate the tax.

Fade back to 1970, when Senator Charles McC. Mathias, Jr., of Maryland sought to make the once-a-year affliction caused by the need to grapple with the 1040 less time-consuming. To help attain that estimable goal, he sponsored the following legislation (known officially as Senate bill 3719, 1970):

> Be it enacted by the Senate and House of Representatives of the United States of America in Congress assembled, that it is the intent of Congress that, for the relief and assitance of American taxpayers, all forms, schedules, returns, declarations, manuals, instructions, tables, and other materials prepared and distributed by the Internal Revenue Service for public use shall be as clear, concise, and comprehensible as possible. It is the further intent of Congress that common everyday American English shall be used wherever and whenever possible in all such materials intended or required to be used by large numbers of individual taxpayers.

Fortunately for the national interest, as well as for tax mavens like me who get paid to explain the Internal Revenue Code and have families to feed, an understandably upset IRS persuaded Congress it would be a dereliction of legislative responsibility for the Gang of 535 to approve such a proposal.

Should you go it alone or hire someone to fill out your 1040? The answer depends on your particular situation. Is your income mainly from salaries, with some interest and dividends, and you take the standard deduction (see Chapter 1) or it is easy to compute your itemized deductions for charitable contributions (Chapter 8), real estate taxes, mortgage interest, and state income taxes? You probably are able to file without paid help or with free help available from taxpayer assistance programs offered by the IRS, state agencies, and many volunteer organizations, such as the American Association of Retired Persons.

Odds are, though, that tax help is advisable when, for instance, you have business or rental income, buy or sell a personal residence (see Chapter 3 for home sales), start or end a marriage (Chapter 4), make a job-related move (Chapter 5), invest in limited partnerships, receive a severance package from an employer, or withdraw money from IRAs, 401(k)s (Chapter 10 for IRAs and 401(k)s), Keogh plans, or other retirement arrangements.

Tip. The complex changes introduced by the Tax Reform Act of 1986, as well as by later law revisions, might compel you to use a paid preparer. Before you choose one, here are some important points to note.

- Anyone can set up shop and hang out a shingle as a tax preparer. There are no national educational and professional requirements.
- Your best bet to find suitable help: word-of-mouth recommendations from relatives, friends, or those with business and financial situations similar to yours.
- Ask about the fee structure. Be suspicious of someone who fails to review your return for last year before deciding how long it will take and how much it will cost to do this year.

Tip. Want to cut the cost considerably? Prepare the return yourself and take it to a qualified tax professional who is willing to charge a greatly reduced fee for its review. Should it prove necessary to redo the return, you pay a lot less because you have already done a good deal of the work.

Caution. The fees you pay are likely to be only partially deductible, if at all. The hitch is that tax reform drastically restricts deductions for payments to return preparers. Those outlays, along with safe deposit box rentals, union dues, and most other miscellaneous expenses that are listed as itemized deductions on Schedule A of Form 1040 are allowable only to the extent that their total exceeds 2 percent of your AGI, short for adjusted gross income.

Example. If your AGI is $40,000, the 2 percent floor bars a write-off for the first $800 of preparer fees and other miscellaneous expenses. AGI is governmentalese for the amount you enter on Form 1040 after reporting salaries, dividends, and other kinds of income and deducting such items as contributions to retirement plans and alimony payments. The AGI figure is before claiming the standard deduction or itemizing for outlays like charitable donations.

Exception for Schedule C, E, or F preparation. You get a break for the portion of your fees that are allocable to Schedule C (business income from self-employment), Schedule E (rental income from stores, vacation homes, or other properties; royalties; and partnerships) or Schedule F (farm income). List such fees as "above-the-line" adjustments that you subtract from gross income to arrive at AGI. Consequently, you can fully deduct them on Schedule C, E, or F, instead of as a miscellaneous deduction subject to the 2 percent floor. (For the rules on miscellaneous deductions, see the discussion in Chapter 9.)

Tip. Turning records over to your return preparer? It is prudent to photocopy all vital checks and other documents that support deductions and other items on your return. Documents do get lost.

Commercial Preparers

Most individuals who seek paid help use commercial return-preparation services. Some of these firms do business only on a local basis, whereas others maintain offices throughout the country—the best known being H&R Block (with which I have no connection, despite the same last name). Before you go that route, however, here are some points to keep in mind.

Every year, consumer protection agencies are inundated with complaints from victimized taxpayers about their frustrating experiences with commercial return-preparation services, companies that are not of equal quality. Some tax services do a much better job of training their helpers than others.

Consider this annual scenario: Many commercial preparers are hard put to hire enough trained help during the filing season, a circumstance that forces them to use moonlighters with little return-related experience. To make matters worse, a high percentage of these employees are hired just before the tax season starts and put through fast training courses that make them only slightly more knowledgeable than their customers about how to properly fill out forms. Worse yet, they are paid on the basis of the number of returns completed.

Predictably, the key complaints about commercial preparers are always the same— dishonest advertising that conceals hidden charges so that clients wind up shelling out more than they save in taxes, and slipshod work by self-designated "experts" that leaves taxpayers in trouble and in debt to the tax collectors.

What if something goes wrong with your return? At a minimum, you'll be involved in some correspondence with the IRS; at the worst, you might be hauled in by the IRS for an audit and asked to justify certain facts and figures on your return. More often than not, an audit means extra taxes, interest charges that, like other kinds of consumer interest payments, are nondeductible (see the discussion of interest deductions in "Timing Payments of Deductible Expenses" in Chapter 1), and perhaps penalties, also nondeductible.

Tip. To spare yourself some unnecessary grief, follow these recommendations from New York City's Department of Consumer Affairs on how to deal with commercial return preparers:

- Read the company's advertisement carefully. Will the firm actually fill out your return or, as some do, just charge you a consultation fee for tax advice?
- Watch out for "lowball" operators who attract customers with minimum price advertisements that quote a fee of, say, "$20 and up." That $20 is the absolute minimum you can expect to pay.

Caution. Avoid being hit with a hefty "and up" charge for "extras" such as completion of state forms. Tell the firm exactly what type of help you need; then ask for a written statement of the complete cost of its services.

- Don't be misled by the advertisements that read "$10 per tax return." Odds are that this fee covers only the cost of filling out federal or state short forms that call for little information.
- Ask the preparer to identify him- or herself and state what kind of training he or

she has before you allow that person to deal with your returns.

- Find out what responsibility, if any, the preparer assumes for the accuracy of your returns. If he or she assumes any responsibility, make certain to request a written guarantee.
- Insist that the preparer sign your returns, insert his or her address and identifying number on them, and provide you with copies. The law requires paid preparers to do so. (See "Penalties for Preparers" later in this chapter.)
- Be sure to ask for—and to keep—a written receipt for all the money you pay to a tax service.

Tip. You can include the payment with your other itemized deductibles under "miscellaneous deductions" on Schedule A of Form 1040 for next year, and you need the receipt in case the IRS questions your deductions. But most miscellaneous itemized deductions are allowable only to the extent that their total in any one year exceeds 2 percent of your adjusted gross income. (For the rules on miscellaneous deductions, see the discussion in Chapter 9.)

- Report any deceptive ads or other irregularities to your state or local consumer protection agency.

The burden is still on you. It's not just consumer protection agencies that have misgivings about some return preparers. The IRS issues this yearly warning to those who plan to hire help at tax time: "You are still responsible for the accuracy of every item entered on your return. If there is any underpayment, you are responsible for paying it, plus any interest and penalty that may be due. There-

fore, you should be careful to choose someone who understands tax matters and will prepare a complete and accurate return."

Here are some reminders from the IRS on how to guard against dishonest preparers.

1. Beware of an adviser who "guarantees" you a refund before completing your return, or who bases the fee charged on a percentage of the refund, or who claims to "know all the angles." Most likely, such an adviser will not be around to answer any questions that might arise after the return has been filed.
2. Never use a preparer who suggests that you omit income, overstate deductions, or claim fictitious dependents.
3. Do not allow a refund check to be mailed directly to the preparer, rather than directly to you.
4. Never sign a blank return; that's like signing a blank check.
5. Never sign a return prepared in pencil, because the computations can be changed later.

Enrolled Agents

Does your return require more knowledgeable and comprehensive assistance than commercial preparers usually are able to provide? Your choices are not limited to certified public accountants or attorneys. Another option, often overlooked, is Enrolled Agents (EAs). They are the only tax preparers required by the IRS to demonstrate special competence in the field of taxation.

There are two ways for EAs (who are not state-licensed CPAs or attorneys) to earn their designation. They have worked for the IRS for at least five years or have successfully completed a rigorous two-day exam on taxes. The yearly IRS-administered test is no snap. Typically, only 30 percent of the test-takers pass.

Moreover, the IRS insists that EAs stay on top of continual law changes. To maintain their IRS accreditation, they have to take continuing professional education courses courses in federal taxes—another confidence builder for prospective clients.

Fees. EAs typically charge more than commercial preparers but less than CPAs and attorneys, who are not necessarily tax experts, unless they have chosen to develop their expertise in that area. Like CPAs and attorneys, many EAs calculate their charges on an hourly basis, as what they are selling is their knowledge of how to use the tax laws to your advantage.

How to find an enrolled agent. There are over 30,000 EAs nationwide. To obtain a free list of EAs in your area, call the National Association of Enrolled Agents (NAEA) at its toll-free number, 1-800-424-4339, or write to the NAEA at 200 Orchard Ridge Drive, Suite 302, Gaithersburg, MD 20878. Many EAs are also listed in the Yellow Pages under "Tax Preparation."

Audits. Besides preparing returns, EAs can represent taxpayers at audits and at all stages of the IRS appeals process following audits, just the same as CPAs and attorneys. You do not have to appear with a representative if you have granted that person a power of attorney (IRS Form 2848) to negotiate a settlement or appeal the findings of an IRS examiner.

Unlike lawyers, CPAs, and EAs, commercial preparers cannot represent taxpayers, though many of these firms advertise that they will "accompany" their customers before the IRS. For example, the IRS allows an

H&R Block employee to attend an audit with you only to explain how the figures on your return were computed. This can be an important distinction in the event that the feds question your return and you are unable to settle a disputed item with the examining agent. (For more information on audits, see Chapter 11.)

CPAs and Attorneys

Depending on what kinds of income you have and the complexity of your financial life, you might be a prime candidate for a CPA or attorney, many of whom offer year-round help as return preparers and tax planners. Typically, you need more than return preparation when, say, you start a business or have a variety of investments, or there are tax implications to an important change in your life, such as marriage, divorce, retirement from a job, or a move to a new state. Attorneys tend to charge higher fees than CPAs, and both groups charge more than commercial preparers or EAs.

Help from the IRS

The IRS provides a broad variety of services without charge if you are an intrepid individual who is willing to go one-on-one with the feds by filling out your own tax forms or if you just want to check the accuracy of the person you hire to complete your return. For starters, there is the agency's annual best-seller, *Your Federal Income Tax* (also known to the tax man as Publication 17).

Your Federal Income Tax can be invaluable because it furnishes far more information about specific situations than is supplied in the instructions that accompany your return. The publication's several hundred pages contain numerous examples, as well as sample filled-out forms that take you on a line-by-line journey through the perplexities of Form 1040 and other schedules and forms that you may have to submit.

This tax manual thoroughly covers such items as reporting income from salaries, dividends, and other sources (for more on what must be reported, see "Adding Up Your Taxable Income" later in this chapter) and whether to itemize your outlays for donations to charities and the like or to take the standard deduction that you automatically get without having to itemize (see "Itemizing versus Standard Deduction" in Chapter 1). Its front section highlights important changes in the tax rules over the past year so that you can take these changes into account before filling out your return.

According to the IRS, its comprehensive tax guide provides nearly all the answers to questions and problems that are likely to come up when you do your returns. For the most part, it does give complete explanations in plain, uncomplicated language. Some segments, however, can be tough reading if your IQ is below 180; others are helpful only if you have difficulty falling asleep.

Besides *Your Federal Income Tax,* the feds offer a laundry list of other helpful booklets that focus on specific subjects. The topics include Individual Retirement Accounts and the kiddie tax on investment earnings of children under age 14. (For the rules on IRAs and kiddie taxes, see Chapter 10). IRS Publication 910, *Guide to Free Tax Services,* provides a complete list of booklets and explains what each one covers. All of these publications are free, which means that your tax dollars already paid for them.

There are several ways to obtain copies of IRS publications. You can call 1-800-TAX-FORM, use the order form in the instruction booklet for Form 1040 (during the filing season, allow at least 10 work days for delivery of publications ordered by telephone or letter), or stop by the IRS office serving your area to get them immediately. Many libraries also have copies of IRS tax guides.

Reach out and touch the tax takers. The Form 1040 instructions include a list of IRS toll-free telephone numbers to call for answers to your federal tax questions. The instructions also reveal that IRS supervisors occasionally listen in on these conversations to ensure that "employees give courteous responses and accurate information." But the IRS swears that "no record is kept of any taxpayer's name, address, or Social Security number," except where, at the taxpayer's request, a follow-up telephone call must be made.

The monitoring of conversations was, in part, triggered by IRS surveys. These surveys revealed numerous errors made by staff members who handled millions of telephone and walk-in inquiries from persons who needed help with their returns. Surprisingly, many of the errors were in favor of the taxpayers.

Other shortcomings in the assistance that the IRS provides were uncovered in surveys conducted by Congress. For example, many persons who dialed for answers to their questions were stymied by busy signals or gave up after being put on "hold." To really twist the knife, many who endured a lengthy wait on hold were eventually rewarded for their perseverance with a recorded announcement that the office was closed for the day.

Tip. To get through more quickly during the filing season, telephone during the middle or end of the week, but not at midday. Throughout the week, the period of peak demand for assistance is around noon, when people devote their lunchtimes to tax time. Avoid Mondays, which are usually the busiest days.

Some Words of Caution

Despite the numerous errors made by the IRS, the law permits the agency to disclaim all responsibility for inaccurate information that its employees give as answers to telephone or walk-in inquiries or that it prints in its publications. For instance, you cannot absolutely rely on the advice in *Your Federal Income Tax,* which warns that "you are still responsible for payment of the correct tax." This has been made expensively clear to more than one person.

Consider the New York taxpayer who relied on a mistaken comment, since corrected, in *Your Federal Income Tax* and deducted a loss on the sale of his home. When the IRS disallowed his write-off, he took his case to the Tax Court, where he ran afoul of a long-standing rule. The only authoritative sources of law in the tax field, noted the court, are the Internal Revenue Code and the IRS's administrative regulations. An informal IRS publication simply isn't authoritative.

In another case involving IRS misinformation, the judge ruled that it was "not reasonable" to rely on the word of an IRS employee, because a taxpayer's "only recourse is to vigilant self-protection of his interest."

Another drawback to IRS help: Its publications reflect only the agency's point of view on how to interpret the frequently fuzzy language in the tax statutes. In most cases,

that is all that matters. But tucked away inside the front cover of *Your Federal Income Tax* is the warning that it "covers some subjects on which a court may have made a decision more favorable to taxpayers than the interpretation of the Service. Until these differing interpretations are resolved by higher court decisions or in some other way, this publication will continue to present the interpretation of the Service." Put less elegantly, the publication ignores court decisions that often interpret the law more liberally than the IRS does.

Tip. Because *Your Federal Income Tax* is not copyrighted, you can pick up a commercial version of it at drugstores and supermarkets during the filing season. Some enterprising publishers simply remove the cover from *Your Federal Income Tax,* replace it with their own—calling it "Official Tax Guide," or some similar title—and sell information that the IRS provides for free.

One last reminder: Whether you rely on paid preparers or free taxpayer assistance programs, you are ultimately responsible for the accuracy of your return. By knowing what kinds of advice to avoid—and where to get sound tax information—you will save yourself some big headaches down the road.

PENALTIES FOR PREPARERS

Figuring out your income tax has become so complicated it's created a whole industry that provides work for thousands of people—high-powered tax lawyers and accountants and thriving businesses such as H&R Block. In

times when unemployment is so high that could be considered a boon to the economy.
—*The Wall Street Journal*,
July 28, 1982

If you decide to use a return preparer, don't be surprised if you are asked to provide detailed information about income, deductions, and other items. Despite a longstanding rule that holds you responsible for errors on your return even if you pay someone to complete it, the preparer may have to shoulder some of the blame if the tax liability is understated.

The law authorizes the Internal Revenue to exact penalties from a preparer. One of these sanctions is a nondeductible penalty of $250 for an understatement of tax that is due to the preparer's taking an "unrealistic position" in the case of a deduction or some other item on the return. The penalty, which is assessed on a per-return basis, rises to $1,000 for an understatement due either to (1) willfulness or (2) negligent or intentional disregard of IRS rules. Moreover, the feds do not have to unduly exert themselves to establish willfulness, as the following case demonstrates.

James Pickering, a CPA, had been preparing the tax returns for A.P.T. Construction Company. An IRS audit revealed that A.P.T. had paid and taken deductions for a number of personal expenses of the company's shareholders, including telephone service and gasoline and repairs for cars.

A federal district court held Pickering was liable for a penalty of $1,000 for willfully understating A.P.T.'s tax liability. In his appeal to the Eighth Circuit, he claimed that although he might have made a mistake, there was insufficient evidence to show "willfulness" on his part. The appellate court disagreed. True, the evidence against him was "weak." Nevertheless, there were more than enough facts to hang him.

Most damning was the testimony of the company's bookkeeper. She'd been aware that A.P.T. paid many personal bills for shareholders. On one occasion, the bookkeeper asked Pickering "what the IRS was going to say about some of our personal expenses if they ever came to audit." Pickering's response: "Don't worry about it."

Both the trial and appellate courts agreed that Pickering couldn't ignore a red flag like that. The bookkeeper's statement called for further investigation on his part. The CPA's failure to probe deeper amounted to "willfulness." That doesn't require fraudulent intent or an evil motive, only a "conscious act or omission made in the knowledge that a duty is therefore not being met."

The hefty penalties that the IRS routinely collects from accountants, attorneys, and other tax professionals underscore the intention of the agency to push enforcement of these sanctions to pressure preparers to act less like representatives of their clients and more like revenue agents in disguise. Consequently, even those risk-taking preparers who once seemed eager to go to the mat with the tax gatherers are no longer willing to accept without question all the figures submitted by you and to fill out a return on the basis of those figures. To protect themselves, most reputable preparers will ask searching questions to make sure that the figures you furnish are supported by evidence, where necessary, and they may ask for additional information where such information may change the tax effect of the figures furnished.

To add clout to the penalty drive, IRS computers are programmed to identify preparers *and their clients*. So when the feds want information about a particular preparer, they are able to obtain the identities of all clients for whom that person prepared Form 1040s. This provides the IRS with ready access to clients of any preparer hit with a number of preparer penalties in the event that the agency decides to check out more of the returns he or she prepared.

The Internal Revenue Code authorizes a host of other penalties for preparers. There are penalties for, among other things, failing to furnish copies of returns to taxpayers and failing to sign their names or to list their identifying numbers on those returns.

Tip. The preparer penalties apply only to persons who do returns for compensation. *Result:* They need not concern you if you do your neighbor a favor and fill out a Form 1040. The law does not consider you to be "compensated" if your neighbor insisted on inviting you to dinner or mowed your lawn in return.

Caution. The preparer penalties are in addition to other penalties that the IRS can slap on John or Jane Q. Taxpayer for their own miscues, such as improper deductions, late filings (see "Late-Filing Penalties" in Chapter 14), or tardy payments.

How to Avoid a Hassle with the IRS

The Income Tax has made more Liars out of the American people than Golf has. Even when you make one out on the level, you don't know when it's through if you are a Crook or a Martyr.

> —Will Rogers,
> "The Illiterate Digest," 1924

Pay taxes early and do paperwork correctly. When it comes to the IRS, it's not just the substance that counts, it's the form as well.

> —from an IRS TV commercial

There can be trouble ahead if the Internal Revenue Service spots a mistake on your return. At a minimum, you will be involved in some time-consuming correspondence with the IRS. At the other extreme, your return might wind up being subjected to an audit, with proof demanded to justify exemptions, deductions, and other facts and figures. So avoid mistakes that direct the attention of the IRS to your return and spare yourself some unnecessary grief.

General Reminder. Here are some reminders on items to check before you sign your return and send it in, along with some tips on steps to take after you file.

- Get an early start on the preparation of your return, particularly if you have a refund coming. Even if you will owe Uncle Sam more money, an early start gives you additional time to plow through often complex filing instructions, track down misplaced records, and get extra tax forms and instruction booklets on subjects that intrigue or confuse you. There is no way more certain to generate errors or overlook opportunities to save than scrambling to complete a return at the last minute.

Tip. Do you need forms or booklets as the filing deadline approaches? Try your local library for booklets and blank forms that you can photocopy. That might be the fastest way to get the ones you need when your fellow taxpayers are inundating the IRS with demands for help.

- Using a return preparer? Meet as early as possible during the filing season. The earlier your appointment, the more time the preparer has to uncover opportunities to save you money.
- First meeting with the preparer? Bring along prior returns. In some cases, reviewing past filings uncovers miscues that require amending (see "Refund Claims" in Chapter 14) or ways to trim the tab that you might now be overlooking.

Tip. Need a copy of an old return, but unable to find it? Use IRS Form 4506 (Request for Copy of Tax Form) to obtain a copy. (For more information on Form 4506, see "Paperwork" in "Coping with the IRS after April 15" in Chapter 14.)

- Read carefully the instructions that come with your Form 1040. Those instructions, which include plain-language explanations of changes in the tax laws, are essential in accurately preparing your return.
- File early if you expect a refund. The earlier you file, the quicker IRS sends it; the sooner the money is in your hands, the earlier it begins earning interest.
- Procrastination pays if there will be a balance due when filing Form 1040. By waiting until April 15 to send in the payment, the money continues to earn interest for you.

- Unable to complete Form 1040 by the April 15 due date? By April 15, submit IRS Form 4868, which lets you push the deadline back until August 15. (See "More Time to File Your Return" in the next section of this chapter.)
- Don't time your return based on your audit odds. It makes no difference whether you file early, late, or in between. All returns, regardless of when filed, go through IRS computers that evaluate them for audit potential. (See "Audit Odds" in Chapter 11.)
- Be certain that you check the correct box indicating your filing status and the correct boxes for exemptions. For instance, don't check the box for "single" instead of "head of household."

Tip. Married couples cannot switch from joint to separate returns after the filing deadline expires. But they can switch from separate to joint filing within three years after the deadline.

- Can you be claimed as a dependent on the return of someone else, such as your parent? You must check a box to indicate that is so. There is a reason for this requirement. As a dependent of another person, you cannot claim an exemption for yourself on your own return.
- Are you a noncustodial parent who is claiming a child as a dependent? You need to submit IRS Form 8382 with your return.
- List Social Security numbers for children and other persons one year or older who are claimed by you as dependents. Failing to report the numbers or listing incorrect ones could subject you to a penalty of as much as $50, as well as the possible

disallowance of an exemption. (See Chapter 2 for dependency exemptions.)

Reporting Income.

- Use the correct line to list income, deductions, or other items, such as the amount of tax due or to be refunded. Fill in all the lines that apply to you.
- Attach a Copy B of each W-2 form you receive that shows wages paid and tax withheld. Keep Copy C for your own records. Incidentally, hold on to your payroll stubs until you get your W-2 form and double-check its accuracy. If you do not receive your W-2 form from your employer by January 31 or the one you have is incorrect, contact your employer and ask that the W-2 form, or a corrected one, be sent to you.

Tip. If you are unable to obtain your W-2 by February 15, contact your local IRS office for Form 4852 (Employee's Substitute Wage and Tax Statement). As a substitute for an unreceived W-2, you can submit Form 4852. On it, you give your best estimate of the amounts that would have been shown as wages paid and taxes withheld on the missing W-2.

Caution. If you subsequently receive a W-2 with amounts that differ from those on the Form 4852, you may need to file an amended return. (For more information on amended returns, see "Refund Claims" in Chapter 14.)

Tip. Suppose you file your return but forget to include a W-2 or some other attachment. What to do: Wait until the IRS notifies you to send in the missing document. If you submit it without the notice, the chances are

much greater of its becoming lost or misplaced and your becoming involved in otherwise avoidable correspondence.

- Don't attach 1099 forms, which are those information slips you get from banks and other institutions showing the amount to report as interest, dividends, or other types of income. The IRS gets its own copies.
- Report all income shown on 1099 forms and list the payers exactly as they are shown on the forms.

Example. You have total dividend income of $800, consisting of $500 from Corporation M and $300 from Corporation N. Your shares are held in a street name; that is, the dividend checks come directly from your broker, not from M and N.

To avoid running afoul of the IRS computers, list the broker as the source of the $800 dividends on your Schedule B (Interest and Dividend Income) of Form 1040, rather than listing $500 from M and $300 from N. That way, your Schedule B does not differ from the information listed on the 1099 from the broker, and subsequent IRS matching of 1040 returns and 1099 forms will not result in the agency mistakenly billing you for additional taxes, interest, and penalties on unreported dividends from M and N.

Caution. Check 1099s to make sure that they do not overstate the amount of income you received. Mistakes show up often enough to make the checking worthwhile.

Let's say Corporation P sends a 1099 that erroneously states you received dividends of $800, instead of $500. Do not just list the $500 you deem to be correct on your return without first asking P to send a corrected 1099. P is then supposed to send a revised 1099 that is marked "corrected" to you and to the IRS. If you fail to obtain a corrected 1099, odds are that the IRS will send a notice that asks you to explain the seeming $300 understatement.

Also check 1099s to see whether there has been any backup withholding, either because of a mistake or because you did not fill out a Form W-9 for an account with a bank, broker, or mutual fund that pays you dividends or interest. You are entitled to a credit for any taxes that have been withheld. In that event, add the amount withheld on 1099s to the withholding from salaries shown on W-2s, enter the total on the Form 1040 line for "Federal income tax withheld," and check the box on that line to show that some of the taxes listed are from backup withholding. Otherwise, you will be overpaying your taxes.

Tip. Many mutual fund investors overstate their profits or understate their losses from sales of fund shares because they fail to add dividends automatically reinvested in additional shares (on which they have already been taxed) to the cost of their original investments.

- On the Form 1040 line for "tax-exempt interest," list any you have, though it is not taxed. The interest is taken into account in determining the taxability of any Social Security benefits (see Chapter 15).
- Rental property losses come under complex rules. Generally, losses from tax shelter deals can offset only income from similar investments. Shelter losses cannot shield from taxation nonshelter income, such as wages. These tough restrictions are subject to several exceptions, including a special break for most owners of rental property who qualify as "active" managers—legalese for those helping to make decisions on such things as okaying tenants, setting rents, and approving capital improvements. They can deduct up to $25,000 in losses against other income. That break, though, begins to phase out when adjusted gross income (AGI) exceeds $100,000, and it vanishes when AGI surpasses $150,000. (Losses on rental properties are discussed in Chapter 10.)

- On the Form 1040 line for "other" income, remember to explain the source of what you receive from, say, gambling winnings or prizes.

Adjustments to Income

- Tax reform restricts deductions for Individual Retirement Accounts. Under the law applicable to tax year 1994, you are still eligible for this deduction of up to $2,000 if you are employed and neither you nor your spouse is covered by a pension plan at work. But limitations do apply if you file jointly and either of you is covered by a pension plan. To qualify for the full deduction, your AGI has to be less than $40,000 for a married couple filing jointly and $25,000 for a single person. Only a partial deduction is allowed when AGI is between $40,000 and $50,000 for a couple filing jointly and between $25,000 and $35,000 for a single person. Forget about any IRA deduction for someone covered by a pension plan when AGI exceeds $50,000 for joint filers and $35,000 for a single person.

Tip. You can file your return and claim an allowable IRA deduction before actually making the deposit to the IRA. But the money has to be deposited by April 15. Don't have the money available by then? You can borrow the funds or put it on your credit card.

Caution. Did you make a nondeductible IRA contribution? Fill out and submit Form 8606 with your Form 1040. Keep a copy of Form 8606 until you complete withdrawals from all IRAs opened. (For more on IRAs, see Chapter 10.)

Caution. As this book goes to press in the summer of 1994, Congress is considering changes in the rules for IRAs. The proposed legislation includes a provision that would allow more people to deduct contributions to their IRAs.

- The rules are complicated if you withdrew funds from a bank time savings account before the specified maturity date and the bank imposes a penalty in the form of a forfeiture of part of the interest earned and even some of the principal. Claim the forfeited-interest penalty on the line on Form 1040 for "penalty on early withdrawal of savings." It is one of those "above-the-line" adjustments, that is, a subtraction from gross income to arrive at AGI, rather than an itemized deduction.

Tip. You are entitled to deduct the entire penalty even if it exceeds your interest income. Just how much you get to deduct is supposed to be shown on the information return sent to you by the bank.

Caution. On the Form 1040 line for "taxable interest income," you must report the *entire* amount of interest credited to your account during the withdrawal year, *without* subtracting the penalty that you deduct elsewhere. Otherwise, you improperly take a double deduction for the penalty, a miscue that the IRS computers are programmed to detect.

- On the Form 1040 line for "alimony paid," a payer, usually the ex-husband, has to list the Social Security number of his former wife who gets those payments. He should be able to get her Social Security number from copies of returns filed when they were married. If he fails to list her number, the IRS is likely to send him a letter before it will process his return further.

Caution. Armed with a Social Security number, the IRS computers can cross-check the ex-wife's return to see whether his payments are listed as income by her on the Form 1040 line for "alimony received." To help persuade the ex-mate to comply with the information-reporting requirements, the law authorizes the IRS to collect a $50 penalty from her for failing to furnish her number to him in time and from him for failing to include her number on his return. There is no penalty, though, when the failure is due to reasonable cause and not to willful neglect.

Tip. The Form 1040 line for alimony paid provides space to list only one ex-wife's number and the amount paid to her. What should a man do when he makes payments to more than one ex-wife? He should attach a separate statement that lists all other ex-wives, their Social Security numbers, and the amounts paid to them (a computer printout is acceptable). If the ex-husband fails to send along that explanatory note, he should count on hearing from the IRS.

- Moving expenses in connection with a job-related move are allowable only if the new job adds at least 50 miles to your commute. Compute the deduction on Form 3903, which has to go with your Form 1040.

Tip. You have some leeway on the 50-mile minimum. The IRS does not require you to measure the distance on the basis of a straight line on a map. It's okay to calculate the mileage on the shortest of the routes that you would ordinarily travel. (For more on moving expenses, see Chapter 5.)

Itemized Deductions

- Itemizers should make sure not to claim too much on Schedule A of Form 1040 for medical expenses or miscellaneous deductions. Medical outlays count only if they run to more than 7.5 percent of your AGI. Miscellaneous expenses are allowed only for the part above 2 percent of AGI. Remember these rules if you make any last-minute revision in the figure you show for AGI. You must recalculate the nondeductible amounts for medical payments and miscellaneous expenses. And remember to revise your state or city tax forms. (See Chapter 7 for medical expenses and Chapter 9 for miscellaneous expenses.)

- Did you volunteer to raise money for charity or to perform other tasks, such as teaching Sunday school? You cannot take a charitable deduction for the value of your time and services. But your volunteer work does entitle you to claim un-reimbursed expenses as an itemized deduction on Schedule A. These allowables include such items as telephone calls, postage and stationery, supplies used in making baked goods for a charity sale, as well as the cost and cleaning of uniforms not adaptable to ordinary wear that you are required to wear while performing services.

Tip. A frequently omitted write-off is for travel to and from your volunteer work. If you use buses, trains, or taxis, simply record your fares and claim these as charitable travel. If you drive, claim 12 cents a mile (under the rules applicable to tax year 1994, the most recent year for which information is available as this book goes to press) or the actual cost of gas and oil, whichever is greater, plus a separate deduction for parking fees and highway tolls. Also, you can deduct for meals, lodging, and travel expenses on out-of-town trips required by your organization. (See "Volunteer Workers" in Chapter 8.)

Caution. Besides claiming deductions for contributions made with checks or cash, are you claiming a deduction of over $500 for noncash gifts of property like clothing and toys? Complete Form 8283 and submit it with Form 1040.

- On a casualty or theft loss resulting from a fire, auto accident, burglary, or similar event, remember that there is a two-step computation on Schedule A for your deduction. Such losses are deductible only if they amount to more than 10 percent of your AGI. Moreover, unless you use the property in your business, you get no deduction for the first $100 of each casualty or theft loss. (See "Casualty and Theft Losses" in Chapter 9.)

- Mortgage points are 100 percent deductible on Schedule A in the year of payment if you pay them to obtain a loan to buy, build, or improve (as when you add or remodel a room) your "principal residence," a term which is legalese for a year-round home, as opposed to a vacation retreat or property for which you charge rent. In most cases, there is no immediate deduction for points paid to refinance (with none of the proceeds used to pay for improvements) a mortgage on your principal residence. The points are deductible over the life of the loan. (For more information, see " 'Points' for Home Mortgages" in Chapter 9.)

- Gambling losses are allowed to the extent of winnings; but they can be claimed only as an itemized deduction. Use the standard deduction and you forfeit the loss deduction (see Chapter 12).

Caution. You suffer a partial disallowance of your allowable write-off for most itemized deductibles if your AGI is above a specified amount that is adjusted annually to reflect inflation—$111,800 for 1994. The disallowance is 3 percent of the amount by which your AGI surpasses $111,800. Put another way, you lose $300 in total deductions for every $10,000 of AGI above $111,800. The $111,800 figure drops to $55,900 if you are married and file a separate return; going that route does not raise the threshold for a couple to a combined $223,600. At the bottom of Schedule A are instructions that direct a person with an above-$111,800 AGI to a worksheet that is used to calculate the disallowance. (See "Curtailment of Most Itemized Deductions for Individuals with AGIs above a Specified Amount" in Chapter 14.)

Final Reminders.

- Set aside time to rummage through your personal records, including checkbooks, credit card statements, receipts, appointment calendars, and bills. Your objective: to find deductible expenses that would otherwise go unclaimed.

- Look for deductible items that usually do not appear in the checkbook. These include travel costs incurred to obtain medical care (see "Transportation Expenses" in Chapter 7), worthless loans (see "Lending Money to a Relative or Friend" in Chapter 9), worthless stocks (Chapter 10), and gambling losses, which are deductible up to the amount of winnings (Chapter 12).

- Review last year's return. See if there are items to be carried forward, such as capital losses from sales of stocks and other investments, which go on Schedule D of Form 1040 (see "Capital Gains and Losses" in Chapter 10), or a net operating loss from the active operation of a business (see "Business Losses" in Chapter 9).

- Be sure to securely attach to your return all required schedules and statements—for example, Schedules A and B, on which you itemize deductions and list interest and dividend income, or Schedule D, which lists gains and losses from sales of assets. Include your name and Social Security number on any IRS schedule or your own statement. Doing that will make it much easier for the IRS to associate them with your return in case they become separated from it.

Example. Suppose you had a loss on a stock sale in 1993. The cap on a deduction for capital losses might have barred a write-off of the entire loss on your return for 1993; after an offset against capital gains, no more than $3,000 of additional capital losses can be subtracted from ordinary income, such as salaries or pensions. But you can apply any unused 1993 losses against capital gains for 1994, as well as apply any remaining losses against as much as $3,000 of ordinary income.

Caution. Did you sell a personal residence? Report the details on Form 2119 and submit it with your Form 1040. This holds true even if you defer or exclude the entire gain or have a nondeductible loss. Note, too, that the real-estate broker or other person handling the settlement must report the sales proceeds to the IRS. This makes it easier for the feds to target homesellers who fail to declare their profits (see Chapter 3).

- Recheck your return and schedules to make sure you have no errors in your computations. If possible, have someone else review them, too.

A frustrated Los Angeleno telephoned his local IRS office because he kept getting a negative amount on his return. As he told the IRS, "The instructions said to subtract line 8 from line 7, and when I subtract 8 from 7, I keep getting minus one."

- Sign your return. On a joint return, both husband and wife must sign. Any person paid to prepare your return must also sign it as the preparer.

Caution. Your return is considered incomplete until you sign. A point worth noting is that the statute of limitations for an audit does not start to run on an unsigned return.

- Check the pre-addressed peel-off label on the cover of the forms package that you receive in the mail before you place it in the name and address block of the return you file. Be sure your name, address, and Social Security number are correct. Make necessary corrections on the label.

Caution. First write the information in pen in the name-and-address portion and then place the peel-off label over it. This could prevent your return from getting lost in case the label falls off or catches on something and is mistakenly ripped off. List your Social Security number if you do not use the label (or if you have not received a forms package for some reason). Transposed digits in a Social Security number can cause untold grief. If it's a joint return, the IRS asks that you list both of your numbers, even if one of you had no income at all.

Tip. Oddly enough, many taxpayers refuse to place the labels on their returns because they suspect that the codes and other symbols on the labels somehow aid the IRS in the selection of returns for audit. However, IRS officials insist that this is untrue; the agency uses these markings only to make it easier for the postal service to deliver blank forms and then to speed up the processing of completed forms and the issuance of refund checks.

When the label is attached to a taxpayer's return, the IRS transcription operator does not need to enter the taxpayer's name or address, provided no changes have been made to the label. Therefore, label usage helps to decrease processing time and costs.

- Use the pre-addressed envelope that came with your return. If you do not have one, or if you moved during the year, mail it to the IRS Service Center for the area where you now live.

Tip. The bar codes on pre-addressed envelopes represent postal ZIP codes and tax-form type that allow both the Postal Service and the IRS to machine-sort the envelopes. Machine sorting is faster and less costly than hand sorting.

- Make certain that mailings to the IRS bear the proper amount of postage and show a full return address. Otherwise, you could be hit with a hefty, nondeductible late-filing penalty. (See "Checks Payable to the IRS" in Chapter 14.)
- You are responsible for the accuracy of every line on your return even if you pay a preparer or you prepare it yourself with free help from an IRS taxpayer assistance program. That is why the IRS issues a yearly warning to choose a preparer "who understands tax matters and will prepare a complete and accurate tax return."

Planning Ahead

- Did you receive a large refund? To avoid a repeat, you might want to file a new Form W-4 (Employee's Withholding Allowance Certificate) with your employer and increase the number of withholding "allowances" (exemptions) that you take. (See "Is Your Withholding Out of Whack?" in Chapter 14.)
- Just because you receive a refund does not mean that you can forget about an audit. All it means is that IRS computers have checked arithmetic and other basic items. So make sure to file away those checks and other records that back up deductions and other items, as well as a copy of your return. You will need them

if the computers bounce your return. Generally, the IRS has up to three years to audit your return after you file it. (For a discussion of how long to keep records, see Chapter 11.)

- As one last step, open a file now for this year and start to save the information that you will need next year at tax time. (See "Make Tax Planning a Year-Round Job" in Chapter 1.)

ROUNDING OFF RETURN FIGURES

To cut down on arithmetic errors, the Internal Revenue Service allows rounding off figures to the nearest whole dollar, provided you do so for all entries on your return and accompanying schedules. This means that you drop amounts under 50 cents and increase amounts between 50 and 99 cents to the next dollar. For instance, $25.32 becomes $25.00 and $25.50 becomes $26.00.

If you have to add two or more amounts to figure the total to enter on a line of your return, include cents when adding the amounts and only round off the total.

Example. You receive two W-2 forms from employers; one showing wages of $5,000.55 and one showing wages of $18,500.73. On your Form 1040, you would enter $23,501 ($5,000.55 plus $18,500.73 equals $23,501.28), instead of $23,502 ($5,001 plus $18,501).

Caution. For most filers, rounding off usually makes little difference in their total tax. But the way the IRS sets up its Tax Tables, not keeping a close eye on the pennies can cost you a few dollars.

The Form 1040 instructions include Tax Tables that are supposed to make it easier for most persons to figure their tab. They show the tax due on taxable income (what is left after claiming deductions and exemptions, but before claiming credits) up to $100,000. But because the tables use $50 brackets, a difference of as little as one cent in taxable income can mean a difference of enough to notice in what you owe or get back.

Example. You file a joint return that lists taxable income of $36,949.99. Under the rules applicable to tax year 1993 (the most recent year for which information is available as this book goes to press in the summer of 1994), you pay tax of $5,542.00. But if your taxable income is $36,950.00, the table jumps your tax to $5,556.00, or $14.00 more.

Just how much more, or less, the one cent will cost depends, of course, on your table bracket and whether your filing status is single, married filing jointly, married filing separately, or head of household.

MORE TIME TO FILE YOUR RETURN

Death and taxes and childbirth! There's never any convenient time for any of them!
—Margaret Mitchell,
"Gone With the Wind," 1936

The law authorizes the IRS to assess stiff, nondeductible penalties against late filers who forget to obtain filing extensions, which are discussed below, and submit their Form 1040s after the usual April 15 deadline. Those penalties are in addition to interest charges.

For openers, there is a 5 percent late-filing penalty (see Code Section 6651). Generally, this penalty is 5 percent of the balance due (*after* subtracting taxes previously paid through withholding and estimated payments) for each month that the Form 1040 is late, up to a maximum of 25 percent. If the late filing is fraudulent, the monthly penalty is 15 percent, up to a maximum of 75 percent.

A special rule applies when a Form 1040 is at least 60 days late. The late-filing penalty is $100 or the balance due with the return, whichever is the lesser figure. *Translation:* No late-filing penalty when there is no balance due.

Sometimes the IRS will forget about a late-filing penalty. To get the tax collectors to undo an overdue-return penalty, you have to convince them that there was "reasonable cause" for your tardiness—say, destruction of your records by fire or flood. Not having enough cash on hand to settle the tab at filing time, even if you can prove it, is not reasonable cause that will get you off the hook for the late-filing penalty. (For what constitutes reasonable cause, see "Late-Filing Penalties" in Chapter 14.) Worse yet, a flagrant procrastinator may even wind up facing criminal charges. (See "Fear of Filing" in "Criminal Investigations" in Chapter 11.)

But an understanding IRS wants to help; it says that there is no need to panic if you need additional time to complete your return. You can get an automatic four-month extension to August 15 for filing Form 1040.

You do not have to explain why you seek to postpone the inevitable; all you have to do is fill out Form 4868, which is an easily completed application for extension.

There are several ways to obtain Form 4868. You can call 1-800-TAX-FORM, use the order form in the instruction booklet for Form 1040 (allow at least 10 work days for delivery of any form or schedule ordered by telephone or letter), or go to your local IRS office.

The fastest way to get Form 4868 might be to visit your local library. Every filing season, the IRS provides libraries with sets of tax forms for photocopying—among them Form 4868.

Make sure to mail Form 4868 by April 15, along with a check covering what you estimate you owe, after subtracting taxes previously paid through withholding from salaries and estimated payments. (See "Is Your Withholding out of Whack?" in Chapter 14.) That estimate of the balance due, as explained below, must be in good faith.

Include on any check payable to the IRS all the information necessary to credit the money properly—Social Security number, the tax year, and the form number. (See "Checks Payable to the IRS" in Chapter 14.)

Tip. Is it worth the bother to send Form 4868 by certified mail and get a return receipt from the post office from which the extension application is sent? The official IRS position is that a post office receipt is not conclusive proof; it shows only that you mailed something in an envelope, not necessarily your Form 4868. Still, it can't hurt to get a receipt if you fear that your application might be lost in the mail or by the IRS.

Do you want to really nail things down? Hand-deliver the application to your local IRS office; a clerk will stamp the receipt date on both the filed Form 4868 and the copy you keep. Then there should be no question that your request for an extension was submitted in a timely fashion.

Caution. An often-misunderstood rule is that an extension of time to file a return does NOT extend the deadline of April 15 to open and make a tax-deductible payment to an Individual Retirement Account. (For more on IRAs, see Chapter 10.) But a filing extension can give you additional time to decide whether to make a payment to a retirement plan for a self-employed person, whether a Keogh or a SEP (simplified employee pension plan), which is like an IRA, but without a $2,000 cap on deposits.

Tip. When you finally file your return, be sure to enter any payment you made with Form 4868 on the Form 1040 line for "amount paid with Form 4868."

Waiver of late-filing penalties. The IRS has relaxed the rules if you are unable to pay the balance due when you submit Form 4868. Previously, the IRS usually considered the application request on Form 4868 to be invalid and the return delinquent. Therefore, it assessed the late-filing penalty. Now, though, the IRS will waive the penalty. To qualify for the waiver, you must meet an August 15 deadline. By that date, you have to make full payment or arrange for partial payments in installments.

The IRS makes it easy to schedule installment plans. Just fill out Form 9465 (Installment Agreement Request) and attach it to the front of your return. Form 9465 allows you to request a monthly payment plan and specify the amounts you are able to pay each month and the monthly due date. (See "Unable to Pay Your Taxes? Ask to Pay IRS Monthly" in Chapter 14.)

Interest charges and late-payment penalties. There are a couple of possible hitches. For one thing, an extension of time to file is not an extension of time to pay. If it turns out that you underestimated the amount to send with Form 4868, you will be charged interest from April 15 on the balance due with your delayed return.

Caution. Like other kinds of consumer interest payments, interest on overdue taxes is nondeductible. (See the discussion of interest deductions in "Timing Payments of Deductible Expenses" in Chapter 1.)

Besides collecting interest, the IRS can charge a late-payment penalty if the balance due is either (1) more than 10 percent of the tax shown on your return or (2) not paid by August 15. Generally, the late-payment penalty is one-half of 1 percent of the unpaid amount for each month or part of a month, up to a maximum of 25 percent, unless you can show reasonable cause for late payment.

Low estimate can void extension. Carefully estimate the tax you owe, especially if you have income from sources not subject to withholding—for instance, earnings from self-employment, profits from sales of investments, or alimony. If you are too casual, the IRS has the authority to retroactively revoke your extension, notwithstanding that the agency originally accepted your application, and tack on those penalties for late filing and payment.

You do not have to "assemble an exact picture of your income" before asking for an extension. Nor does a sizable error make an estimate improper, according to a Tax Court decision, which approved the revocation of an extension obtained by Otis Crocker, a Mississippi attorney. But to challenge a revo-

cation, warns the Tax Court, there must be evidence to show that you searched your records, attempted to find missing documents, and gathered the data needed to make a good faith estimate.

Additional Extensions

Do you need a special extension of more than four months? To get an extension from August 15 to October 15, you must file Form 2688 or write a letter to the IRS explaining the circumstances. But if you have not taken advantage of the automatic extension, you will not get approval for a special extension unless you can show "undue hardship"—for instance, inability to apply for an automatic four-month extension on Form 4868 because you cannot estimate your taxes due to your receipts and canceled checks being destroyed in a fire or unavailable, as in a situation where the records are in the possession of your future ex-spouse, who refuses to make them available until after the divorce becomes final.

State Tax Returns

Requirements vary from state to state. Some states accept Form 4868 for extending the due date of your state return, while others require a separate application. Check the rules of the state in which you have to file returns, including the penalties for any underpayments of state tax.

ADDING UP YOUR TAXABLE INCOME

Count the day won, when, turning on its axis,
this earth imposes no additional taxes.
—Franklin Pierce Adams,
American columnist and author
and member of the Algonquin
Round Table (1881–1960)

Are you one of those taxpayers who think of the IRS as an insatiable beast that feasts on all of your income? Take heart. As a general rule, the law does authorize the IRS to cut itself in for a share of each dollar of your income, whether from earnings, investments, or what have you. But you should be aware that no taxes are due on a lot of the income that people receive. Knowing the more common exceptions may help to erase the tax bite when filing time rolls around.

Here are reminders on some forms of income that completely or partly escape taxes.

- Social Security benefits are taxable only if you are a middle- or upper-income retiree. Starting with returns for 1994 to be filed in 1995, you are taxed on up to 50 percent of those benefits when your pension, dividends, and other sources of income, *including* tax-exempt interest, is *above* a specified amount—between $25,001 and $34,000 for single persons or between $32,001 and $44,000 for couples filing jointly. You are taxed on up to 85 percent of those benefits when such income *exceeds* $34,000 for singles and $44,000 for joint filers.

    For 1993 and previous years, the IRS winds up with a lesser amount. You are taxed on up to 50 percent of those benefits when such income *exceeds* thresholds of $25,000 for singles and $32,000 for joint filers. (Taxation of Social Security benefits is discussed in Chapter 15.)

- Pension benefits are also subject to special rules. Just how much Uncle Sam siphons off from an employer-provided pension depends on whether you contributed your own funds to the plan. If you did, you are not taxed on your benefits to the extent that they represent a recovery of what you yourself contributed. If you did not, you are taxed on all of your benefits.

- Workers' compensation and similar payments are fully exempt from taxes. But what if you continue to receive your salary during the time that you are recovering and your employer requires you to turn over your compensation benefits to the firm? In that event, no tax is due on the part of your salary equal to the benefits that you turn over.

- Jury duty pay is taxed. But you are relieved of taxes on the jury pay if you must turn it over to your employer because your employer continues to pay your salary while you serve on the jury. You still have to list the pay on the line for "other income" on Form 1040, but you can deduct the amount turned over to your employer as an adjustment to income. Include that amount in the "total adjustments" deduction on the front of Form 1040. Note on the dotted line next to the total-adjustments figure that jury pay is included, and show the amount.

- Welfare payments are exempt from taxation, though they are taxable where fraudulently obtained, just the same as income from other illegal activities, such as embezzlement (Rev. Rul. 78-53).

- Ditto for veterans' benefits, such as

educational payments for college or other study and training or subsistence allowances.

- Money or other assets received as gifts or inheritances are never diminished by *income* taxes, although the IRS may exact separate *gift* or *estate* taxes on property transfers that exceed certain amounts. (For the rules on gift and estate taxes, see Chapter 16).

Tip. The IRS does collect income taxes on any interest, dividends, rentals, or other earnings that you later derive from investing such largesse.

Gift or pay. The courts are often asked to decide the troublesome issue of whether the money in question is compensation for services that should be listed on Form 1040 or a gift that completely escapes taxes.

Consider the unusual case of Rosa Runyon, who received $10,000 from her former bosses, Franklin Burford and Edsel Lucas, and was told by them that the money was a gift. Franklin and Edsel decided to be generous because they made windfall profits of more than $4 million apiece from the sale of their coal-mining company.

Several weeks after the sale, they each gave a personal check for $5,000 to Rosa; she had been a bookkeeper and receptionist for the company for seven years, but had left her job six years before the sale. The checks were accompanied by a handwritten note from Edsel advising her of the sale of the company by him and Franklin and of their awareness of the important role she had played in the formation of the company, especially during the hard, lean years, and that they wanted to show their appreciation for her contribution to the company's success by saying "Thanks,

Rosa" and by enclosing a check from each of them for $5,000.

Rosa asked her two benefactors whether she had to list the unexpected $10,000 on her Form 1040. Edsel told her it was a gift and not taxable to her, as did Franklin, an attorney who had practiced tax law for 10 years and taught the subject at a law school for three years. Yet her ex-bosses subsequently filed gift tax returns that did not include the payments to Rosa and similar payments by them to several other employees and former employees of the company. Moreover, both Franklin and Edsel wrote off as business expenses on their own Form 1040s the payment to Rosa and the other employees.

The IRS went after Rosa for income taxes on the $10,000, but the Tax Court held that the money was a nontaxable gift. The owners were in no way obligated to pay Rosa; she had been adequately compensated by the company for her services, had never been an employee of Edsel or Franklin, and did not expect to work for them in the future.

Franklin and Edsel also took business-expense deductions for payments of $30,000 to Jamie Abdella, another employee of the company. The Tax Court held that Jamie had received a gift. Said the court of the deductions claimed by Franklin and Edsel and their testimony that the payments were compensation: "Their generous impulse to make a gift was transformed by the time of the trial into a new economic impulse to save on their personal taxes. Regrettably, what was conceived and born in generosity was later debauched and disowned in avarice."

Tip. Severance pay counts as reportable income, just like regular salary; it is not a tax-free gift.

Usually, as explained below, scholarships

for tuition escape taxes. But the IRS has ruled that scholarships received by winners of beauty contests are payments for services rendered and taxes are due.

Election-night partying is an inherent part of campaigning; so, says the IRS, campaign funds can pay for the partying without the costs counting as reportable income to the candidate.

- Life insurance proceeds paid to you because of the death of the insured are not taxable.

- Earnings from working abroad, up to specified ceilings, are excused from taxes.

- Scholarships and fellowship grants come under special rules introduced by tax reform. Scholarship payments for tuition, fees, books, supplies, and equipment remain tax-free, provided you are a degree candidate. But scholarship funds that cover room, board, and other expenses are taxable. Ditto for payments for teaching, research, or other work required to receive the grant. And if you are not seeking a degree, even scholarship dollars used for tuition are taxable.

- Interest on bonds or other obligations issued by state or local governments is completely free of federal taxes. This break also applies to exempt-interest dividends received from mutual funds that invest in these bonds.

- Interest from U.S. Savings Bonds is reportable income. But the interest from Series E or EE bonds does not have to be reported until you cash in the bonds. Alternatively, you can report the interest as it builds up each year without cashing in the bonds.

Special rules for bonds bought in 1990 and later years. These rules excuse some indi-

viduals from taxes on interest from EE bonds that they redeem to pay educational expenses. The interest exemption break is available if these requirements are met. The EE bonds must be bought after 1989, owned by individuals age 24 or older at the time of issuance, and cashed in by them during a year when they pay tuition and fees at colleges and universities for themselves or for children or others for whom they can claim dependency exemptions. There is no break for bonds bought in the name of a child under the age of 24 or redemption proceeds used to pay for room and board. Also, there is an income test that disqualifies many individuals. The exemption begins to phase out when adjusted gross income is above a specified amount that is adjusted annually to reflect inflation. For tax year 1994 (the most recent year for which information is available as this book goes to press), the amount is $61,850 for joint filers and $41,200 for singles and heads of households. (For more on this exemption, see "The Kiddie Tax" in Chapter 10.)

Proposed legislation. As this book goes to press in the summer of 1994, Congress is considering a proposal to end the phaseout of the exclusion.

- Dividends, interest, or other earnings on funds in an Individual Retirement Account, Keogh plan, or similar retirement arrangement accumulate without being taxed. No tax is due until you begin withdrawals from the retirement plan. (IRAs and Keoghs are discussed in Chapter 10.)

- Car pool payments that you receive from riders are not taxed unless they run to more than your expenses. (See "Commuting Deductions" in Chapter 5.)

- Child support payments are not considered taxable income to the recipient, provided the divorce decree specifically distinguishes these payments from alimony, which is taxable.

- Rebates should not be mistaken for income. A rebate on the purchase of, say, a car is not income. It is considered a reduction of the car's price. (Note, though, that if you use the car in a business, the rebate reduces the available tax incentives, such as depreciation deductions.) Similarly, you are not required to report "dividends" on life insurance policies that actually are a return of some of your premium payments.

- A profit on the sale of your house or condominium qualifies for special tax breaks that allow you to postpone or even escape taxes. At any age, you can defer taxes on the gain from the sale of a principal residence, provided you buy or build and move into a more expensive dwelling. (If the second home costs less than the first, only the portion of the profits you invest in the second home is tax deferred.) The postponed profits will be taxed when you sell the second house, unless you again reinvest the proceeds in a home.

  Another break becomes available if either you or your spouse is 55 or over when you finally sell, provided you lived in the house for at least three years out of the five-year period ending on the sale date. You escape taxes on up to the first $125,000 of profit, including deferred gain from the prior sale of a home or homes. (For the rules on home sales, see Chapter 3.)

Proposed legislation. As this book goes to press in the summer of 1994, Congress is considering a proposal to index for inflation the once-in-a-lifetime $125,000 exclusion for a gain on the sale of a principal residence.

- Vacation-home rentals also come under special rules. If you rent out your cottage or condo for less than 15 days during the year, you do not have to declare any of the income you receive. This unique exemption provides a valuable loophole for less-than-15-day landlords with vacation homes (or year-round homes, for that matter) near annual events where rents soar for short periods—Indianapolis for the Memorial Day race, Louisville during Derby week, New Orleans during Mardi Gras, and Augusta during its Masters golf tournament, to cite examples. But go beyond the less-than-15-days limit and all the rental income becomes reportable. Check the rules carefully because the IRS can be sticky.

Proposed legislation. As this book goes to press in the fall of 1994, Congress is considering a curtailment of the exemption for vacation-home rentals of less than 15 days.

Help from the IRS

For more information, see IRS Publication 525, *Taxable and Nontaxable Income.* For a free copy, call 1-800-TAX-FORM (allow at least 10 work days for mailing) or stop by the IRS office serving your area to obtain one immediately. Many libraries also have copies of this and other IRS tax guides. IRS Publication 910, *Guide to Free Tax Services,* provides a complete list of booklets and explains what each one covers. (For a discussion of IRS publications, see "Get the Right Help at Tax Time" at the beginning of this chapter.)

Tip. Don't rely absolutely on IRS advice, whether it is information that employees give to telephone or walk-in inquiries or instructions that the agency prints in its publications. Mistakes in instructions or advice are inevitable, and the IRS is not bound by them.

AWARD WINNERS ARE LOSERS UNDER TAX REFORM

Senator Russell Long of Louisiana's definition of tax reform: Don't tax you, don't tax me. Tax that fellow behind the tree.

One of the sneakier consequences of the Tax Reform Act of 1986 is a limitation on a long-standing break for prizes and awards that honor the accomplishments of outstanding individuals, such as authors John Steinbeck, Issac Bashevis Singer, and Saul Bellow.

By way of background, you are liable for taxes on your winnings from lucky number drawings, television or radio quiz programs, beauty contests, and similar events, just as you are for bonuses and other awards received from your employer for outstanding work or suggestions.

Prior law, however, entitled you to an exemption from taxes for awards bestowed primarily in recognition of your past achievements in religious, charitable, scientific, artistic, educational, literary, or civic fields. Awards that can pass muster as tax-free

prizes include the Nobel Prizes, which were worth $1,600,000 in 1993.

This exclusion from taxable income is available only if you pass a two-step test. The first requirement is that you were named the winner without any action on your part, that is, you did not specifically apply for the award by entering the contest or proceeding. The second stipulation is that you are not obligated, as a condition of receiving the award, to perform substantial future services, such as teaching.

The revised rules retained the not-personally-seeking and no-future-services requirements and added a third one. The third requirement makes the tax break meaningless.

The law now grants tax relief for your award only if you assign it away from yourself to a charity. Specifically, you must "designate," that is, instruct the award-conferring organization to turn the proceeds over to one or more governmental agencies at federal, state, or local levels or to certain charities, such as schools or churches.

Predictably, the law includes some fine print that you ignore at your peril. The key condition is that there is a deadline for the designation. You become ineligible for the exclusion and have to count the award as reportable income if you fail to meet the deadline.

To stay in the good graces of the IRS, your designation and the awarding organization's fulfillment of that designation must occur before any prohibited use by you of the money or other property awarded. In the case of a cash award, the designation/fulfillment has to take place before you spend, deposit, or otherwise invest the funds. Also, you run afoul of the prohibited-use rule if you allow use of the property by someone else, such as a family member, in advance of the designation/fulfillment.

No double break. Can you convert what is supposed to be a restriction into a double break by combining tax-free treatment of the award with a charitable deduction for assigning the proceeds to, for example, your Uncle Sam or your alma mater? Not surprisingly, the feds anticipated that maneuver. The law specifically instructs the tax gatherers to disallow a charitable write-off for an assigned award.

THOSE TAXING AFFAIRS

To tax and to please, no more than to love and be wise, is not given to man.
—Edmund Burke, British political writer and statesman (1729–1797)

Our tax laws are usually spelled out precisely; it's real-life situations that don't always fall conveniently into place. For instance, there is a mile-wide definition of income that entitles the IRS to share in "all income from whatever source derived," including payments that are "compensation for services." On the other hand, the term "income" doesn't include gifts. As a result, the courts often have to resolve the troublesome question of whether a tax-free "gift" was actually a payment for services rendered. Not surprisingly, the question has come up when the IRS insisted on its share of sizable amounts received by women from men who were not their husbands.

Consider the unusual case of Thelma Blevins, a Louisville divorcee who was a jack-of-all-trades and became the target of a painstaking IRS investigation. Besides supervising a staff engaged in the oldest of professions, she occasionally filled in herself and staged unique shows for her guests. Among other things, the IRS charged that Jim Mulhall enjoyed a close relationship with Thelma and that the money he gave her before and after her divorce should have been reported on her returns.

Thelma and Jim told the judge that these payments were gifts that had been made "in contemplation of marriage" and not compensation. But the judge accepted the IRS's version of what these payments were for because they spanned a 12-year period and Jim made no attempt to shed his wife during that period.

Another gift-or-income bout involved Margaret Brizendine, a lady with a similar background. The way Margaret told it to the judge, she met a gentlemen at a restaurant in Roanoke, Virginia, and became his friend. During the next five years, he provided her with a house, a fur coat, and a weekly allowance. Margaret thought these items were gifts because she received them in exchange "for her promise not to engage in prostitution and to grant him her companionship." But the judge thought it was stretching things to call them gifts. In fact, he took a damned-if-you-do-or-don't approach and said payments for vowing to abstain are just as taxable as payments for services rendered.

Fortunately, the Tax Court doesn't always side with the IRS, and an understanding judge came to the rescue of Greta Starks. It all began in the pre-inflation 1950s when Greta, then in her twenties and employed occasionally as a Detroit fashion model, became involved in what the Tax Court discreetly described as a "very personal relationship" with a married gentleman in his fifties. He proceeded to spend a minimum of $65,000 on a shopping list that included a home, a new car, a piano, jewelry, furs, and clothes from Saks Fifth Avenue.

Somehow, the IRS discovered their arrangement and, besides arguing that Greta should have paid income taxes on the $65,000, it tried to collect self-employment taxes on the grounds that she had been engaged in a business venture.

Greta testified that the items in question were gifts and was backed up by her friend. He said the payments were made "to insure her companionship and were more or less a personal investment in my future." Though less than impressed with his testimony, the court decided that Greta had not performed services for pay and relieved her of any tax liability.

WHEN INCOME IS REPORTABLE

The President, when the IRS is concerned, I assure you, is just another citizen and even more so.

—President Richard Nixon, notes the April 15, 1974 issue of *Time* mazagine, "offered that wry observation exactly one month ago, when advance warnings had been posted that he might owe half a million dollars in back taxes."

When the Internal Revenue Service sends the forms for their annual reckoning, most individuals list their deductions and income on a "cash" basis. They deduct all their expenses in the year that they actually pay them and report all income items in the year they actually receive them.

Cash-basis taxpayers are also subject to a "constructive-receipt" rule. This rule requires them to declare as income amounts that, though not actually received, have been credited to their account (interest on savings, to cite a common example) or made subject to their control or set aside for them.

Similarly, you must count as income for the current taxable year a check that you receive in the mail on December 31, even though you receive it after banking hours and cannot cash it or deposit it to your account until January 2. Moreover, the IRS is unwilling to draw a distinction between the actual delivery of regular mail and the attempted delivery of certified mail. According to an IRS ruling, you constructively receive certified mail that arrives on December 31 when you are not home to sign for the mail (Rev. Rul. 76–3).

But an important point sometimes overlooked is that a revenue ruling is by no means the last word. It merely reflects the official IRS position on an issue and is not binding on the courts.

A case in point was the refusal of the Tax Court to rigidly apply the IRS guidelines on constructive receipt to Beatrice Davis. She was not home on the last day of 1974 when the Postal Service tried to deliver a letter sent certified mail, return receipt requested. By the time Beatrice arrived home to find notification of the office at which she could pick up the letter, the office had closed for the day. When the office reopened on January 2, she got some surprising news. Instead of an expected notice of a rent increase, the letter contained a $17,000 severance payment from an employer who had told her that the several months' processing required for a severance payment meant that the check would arrive well beyond 1974.

Along with her income tax return for 1974, Beatrice attached an explanation of why $17,000 that had been listed on her W-2 for

1974 was actually reportable income for 1975. The IRS, nevertheless, insisted that the $17,000 moved her into a higher-than-expected bracket for 1974 because the employer had committed the money to her that year.

That argument failed to sway the Tax Court. It pointed out that the payment must be made available without substantial limitations. "Implicit in availability is notice to the taxpayer that the funds are subject to his will and control." Such notice was lacking, the court noted, since Beatrice "had no expectation" that the payment would arrive in 1974. The Tax Court saw no reason to apply the constructive-receipt rule simply because Beatrice received notice of attempted delivery on December 31, where she had "no inkling" that the certified mail was her severance pay.

The Tax Court also sided with football star Paul Hornung, who ran afoul of the constructive-receipt rule when he was rewarded with a car on December 31 for setting a league record for scoring points in a championship game. Paul received a Corvette from *Sport* magazine for being named the outstanding player in the National Football League Championship game of 1961, which was played in Green Bay, Wisconsin. Shortly after the game ended, *Sport*'s editor told Paul of his selection as most valuable player that Sunday afternoon and that the key and title to his Corvette could be picked up at a car dealer in New York City.

Although Paul actually received his prize at an awards luncheon several days later, the IRS counted the car as income for 1961. But the Tax Court picked 1962, because there was no way Paul could claim his award until that year. *Sport* magazine had not arranged for the Corvette to be available immediately because the game was held in Green Bay and,

as the editor put it: "It seemed a hundred-to-one that the recipient of the award would want to come to New York on New Year's Eve to take possession" of the prize.

But the Tax Court held that the IRS properly refused to permit an executive to defer reporting part of a severance payment beyond the year in which he received the disputed funds in a lump sum. Joseph Ewers' job as a bank president came to an end on October 1. The bank's board of directors intended to send severance of $47,000 to him in equal amounts over a seven-month period, starting October 1. Instead, for reasons unknown, Joseph received all of his severance within a month after he lost his job.

Joseph reported three-sevenths of this amount on his return for the year in which he received the severance pay and the remaining four-sevenths on his return for the subsequent year. But the court held he had to declare the entire amount as income in the year of receipt, regardless of what the bank actually intended to do; there were no restrictions on his use of the money in that year.

A constructive receipt can occur when money is paid to someone else for you. This could happen, for instance, if your employer had to withhold part of your pay from you and turn it over instead to a creditor who had attached your salary. Although you never saw the money, you constructively received it and are taxed on it.

The Tax Court invoked this rule against Edwin Pilipski when the IRS levied on his IRA account of $14,000 to help pay part of a liability of $46,000 that had been assessed against him because of his failure to pay taxes withheld from the paychecks of his corporation's employees. (See "Hefty Penalty for Using 'Withheld' Dollars" in Chapter

14.) Hence, it made no difference that the IRA withdrawal had not first wound up in Edwin's hands before it was turned over to the IRS.

ANSWERS TO COMMON TAX PROBLEMS

Continual changes in the tax rules make it more important than ever to familiarize yourself with steps that can cut the tab at filing time. To help ease the annual chore, here are answers to some of the most frequently asked questions on what or how much is deductible, as well as tips on how to steer clear of pitfalls and take maximum advantage of often-overlooked breaks. If you need additional information in specific areas, contact the IRS or consult your tax adviser.

Joint or Separate Filing

Q. *My wife died this year. Does this mean I cannot file a joint return?*

A. Don't make the common mistake of figuring your tax bill by using the higher rates for singles or head of household just because you are a widower. You are entitled to file jointly for the year you become a widower (or widow).

What's more, check later on whether you qualify for the special break that allows a widower or widow with a dependent child—in tax jargon, a "surviving spouse"—the benefit of joint-return rates for two years after the spouse's death. And even if you don't meet all the tests for a surviving spouse, you may still be entitled to cut your tax by filing as head of household, instead of as a single person. (For more informa-

tion, see "Joint-Return Rates for Surviving Spouses" in Chapter 4.)

Q. *We can lower our taxes considerably by filing a joint return. But we did not get married until late October of 1994. Can we still file jointly for tax year 1994?*

A. Absolutely. It is your marital status as of December 31 that usually determines your filing status for the entire year. Therefore, the IRS considers you a married person for all of 1994, even if you had wed as late as December 31.

Going in the other direction, a divorce or legal separation, even one that took place as late as December 31, bars you from filing jointly for 1994. You are considered a single person for all of 1994 and must use the rates for singles or heads of households. (For more information, see "Marriage or Divorce as a Tax Shelter" in Chapter 4.)

Q. *My wife recently died. How should I sign our joint return?*

A. Assuming an executor or administrator has not been appointed, you should sign your name and add after your signature: "Filing as surviving spouse."

Q. *I live with another person of the same sex, and we enjoy a closer relationship than most of our married friends. Does that entitle us to save taxes by filing jointly?*

A. No. As things stand now, the IRS allows joint filing only by heterosexual couples who are legally married. Nor can either of you cut the tax bite by filing as head of household.

Q. *It pays for me to file jointly. But I don't want to reveal my income to my wife. Suppose I have her sign a blank return and then fill in the figures?*

A. Don't bother. She's entitled to a copy of the return from the IRS.

Q. *My wife refuses to sign our joint income tax return, just because our marriage may be going down the tubes. What can I do?*

A. A joint return must be signed by both spouses, even if only one had income. Since your wife refuses to sign a joint return, you must each file a separate return if either of you had income above a specified amount —$2,450, in the case of a return for tax year 1994.

Q. *If I file separately, claiming all the itemized deductions, can my wife file using the standard deduction for nonitemizers?*

A. No. Both individuals must use the same method of handling deductions. If you itemize, so must your wife.

What Is Reportable

Q. *I received a refund in 1994 of my state income taxes for 1993. Do I have to report that refund as income on Form 1040 for tax year 1994?*

A. Only if you claimed an *itemized* deduction for those taxes on your Form 1040 for tax year 1993 and the deduction decreased your 1993 federal taxes. But you do not have to report that refund on your 1994 form if you either (1) figured your tax the regular way for 1993, passed up itemizing, and used the standard deduction, or (2) were subject to the alternative minimum tax for 1993, which applies only when it produces a higher tax bill than the tax figured the regular way and, among other things, bars a deduction for state income taxes. (For more on the alternative minimum tax, see Chapter 14.)

Tip. Does your reportable income on Form 1040 include a refund of state taxes? Check the rules of the state in which you have to file a return. The refund generally escapes taxes when figuring your income for purposes of state income taxes. In New York, for example, it is a subtraction on page one of the return when computing New York taxable income.

Q. *I plan to spend my retirement years in Mexico. Does moving south of the border mean an otherwise reportable pension can escape the clutches of the IRS?*

A. Moving anywhere outside of the country won't help, because Uncle Sam taxes citizens wherever they live. Nor does going abroad mean you can disinherit the IRS when it comes to estate taxes. (For the rules on estate taxes, see Chapter 16.)

Q. *I had a jobless spell. Where in the Form 1040 instructions is the explanation of how to calculate the part of my unemployment compensation that escapes income taxes?*

A. Report the entire amount on the Form 1040 line for "unemployment compensation." Tax reform abolished the exemption from taxes for part or all of unemployment benefits, making jobless pay fully taxable.

Q. *My fiance decided to break our engagement two days before the wedding. So I kept his engagement gifts, including a very expensive ring. Must I pay taxes on these gifts?*

A. No. Gifts are not reportable as income on your tax return.

Q. *I received $50,000 for injuries I suffered in a car accident. Is it taxable?*

A. No. Compensation for personal injury or illness is not taxed, no matter how high.

Q. *My insurance company sent me a statement saying it paid dividends and interest on* *my life insurance policy. The company did not actually send me a check. Does any of the payment have to be shown on my 1040?*

A. The dividends are not taxable unless the dividends you have received exceed the premiums you have paid. Interest on dividends left on deposit is taxable.

Q. *I received a refund on my Form 1040, plus some interest. I know the refund is not reportable income, but what about the interest?*

A. The interest is taxable, just the same as interest from a savings account.

Q. *I own a building in which I leased space to an accountant last year. Since then, the accountant has made substantial improvements to her office. Do I have to report the value of these improvements as part of my rental income?*

A. No, provided the improvements are not a substitute for regular rental payments. (Internal Revenue Code Section 108). But you get no depreciation deductions for the improvements as you did not pay for them yourself.

When to Report

Q. *My bank credited interest of $500 to my savings account last year, but I didn't have it entered in my passbook until February of this year. Do I report the interest on my Form 1040 for the last year or this year?*

A. Report it on your return for last year. The $500 will be included in the Form 1099 for last year that you receive from the bank. (See "When Income Is Reportable" earlier in this chapter.)

Q. *Last week, I won $25,000 in our state lottery. Since I expect to be in a much lower tax*

bracket next year, can I wait until then to cash my ticket and thereby cut the IRS's share?

A. No. The money is yours for the asking; therefore, you must report all of it on this year's return, even if you do not collect your prize until next year.

Q. *My employer has given me an expense-paid vacation to Mexico next January as an award for my reaching the million-dollar sales mark. How will this affect my income taxes?*

A. You are liable for taxes on rewards and bonuses, including vacation trips paid to you for outstanding work. If such an award is payable at some future time at the option of your employer, it is not taxable until you receive it or your employer makes it available to you.

Moving Expenses

Q. *What requirements must I meet to deduct the cost of a job-related move?*

A. The key stipulation is that the new job location has to be at least 50 miles farther from your old residence than your old job was. An example: If the distance between your old home and your old job is 20 miles, the distance between your old home and your new job has to be at least 70 miles.

To do the paperwork, first compute your deduction on Form 3903. Then the amount entered on Form 3903 is carried to, and entered on, the Form 1040 line for moving expenses. (See "Moving Expenses" in Chapter 5.)

Q. *My company will reimburse several new employees for their moving expenses. According to my accountant, an employer is excused from withholding income and Social Security taxes from these payments. It this true?*

A. These withholding exemptions apply only to the extent that an employer "reasonably believes" an employee qualifies for the moving-expense deduction [Internal Revenue Code Section 3401(a)(15).] For example, these exemptions do not cover reimbursements for an employee's nondeductible outlays, such as a loss on the sale of a personal residence.

Taxes

Q. *For tax year 1994, how do I calculate my itemized deduction for state and local income taxes on Schedule A?*

A. Your allowable deduction includes taxes taken out from your pay during 1994, plus any estimated tax payments that you made during 1994. Also, be sure that your deduction includes any payments for 1993 or earlier years that you made during 1994. If there is a balance due on your 1994 state or city returns, take it as an itemized deduction on your Form 1040 for the year that you pay it.

Q. *Since so much of the cost of liquor and cigarettes goes for taxes, can I claim those taxes with my other itemized deductions?*

A. No deduction is allowed for federal or local cigarette or liquor taxes.

Q. *Can I deduct personal property taxes?*

A. Only if you forgo the standard deduction and itemize. In that case, a personal property tax may be deducted, provided it meets the following three conditions: (1) The tax must be based on the value of the personal property. (2) The tax must be imposed on an annual basis. (3) The tax must be imposed on personal property.

Q. *Are water and sewer taxes deductible?*

A. No. Generally, water and sewer taxes are nondeductible personal expenses.

Q. *Am I allowed to deduct Social Security taxes withheld from my wages?*

A. These taxes are never deductible.

Q. *Can I include the cost of lottery tickets with my itemized deductions for state taxes or charitable contributions?*

A. No. IRS rules for gambling losses apply to lottery tickets. The cost of those tickets can be taken as an itemized deduction to offset any kind of gambling winnings—lotteries, horse racing, cards, etc. But if there are no winnings, there's no deduction. (For the rules on gambling losses, see Chapter 12.)

Interest Deductions

Q. *Can we file jointly and also deduct mortgage interest and real estate taxes on our home when I'm the only one reporting income and the home is held in the name of my wife only?*

A. Yes. The IRS says a married couple can file jointly even if only one of them reports income. What's more, you don't lose out on the deductions for interest and taxes enjoyed by homeowners merely because title to your home is held in the name of a spouse who doesn't report any income.

Q. *Right after my son bought his home, he lost his job and was unemployed for four months. I made the mortgage and real estate tax payments for those four months, while he took care of some other obligations. Am I allowed to include my payments of his interest and taxes with my other itemized deductions on Schedule A?*

A. Forget about any tax break for your

generosity. Those expenses can be claimed only by the person who is legally bound to pay them—the property owner, ordinarily. *Result:* Both you and your son are ineligible for the write-off. What disqualifies you is that the payments are not your obligation; what disqualifies him is that he did not make the payments.

Tip.   If you again need to help out, the way to preserve your son's deductions for interest and taxes is for you to give or lend the money to him and allow him to pay those expenses.

Education Expenses

Q.   *Now that all my children are old enough to attend school, I want to complete my college education. What are the tax rules on deduction of educational expenses?*

A.   The IRS rules out any deduction if the expenses were incurred primarily either (1) to meet the minimum educational requirements for qualification in your *future* employment or trade or business, or (2) to qualify you in a *new* trade or business. This is so, even though the education maintains or improves skills required by you in your present employment or trade business or meets the requirement of your employer or requirements of law or regulations. But the IRS says you can claim a deduction for expenses for education if incurred primarily either (1) to meet the specific requirements of your employer or requirements of law or regulations for keeping your *present* salary, status, or employment, or (2) to maintain or improve the skills required in performing the duties of your *present* employment or trade or business.

Here's an IRS-approved example of how these rules work. You cannot deduct the cost of courses to meet the minimum requirements for obtaining a license to teach, say, art. But suppose you already teach art at a high school and want to switch to teaching mathematics. You can deduct the cost of courses to qualify as a math teacher.

For more information, get a free copy of IRS Publication 508, *Educational Expenses.*

Caution.   There is another hurdle before you can deduct educational expenses and other unreimbursed employee business expenses. They must be included with your other itemized deductibles under "miscellaneous deductions" on Schedule A of Form 1040. Most miscellaneous expenses are allowable only to the extent that their total in any one year exceeds 2 percent of your adjusted gross income (AGI). (For the rules on miscellaneous deductions, see the discussion in Chapter 9.) Moreover, educational expenses and other miscellaneous deductions are among the itemized deductions subject to a partial disallowance when you have an AGI above a specified amount, which is adjusted annually to reflect inflation—$111,800 for tax year 1994. The disallowance is 3 percent of the amount by which your AGI exceeds $111,800. (See "Curtailment of Most Itemized Deductions for Individuals with AGIs above a Specified Amount" in Chapter 14). Note, too, that there is no deduction for travel itself as a form of education. (See "Educational Travel Not Deductible" in Chapter 5.)

Q.   *I recently suffered a back injury that prevents me from doing chairside dentistry. I plan to return to school to obtain a degree in health administration. As I plan to continue working in the dental field, though in an administrative capacity, does that qualify me for an education expense deduction?*

A. Yes. In a situation comparable to yours, the IRS approved educational expenses incurred by a practicing dentist who returned to school full-time to study orthodontics. After completion of his schooling, he limited his practice to orthodontics. His postgraduate courses improved his professional skills as a dentist; they did not qualify him for a new profession, which would have made his outlays nondeductible (Rev. Rul. 74–78).

Q. *How will an IRS examiner react if a physician in general practice claims an education-expense deduction for courses that qualify him or her as a surgeon?*

A. No problem. As in the case of the dentist in the preceding question, the law allows a doctor to deduct the costs of qualifying for a speciality within the medical profession.

Dependent Care

Q. *My elderly aunt came to live with us after her retirement, and we take a dependency exemption for her. But we also have to pay someone to stay with her while we are at our jobs. Do those payments entitle us to claim a dependent-care credit?*

A. Only if she is disabled, which means a person who suffers from physical or mental disabilities that prevent her from dressing or feeding herself or tending to her personal hygiene without the help of someone else, or who needs constant attention to prevent her from injuring herself or others. (For more information, see "Qualifying Dependents" in the discussion of child- or dependent-care expenses in Chapter 6.)

Q. *We intend to send our son to day camp and our daughter to sleep-away camp. Which payments count toward the child-care credit for working parents?*

A. The cost of the day camp qualifies, as long as your son is under the age of 13, but not the fee for sleep-away camp.

Divorce

Q. *Under our divorce decree, I have to pay alimony to my ex-wife. The decree also requires me to repay a loan that I received from her before we married. Does the loan repayment count as part of my tax-deductible alimony?*

A. No. You get no write-off for the repayment of a loan, even if a divorce decree orders you to do so.

Q. *I'm filing for a divorce. Since my husband is again between jobs, I'm stuck with paying my legal fees, and they're out of sight. How much of a tax break do I get for my legal fees?*

A. Not much, unfortunately. You get an itemized deduction for legal fees incurred to obtain a divorce or separation only to the extent that those outlays are for tax advice. Moreover, revised rules curtail write-offs for miscellaneous itemized deductions, a category that includes payments for tax advice. Most miscellaneous deductibles are allowed only to the extent that their total in any one year exceeds 2 percent of your adjusted gross income. Anything below the 2 percent floor is nondeductible.

Tip. If your attorney's services include tax advice, make sure that the bill shows a breakdown between the nondeductible portion charged for the divorce and the deductible amount charged for tax advice that can be included with your other itemized deductibles. That way, assuming you surpass the 2 percent threshold, you can back up your deduction in case the IRS later asks any questions. (See "Legal Fees for a Divorce" in Chapter 4.)

Q. *For my second marriage, my first husband surprised me with an additional alimony payment, a gesture not required by our divorce decree. According to his attorney, my ex-mate gets a deduction and I have to report the payment. My new husband disagrees. Who is right?*

A. The attorney gave bum advice. As your former husband is under no legal obligation to pay that money to you, it is a gift; nothing is deductible by him or reportable by you.

Q. *I receive child support payments from my former husband. What are the tax rules?*

A. You do not have to report them, and he cannot deduct them.

Casualty and Theft Losses

Q. *I signed for lessons with a Florida dance studio and paid in advance. Then I moved to Oregon. Can I deduct the unused lessons?*

A. There is no deduction for personal expenses of this type.

Q. *With all the kidnappings that go on, what's the tax situation for parents who are forced to make ransom payments?*

A. IRS says payments to ransom a kidnapped child are deductible under the rules for theft losses.

Q. *When my wife moved out, she took all my furniture with her. At tax time, can I claim a theft loss for the furniture?*

A. It all depends on what the law says where you live. You are not entitled to any

deductions unless the law in your state says a theft occurred when your wife took the property without your consent. (See "Casualty and Theft Losses" in Chapter 9.)

Business Deductions

Q. *I had an out-of-town assignment for three weeks. It cost more for me to come home each weekend than it would have to stay over, but my company only paid what the cost of room and meals to stay would have been. Can I deduct the difference?*

A. No.

Q. *It's a constant struggle to meet my alimony payments and support my girlfriend at the same time. And after the IRS takes its cut, I'm really strapped for funds. One way to at least ease the tax bite for my business is to hire my girlfriend as a secretary, since she's also good behind a desk. But I'm concerned that the IRS will challenge my tax write-off for her salary. Am I asking for trouble?*

A. You should have no problem so long as your girlfriend actually works as a secretary and her salary is not higher than the going rate for other secretaries who render services only at the office.

Q. *I own all the shares of a family-run corporation. For many years, I have given a yearly bonus, equal to 3 percent of my net profit, for outstanding work performed by a key, long-time employee who is not related to me. Since this arrangement is informal, it does not obligate me to pay any bonus.*

The way I see things, my employee should not be liable for income taxes on this money because it is a gift. That would also excuse me from withholding income taxes and Social Security taxes. But now, an IRS agent insists that these payments are not gifts but compensation for services and that I am responsible for back payroll taxes, plus interest charges. Should I hire a tax expert to show the IRS that it is wrong?

A. No. Your arguments would get exactly nowhere with the IRS. Nor would it pay to take your case to court. The judge must be guided by what the Internal Revenue Code says. Unfortunately, Section 61 uses a mile-wide definition of income that entitles the IRS to share in "all income from whatever source derived," including payments that are "compensation for services." Whether or not your arrangement is in writing or you took deductions for those payments, the courts routinely hold that they are actually for services rendered.

Q. *I ran up sizable travel and entertainment expenses for my corporation, for which I'm entitled to get reimbursed. But I neglected to get reimbursed for them before the corporate return was filed. To keep things simple and to get an immediate tax deduction, can't I just claim them on my own return as employee business expenses?*

A. The IRS will automatically disallow them because you're entitled to reimbursement. It's the corporation's expenses, not yours. And it makes no difference even if you're the only stockholder. You still can't deduct expenses you pay on the corporation's behalf. Collect your tax-free reimbursement now and deduct the expenses on your corporation's next return.

Q. *I recently started a business and soon will need some extra help. I'm thinking about hiring my husband or asking my two daughters to help out after school. A customer told me that I do not have to pay Social Security taxes on their wages. Can that be true?*

A. You might be off the hook for one or both of your daughters, but not for your husband. There is one set of rules for them and another for him.

As for your daughters, the answer depends on their ages and whether you operate as a sole proprietorship, a husband-wife partnership, or a corporation. The Internal Revenue Code [Section 3121(b)(3)(A)] authorizes an exemption from Social Security taxes for wages paid to a son or daughter under the age of 18 by a family business that is run as a sole proprietorship or a husband-wife partnership, but not one that is incorporated.

There is no exemption at all in the case of your husband. You are stuck with taxes on wages paid to him, just the same as any other person you employ.

Through 1987, the rules were more favorable for sole proprietorships and husband-wife partnerships. The son or daughter could be as old as age 21. Moreover, assuming a sole proprietorship, there was an exemption for wages paid to a spouse. (For more information, see "Tax Breaks for Hiring Your Youngsters" in "The Kiddie Tax" in Chapter 10.)

Q. *I contribute lots of unpaid overtime to my employer. Can I take a tax deduction for it?*

A. No, whether the overtime is voluntary or required.

Q. *How does a doctor deduct his payment of a fee for lifetime nontransferrable privileges of practicing in a hospital he and other doctors organized?*

A. According to an IRS ruling, the fee is a capital outlay rather than an immediately deductible business expense. It purchased an intangible asset with a useful life of more than one year. Thus, the IRS concluded that he can use his life expectancy as the period for writing off the fee.

Q. *I acquired a building which I plan to demolish, and then construct a replacement for my business. Can I take an immediate deduction for the demolition cost? What about the building itself?*

A. The cost of the entire property has to be allocated to the land. Because the land is considered to have a zero cost basis for tax purposes, there is no loss when the building is demolished. Also, the cost of demolition is added to the land.

Q. *Can a call girl who poses as a stenographer claim depreciation of her typewriter?*

A. No, says the IRS. Use it or lose it.

Q. *I am a free-lance writer. A magazine asked me to do an article for $1,500 and reimbursement of expenses. In the course of researching the article, I incurred travel, telephone, and other expenses of $500. But I received nothing because the magazine went bankrupt. I know where what expenses go on which lines of Schedule C of Form 1040. But what about that unpaid $1,500? In the expenses part of Schedule C, there is a line headed "Bad debts from sales or services." Is that where I list my bad-debt deduction for the unpaid $1,500?*

A. No. Unfortunately, despite that heading, you cannot take any deduction for the $1,500. The snag: You are what is known as a "cash-basis taxpayer." That is IRS jargon for individuals who do not have to report payments for articles and other income items until the year that they actually receive them and do not get to deduct their expenses until the year that they pay them. As you did not previously count the $1,500 as reportable income, you are not allowed to deduct an equivalent amount.

Figuring Taxes

Q. *My income soared because of an unusually large bonus. What is the form I use to take advantage of income averaging?*

A. You have to calculate your taxes the same as anyone else. Averaging is one of the many breaks ended by tax reform.

When to File

Q. *My father died this year. How quickly must I file his final return?*

A. You still have until April 15 next year.

14 FIGURING AND PAYING YOUR TAXES

This is too difficult for a mathematician, it takes a philosopher.

—Albert Einstein, on
completing his tax return

We don't pay taxes. Only the little people pay taxes.

—Leona Helmsley

THE 1913 FORM 1040

I guess you will have to go to jail. If that is the result of not understanding the Income Tax Law, I shall meet you there. We shall have a merry, merry time, for all of our friends will be there. It will be an intellectual center, for no one understands the Income Tax Law except persons who have not sufficient intelligence to understand the questions that arise under it.

—Senator Elihu Root of New York
on the 1913 income tax law.

Say "1040" and most of us think of the income tax returns we file on April 15. But it is only because of the element of chance that we fill out 1040s, instead of 1039s or 1050s, notes the Internal Revenue Service's "Statistics of Income Bulletin."

Why is that? Because the number 1040 was simply the next number up in the system of sequential numbering of forms developed by the Bureau of Internal Revenue, the predecessor of today's IRS.

On January 5, 1914, the Department of the Treasury unveiled the new Form 1040. The deadline for filing the form with the local tax collector's office was less than two months away, March 1, 1914.

Including one page of instructions, the 1913 version of 1040 was four pages long and its list of deductions was spartan, compared to today's sumptuous array of write-offs for money put in IRAs and retirement plans, alimony payments, itemized deductions for charitable contributions, etc., standard deductions for nonitemizers, dependency exemptions, and the like.

The first modern tax return authorized a deduction of $3,000 for singles and $4,000 for marrieds. Spouses could file joint or separate returns, but in no case could their combined deductions be more than $4,000. The $3,000/$4,000 write-off alone was sufficient to relieve all but a comparative handful of individuals from liability for income taxes. Other authorized deductions included personal interest paid (a deduction deep-sixed by the Tax Reform Act of 1986), business losses and uninsured losses from "fires, storms, or shipwreck" (unsurprisingly, no mention of plane crashes), all other taxes paid, such as real estate taxes, bad debts, and "reasonable" depreciation of business property.

For 1913's taxpayers, the brackets were

way below today's rates; and that's without taking intervening decades of inflation into account. For singles and joint filers, the 1913 brackets started at 1 percent on taxable income (what is left *after* reportable income is offset by deductions) of up to $50,000. The next brackets were 2 percent (income between $50,000 and $75,000), 3 percent (between $75,000 and $100,000), 4 percent (between $100,000 and $250,000), 5 percent (between $250,000 and $500,000) and a top rate of 6 percent (above $500,000).

Contrast those levels with tax year 1994's brackets—15, 28, 31, 36, and 39.6 percent (the latest year for which information is available as this book goes to press in the summer of 1994; see "What Is Your Real Tax Bracket" later in this chapter). The 15 percent bracket applies to income of up to $22,750 for singles and $38,000 for joint filers. The next brackets are 28 percent (between $22,750 and $55,100 for singles and $38,000 and $91,850 for joints), 31 percent (between $55,100 and $115,000 for singles and $91,850 and $140,000 for joints), 36 percent (between $115,000 and $250,000 for singles and $140,000 and $250,000 for joints) and a top rate of 39.6 percent (above $250,000 for singles and joints).

Back then, after filling out their forms, taxpayers had to sign "under oath or affirmation" before "any officer authorized by law to administer oaths." Nowadays, taxpayers simply sign them.

Just over 350,000 1040's were filed in 1914, and the feds audited 100 percent of them. This filing season, the IRS expects to receive about 115 million 1040's and plans to audit about one percent of the filers. (See "Audit Odds" in Chapter 11.)

Is Your Withholding Out of Whack?

When you settled with the Internal Revenue Service last April, did you discover that you were entitled to receive a hefty refund or obliged to pay a sizable sum? The hitch could be that your withholding was out of whack and your employer took out too much or too little from your paychecks for the year.

Worse yet, the chances are that the same thing will happen again unless you act now to revise the amount subtracted from your pay to make sure that it will be in rough balance with what the tax tab will be when filing time rolls around.

Overwithholding means that the IRS gets the interest-free use of your money from the time it is taken out of your paycheck until you recover it as a tax refund the following spring. Of course, you can stay overwithheld each payday if you prefer that as a way of forcing yourself to save.

Underwithholding means you have to fork over the balance due all at once and may be hit with a nondeductible estimated tax penalty because not enough was taken out. Here are some points to keep in mind if you need to file a new Form W-4 (Employee's Withholding Allowance Certificate) with your employer on which you indicate the number of withholding "allowances" (exemptions) that you want to take.

Overwithholding

This often occurs because of confusion about withholding allowances and dependency exemptions. Contrary to what many working persons mistakenly assume, the number of dependency exemptions that you can claim on Form 1040 for yourself and your spouse, children, and other dependents does not set the ceiling on the number of withholding allowances that you are authorized to claim on a W-4. (For the rules on dependency exemptions, see Chapter 2.)

Actually, the law entitles you to claim extra withholding exemptions to reduce the over-withholding that otherwise results when you have sizable itemized deductions, alimony payments, credits for child- or dependent-care expenses, or other adjustments, such as deductible payments to an IRA. Each exemption frees $2,450 of salary or other compensation from withholding. (This figure is for tax year 1994, the most recent year for which information is available as this book goes to press; the amount of the exemption is scheduled to be indexed—that is, adjusted upward to reflect inflation—on returns for 1995 and later years). But if, like many other persons, you prefer to remain overwithheld, you do not have to revise your W-4 just because you are eligible to take advantage of these exemptions. You need to do so only if you want to boost your take-home pay.

The W-4, which contains instructions, lists the special circumstances that allow you to claim extra exemptions.

Tip. You must file a new W-4 within 10 days if the number of exemptions you previously claimed decreases because, for example, you get divorced or stop supporting a dependent.

Caution. The IRS is empowered to exact a civil penalty of $500 from a person who does not have a reasonable basis for the exemptions that he or she claims on the form. To add to its enforcement powers, the IRS is also authorized to seek court-imposed criminal penalties on persons who file false W-4s. The penalties are stiff—a sojourn in the slammer of up to a year and a fine of up to $1,000.

Underwithholding

Suppose you have to cope with the reverse problem—too little is taken out. It's just as easy to change your W-4 to claim fewer exemptions than you are allowed and increase your withholding.

Assume, for example, that you are entitled to five withholding exemptions. Simply claim fewer exemptions or none at all in the space provided on the form. If you want to go even further, ask your employer to withhold an additional amount. The W-4 has a line on which you show that figure.

Tip. The marital status section of the W-4 has a box labeled "married, but withhold at higher single rate." This box can be checked by married couples where both spouses work or by a married person with more than one employer, so as to increase the amount withheld.

Sidestepping estimated tax payments. You can use extra withholding to avoid making quarterly payments of estimated taxes (including self-employment taxes; see Chapter 15) otherwise due on income from sources not covered by withholding. Estimated tax payments are discussed in the next section of this chapter.

How withholding came and stayed. The withholding system had a difficult birth, when it was introduced in 1943 in the middle of World War II. The 1943 tax act was so complicated that President Franklin D. Roosevelt vetoed it, saying "the American taxpayer had been promised of late that tax laws and returns will be drastically simplified. This bill does not make good that promise . . . . These taxpayers, now engaged in an effort to win the greatest war this nation has ever faced, are not in a mood to study higher mathematics." Congress, however, overrode FDR's veto, and withholding went on the books.

During that war, Irving Berlin wrote a song that tried to put Americans in an upbeat mood about their taxes. Unlike "White Christmas," another war-time composition that remains a standard, the song now interests only Berlin buffs, a circumstance that is explainable by its refrain:

You see those bombers in the sky?
Rockefeller helped to build them
So did I
I paid my income tax today

In an article on America in the 1940s for the January 3, 1994, issue of *Newsweek,* David Brinkley of ABC News recalled withholding's introduction:

Under pressure of war, the withholding tax was born. It is doubtful that without war Congress would ever have voted for a tax so intrusive and troublesome. Because of the withholding tax, the term "take-home pay" entered the language. Had people been forced to count out their taxes in hard cash for some government collector, taxes in such stratospheric amounts almost certainly could not have been collected.

The cost of the war was so high that the top rate eventually went to about 92 percent. It was explained to Roosevelt that his rich enemies would be soaked, even fleeced, beyond their deepest fears. They paid the 92 percent, hated it, but could not escape. It made Roosevelt so happy, Press Secretary Steve Early told me, that once or twice he saw the president spend hours pouring over records

sent to him from the IRS showing who paid how much.

As for Roosevelt's own finances, all that was ever known was that his mother, Sara Delano Roosevelt, until she died in 1941, every month or so handed him cash in a sealed envelope.

Members of Congress were so happy to find they now had a Niagara of money flooding into Washington, all ready for them to spend. Even when the war was long over, there was never any thought of ending the withholding tax. (They held the top rate at about 70 percent for another 16 years.) Did the enormous tax rates pay the cost of the war? No. Did the government run the war on credit and leave billions in debt? Yes.

A personal comment: Mr. Brinkley fails to persuade me that pay-as-you-fight financing, instead of an increase in the national debt, was the right way to pay for a global conflict's cost.

ESTIMATED TAX PAYMENTS

Who is subject to the requirements for quarterly payments of estimated income taxes (including any self-employment tax, which is discussed in Chapter 15, or alternative minimum tax, which is discussed later in this chapter)? Expect to run afoul of the requirements for estimated payments when you are, say, a self-employed with earnings from a business or profession; a homeowner with a reportable profit from its sale (see Chapter 3); an investor who receives interest, dividends, gains from sales of investments and the like; a divorced person who receives alimony payments; or a retiree with pension payments undiminished by withholding.

The law authorizes the IRS to exact penalties for insufficient quarterly payments or for failure to pay the installments on time as they become due, unless your estimated taxes are below $500. It is immaterial that your final estimates prove sufficient to erase any balance due when you submit your Form 1040 for 1994.

Note, though, that there are exceptions that relieve you of any penalties for underpayments of more than $500. You are excused from penalties as long as you made payments (including withholding taken from your paychecks) for tax year 1994 by the quarterly due dates of April 15, June 15, September 15, and January 15 that exceed a specific benchmark.

Those payments must be more than the *least* of the following three amounts:

1. Ninety percent (66⅔ percent for qualifying farmers and fishermen) of the actual taxes you owe for 1994.

2. One hundred percent of the taxes you paid for 1993. This is so even if the amount due was zero, provided the return covered 12 months. Because the second exception—the prior year's tax—is a fixed number, it is the easiest way for most people to calculate their payments and avoid penalties.

Example. You paid $10,000 in taxes for 1993 and $11,000 through estimates or withholding in 1994. With that set of numbers, you are off the hook, no matter how much your 1994 liability turns out to be.

3. Ninety percent of the actual taxes you owe for 1994, figured by annualizing income actually received by the end of the quarter in question. The third escape clause is most helpful to persons

who receive the bulk of their incomes late in the year.

Restrictions on use of exception for prior year's tax. Starting with estimated payments for 1994, the 100-percent escape hatch remains available if your adjusted gross income (AGI) is under $150,000. It is not available if your AGI is above $150,000. However, it is still possible to avoid penalties. To do so, you have to make timely payments that are at least equal to (1) 90 percent of the actual taxes you owe for 1994 or (2) 110 percent of your tax liability for 1993, whichever is the *lesser* figure.

Example. Your 1993 AGI was over $150,000 and your 1993 tax was $30,000. To avoid estimated tax penalties, you should pay $33,000 (110 percent of $30,000).

Help from the IRS

For detailed information, get IRS Publications 505, *Tax Withholding and Estimated Tax,* and 919, *Is My Withholding Correct?,* which include a worksheet to figure out if too much or too little tax is being withheld from your pay. To obtain free copies, call 1-800-TAX-FORM (allow at least 10 work days for mailing) or stop by the IRS office serving your area to obtain them immediately. Many libraries also have copies of these and other IRS tax guides. IRS Publication 910, *Guide to Free Tax Services,* provides a complete list of booklets and explains what each one covers. (For a discussion of IRS publications, see "Get the Right Help at Tax Time" in Chapter 13.)

UNABLE TO PAY YOUR TAXES? ASK TO PAY IRS MONTHLY

Of all debts men are least willing to pay the taxes. What a satire is this on government!
—Ralph Waldo Emerson, "Politics," 1844

What is the difference between a taxidermist and a tax collector? The taxidermist takes only your skin.
—Mark Twain, "Notebooks," December 30, 1902

Lament for unpaid taxes: IRS employees in the agency's Washington, D.C., office have a choral group whose repertoire includes "The Red, White, and Blue Can't Get by on Your I.O.U."

Judging from the letters I receive, many of my readers have not filed their returns because they owe taxes and are strapped for cash. What follows is a representative request for advice and my response.

Q. *I have yet to file my return for 1993. Nor did I use IRS Form 4868 to ask for a filing extension beyond April 15 to August 15. (See "More Time to File Your Return" in Chapter 13.) My problem is that I had sizable gains from sales of investments and reinvested the proceeds without keeping enough cash to pay taxes on the profits. When I completed my return, there was a balance due of about $20,000, which I simply was unable to pay on April 15.*

A friend insists I should not call attention to myself by submitting my Form 1040 without paying; rather, I should wait to file until I have enough to take care of the entire tab. Is that good advice?

A. Unfortunately, along with many other persons, your friend mistakenly assumes that failing to file is the answer to your tax dilemma—a tactic guaranteed to dig you deeper into debt with the IRS. Instead, what you ought to do is file now to avoid or minimize severe, nondeductible penalties. Those penalties are in addition to nondeductible interest charges.

Late-filing penalty. The stiffest dent in your wallet is a 5 percent late-filing penalty. Generally, this penalty is 5 percent of the balance due (the amount that remains unpaid after subtractions for taxes previously paid through withholdings from wages and quarterly payments of estimated taxes) for each month, or part of a month, that a Form 1040 is late. The maximum penalty is 25 percent of the balance due. (Had you timely submitted Form 4868, the IRS would have waived the late-filing penalty.)

On a balance due of $20,000, that works out to $1,000 per month. The penalty can be as much as $5,000 if your return is more than four months late.

The rules are even harsher in the case of a late filing that is deemed fraudulent. The monthly penalty soars to 15 percent, up to a maximum of 75 percent.

Late-payment penalty. On top of the late-filing penalty, the IRS can exact a late-payment penalty, which kicks in when the balance due is either (1) more than 10 percent of the tax shown on the return or (2) not paid by August 15. Generally, the late-payment penalty is one-half of 1 percent of the unpaid amount for each month, or part of a month, up to a maximum of 25 percent —$100 each month on a balance due of $20,000. However, when the IRS assesses penalties for both late filing and late payment, one partly offsets the other.

Interest charges. Besides penalties for late filing and payment, you owe interest from April 15 on the balance due. Worse yet, no longer is there any deduction for interest on overdue taxes, as is true of other kinds of consumer interest payments, such as charge account and credit card balances and car loans. Also, the IRS charges interest on the penalty for late filing, but not the one for late payment.

The interest rate changes every three months. As this book goes to press in the summer of 1994, the annual rate is 7 percent, compounded daily. (No waiver of the late-payment penalty and interest charge, even for someone who did timely submit Form 4868, cautions the IRS.)

Tip. Given the daunting charges for penalties and interest, it is clear what needs to be done. File as soon as possible, even if you are unable to pay the balance. For instance, the interest charges and penalties for late filing and payment could boost a tax liability of $10,000 to about $14,000 in less than 12 months.

Form 9465. The IRS wants people in your position to at least file returns. So it will allow individuals who owe more in taxes than they can afford to pay to work out payment plans based on monthly installments.

All you need to do is fill out Form 9465 (Installment Agreement Request) and attach it to the front of your return; indicate the amount you propose to pay each month and the payment date, which must be the first through the twenty-eighth day. The IRS is supposed to notify you within 30 days that it approved or denied your request or that it needs more information.

Tip. Form 9465 is mum on two key points: (1) what minimum amount (dollar amount or percentage of the balance) the IRS will accept monthly and (2) over how many months you can schedule the payments. But I have been informally advised by the IRS that if your proposed payments are too low, the agency will contact you to discuss a more suitable schedule.

Some guidelines: IRS statistics reveal that average installment agreements are for about $2,300, and payments are made over 20-month periods. Presumably, the IRS will go along with an offer to pay several thousand dollars, plus interest, in monthly amounts over a less-than-two-year period.

Financial information. Form 9465 does not ask you to disclose financial information—for instance, amounts in bank accounts or sources from which you can borrow. Consequently, you need not exhaust other available means to qualify for installment payments.

The IRS further relaxes the rules if your account balances are under $10,000. No longer do you have to complete a financial statement. If a financial statement is not required and you adhere to the payment schedule, the IRS will show its appreciation: No federal tax lien will be filed.

Caution. A monthly payment plan, warns the IRS, might not be your best option. A bank loan, for instance, could be less costly. As I mentioned previously, the IRS exacts additional charges. Their cost to you is an annual rate of 14 percent on your unpaid amounts—interest (currently 8 percent) and a late-payment penalty (one-half of 1 percent). But paying the IRS relieves you of the need to fill out a bank's credit application and financial statement and, in some cases,

Uncle Sam might be the only one willing to be your source of credit.

Proposed change.   As this book goes to press in the summer of 1994, the IRS announced a proposed charge to cover the costs of administering monthly payment arrangements. Under the proposal, you have to submit a payment of $16 with a Form 9465 that accompanies your return. The charge increases from $16 to at least $20 for a Form 9465 submitted after the filing due date.

CHECKS PAYABLE TO THE IRS

There is a superstition held by the natives of Malaya that the orangutan is really human but that he remains speechless in order to avoid the payment of taxes.

—Anonymous

Before you mail any check to the Internal Revenue Service, make sure to note the following on it:

1. The reason for the payment, the form number, and the year of the return for which the check is being sent (for instance, "balance due on Form 1040 for 1994").
2. Your daytime telephone number and Social Security number, or, if you operate a business, your employer identification number.

Also, the IRS asks that you use separate checks and note the necessary information on each one when you pay two different taxes at once, such as past-due income taxes and interest for an earlier year and an estimated

tax payment for this year. Doing that will make it much easier for the IRS to identify and credit you with the payment if it becomes prematurely separated from the accompanying correspondence or return.

Overlooking this simple step may confuse the computers and, at a minimum, direct attention to your return, and require otherwise avoidable correspondence. Even worse, it may cause those relentless computers to erroneously charge you with a penalty for failing to make a timely payment. (Late-payment penalties are discussed in "More Time to File Your Return" in Chapter 13.)

Tip.   Attach a check on top of any Forms W-2, etc., on the front of a return—*not* on the back or between pages, where it might be overlooked.

Caution.   There can be yet another problem if you are casual about what you write on the pay-to-the-order line of a check going to the IRS. Your tax tab could double if you merely make the check payable to "IRS," instead of "Internal Revenue Service," and it winds up in the wrong hands. That "IRS" can easily be altered to "MRS" followed by a name, or altered to a name by combining the initials "I.R." with a last name—for instance, "I.R. Smith." And some obliging taxpayers even send checks without filling in the payee line.

Tip.   While you're at it, make sure that mailings to the IRS bear the proper amount of postage and show a full return address. Otherwise, you run the risk of being hit with a nondeductible late-filing penalty. (Late-filing penalties are discussed later in this chapter.) Mail without stamps, and that includes tax returns, goes undelivered and is returned to the sender by the postal service.

Worse yet, mail without stamps and without a return address goes to the Dead Letter Office.

WHAT IS YOUR REAL TAX BRACKET?

I have something my tax doctor calls "narco-taxis." Within 20 seconds of hearing someone launch into an explanation of tax laws, my eyes become glassy, my body loses all feeling, and I go into a shallow coma.

—Russell Baker, "Sunday Observer", *The New York Times,* April 19, 1987

Back in 1986, Congress undertook a top-to-bottom restructuring of the Internal Revenue Code, known officially as the Tax Reform Act of 1986. But that was just Act I, as we all know. Congress enacted wide-ranging refinements in each of the following years, most recently in August of 1993.

Why do our lawmakers keep going back to the drawing board? Because of the need to raise more taxes to offset spiraling budget deficits, a situation that means we can look forward to more changes in the immediate future.

The centerpiece of the 1993 legislation was an increase in the top tax rate for individuals by the creation of two new brackets. Worse still, the increase authorized in August applied retroactively to January 1, 1993.

The mostly good news for literally 99 percent of the nation's taxpayers: There continues to be tax brackets of 15, 28, and 31 percent, as well as preferential treatment for long-term capital gains from sales of stocks and other investments owned more than twelve months. More on that later.

The bad news for about 1 percent of the taxpayers, starting with returns for 1993 filed in 1994: A boost in the top tax bracket

from 31 to 36 percent and, for those with above-$250,000 taxable incomes, a surtax that is the equivalent of a tax bracket of 39.6 percent (the surtax is explained later).

The top rate of 36 percent kicks in *only* when taxable income *surpasses*:

- $115,000 for singles;
- $127,500 for heads of households;
- $140,000 for joint filers; and
- $70,000 for married couples filing separately.

Caution. Research shows, says the *New York Times*, that the "nation suffers from a massive case of tax illiteracy that goes beyond the inherent complexity of the system and cuts across every economic and educational stratum." That knowledge gap underlines why I should split some semantic hairs before I proceed further.

Like other tax professionals, my experience has been that most people do not know the difference between "taxable income" and "adjusted gross income" (AGI)—terms that pop up continually in this book and that taxpayers must understand if they want to get an accurate fix on what their top tax bracket really is and how the bracket revisions affect them.

Taxable income means the amount of income that is left *after* AGI is offset by for exemptions for yourself and other dependents (see Chapter 2), as well as itemized deductions for outlays such as charitable contributions or real estate taxes, or, if you do not itemize, the standard deduction, the no-proof-required amount that is automatically available without the need to itemize. (For more on the standard deduction, see "Itemizing versus Standard Deduction" in Chapter 1.) According to the IRS, a taxable income of $140,000 generally corresponds to an AGI of about $180,000.

AGI is the amount that you report at the bottom of page one of Form 1040 after listing salaries, interest, dividends, and other sources of income and claiming certain deductions such as money placed in Individual Retirement Accounts and alimony payments. The AGI amount is *before* claiming exemptions and itemized deductions or the standard deduction.

Incidentally, researchers also found out that only 50 percent of the taxpayers understand the distinction between itemized and standard deductions.

Filing status. Many people also misunderstand how to determine their filing status—married, single, or head of household.

For example, a break often overlooked is that a widow or widower with a dependent child—in bureaucratese, someone defined as a "surviving spouse"—may be entitled to the benefit of joint-return rates, which are more favorable than those for a single person or head of household, for two years after the mate's death. (See "Joint-Return Rates for Surviving Spouses" in Chapter 4.)

Tip. All is not lost if you fail to qualify as a surviving spouse who can use the joint-return rates. You still may be able to avoid the single-person rates and use the more favorable ones for head of household. What if you are no longer eligible for treatment as a surviving spouse, but you remain unmarried and your child lives with you? You might qualify as a head of household even if you are ineligible to claim an exemption for your child.

Similarly, a married person filing a separate return might be able to get the benefit of the more favorable rates for a head of house-

hold and not have to use the rates for a married person filing separately. (See "Lower Rates for Some Marrieds Filing Separately" in Chapter 4.)

Surtax. The bracket overhaul is not limited to the new tax bracket of 36 percent for 1993 and subsequent years. There also is a 10 percent surtax on taxable incomes over $250,000 if you are single, head of household, or filing jointly. The $250,000 figure drops to $125,000 if you are married and file a separate return.

Tip. A surtax is a tax on a tax. It is not an extra tax of 10 percent. So the effect of the surtax is to create a top bracket of 39.6 percent for 1993 and subsequent years.

Indexing of brackets. Under the 1986 Tax Reform Act, the 15, 28, and 31 percent brackets are "indexed," as are the phaseout figures for itemized deductions (see the next section of this chapter) and personal exemptions (see Chapter 2).

Indexing means the brackets automatically adjust each year for inflation, as measured by changes in the Consumer Price Index. What indexing accomplishes is to eliminate bracket creep, which enriches Uncle Sam at the expense of persons whose incomes climb with inflation. Note, though, that the Clinton Administration and Congress agreed that there would be *no* indexing for tax year 1994 of the 36 percent bracket and the 10 percent surtax. As the law now stands, they are scheduled to be indexed for 1995 and later years.

Higher rates make tax-exempt or tax-deferred investments more attractive. The 36 percent bracket for 1993 and subsequent years and the 10 percent surtax enhance the allure of tax-exempt investments, such as municipal bond funds (see "When Tax-Exempt Investments Make Sense" in Chapter 10), and tax-deferred savings arrangements, such as IRAs and 401(k) plans for employees (see Chapter 10) and Keogh plans for self-employeds.

Tip. A slight consolation if you move into a higher bracket is that you get more mileage out of your deductions because they offset income taxed at a higher rate.

Tax rates for capital gains. Special rules govern long-term capital gains from assets owned more than 12 months.

Capital gains continue to be taxed at a top rate of 15 percent for persons in the 15 percent bracket and at a rate of 28 percent for those in the old 28 or 31 percent brackets and the new 36 and 39.6 percent brackets. (See Chapter 10.)

Tip. A cause of much confusion is that the increase in the top tax rate from the old 31 to the new 36 or 39.6 percent (assuming the surtax is applicable) affects *only* upper-income individuals. The tab is *unchanged* as long as taxable income is *below*:

- $115,000 for single filers;
- $127,500 for heads of households;
- $140,000 for joint filers; and
- $70,000 for married couples filing separately.

Social Security recipients. Many recipients who continue to fall within the 15, 28, and 31 percent brackets, which are discussed below, will nevertheless pay more taxes on their Social Security benefits. That is because the

portion of benefits subject to income taxes increases from as much as 50 percent to as much as 85 percent, starting with returns for 1994 to be filed in 1995. (See Chapter 15.)

The 15 percent bracket. This bracket applies to taxable income for 1994 of *up* to:

- $22,750 for singles;
- $38,000 for marrieds filing jointly;
- $30,500 for heads of households; and
- $19,000 for marrieds filing separately.

The 28 percent bracket. This bracket applies to taxable income for 1994 *between*:

- $22,750 and $55,100 for singles;
- $38,000 and $91,850 for joint filers;
- $30,500 and $78,700 for heads of households; and
- $19,000 and $45,925 for marrieds filing separately.

The 31 percent bracket. This bracket applies to taxable income for 1994 *between*:

- $55,100 and $115,000 for singles;
- $91,850 and $140,000 for joint filers;
- $78,700 and $127,500 for heads of households; and
- $45,925 and $70,000 for marrieds filing separately.

Tip. For upper-middle and high-income individuals who fall into the 31, 36, or 39.6 brackets, their top rates actually are higher. Why? Because they suffer a partial disallowance of certain itemized deductions. The disallowance is 3 percent of the amount by which AGI *exceeds* a specific figure that is indexed (adjusted to reflect inflation) each year—$111,800 for tax year 1994. (See the discussion later in this chapter.)

Also, their personal exemptions are phased out when AGI is *between*:

- $111,800 and $234,300 for singles;
- $167,700 and $290,200 for joint filers;
- $139,750 and $262,250 for heads of households; and
- $83,850 and $145,100 for marrieds filing separately.

Individuals in these categories completely lose the benefit of their personal exemptions when AGI exceeds the top figures. (For a more detailed discussion of dependency exemptions, see Chapter 2.)

Top bracket.   Know how to figure out your top tax bracket—the maximum rate you must pay on any part of your income? If not, you have lots of company.

Many individuals, especially those who hire preparers to do their 1040 forms, are unable to get a real fix on what their top bracket actually is, or how much they have to pay. That is not unexpected, though, given the complexities of how taxable income is determined and the additional computation that becomes necessary when the amount exacted by the IRS is increased by the sums that are siphoned off by many states and cities.

Actually, all it takes is some fairly simple paperwork to figure your top bracket if you are in the 15 or 28 percent brackets, though, as I explained before, the calculation becomes daunting if you fall into a bracket that is 31 percent or higher. Conversely, it is easy to determine your effective tax rate; to get this figure, divide the total dollars that you lose to federal and local levies by your gross income. Your reward for your efforts might

be the discovery that your top bracket is higher than you thought, whereas your effective rate is much lower.

To illustrate how to figure your top bracket, let's look at an example: As joint filers, John and Virginia Hickey declare a gross income of $55,000. The Hickeys offset that amount by $15,000 through personal exemptions and itemized deductions. Their taxable income is $40,000, which places them in a top federal tax bracket of 28 percent.

The couple's taxable income can go as high as $91,850 before they are forced into the next bracket, where each added dollar of income is taxed at a 31 percent rate. To ease themselves into the 15 percent bracket, their taxable income must drop below $38,000.

Suppose, though, that the Hickeys are liable for both federal and local taxes. In that case, they have more numbers to crunch.

Their combined top bracket, however, is not the sum of their federal, state, and city brackets. Rather, it is their top federal bracket, plus the state and city brackets, minus the federal tax saving that becomes available because the local taxes can be claimed as itemized deductions on Schedule A of Form 1040.

Let's say the Hickeys are in a 6 percent bracket for state taxes. To determine their top tax bracket, they multiply their 28-percent federal bracket by 6 percent, which equals about 2 percent. They then subtract this 2 percent from 6 percent. Result: a 4-percent tax rate, which, when added to the federally imposed 28 percent, brings their top bracket to roughly 32 percent.

Effective rate.   As noted earlier, gross income of $55,000 and taxable income of $40,000 puts the Hickeys into the 28-percent federal tax bracket. However, not all of their income gets taxed at the 28-percent rate. Their taxable income up to $38,000 is taxed at the 15-percent rate; their income between $38,000 and $91,850 is taxed at the 28-percent rate.

Assuming they have no tax credits, their tax bill is $6,260—the sum of $5,700 on the first $38,000 ($38,000 times 15 percent), plus $560 ($2,000 times 28 percent). To determine their effective rate, the Hickeys divide their tax bill by their gross income ($6,260 divided by $55,000). The rate? A shade above 11.38 percent—nowhere near 28 percent.

Strategy. The key to successful tax planning is to know your top bracket. For example, only if you are able to gauge your real after-tax return are you able to decide whether an investment that is exempt from taxes provides a higher yield than one that is fully taxable.

Example. Victor and Ethel DeVorkin are in a 40 percent federal and state bracket. With their set of numbers, a tax-free return of 6 percent would be equivalent to a fully taxable 10 percent; a tax-free 7 percent would match a fully taxable 11.67 percent. Were the DeVorkins in a 30 percent bracket, tax-free returns of 6 and 7 percent would equal fully taxable returns of 8.57 and 10 percent, respectively. (See "When Tax-Exempt Investments Make Sense" in Chapter 10.)

Knowing how much you get to keep after taxes also helps in other ways. The long list of possibilities includes:

- when it is worthwhile to advance or postpone the payment of deductions or the receipt of income from one year into another (Chapter 1);

- whether it is more advantageous to marry or divorce before or after the close of the year (see Chapter 4);

- when, with no deduction for payments of interest on car and other personal loans, it becomes worthwhile to pay off such loans with savings, where practical, or funds obtained through a home equity loan (you can write off all of the interest on up to $100,000 of home equity borrowing; see the discussion of interest deductions in "Timing Payments of Deductible Expenses" in Chapter 1);

- how much of a salary boost you need to justify a job change; and

- even the amount and kind of property you donate to charity (Chapter 8).

Tip. As you plan your tax strategies, keep in mind that the taxes you *save* can generate high-powered dollars. For instance, if you are in a 35 percent federal and state bracket, a tax savings of $1,000 provides the same purchasing power as $1,539 of added before-tax income (.35 times $1,539 equals about $539; $1,539 minus $539 equals $1,000).

ALTERNATIVE MINIMUM TAX

I apologize for the inequities in the practical applications of the tax, but if we should wait before collecting a tax to adjust the taxes upon each man in exact proportion with every other, we shall never collect any tax at all.

—President Abraham Lincoln
in an 1864 address to the
164th Ohio Regiment

The 1993 tax act increased the alternative minimum tax (AMT), a levy that affects relatively few individuals. The AMT is designed to require the payment of a minimum tax by certain high-income individuals who engage in business and investment ventures that allow them to legitimately use deductions and other breaks to greatly reduce, or even eliminate, their regular income tax.

To make payment of a minimum tax likely, the AMT allows fewer write-offs and counts more items as reportable income than the regular method used to determine your tax liability. (For the regular method, see "What Is Your Real Tax Bracket?" in the preceding section of this chapter.) *Result*: You must calculate your tax both ways—regular and AMT—and pay the higher of the two taxes.

You can run afoul of the AMT's more stringent rules when you have deductions for, among other things, accelerated depreciation, percentage depletion, intangible drilling costs, and tax shelter losses. The IRS dubs these breaks "tax preference items."

What if you have no preference items? The AMT might nevertheless apply if you have substantial itemized deductions that are allowable on Schedule A of Form 1040, but not allowable for AMT purposes such as state and local income taxes (see the discussion of state and local income taxes under "Timing Payments of Deductible Expenses" in Chapter 1), certain interest expenses, and miscellaneous expenses (see Chapter 9).

The AMT rate applies to AMT taxable income (generally, your regular taxable income increased by tax preference items and certain itemized deductions that are added back to income) after claiming an exemption. For tax year 1994, the AMT rate is a two-tiered system. The rate is 26 percent on taxable income of up to $175,000 ($87,500 for married persons filing separately). It moves up to 28 percent on AMT taxable income over $175,000 ($87,500 for married persons filing separately). Previously, the AMT rate was a flat 24 percent.

The exemption is as follows:

- $45,000 for married persons filing jointly, up from $40,000 previously;
- $33,750 for single persons or heads of households, up from $30,000 previously, and;
- $22,500 for married persons filing separate returns, up from $20,000 previously.

However, these exemptions phase out if AMT income exceeds specified levels that vary by filing status.

For tax year 1994, the regular tax rates are 15, 28, and 31 percent, as before, and, first introduced in 1993, rates of 36 and 39.6 percent. The regular rate of 36 percent applies when taxable income (what is left after income is offset by deductions and exemptions) surpasses:

- $115,000 for singles;
- $127,500 for heads of households;
- $140,000 for joint filers; and
- $70,000 for married couples filing separately.

The 39.6 percent rate applies to taxable income over $250,000, whether you are filing jointly, head of household, or single. The $250,000 figure drops to $125,000 if you are married and filing separately.

Caution. Higher AMT rates for everyone and higher regular rates on higher incomes means that the AMT can snare some upper-middle-income individuals who previously did not have to take the AMT into account in mapping out their tax strategies.

Help from the IRS

For detailed information, see IRS Publication 909, *Alternative Minimum Tax for Individuals.* For a free copy, call 1-800-TAX-FORM (allow at least 10 work days for mailing or stop by the IRS office serving your area to obtain one immediately. Many libraries also have copies of this and other IRS tax guides. IRS Publication 910, *Guide to Free Tax Services,* provides a complete list of booklets and explains what each one covers. (For a discussion of IRS Publications, see "Get the Right Help at Tax Time" in Chapter 13.)

CURTAILMENT OF MOST ITEMIZED DEDUCTIONS FOR INDIVIDUALS WITH ADJUSTED GROSS INCOMES ABOVE A SPECIFIED AMOUNT— $111,800 FOR 1994

When the Internal Revenue presented Mark Twain with an 1864 tax bill for $36.82, plus a $3.12 delinquency penalty, he wrote his editor, "I am taxed on my income. This is perfectly gorgeous. I never felt so important in my life."

—*Mark Twain's Letters,* Albert B. Paine, Editor, Harper & Row, 1917

Several years after the overhaul of the Internal Revenue Code by the 1986 Tax Reform Act, Congress took another whack at itemized deductions. Tucked into that re-vamping was a provision that further restricts write-offs by upper-income itemizers—yet another one of those devious backdoor tax increases that our lawmakers favor, especially when they are obliged to enact legislation during an election year.

The law requires you to reduce the amount you are able to claim for most itemized deductions when your adjusted gross income (AGI) is above a specified amount— $111,800 for 1994, up from $108,450 for 1993, $105,250 for 1992 and $100,000 for 1991, when this curtailment first went on the books. You forfeit deductions equal to 3 percent of the amount that your AGI exceeds $111,800. Put another way, you lose $300 in total deductions for every $10,000 of AGI above $111,800 (the $111,800 figure drops to $55,900 if you are married and file a separate return; going that route does not raise a couple's threshold to a combined $223,600).

AGI is the figure you report at the bottom of page 1 of Form 1040 after listing salaries, interest, dividends, and other sources of income and claiming certain deductions like alimony payments and money placed in Individual Retirement Accounts and other retirement plans. The AGI amount is before itemizing for outlays like charitable contributions and claiming dependency exemptions.

The 3 percent restriction applies to deductions for interest on home mortgages, real estate taxes, state and local taxes (see the discussion of these deductions in "Timing Payments of Deductible Expenses" in Chapter 1), charitable contributions (Chapter 8), and miscellaneous expenses (already allowable, in most cases, just for the amount above 2 percent of AGI; Chapter 9).

There are several reprieves, but the exceptions are for deductions that already are subject to limitations. The 3 percent rule does not apply to deductions for medical expenses (deductible only for the amount above 7.5 percent of AGI; Chapter 7), casualty and theft losses (allowable only to the extent such uninsured losses exceed $100 (for each casualty or theft, plus 10 percent of your AGI; Chapter 9), gambling losses (allowable just to the extent of gambling winnings; Chapter 12), and interest on funds borrowed to finance investments, such as margin accounts used to buy stocks (allowable just to the extent of investment income, a category that includes dividends, interest, and, subject to restrictions, capital gains).

Example. Your AGI is $161,800 and your otherwise allowable itemized deductions for charitable donations, home-mortgage interest, real estate taxes, and the like aggregate $20,000. You need no calculator to know that the amount of income above the $111,800 threshold is $50,000, and 3 percent of $50,000 is $1,500. *Result:* Your deductions are limited to $18,500; you forfeit $1,500.

You suffer the same $1,500 disallowance whether your itemized deductions are $30,000 or $100,000, because the disallowance is based on the amount by which AGI surpasses $111,800, not the total of itemized deductions. However, this curtailment cannot cause you to lose more than 80 percent of your total deductions; you still are allowed 20 percent of them.

Strategy. Is it worth the trouble for persons with incomes mainly from investments to move funds into tax-exempt municipal bonds, thereby lowering AGIs and shielding some of their itemized deductions from the 3 percent rule? For most investors, the modest tax savings is insufficient to warrant playing around with investment returns.

Consider, for instance, how slight a reward would be reaped by someone in a 31 percent bracket and an above-$111,800 AGI were he to move more than $125,000 out of taxable investments and into tax-exempts and lower AGI by $10,000. With those numbers, he would salvage itemized deductions of $300 and save less than $100 in taxes.

A better way to lower AGI is to move the maximum allowable amount of deductible contributions into retirement plans, whether Individual Retirement Accounts or 401(k) plans for employees (Chapter 10), or Keogh plans, which are used to shelter earnings of self-employeds. Moreover, you get a tax deferral for the interest or other earnings on your retirement savings.

Caution. After 1994, the $111,800 threshold is scheduled to be adjusted upward to provide relief from inflation, as measured by the Consumer Price Index. However, spiraling budget deficits might compel our lawmakers to further curtail itemized deductions for write-offs like home-mortgage interest and real estate taxes. The backdoor tax hike could take the form of a decrease in the threshold, an increase in the amount disallowed to above 3 percent, or both.

Your Share of the Tax Burden

The income tax is just. It simply intends to put the burdens of government justly upon the backs of the people. I am in favor of an income tax. When I find a man who is not willing to bear his share of the burdens of the government which protects him, I find a man who is unworthy to enjoy the blessings of a government like ours.

—William Jennings Bryan,
Speech to Democratic
National Convention, Chicago,
July 8, 1896

An organization promoting marijuana legalization claims that this would produce needed taxes. Its leader said, "We want to pay higher taxes, something no other group is willing to do."

I'm delighted to pay big taxes. Big taxes mean big income.

—H. Ross Perot, *The New York Times,* April 15, 1988

The budget should be balanced, the Treasury should be refilled, public debt should be reduced, the arrogance of officialdom should be tempered and controlled, and the assistance to foreign lands should be curtailed lest Rome become bankrupt.

—Marcus Tullius Cicero,
106–143 B.C., greatest
Roman orator, famous also as a
politician and philosopher

Do you sometimes feel as though the entire tax load falls on your shoulders? If so, it would not come as a surprise to the Tax Foundation, Inc., a business-oriented, Washington-based research outfit that scrutinizes Internal Revenue Service statistics. According to the Tax Foundation, recent years have seen only slight changes in the share of the tax load borne by basically middle- and upper-income persons.

What follows is a rundown of some interesting statistics gleaned from returns filed for 1991 (the latest figures available). These statistics are compared with the figures for 1986 (when the changes introduced by tax reform first took effect) through 1990.

The comparison is based on AGI, short for adjusted gross income. AGI is the figure shown at the bottom of page 1 of Form 1040 after listing salaries and other sources of income and claiming certain deductions like money set aside in IRAs. The AGI amount is before itemizing for outlays like charitable contributions and claiming dependency exemptions.

- The richer 50 percent of the taxpayers (those showing an AGI higher than $20,108). They shouldered 94.5 percent of the total tax revenues for 1991. The comparable figures are 93.8 for 1990, 93.9 for 1989, 94.5 for 1988, 94.1 for 1987, and 93.8 for 1986.

- The poorer 50 percent (AGI under $20,108). They paid 5.5 percent of the total. The comparable figures are 6.2 for 1990, 6.1 for 1989, 5.5 for 1988, 5.9 for 1987, and 6.2 for 1986.

- The highest 25 percent (AGI over $38,917). They footed 77.2 percent of the tax bill. The comparable figures are 76.3 for 1990, 76.5 for 1989, 77.8 for 1988, 76.7 for 1987, and 76.2 for 1986.

- The richest 10 percent (AGI over $61,952). They chipped in for 55.3 percent of the total tax revenues. The comparable figures are 53.9 for 1990, 54.5 for 1989, 56.9 for 1988, 55.4 for 1987, and 55.5 for 1986.

- The richest 5 percent (AGI over $81,601). They coughed up 43.4 percent of the total. The comparable figures are 42.9 for 1990, 43.6 for 1989, 45.9 for 1988, 43.0 for 1987, and 42.9 for 1986.

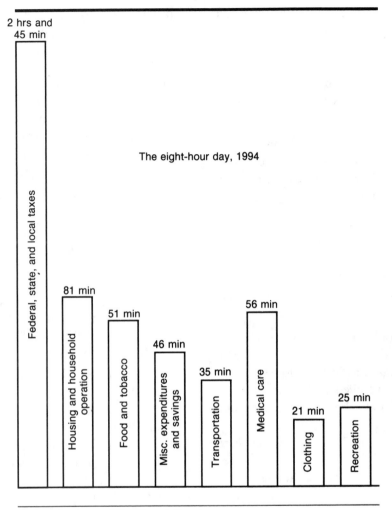

2 hrs and
45 min

The eight-hour day, 1994

Federal, state, and local taxes

81 min

Housing and household operation

51 min

Food and tobacco

46 min

Misc. expenditures and savings

35 min

Transportation

56 min

Medical care

21 min

Clothing

25 min

Recreation

Source: Courtesy of *Tax Foundation, Inc.*

The Tax Foundation also reports that Americans spent more time during 1994 (the most recent year for which information is available) earning money to pay taxes than for any other item in the household budget. Taking the 8-hour workday of the average wage earner, the Foundation calculates that 2 hours and 45 minutes were spent laboring for federal, state, and local taxes, 4 minutes longer than the 2 hours and 41 minutes for 1993.

By contrast, the average American spent 81 minutes earning the money for housing and household operation, 51 minutes for food and tobacco, 35 minutes for transportation, 56 minutes for medical care, 21 minutes for clothing, and 25 minutes for recreation. Consumer expenditures (such items as personal care, personal business, and private education), and savings claimed the remaining 46 minutes' worth of his or her day.

Federal taxes ate up the lion's share of each citizen's tax dollars, demanding 1 hour and 48 minutes, while state and local taxes took 57 minutes from the worker's time on the job.

Each year, Foundation statisticians compute Tax Freedom Day—the day that the average employee finishes working to pay all federal, state, and local taxes, assuming every dollar earned from January 1 on went to satisfy tax obligations, and begins working for him or herself. (The calculations assume all taxes are paid by individuals, including those collected from corporations.) For 1994, Tax Freedom Day fell on May 5, two days later than 1993.

Over the years, tax payments have gradually increased more than incomes; as a result, Tax Freedom Day usually comes later each year. In 1930, for instance, the average worker satisfied all tax burdens on February 13. By 1970, Tax Freedom marched more than two months further into the year, April 26.

The Foundation notes that Thomas Jefferson once observed:

I place economy among the first and most important virtues, and public debt as the greatest of dangers. To preserve our independence, we must not let our rulers load us with perpetual debt. We must make our choice between economy and liberty, or profusion and servitude. If we can prevent the Government from wasting the labors of the people under the pretense of caring for them, they will be happy.

LATE-FILING PENALTIES

As explained in the discussion of filing extensions (see "More Time to File Your Return" in Chapter 13), the IRS exacts penalties from tardy taxpayers who miss the deadlines for filing returns or for making payments. The IRS, however, will not insist on a penalty, provided you can show that the delay was "due to reasonable cause and not due to willful neglect."

The tax enforcers have long-standing guidelines on what this means. Though the agency tells its examiners to judge each case by its own facts, certain circumstances generally will excuse a late filing or payment.

So what cause is reasonable? Here are some IRS examples of acceptable excuses.

- For reasons beyond the taxpayer's control, records necessary to compute the tax were not obtainable.
- While the taxpayer mailed the return or payment in time to reach the IRS by the deadline, through no fault of his, it was delivered late.
- The taxpayer failed to file the return or pay the tax in a timely manner after receiving erroneous information from an IRS employee; or the necessary forms and instructions were not provided by the IRS in time, despite a timely request.
- Taxpayer's residence, place of business, or business records are destroyed due to a fire, other casualty, or civil disturbance.
- The death or serious illness of the taxpayer or a member of his or her immediate family occurred. Where the taxpayer is a corporation, estate, trust, or the like, the individual affected must be the person who has sole responsibility for executing the return or making the deposit

or payment, or is a member of that person's immediate family.

- The taxpayer is unavoidably absent. Again, in the case of a corporation, estate, trust, etc., the absent person must have had sole responsibility for executing the return or making the deposit or payment.

- The taxpayer can prove that he personally visited an IRS office before the filing date to get information or aid to make out the return and, through no fault of his own, he was unable to meet with an IRS representative.

Tip. How do you prove that you were there and did not see someone? Presumably, you do so by the testimony of the person you did not see. This tactic is what the lawyers call "proving a negative." I do not recommend it. Death or serious injury is more persuasive.

- The taxpayer relied on the incorrect advice of a competent tax professional, used normal prudence in determining whether further advice was needed and, as a result, came to the conclusion that a return was not required.

Caution. Is there reasonable cause that excuses a late-filing penalty where a taxpayer relies on an attorney or accountant to make a timely filing? No, according to a decision by the Supreme Court.

It all began when Robert Boyle was appointed executor for the estate of his mother. Although Boyle lacked experience in estate taxes, he had previously acted as executor for the estate of his father. The attorney who Boyle hired to handle the legal work for his mother's estate told him of the need to file an estate tax return, but did not tell him the due date for the return. He pro-

vided the attorney with all relevant records and asked several times about the return. The attorney assured Boyle that it would be prepared and filed "in plenty of time." Unfortunately for Boyle, a clerical over sight caused the attorney to miss the nine-month deadline by three months, an oversight that led to a late-filing penalty of $17,000.

The Seventh Circuit Court of Appeals agreed with Boyle that he should be held blameless. Reliance on one's attorney to do the job on time, said the appeals court, is reasonable cause for an overdue return when the taxpayer: (1) is unfamiliar with the tax law; (2) makes full disclosure of all relevant facts to the attorney that he relies on and maintains contact with the attorney from time to time during the administration of the estate; and (3) has otherwise exercised ordinary business care and prudence.

But Boyle struck out with the Supreme Court. It unanimously concluded that the taxpayer is stuck with the penalty even when an attorney causes the delay. Congress chose to place the burden of complying with filing deadlines on the taxpayer, not on an attorney or accountant or some other agent or employee of the taxpayer. "One need not be a tax expert to know that returns have fixed filing dates and that taxes must be paid when they become due."

There is a rose in this bed of thorns. The Supreme Court noted that a different issue arises when a taxpayer relies on the advice of a lawyer or other professional on a question of tax law, such as whether a liability exists. It is reasonable for a client to rely on such advice, though it proves erroneous. "Most taxpayers are not competent to discern error in the substantive advice of an accountant or attorney. To require the taxpayer to challenge the attorney, to seek a second opinion, or to try to monitor counsel on the provisions of the Internal Revenue Code himself would nullify the very purpose of seeking the advice of a presumed expert in the first place."

So you are on fairly safe ground when you rely on the advice of a tax expert that a return need not be filed. If it turns out that your tax pro goofed, odds are that the IRS will be forgiving.

For instance, the Tax Court refused to approve assessment of a penalty for late filing of an estate tax return where an executrix was erroneously advised by her attorney that no return was due until a dispute between her and a beneficiary was resolved.

Tip. There can be situations where a tax pro provides erroneous advice on the deadline for submission of a return. This may be due to a misunderstanding of what the law says is the deadline to file (for instance, telling a client that the due date for an estate tax return is 15, rather than nine, months after the death of the decedent) or to a mistake in counting (say, counting nine months from January 15 and determining that the return is due November 15). Presumably, there is reasonable cause for a late filing in either of these situations.

Caution. The executor or administrator of an estate should ask the lawyer or accountant early and often when federal returns have to be filed and how they are progressing. It's also wise to inquire about state returns.

There was no reasonable cause to excuse a late-payment penalty for estate taxes where the delay was caused by the heirs squabbling over who was liable for the taxes. Nor, held the Tax Court, should John R. and Geraldine M. Gore of Hobart, Indiana, be relieved of a late-return penalty just because their tax adviser recommended a delay to avoid an audit.

How Penalties Are Assessed

Generally, the penalty for late filing is 5 percent of the tax not paid by the due date for each month (or fraction thereof) that the return is late, up to a maximum of 25 percent.

Assuming there is no reasonable cause for the late filing, a measure of relief may be available under what is known as the "timely mailed, timely filed" rule (see Code Section 7502). A tax return is treated as filed on the date it is mailed to the Internal Revenue Service. Thus, the IRS will not assess the usual penalty against a taxpayer whose return is mailed by the filing deadline, even if it's delayed or lost in the mails.

But the IRS warns that this rule doesn't shield a return that is not mailed until after the deadline (Rev. Rul. 73–133). Worse yet, a late mailing can turn out to be considerably more expensive than you might think if the mail is slow.

The IRS computes the late-filing penalty for a delinquent return from the date it is *received*, not the date mailed. The difference can mean an extra 5 percent penalty if the return is delayed for as little as one extra day.

This was underscored in a dispute involving a return that was due on April 15, but not mailed until May 14, just under a month late, and not received until May 19, a bit over one month late. The penalty should be 10 percent rather than 5 percent, said the IRS, and the Tax Court agreed.

STILL WAITING FOR A REFUND? IF YOU MOVED, TELL THE IRS

Every filing season, the IRS is unable to deliver thousands of refund checks that belong to persons who moved without sending their new addresses to the tax collectors. Many of these undelivered checks are owed to recent retirees whose final months on the job constituted less than a full year. Their employers withheld taxes at an annual rate based on an anticipated total that they failed to reach; hence, the refunds.

If you move or otherwise change your address after filing your return and you are expecting a refund, notify the IRS. To report an address change, use IRS Form 8822 (Change of Address).

It is easy to fill out: Just insert your old and new addresses and your full name and Social Security number, as well as the full name and Social Security number of your spouse if you file jointly. Mail the form to the IRS Service Center that handled your last return. Notifying the Post Office is not sufficient.

As of November 1993, the agency was the unwilling holder of refund checks totaling over $50 million that could not be delivered to over 96,000 taxpayers, with an average refund of $518. *Reasons:* The addresses were wrong or the taxpayers moved away without leaving forwarding addresses. Some of those checks are for more than $10,000, according to a report prepared by the General Accounting Office, a congressional agency that monitors the operations of the federal bureaucracy.

It is not just individuals who cannot be located; the IRS also holds refunds due corporations and other businesses. In commenting on the GAO report, an IRS spokesperson revealed that a New York company's undelivered refund check is for "many tens of thousands of dollars."

Those entitled to these refunds can recover them, regardless of how many years have passed. The only thing is, to collect, the taxpayers will have to remember that they have the money coming.

To help reunite these taxpayers with their money, IRS district offices list the names of persons who have not claimed their refund checks. Those lists are published yearly, usually around November. That's about all the help that the IRS provides.

Your move.   Think that you are due a refund? To recover it, you must file Form 3911 (Taxpayer's Statement Regarding Refund), on which you give your Social Security number, the date that the return was filed and the address you used when the return for that year was filed.

Caution.   The U.S. Postal Inspection Service warns taxpayers to beware of mailings from companies that offer to help you get your refund for a small fee. Although the offers may look official, these companies cannot get your refund for you. Instead, they will send you a Form 3911, which you can get free from the IRS.

IRS research shows that almost all undeliverable refund checks are caused by taxpayers not using the preaddressed peel-off label (discussed in "How to Avoid a Hassle with the IRS" in Chapter 13) provided to them with their return.

Tip. Lost refunds are yet another reason to keep copies of your tax returns, which, in any case, are always helpful as guides for future 1040 forms or amending previously filed returns. (For how to amend a return, see the next section of this chapter.)

All is not lost if you failed to copy your return and now need it; get IRS Form 4506. (For more information on Form 4506 (Request for Copy of Tax Form), see "Paperwork" in "Coping with the IRS after April 15" later in this chapter.)

Help from the IRS.   To obtain Forms 3911, 4506, or 8822, telephone 1-800-TAX-FORM (allow seven to ten work days for delivery of these forms and at least 45 days for delivery of a copy of your return) or stop by the IRS office that serves your area to get the forms immediately. (See "Get the Right Help at Tax Time" in Chapter 13.)

But did you have your return filled out by a paid preparer? Check first to see if you are able to get it from the preparer. This may save you some time and money, as the IRS imposes a charge of $4.25 (the standard fee as this book goes to press in the summer of 1994) for a copy of a Form 1040.

Refund Claims

Death and taxes may be life's only certainties, but at least with taxes, we get a second chance. If you goof on a tax return, the IRS gives you three years to correct it. And if that results in a refund, you'll even get interest on your overpayment.

—*Medical Economics,*
February 21, 1994

There is no need to panic if you rechecked a copy of your Form 1040 after it was filed and discovered an error—an overlooked deduction, exemption, or credit, overstated income, or some other slipup that could change your tax liability. An obliging IRS provides a relatively easy way to correct a mistake or to take advantage of a retroactive change in the law, without the bother of completely redoing the return or going through any complicated red tape.

Just contact the Revenue Service for Form 1040X (Amended U.S. Individual Income Tax Return), a simplified form consisting of two pages, plus a set of instructions on how to explain the change you wish to make and compute the refund or balance due.

No matter how meritorious your claim or how sympathetic the IRS is, you are not entitled to a refund unless you satisfy certain procedural requirements and file a timely claim. Here are some tips on how to avoid delaying correspondence and to speed up the processing of your refund claim.

- File a separate Form 1040X for each year for which you are claiming a refund. A claim filed for one year does not put the IRS on notice that you also seek a refund for another year. It's immaterial that the error in issue is identical for more than one year.

- With your claim, you should submit any applicable correspondence from the IRS or tax return schedules and forms. Attach a copy of any IRS notice relating to your refund claim or previously filed return. To correct your return to, say, retroactively take advantage of the childcare credit, submit Form 2441, just as you would have if you had claimed the credit on your original return. If you are correcting the amount of wages or tax withheld that you reported for the year in question, attach a copy of any additional or corrected W-2 forms that you got after you filed your original return.

- Your claim has to set forth in detail each of the grounds upon which you seek a refund. If you are uncertain about what grounds to list, it's permissible to cite alternate, or even inconsistent, grounds. You can, for instance, state that the write-off in question is deductible as a loss resulting from a theft or a bad debt. In addition, the Form 1040X must include facts sufficient to inform the IRS of the items or transactions that it must check to substantiate your claim.

- State an amount to be refunded, although you need not list an exact amount. To leave the door open for a refund in excess of the amount specified, tax pros routinely add this language to the claim: "or such greater amount as is legally refundable, with interest."

- Don't overlook signing Form 1040X.

Tip. Have you moved? After you complete Form 1040X, send it to the IRS Service Center where your return was filed, not to the Service Center for your current address.

Caution. According to IRS officials, filing Form 1040X does not mean that your return will be automatically flagged for examination. The original return, plus the correction indicated on Form 1040X, are supposed to be reviewed just the way the agency would have reviewed your return, had you originally filed a correct one. Nevertheless, you should be aware that an amendment of your Form 1040 for any reason might prompt the

IRS not only to question other items on your return but also to take a look at your returns for earlier years.

It's wise to determine in advance of an audit whether, say, some of your deductions can stand a closer look. The examination could conceivably uncover errors that erase the hoped-for refund and entitle the IRS to exact back taxes plus interest. Note also that approval of a refund claim does not bar a later audit.

Deadline for filing an amended return. The deadline is fairly liberal. Generally, the law requires you to submit Form 1040X within (1) three years from the date (including any filing extension) you filed your original return (a return filed before the due date is treated as having been filed on the due date), or (2) within two years from the time you paid the tax, whichever is later.

Example. You want to correct an erroneous Form 1040 for 1992 that you filed in February 1993. Ordinarily, the statute of limitations for filing Form 1040X runs out on April 15, 1996. Note, though, that if you obtained an extension of your filing deadline (for filing extensions, see Chapter 13), that also extends your amending deadline.

Caution. The statute of limitations bars a refund claim even when the failure to file a timely claim is due to a delay caused by IRS-supplied information that proves erroneous.

Tip. The general rule is subject to some exceptions that extend the statute of limitations when, among other things, you failed to take deductions for bad debts (see "Loaning Money to a Relative or Friend" in Chapter 9) or worthless securities (Chapter 10). In those cases, you have seven, instead of three, years to submit a refund claim.

Caution. Most refund claims and other documents reach the IRS without incident and are properly handled there. But suppose your Form 1040X is among those mismailed, misfiled, or mislaid by the Post Office or the IRS, and after the deadline passes, the tax collectors contend that you failed to beat it. To save yourself a possible headache, get and keep proof of mailing Form 1040X. Send it certified mail, return receipt requested, and staple the receipt to the copy you retain. Even better, hand-deliver Form 1040X to the IRS and have an agency clerk stamp the receipt date on your retained copy.

State tax returns. A change to your Form 1040 also may mean that you have to amend your state return. If so, you should file the appropriate state form.

Protective Claims

In certain situations, it may be necessary to file a "protective" refund claim, which is prepared and filed like any other refund claim. A prospective claim allows a taxpayer to keep open, beyond the usual statute of limitations, a claim on an issue where, for example, there is reason to hope that the IRS may reverse its position in the event that it loses a pending case involving another taxpayer.

More than one taxpayer has discovered too late that failing to file a protective claim means forfeiting a refund that would otherwise be routinely allowed. Consider, for example, the plight of Bob Hindes, a tax-

conscious owner of some real estate that had gone up in value.

Bob's troubles started when he formed a corporation solely to buy his property on the installment method and resell it for cash to a third party. He used installment reporting to spread out his tax bite, while the corporation reported the entire gain. (The tax code no longer allows this maneuver.) But the IRS refused to recognize his sale to the corporation on the ground that the corporation was a dummy and dunned him for taxes on the entire gain. Bob then took the issue to court, but overlooked the need for the corporation to file a protective refund claim. By the time the court decided he owed taxes on the entire gain, which meant the corporation owed no taxes, the corporation was barred from recovering a refund by the expiration of the statute of limitations.

Tip. Don't delay the filing of a prospective claim merely because you're uncertain about the amount due. File it while the limitations period remains open whenever you learn of something that supports your position, even though the exact amount due is undeterminable.

Help from the IRS

For more information about refund claims, see IRS Publication 556, *Examination of Returns, Appeal Rights, and Claims for Refund.* For a free copy, call 1-800-TAX-FORM (allow at least 10 work days for mailing) or stop by the IRS office serving your area to obtain one immediately. Many libraries also have copies of this and other IRS tax guides. IRS Publication 910, *Guide to*

Free Tax Services, provides a complete list of booklets and explains what each one covers. (For a discussion of IRS publications, see "Get the Right Help at Tax Time" in Chapter 13.)

Tip. Don't rely absolutely on IRS advice, whether it is information that employees give to telephone or walk-in inquiries or instructions that the agency prints in its publications. Mistakes in instructions or advice are inevitable, and the IRS is not bound by them.

HEFTY PENALTY FOR USING "WITHHELD" DOLLARS

The law empowers the IRS to act firmly and swiftly against companies that fail to timely turn over to Uncle Sam the withholding and payroll taxes for their employees. The typical culprits are small or medium-sized, closely held companies that find themselves short of operating cash and unable to borrow from banks or other conventional sources.

The problem that confronts these companies is how to come up with sufficient funds to meet the gross payroll and also pay apprehensive suppliers who are unwilling to extend additional credit. Their solution is what gets these businesses into bad tax trouble. Management opts to pay employees their net salaries or wages and not to make required deposits with the IRS. After all, reason the ever-optomistic officers, they will take care of the "borrowed" taxes just as soon as business picks up.

Many thousands of individuals who played games with withheld taxes later were stunned to discover that they were personally liable if their company failed to pay such taxes. Buried in the Internal Revenue Code

is a provision, Section 6672, that authorizes the IRS to assert a 100 percent penalty against persons required to collect and pay over taxes and who willfully failed to do so.

Pursuant to revised procedures that took effect early in 1993, a kinder and gentler IRS no longer refers to the penalty packing possibly the severest wallop in its arsenal as the "100 percent penalty." Instead, an image-conscious agency has come up with a bland term—the "trust fund recovery penalty."

Generally, the feds pursue the owners or top officers of an organization. The official policy is not to assert the penalty against "non-owner employees of the business, who act solely under the dominion and control of others, and who are not in a position to make independent decisions on behalf of the business entity"—for instance, secretaries, clerks, and bookkeepers. However, the tax enforcers have lots of leeway on just who should be dunned.

Consider, for example, the plight of Ted Neckles. When the IRS first became aware that Task Enterprises, Inc., had failed to remit hundreds of thousands of dollars in withheld taxes, there seemed to be little that the government could do to get its mitts on the money. Task had folded within a year of its incorporation. The IRS looked into the pockets of former officers but found nothing.

The agency finally focused on Ted, one of the original organizers and investors, but not an officer or employee of Task. IRS sleuths discovered that Ted had always been around and had significant control over disbursement of funds. Though without any title and unsalaried, he was authorized to draw on all corporate accounts and signed most of the checks on the firm's general account. Ted made decisions as to which creditors would be paid and when. What is more, he knew of the withheld, but unpaid, tax money.

The IRS invoked Section 6672 and forced Ted to pay the withheld funds. He filed suit to recover the payment. But the court concluded that he was what the lawyers call a de facto, that is, in reality, Task employee. Clearly, he was someone who could have seen to it that the withheld taxes were paid over. Because Ted had the power and the authority to pay creditors and was aware of the tax arrears, he was a "responsible person" within the meaning of Section 6672 and was therefore liable for the taxes.

Fortunately, there are some limits on who can be held liable when a business goes belly up. In another dispute, the court snubbed the invitation of the IRS to impose liability on Catherine Barrett, an officer who was a mere figurehead, with no real authority. Catherine, the president's wife and subsequently his widow, had been authorized by him to sign company checks. But there was believeable testimony that she had done so only at the command of her husband, who ran the business "with an iron hand" and forced her to sign checks by "berating her publicly, threatening her and at times beating her." The court found that the real authority to decide whom to pay and when rested solely with him.

Tip. To improve its collection prospects, the IRS can assess the same 100 percent penalty against more than one person where there is more than one responsible corporate officer. The agency, however, can collect only once, though it is free to choose the parties who get stuck.

COPING WITH THE IRS AFTER APRIL 15

There can be trouble ahead if you assume that filing your Form 1040 means that you are finished with the feds for another year. For instance, the IRS may want to chat about your return. Usually, they will insist on extra taxes plus interest, unless you have records to back up your deductions and other items on the form. But just how long do you need to hang on to your records? And what if you discover you overpaid your taxes? Here are some tips on how to cope with audits, refund snafus, and other post–April 15 encounters with the tax takers.

Refunds

Q. *Although I filed my tax return in the early part of April, I have not yet received my refund. How long should I wait before I check to see whether something went wrong?*

A. Normally, you will receive your refund check about six weeks after filing your return. The IRS says you should wait at least eight weeks after filing before inquiring about a refund.

For instructions on how to call a toll-free telephone number in your area for information on the status of your refund, see the instruction booklet that comes with Form 1040. Be sure to have a copy of your tax return available; when calling, you must provide the first Social Security number shown on your return, your filing status (single, married filing jointly, etc.), and the exact amount of your refund.

Tip. Many times, says the IRS, it turns out that a refund is "lost" because one spouse has cashed the check unbeknownst to the other.

Q. *Thanks to an IRS computer goof, I received an unexpected windfall. Instead of an expected refund of $600, I received a check for $6,600. Can I simply hold on to the money until the IRS discovers the error or would I be better off returning it immediately?*

A. Because you have use of the money, the IRS will charge you interest which, like other kinds of consumer interest payments (discussed in "Timing Payments of Deductible Expenses" in Chapter 1), you cannot deduct. To avoid an interest charge, immediately return the overpayment. You can either return the $6,600 check in full or deposit it and send your own check for $6,000.

Tip. An IRS official informally advises that you will do better to send your own check for the excess payment. If you return the IRS check, you will have to wait about eight to ten weeks to get a check for the correct amount. In addition, if your check goes astray, you can stop payment and send another check. If you return the IRS check and that happens, it can be more difficult getting the matter straightened out.

Interest on an erroneous refund. The law entitles the IRS to collect interest on an erroneous refund, as an Arizona couple belatedly discovered. Charles and Patricia Lasbury filed a 1979 return that showed a balance due of $1,000. Because of a computer blunder, they received an unexpected windfall in April of 1980—a refund of $22,000.

It was not until April 1982 that the IRS sent a letter telling the Lasburys to repay the $22,000 mistakenly sent to them. The letter made no mention of interest charges. The couple voluntarily repaid the $22,000 before the IRS began any court action.

Fade to August 1982, when the IRS sued them for interest on the money while they held it. *Verdict:* It made no difference that the IRS had erred or that the Lasburys voluntarily repaid the money. The court held the IRS was entitled to $5,500 interest, plus interest from the date the agency filed its suit.

Q. *The tax refund check I received from the IRS is less than the amount I claimed on my return. There was no explanation accompanying the check. Should I cash it?*

A. Yes. The IRS issued your refund check for the amount clearly owed to you. And it may be holding the refund balance because of an error on your part. For instance, you may have neglected to check the box indicating you file as a head of household, thereby forcing the IRS to mistakenly figure your tax at the higher rates for a single person. So cashing your check will in no way prevent you from getting any refund balance to which you are entitled.

Amending Returns

Q. *I rechecked a copy of my tax return after it was already filed and discovered an error. How do I correct it?*

A. Use Form 1040X to explain the change you wish to make and to compute the refund or balance due. (For more information, see the discussion of refund claims in the preceding section of this chapter.)

Q. *Because of marital problems, my husband and I filed separate returns last year. Now that we've reconciled, can we switch to joint returns for that year?*

A. Yes, provided you do so by filing an amended return within three years from the filing deadline for your return.

Remember, though, that you can't make the opposite switch. If you file jointly, you can't switch to separate returns once the filing deadline has passed. That election is binding on you.

Q. *We filed jointly and then divorced. Now my former husband threatens to disavow our joint return and file a separate return. Can he get away with forcing me to pay more taxes?*

A. Relax. It's too late now for him to switch from filing jointly to filing separately.

Q. *We filed a joint return and took the standard deduction. Now we find it would have been to our advantage to itemize our payments for interest charges on home mortgages, charitable contributions, and the like. Are we stuck with the standard deduction?*

A. No. You can amend your return and switch from the standard deduction to itemizing, or vice versa, provided you do so no later than three years after the filing deadline for your return.

Audits

Q. *My husband and I disagree about how long we should keep the backup records for old tax returns. I say six years; he says three. Which one of us is right?*

A. It all depends. You should retain receipts and whatever else might help support deductions or other items on your return, at least until the statute of limitations runs out for an IRS audit or for you to file a refund claim, should you find an error after filing.

As a general rule, the IRS has three years from the filing deadline to take a crack at your return. (For more information on IRS audits and how long to keep records, see Chapter 11.)

Q. *The IRS wants to audit my return. At the time I filed it, I lived in a different state. Must I return to that state for the examination?*

A. No. You can ask the IRS to transfer your case to its office for the area in which you now reside.

Q. *I didn't file a tax return for last year because I feared that doing so would alert the IRS to my failure to file for earlier years and it would bring charges that could lead to imprisonment, as well as civil penalties. If I make a voluntary disclosure of my failure to file, will that end all of my problems?*

A. Usually, the government does not bring criminal charges against a person who makes a truly voluntary disclosure *before* an investigation begins. But a voluntary disclosure will not shield a repenting taxpayer from hefty civil penalties for fraud or for late filing, plus interest charges on back taxes, that are routinely exacted from a cheater who is spared criminal prosecution. (For more on voluntary disclosures, see "Criminal Investigations" in Chapter 11.)

Q. *The IRS claims the increase in my net worth doesn't jibe with my reported income. To help track down my spending, it wants my attorney to turn over copies of his bills and testify about them. Can it force him to reveal confidential information?*

A. Fee arrangements between an attorney and his client are not shielded by the attorney-client privilege.

Q. *The IRS has issued a summons for my tax records. Am I or my attorney entitled to be reimbursed for the cost of locating, copying, and transporting the records?*

A. No. The IRS is only required to reimburse third parties such as banks. (IRS summonses are discussed under "Criminal Investigations" in Chapter 11.)

Q. *A South Dakota court convicted me on charges of indecently exposing myself to members of the opposite sex. But the way I see things, the tax rules that grant dependency exemptions for children encourage married couples to engage in the same kind of conduct that caused my conviction. Since these rules encourage behavior that South Dakota says is criminal, shouldn't that excuse me from paying taxes?*

A. That's the very argument Raymond Rau made. But a baffled Tax Court was unimpressed with his argument and ordered Raymond to pay his taxes.

Q. *What's the difference between tax avoidance and tax evasion?*

A. Tax *evasion* is a criminal offense that carries a jail sentence of up to five years, plus a fine of up to $100,000. Tax *avoidance,* on the other hand, is perfectly legal; for example, if you know your tax bracket will be higher for this year than next, you would be wise to concentrate charitable contributions and other deductibles into this year, because the deductions will generate a greater tax savings in the higher-bracket year. (See "Criminal Investigations" in Chapter 11.)

Penalties

Q. *I thought that I had paid my taxes, and I've received a notice from the IRS saying I owe more, plus an estimated tax penalty. How can that be?*

A. There could be several reasons. You might not have had enough income tax withheld from each of your paychecks, or perhaps an error was made in the preparation of your return. Are you a self-employed person? What prompted the notice might be that you missed making the required quarterly estimated tax payments.

Q. *Because of a blunder by my return preparer, I was hit with an estimated tax penalty. What's the tax situation if the preparer pays the penalty?*

A. According to an IRS ruling, you must report the payment as income (Ruling 77449029).

Q. *How does the IRS calculate the running of an underpayment penalty for estimated taxes?*

A. The penalty runs from the deadline for the installment payment to the date of payment, but not beyond the filing deadline for Form 1040.

Note that although further running of the penalty on an insufficient earlier installment can be *stopped* by an overpayment of a later installment, to the extent it erases the arrears, an overpayment *will not wipe out* the penalty for an earlier underpayment.

Q. *Besides my salary, I receive taxable alimony from my ex-husband. Is there any way I can avoid the bother, not to mention the difficulty of coming up with the money, of payments of quarterly installments of estimated income taxes on my alimony?*

A. Yes. Arrange to have your employer increase the amount withheld from your salary by enough to excuse you from making estimated tax payments.

Tip. Salary withholdings are treated as taken out in equal amounts during the four quarters, regardless of when they are actually deducted. Consequently, extra withholding as late as December 31 can *retroactively offset* an underestimate as early as April 15 and eliminate a penalty for underpayment of estimated taxes. (For more on withholding and estimated payments, see the discussion earlier in this chapter.)

Q. *Do I need to worry about a late-filing penalty if I turned my records over to a return preparer who filed my Form 1040 after the due date?*

A. Reliance on your adviser is not an acceptable excuse. (See the discussion of late-filing penalties earlier in this chapter.)

Q. *I did my neighbor a favor and filled out his return for free. In case he's audited, am I subject to those tough rules that penalize preparers who negligently or intentionally disregard the IRS rules or regulations?*

A. No. Those rules apply only to someone who prepares a return for compensation. For penalty purposes, you are not considered "compensated" if he insisted on inviting you to dinner or mowed your lawn in return. (For penalties imposed on persons who prepare returns for compensation, see "Penalties for Preparers" in Chapter 13.)

Q. *Suppose I don't turn over to the IRS the income and Social Security taxes withheld by my company from its employees. What can happen?*

A. Quite a bit. You are personally liable for the unpaid taxes. That means the IRS can slap a 100 percent penalty equal to the unpaid taxes against you when you neglect your duty to collect and pay over the taxes. And worse yet, the IRS can also grab your assets to satisfy the penalty without first trying to collect from your company. (See the discussion earlier in this chapter of "Hefty Penalty for Using 'Withheld' Dollars.")

Q. *How can I keep track of all the federal deadlines for filing returns and sending in tax payments?*

A. One way is to ask IRS for its free Publication 509, *Tax Calendars*. To obtain a copy, call 1-800-TAX-FORM (allow at least 10 work days for mailing) or stop by the IRS office for your area to obtain one immediately.

Paperwork

Q. *After suffering through years of my husband's out-of-control gambling and high-frequency infidelity, I finally have decided to file for divorce. Before the split becomes final, I need to negotiate a financial settlement that will adequately provide for myself and our children. My lawyer will not be able to hammer out an agreement until I can provide detailed information about my husband's finances—the amounts and kinds of gambling winnings, how much he earns, and where he has savings accounts, as well as his other sources of income.*

I know that he has to disclose this information on our 1040 forms. Like lots of other wives, though, I foolishly signed a blank 1040 when tax time rolled around each April. That's the last I saw of our joint returns, which were filled out by a certified public accountant, a woman that I have good reason to suspect has been romantically involved with my husband for several years.

Not surprisingly, I am being stonewalled by my future ex-husband, who absolutely refuses to give me his retained copies of our returns. Do I have to pay even more to my attorney for suing to get ahold of them? My legal fees are already astronomical.

A. Your lawyer ought to have advised you that there is no need to go before a judge. In fact, this is one chore that you readily can handle without help from an attorney or anyone else.

The law, in most cases, requires a paid preparer, such as your husband's CPA, to keep copies of returns for at least three years after the filing due date—for instance, at least until April 1996 in the case of a return for tax year 1993, with a filing due date, for most persons, of April 1994. Consequently, you should be able to obtain copies from her, though she might try to stall for a while.

Going the preparer route, notes the IRS, can save you both time and money, as the agency imposes a charge of $4.25 for each return requested. (As this book goes to press in the summer of 1994, the IRS announced that it proposes to raise the fee from $4.25 to $12.00.) But if, as is understandable, you prefer to avoid any contact with an allegedly adulterous accountant, all is not lost. You are entitled to get copies from the IRS. This is so even if all the jointly reported income was your husband's.

There is a bit of easy-to-complete paperwork involved when you ask the IRS to provide copies of returns and all attachments, including W-2 forms. You have to use IRS Form 4506 (Request for Copy of Tax Form), available by telephoning 1-800-TAX-FORM (allow at least 10 work days for mailing) or by stopping by the IRS office that serves your area to get it immediately.

Have you moved? After you complete Form 4506 (to ease your burden, it need *not* be signed by your husband), send it to the IRS Service Center where the returns were filed, not to the Service Center for your current address. Use a separate Form 4506 for each Service Center from which you are requesting a copy of your return. Allow at least 45 days for delivery of copies.

Q. *My wife and I plan to open a joint savings account, and the bank will ask for a Social Security number. Should I use mine or hers?*

A. If the money belongs to one of you, furnish that person's number. If you both chipped in, furnish either number. From the income tax viewpoint, if you file a joint return, it makes no difference which number you use.

Q. *My one-year-old received some cash gifts on his birthday and I intend to open a savings account for him. Does he need a Social Security number?*

A. Yes, even if he doesn't have to file a return. To apply for a Social Security number, you should use Form SS-5, available from any Social Security Administration Office. Moreover, you must report Social Security numbers for children and other persons one year or older who are claimed by you as dependents. (For the rules on dependency exemptions, see Chapter 2.)

Q. *My father is 68 and still works part-time. Since he is receiving Social Security benefits, is his employer correct in withholding Social Security from his pay?*

A. Yes. His pay remains subject to Social Security withholding even if he is already receiving benefits.

Q. *I plan to hire my first employee and will have to withhold taxes from his wages. How do I get an employer identification number?*

A. Application for an employer identification number is made on Form SS-4, available at any Internal Revenue office. Mail the completed application to the IRS Service Center designated in the instructions on the form.

Q. *I recently incorporated my business. Can my new corporation still use my old employer identification number?*

A. No. A new corporation must apply for its own employer identification number on Form SS-4.

15 SOCIAL SECURITY TAXES

HOUSEHOLD HELP

The Internal Revenue Service can play rough when it tracks down people who hire household help and fail to fork over Social Security taxes on their wages. Despite what you may have heard, warns the IRS, you are not off the hook for withholding just because a hard-to-hire housecleaner is unwilling to work unless you agree to forget about Social Security taxes.

While it may take years for the IRS to uncover what you have left undone, the delayed day of reckoning can come when your helper retires and applies for Social Security benefits based on earnings that should have been reported in earlier years. Worse yet, your tax tab can turn out to be a lot more expensive than you might think.

The IRS can hit you with a bill for all back taxes (not just *your* share, but also the *employee's* share that you were supposed to withhold), as well as interest, plus a slew of penalties for late payment and late filing. There is no time limit on when the IRS can begin an audit if you fail to file Form 942 (Employer's Quarterly Tax Return for household employees), which is discussed below. (For more on the time limit for audits, see "How Long to Keep Tax Records" in Chapter 11.)

This was made clear a number of years ago to a Mississippi woman who employed two domestics for several years and opted to "let a sleeping dog lie" when it came to Social Security taxes. She wound up paying over $3,700 in taxes, interest, and penalties. Nowadays, her tab would be more than twice as much.

Unpaid Social Security taxes derailed the nomination of Zoe Baird, the $507,000-a-year senior vice president and general counsel for the Aetna Life and Casualty Company who was nominated for Attorney General by President Clinton at the start of 1993. Zoe withdrew from contention for the post after revelations that she and her husband, Yale law professor Paul Gewirtz, needed a driver and a nanny for their infant son, Julian, had hired illegal aliens, a Peruvian couple, and had failed to pay Social Security taxes on the couple's weekly salary of $500.

To make amends, the two lawyers had to pay $12,000 taxes, penalties, and interest, plus a fine of $2,900 for knowingly hiring undocumented workers. Presumably, Zoe, who went back to Aetna, and Paul filed amended returns for child-care credits (see Chapter 6) on the wages they paid for Julian's care.

Unlike Zoe and Paul, you don't have to preside over a household staff or pay a lot to become liable for Social Security taxes. You are stuck with those taxes once you pay cash wages of $50 or more in a three-month calendar quarter to a household employee. The $50 figure has languished unadjusted since it went on the books in 1950 and works out to as little as $4 a week.

Also, the IRS broadly defines "household employee" to include babysitters, whether adult or teenage, cooks, maids, and companions for the elderly or convalescents, but not persons who work for you as independent contractors—for instance, painters or plumbers.

All cash payments count. This holds true even if part is paid to cover the cost of board, room, or bus fare. But you do not have to count the value of room and board, clothing, or other noncash items. Nor are any taxes due on what you pay to your spouse or to a son or daughter under 21 for household chores.

When Social Security taxes fall due, you must file Form 942, along with your check for the Social Security tax of 15.30 percent on the earnings (the employee's 7.65 percent and the employer's matching 7.65 percent), plus any income taxes that your employee authorized you to withhold. You are responsible for paying the entire 15.30 percent, whether or not you subtracted the domestic's share from his or her wages.

The filing deadline is the last day of the month following the end of the calendar quarter. For instance, the deadline is January 31 for the quarter ending December 31.

Proposed legislation. As this book goes to press in the summer of 1994, Congress is considering several proposals to replace the quarterly threshold of $50 for Social Security taxes with a higher yearly one, starting in 1995. The proposed benchmarks range from $630 to $1,250. An employer paying less than the revised threshold would not have to pay any Social Security taxes for that person. Also eliminated would be Social Security

taxes for wages paid to household employees under age 18.

The highest proposed yearly threshold of $1,250 works out to slightly more than $24 for one day's work by a housecleaner each week. For many years, that has been well below the going rate where I live. Nevertheless, even as modest a yearly figure of $630 would be a greatly overdue revision upward of the $50 quarterly threshold.

Whatever the threshold becomes, that figure would be indexed—that is, adjusted upward to reflect average wage increases.

Tip. One controversial proposal authorizes an amnesty for employers who have avoided Social Security taxes and are either caught or want to make amends. There would be a retroactive adjustment of the $50 threshold to reflect post-1950 average wage increases. For, say, 1994, the retroactive yearly threshold could become $1,200.

Caution. No refunds, though, for those who paid their Social Security taxes, whether timely or belatedly. Those out of luck include Stephen G. Breyer, a 1994 appointment to Supreme Court and previously, while on the United States Court of Appeals for the First Circuit, a finalist for the Supreme Court post that eventually went to Ruth Bader Ginsburg, and Bobby Ray Inman, who withdrew as President Clinton's choice as Defense Secretary; ultimately, they were only two more names on the long list of battered victims of the selection process in the first two years of the Clinton Administration.

Tip. The proposal would vastly simplify the procedures for filing and payment of taxes. Form 942 and the accompanying payments would no longer have to be submitted quarterly. Instead, an employer would be able to pay Social Security taxes on household help each April 15, as part of the once-a-year filing of the employer's Form 1040.

To avoid the need for a lump-sum payment of Social Security taxes on household help to accompany the Form 1040, the employer could arrange to have these Social Security taxes paid through regular estimated payments or withheld from the employer's own paychecks. Presumably, Form W-4 (Employer's Withholding Allowance Certificate; see Chapter 14) would be revised to authorize the withholding.

Tip. To now monitor Social Security compliance, the IRS can check information forms filed by employers. For instance, the form filed by persons who claim child-care credits for payments to babysitters and other care providers (see Chapter 6) must list the names, addresses, and Social Security numbers of the care providers, unless a provider is a tax-exempt organization, such as a church or other charity. Moreover, employers must show total wages and taxes paid on W-2 forms and give copies to both the employee and the IRS. The IRS can slap penalties on employers who fail to do so.

ANOTHER INCREASE

From "Security in Your Old Age," a federal government pamphlet issued in 1936 to explain the brand-new system of Social Security taxes that was to take effect the following year:

Your Part of the Tax
The taxes called for in this law will be paid both by your employer and by you. For the next 3 years you will pay maybe 15 cents a week, maybe

25 cents a week, maybe 30 cents or more, according to what you earn. That is to say, during the next 3 years, beginning January 1, 1937, you will pay 1 cent for every dollar you earn, and at the same time your employer will pay 1 cent for every dollar you earn, up to $3,000 a year. Twenty-six million other workers and their employers will be paying at the same time.

After the first 3 years—that is to say, beginning in 1940—you will pay, and your employer will pay, 1½ cents for each dollar you earn, up to $3,000 a year. This will be the tax for 3 years, and then, beginning in 1943, you will pay 2 cents, and so will your employer, for every dollar you earn for the next 3 years. After that, you and your employer will each pay half a cent more for 3 years, and finally, beginning in 1949, twelve years from now, you and your employer will each pay 3 cents on each dollar you earn, up to $3,000 a year. *That is the most you will ever pay.* [Emphasis added.]

That tax assurance from out of the past notwithstanding, you might have had to reckon with yet another rise in 1994 for FICA (Federal Insurance Contributions Act) taxes, also known as Social Security taxes, whether you did the budgeting for your family or your business.

Those FICA withholdings of payroll taxes from salaries and wages that started with January's paychecks lasted longer for anyone with earnings above $57,600 for 1994. This was the result of an increase in the "wage base," that is, the maximum amount of earnings on which FICA taxes are assessed.

The FICA tax rate for 1994 of 7.65 percent for both employers and employees remained unchanged from 1993. But the latest change in the maximum wage base (which has gone up every year since 1971, when it was $7,800) boosted the base for the 6.20-percent Social Security benefits tax from $57,600 for 1993 to $60,600 for 1994, an increase of $3,000.

High-income earners took another hit. That is because the 7.65 percent FICA tax has two components—a rate of 6.20 percent for the old age, survivors, and disability insurance fund, commonly referred to as the Social Security benefits portion, and a rate of 1.45 percent for the federal hospital insurance program for the elderly, the Medicare fund.

Before 1991, there was only one wage base for the entire 7.65 percent tax. Now however, the law mandates separate wage bases for the Social Security and Medicare parts.

For 1993, the Social Security and Medicare wage bases were $57,600 and $135,000, respectively. So while withholding for Social Security ended at $57,600, it continued just for the smaller Medicare part on wages of as much as $135,000.

The rules for 1994 were drastically revised. Social Security's wage base continues capped ($60,600 for 1994). No longer, though, is there a ceiling on Medicare's wage base. The result is that while Social Security's withholding stopped at $60,600, above-$135,000 earners were stuck with Medicare taxes on *all* of their salaries, bonuses, commissions, vacation pay, etc.

For someone who earned $60,600 during 1994, the added annual assessment amounted to $186.00 ($60,600 minus $57,600, times 6.20 percent). Put another way, a worker whose wages topped $60,600 suffered a total drop in take-home pay of at least $186.00. For each $1,000 above $60,600, he or she lost $14.50 to Medicare taxes.

For high-earning, two-paycheck couples, that drop in take-home pay might have doubled. Many self-employeds also paid more, as explained in the next section of this chapter.

Tip. The 7.65 percent FICA tax now exacts a bigger bite than federal income taxes for many middle-income earners, especially those who have sizable deductions or dependency exemptions. Things have come a long, expensive way since FICA taxes went on the books in 1937, when they were capped at $30 for both employer and employee (1 percent of the first $3,000 of earnings), and stayed that way until 1950; since then, they have risen every year.

The table on the next page illustrates how FICA taxes have ballooned, especially since 1990.

SELF-EMPLOYMENT TAXES

Social Security taxes also went up in 1994 for many self-employed individuals who operate businesses or professions as sole proprietorships, in partnerships with others, or as independent contractors. The tax rate of 15.3 percent on net self-employment earnings (receipts minus expenses) remained unchanged from 1993. But, as is true of FICA taxes (discussed in the previous section of this chapter), the 15.30-percent tax has two components—12.40 percent for Social Security and 2.90 percent for Medicare.

The base figure for the Social Security part went from earnings of $57,600 for 1993 to $60,600 for 1994. As for the Medicare part, no longer is there a ceiling on earnings, starting in 1994.

For an individual whose earnings during 1994 surpassed $60,600, the self-employment tax increased by at least $372 ($60,600 minus $57,600 times 12.40 percent). For each $1,000 above $60,600, a self-employed lost $29 to Medicare taxes. However, the law authorizes an income-tax deduction for one half of the self-employment tax.

Year	Yearly wages subject to tax	Maximum tax on a worker
1937–49	$ 3,000	$ 30.00
1950	3,000	45.00
1951–53	3,600	54.00
1954	3,600	72.00
1955–56	4,200	84.00
1957–58	4,200	94.50
1959	4,800	120.00
1960–61	4,800	144.00
1962	4,800	150.00
1963–65	4,800	174.00
1966	6,600	277.20
1967	6,600	290.40
1968	7,800	343.20
1969–70	7,800	374.40
1971	7,800	405.60
1972	9,000	468.00
1973	10,800	631.80
1974	13,200	772.20
1975	14,100	824.85
1976	15,300	895.05
1977	16,500	965.25
1978	17,700	1,070.85
1979	22,900	1,403.77
1980	25,900	1,587.67
1981	29,700	1,975.05
1982	32,400	2,170.80
1983	35,700	2,391.90
1984	37,800	2,532.60
1985	39,600	2,791.80
1986	42,000	3,003.00
1987	43,800	3,131.70
1988	45,000	3,379.50
1989	48,000	3,604.80
1990	51,300	3,924.45
1991	125,000	5,123.30
1992	130,200	5,328.90
1993	135,000	5,528.70

Caution. You become subject to the self-employment tax when your net earnings surpass $400 for the year. You must, warns the IRS, report your earnings and pay the self-employment tax, even if you are not otherwise obliged to file Form 1040, regardless of your age and even if you receive Social Security benefits. At filing time, do the paperwork on Schedule SE (Social Security Self-Employment Tax), which goes with your Form 1040.

Tip. The law authorizes a break when you have more than one self-employed operation. You can combine the earnings from all of them; consequently, the losses from one or more businesses offset the earnings from those that are profitable.

Consulting Fees Received by Retired Executives

The Tax Court agrees with the IRS that self-employment taxes are due on fees received by retired executives who perform consulting chores for their former employers. It makes no difference, says the court, that a retired exec makes himself available only to his former company and not to others or that he actually renders no consulting services during the years in issue.

When James Hornaday retired as chairman of the board of Guilford Mills, the company agreed to give him an annual payment of $40,000 for life for consulting services on an as-needed basis. During the first few years of the agreement, Guilford sought his expertise on real estate and plant expansion matters. But for the three later years under scrutiny, the company did not ask for his advice.

Hornaday argued that he was not liable for self-employment taxes of thousands of dollars on the annual payments, as Guilford was his only client and he actually provided no services. But the court disagreed. What counts is the extent to which a person is contractually obligated to perform services when called upon, not the extent to which he actually performs. Hornaday had not abandoned his consulting business; he was inactive because of forces outside of his control.

Tip.   Be aware that the law imposes penalties on self-employeds who deliberately fail to deduct from their earnings any allowable deductions, such as depreciation, so as to obtain or increase Social Security benefits.

Tax Protesters

The courts consistently agree with the IRS that the law does not excuse individuals from liability for self-employment taxes because, in their view, the Social Security system is unconstitutional. Consider, for example, how the Tax Court responded when Bruce Hunsberger, a service station operator in Indiana, argued that he was the victim of an unconstitutional, government-sponsored scam because the system is "not likely to have enough money to pay his benefits when they become due, especially since the laws are constantly changed." Bruce must continue to cough up self-employment taxes even if he ultimately collects no benefits. The system, said the court, "does not provide the contractural rights normally thought to characterize an insurance program."

Similarly, the Sixth Circuit Court of Appeals approved the collection of self-employment taxes from George Lee Kindred, the recipient of fees for a series of speeches in which he urged his audiences to revolt against the income tax system. (For more on tax protesters, see "Family Trusts and Other Tax Scams" in Chapter 11.)

Help from the IRS

For more information on the often-confusing rules, see IRS Publication 533, *Self-Employment Tax.* For a free copy, call 1-800-TAX-FORM (allow at least 10 work days for mailing) or stop by the IRS office serving your area to obtain one immediately. Many libraries also have copies of this and other IRS tax guides. IRS Publication 910, *Guide to Free Tax Services,* provides a complete list of booklets and explains what each one covers. (For a discussion of IRS publications, see "Get the Right Help at Tax Time" in Chapter 13.)

Tip.   Don't rely absolutely on IRS advice, whether it is information that employees give to telephone or walk-in inquiries or instructions that the agency prints in its publications. Mistakes in instructions or advice are inevitable, and the IRS is not bound by them.

TAXATION OF BENEFITS

One sure way to determine the social conscience of a government is to examine the way taxes are collected and how they are spent. And one sure way to determine the social conscience of an individual is to get his tax reaction. Taxes, after all, are the dues that we pay for the privileges of membership in an organized society.

—Franklin D. Roosevelt,
campaign address,
Worcester, Massachusetts,
October 31, 1936

Tucked into the 1993 overhaul of the Internal Revenue Code is a back-door provision that increases income taxes on Social

Security benefits for many middle-income retirees otherwise unaffected by the boost in the top tax rate (see "What Is Your Real Tax Bracket?" in Chapter 14) from 31 percent to 39.6 percent. The increase from as much as 50 percent to as much as 85 percent in the amount of Social Security benefits subject to income taxes takes effect starting with returns for 1994 to be filed in 1995. Most Social Security recipients, though, continue to escape income taxes completely on all of their benefits.

Gift of the MAGI.   When does the law say that you must count benefits as reportable income? Only when your income—in tax jargon, your MAGI, short for modified adjusted gross income—*exceeds* specified amounts. In calculating whether income exceeds the thresholds for benefits to be taxed, the MAGI rules require you to count not just salaries, pensions, dividends, capital gains, rents, and the like, but *also* whatever you receive as tax-exempt interest from obligations issued by state and local governments or from mutual funds, as well as 50 percent of your benefits.

For 1993, you were taxed on up to 50 percent of those benefits when your MAGI exceeded $25,000 for singles and $32,000 for joint filers.

Beginning in 1994, you were taxed on up to 50 percent of those benefits when your MAGI is between $25,000 and $34,000 for single persons or between $32,000 and $44,000 for couples filing jointly, which is no different than the rules for 1993. In addition, however, you are taxed on up to 85 percent of those benefits when your MAGI is above $34,000 for singles and $44,000 for joint filers.

Caution.   The $32,000 threshold drops to zero if you are married and file separately, unless you do not reside with your spouse at any time during the taxable year.

Translation: a married couple who live together for just a day and file separate returns do not become entitled to a base amount of $25,000 each.

Proposed legislation.   As this book goes to press in the summer of 1994, Representative Dan Rostenkowski, the former chairman of the Ways and Means Committee, proposed that Congress pass a measure to tax as much as 85 percent of the benefits when your MAGI is above $25,000 for singles and $34,000 for joint filers.

Inflation Ignored

The tax-rate brackets of 15, 28, and 31 percent (but not the brackets of 36 and 39.6 percent), dependency exemptions, and standard deductions are indexed to keep pace with inflation, whereas the tax-triggering figures of $25,000 or $32,000 are not indexed. *Result*: If inflation, which is now mild compared to the pace in previous years, persists at even its present low levels, the IRS is assured of a growing share in the Social Security benefits eventually received by many of today's younger workers. That will be Uncle Sam's version of the golden parachute for workers who retire with employer-sponsored pensions that are fully taxed and who supplement their Social Security and pensions with withdrawals of money that they conscientiously socked away for their old age in 401(k)s or IRAs, likewise fully taxed (other than withdrawals attributable to nondeductible 401(k) or IRA contributions), as is income received from other savings and investment arrangements.

Still, taxation of Social Security benefits should not stop workers from accumulating funds in tax-deferred retirement plans; they will remain a worthwhile option, particularly because of continued concern that the need to raise revenues (governmentalese for increase taxes) to offset spiraling budget deficits will compel Congress to again address itself to the unpleasant question of how to really keep the Social Security system solvent.

Divorce as a Tax Shelter

Whether by design or inadvertence, Congress crafted rules for taxation of Social Security benefits that require a person to pay more taxes on benefits solely because he or she is married. This is so because two single persons who share quarters without benefit of clergy have a combined base amount of $50,000 ($25,000 each), which gives them an advantage of $18,000 (the excess of $50,000 over $32,000) over a married couple—an aspect of the law, that, depending on one's point of view, is a "marriage penalty" or a "sin subsidy."

Certainly, no couple is going to get divorced just to trim the taxes on their Social Security benefits. But for a tax-conscious couple contemplating an unhitching, the prospect of a sizable savings at filing time could well be the clincher.

How does this break for singles help a couple? To put more, or even all, of their Social Security benefits beyond the reach of the IRS, all that they would need to do is divorce and then live together out of wedlock. Assuming their unaltered arrangement re-

mains unaltered, each would become entitled to use the base amount of $25,000 for a single person. Their unhitching (or forgoing that walk down the aisle to begin with) would enable them thereafter to live a more prosperous life in unwedded bliss.

Tip. Divorce provides another tax advantage for two-income couples with relatively equal incomes. The law mandates that marrieds combine their incomes and be taxed at the same rate for the first dollar of the second income as the rate for the last dollar of the first income. Therefore, their tab as marrieds is more than it would be as two singles who report exactly the same incomes. (See "Marriage or Divorce as a Tax Shelter in Chapter 4.)

Tax-Exempt Interest

Moving money into tax-exempt investments can significantly lower the total tax bill for retirees, just as it does for others, as well. But that maneuver will not diminish the taxes paid on Social Security benefits by retirees who also receive tax-exempt interest. As mentioned earlier, tax-free interest must be added to funds received from pensions and other sources to determine whether a Social Security recipient's income is greater than the $25,000/$32,000 thresholds. So, tax-exempt interest can cause a recipient's income that otherwise would be below the $25,000/$32,000 base amounts to exceed the figure at which benefits begin to be taxed.

Estimated Tax Payments

If you have to make estimated tax payments (see Chapter 14), you may need to set aside more for each installment to reflect your liability for taxes on Social Security benefits.

Help from Uncle Sam

For additional information, contact your local Social Security or IRS office for a free copy of Publication 915, *Social Security Benefits and Equivalent Railroad Retirement Benefits.*

State Tax Returns

Does your reportable income on Form 1040 include Social Security benefits? Check the rules of the state in which you have to file a return. In many states, those benefits escape taxes when figuring your income for purposes of state income taxes. In New York, for example, they are a subtraction on page one of the return when computing New York taxable income.

16 ESTATE PLANNING

MINIMIZING GIFT AND ESTATE TAXES

I don't see why a man shouldn't pay an inheritance tax. If a country is good enough to pay taxes to while you are living, it's good enough to pay in after you die. By the time you die you should be so used to paying taxes that it would just be almost second nature to you.

—Will Rogers, 1926

Congress knocked the rich in the creek with a [72 percent raise in the] income tax, then somebody must have told 'em "Yes, Congress you got 'em while they are living. But what if they die on you to keep from paying it?" Congress says, "Well, never thought of that, so we will frame one that will get 'em alive or living, dead or deceased." Now they got such a high inheritance tax on 'em that you won't catch these old rich boys dying promiscuously like they did. This bill makes patriots out of everybody. You sure do die for your country if you die from now on.

—Will Rogers, 1932

The rules governing federal estate and gift taxes have undergone repeated changes in the last few years. Why does Congress keep going back to the drawing board? The main reason is to alleviate the impact of estate and gift taxes on the steadily mushrooming number of individuals in the middle- to upper-middle income group—those whose homes and other assets have been swelled by decades of inflation to the several hundred thousand dollar range.

Here are some points to keep in mind as you choose and implement strategies to lessen or completely avoid these taxes. Current law eliminates estate and gift taxes for all estates of up to $600,000. Previously, there were separate exemptions of only $30,000 from gift taxes and $60,000 from estate taxes.

Congress decided to replace the exemptions with a "unified estate and gift tax credit," which is governmentalese for a single credit. This credit provides the equivalent of an exemption from gift and estate taxes. It is subtracted from the combined gift-estate tax. For the most part, the credit lumps together the cash or other assets that you will leave at death, along with the gifts that you make while alive. There is, however, a big loophole. Lifetime transfers count only to the extent that they exceed the annual exclusions from gift taxes; more on that break in a moment. The credit is used first to offset any gift taxes that you would otherwise pay during your lifetime, with the remainder used to lower or wipe out estate taxes after your death.

The law now on the books authorizes a credit of $192,800. This works out to an exemption from the amount of tax on the first $600,000 of gifts and bequests.

For taxable transfers (gifts and bequests) in excess of $600,000, the rates begin at 37 percent and gradually climb to as high as 55 percent—pretty steep numbers. But the Internal Revenue Service makes a condolence call only on someone who dies and leaves a net taxable estate that runs to more than $600,000. That $600,000 benchmark is *after* assets such as stocks, cash, and real estate are offset by deductions for debts, funeral expenses, administrative outlays for executor's and attorney's fees and similar charges, as well as for gifts to charities *and* without counting any property left to a surviving spouse.

> Last word department. A Michigan tax lawyer on his death left word that his obituary should contain this sentence: "The deceased requested that, to eliminate the middleman, memorials be sent directly to the Internal Revenue Service."
> —*American Bar Association Journal,* March, 1980

Marital deduction. In addition to the exemption of $600,000 that all estates enjoy, there is a special break for married couples—an unlimited marital deduction. Uncle Sam treats a husband and wife as, in effect, a single economic unit and allows unlimited transfers of property from one spouse to another, undiminished by gift or estate taxes. *Result:* No estate tax on the death of a married person, no matter how sizable the estate, provided all assets in excess of $600,000 are left to the surviving spouse and the survivor is a citizen of the United States. As explained below, there is no unlimited marital deduction when the survivor is not a U.S. citizen.

What about estate taxes when the surviv-

ing spouse dies? The survivor is limited to an exemption of $600,000 unless she or he remarries. But an affluent widow or widower with assets in excess of $600,000 can lower or even escape estate taxes on the excess by a carefully planned program of lifetime transfers to children and other prospective heirs, as explained below in the discussion of annual exclusions.

The unlimited marital deduction relieves a married couple of the threat of less property going to their family because of two estate taxes—the first when one spouse dies, the second when the surviving spouse dies. Moreover, a married couple is able to put up to $1,200,000 (exemption of $600,000 for each) beyond the reach of the federal tax collector.

Caution. A law change enacted in 1988 ended the unlimited marital deduction for property passing to a surviving spouse who is not a U.S. citizen. It makes no difference that the spouse resides in the U.S. However, the law left a loophole—a special trust for a spouse who is not a U.S. citizen, known officially as a "qualified domestic trust." The unlimited deduction remains available for assets put in such a trust, as long as they are not distributed to the survivor. The widow or widower is entitled to draw all the income from the trust without triggering estate taxes. But if the survivor were to withdraw any of the assets placed in the trust, the amount removed would be subject to estate taxes.

Tip. Even without such a trust, there is still an exemption of $600,000 from estate taxes for property left to a noncitizen spouse. In the case of lifetime gifts, which are discussed below, there is no unlimited marital deduction for gift taxes on gifts to a noncitizen spouse. Instead, there is an annual limit of

$100,000 on such gifts that can be made free of gift taxes.

> Most people never do the necessary planning to reduce the taxes on their estates for two good reasons; they don't want to think about dying, and they refuse to give away money just so their heirs will pay less tax.
> —*The New York Times,*
> October 17, 1993

> In the end, of course, you *will* give away all your wealth. Some may go to family, some to charities, some to lawyers and some to the Internal Revenue Service. Estate planning allows you more say in who gets what.
> —*U.S. News & World Report,*
> July 30, 1990

Annual exclusions from gift taxes.   Yet another revision raised the amount that you can give away each year without payment of a gift tax. This break is dubbed the "annual exclusion." The annual exclusions are for gifts in any single year to any one person. The gifts can be money or other assets, including securities, real estate, life insurance, jewelry, and works of art. The exclusion figure went from $3,000 (an outdated figure that remained unchanged from 1942 through 1981) to $10,000.

These exclusions permit you to pass along as much as $10,000 a year to each of as many of your children, grandchildren, other relatives, or friends as you like and can afford, provided none of them receives more than $10,000. The $10,000 figure doubles to $20,000 when your spouse consents to "gift splitting," which treats a gift of property owned by only one spouse as though half was given by the husband and half by the wife.

What if you exceed the yearly tax-free ceiling? In most cases, you need not worry. You may still avoid the gift tax by using up, in advance, part of your exemption of $600,000 from gift and estate taxes. (Of course, you are not entitled to take an income tax deduction for such gifts.)

The exclusions allow great flexibility. You can use them to give away a lot.

Consider this example. You and your spouse can steer clear of gift taxes on a transfer of $40,000 to each of your youngsters within a period of as little as several days. All you need to do is place $20,000 in a custodian account or comparable arrangement in late December of the current year and transfer another $20,000 in early January of the following year. Similarly, you and your spouse can make annual gifts of $20,000 to a child and another $20,000 to his (or her) spouse before you start to use up any of your exemption.

Proposed legislation.   In recent years, Congress considered, but failed to enact, proposed legislation that would have substantially affected gift and estate planning. Those proposals included a measure to abolish your unlimited annual exclusions of $10,000 and limit you to an annual exclusion of $30,000, with a cap that doubles to $60,000 when you are married and your spouse agrees to gift splitting. As this book goes to press in the summer of 1994, budget pressures might cause Congress to resurrect and enact some type of curtailment on annual exclusions. Another proposal is to lower the present exemption from estate taxes of $600,000.

Tip.   Whether or not the rules become less favorable, it is best not to wait until year end to make annual gifts to relatives and others to trim the taxable assets that will be left in your estate; earlier gifts let you shift the income tax on the earnings of the assets from yourself to recipients in lower brackets.

No carry-forward for unused exclusions. You are entitled to the exclusions each year even if you make gifts to the same recipients. Remember, though, that you forfeit forever your annual exclusions for any one year unless you make the gifts by December 31. For instance, you cannot carry forward any unused portion of exclusions for 1994 to 1995 or any later year.

Note also that you should be mindful of the calendar when you make a gift by check near the end of the year. Be sure that the donee deposits the check in time for it to clear your bank before the year comes to a close. Otherwise, it counts as a gift for the following year and will be applied against your exclusion for that year, says the IRS, though some courts' decisions disagree. To avoid a dispute with the IRS, pay with a certified check, which immediately removes the money from your bank account.

Unlimited exclusion for payments of educational and medical expenses. There is what the law refers to as an unlimited exclusion— meaning you sidestep any liability for gift taxes—when you pay someone else's school tuition or medical expenses. To take advantage of this break, you must *directly* pay the educational institution or medical care provider, rather than reimburse the person you want to assist. Go that route and your outlays do not count for gift tax purposes.

Caution. You lose out on this break when you turn funds over to the person you want to help. This is so even if that individual uses the money to take care of tuition or medical charges.

You must make your payment to a qualifying educational organization, defined by IRS regulations as one with a regular faculty, an established curriculum, and an organized student body. What can your payments cover? Direct tuition costs for full-time or part-time students, but not books, supplies, dormitory fees, board, and similar expenses.

As for qualifying medical expenses, they are the same ones for which you can take tax deductions. Be mindful of the rules if you originally pay a medical expense for some other person and that expense is then reimbursed. In that event, you are ineligible for the unlimited exclusion and considered to have made a gift when that person receives the reimbursement.

Also consider the income tax deduction that might become available to that person if he or she makes the medical payment. (For a discussion of medical expenses, see Chapter 7.)

Tip. The unlimited exclusion provides an ideal estate-planning opportunity for someone, such as a grandparent, to make tuition payments on a grandchild's behalf and remain entitled to take advantage of the annual $10,000 exclusion.

Whether or not you can benefit from the unlimited exclusion, for gift tax purposes, you have not made gifts when you make legally required tuition or medical payments, as when you do so on your youngster's behalf.

Planning pays off. Estate planning, with an eye particularly on taxes, is rewarding for many persons. Your potential estate may be much larger than you realize, not just because of the steady increase in the value of most homes and other properties, as well as the growth of fringe benefits in business and industry, but also because of the way the IRS calculates your taxable estate. Moreover, don't overlook the possibility that your continually growing estate may eventually exceed even the tax-free limit of $600,000 authorized by current law.

In totaling your taxable estate, the Internal Revenue counts the date-of-death value of your assets, not what you originally paid for them. Here are some examples of why you may be worth a great deal more than you think, at least for estate tax purposes.

The likelihood is that there has been a marked rise in the value of such assets as your year-round home, that vacation retreat in the country or at the seashore, jewelry, or antiques. Those increased values will show up in your estate, as will the proceeds from life insurance policies. Count the face value of all policies you hold (some of which probably call for a double-indemnity payment in case of accidental death), including those group policies with no cash surrender value that you acquire as a fringe benefit where you work or by becoming a member of a professional or fraternal association. It makes no difference to the tax collectors that the insurance proceeds are paid to a beneficiary and not to your estate.

Own property jointly? Your taxable estate includes half the value of bank accounts or other property owned jointly with the right of survivorship with a spouse, and possibly the entire value when property is jointly owned with someone other than your spouse, such as a son or a sister.

Tip. To find out whether you now have enough property to pose estate tax problems, you should set up a complete and accurate listing of your net worth—what you own minus what you owe. Then consult a tax expert if you plan to use any of the strategies listed previously.

Once you have a plan in place, check regularly with your adviser about tax-law changes or other legislation that may make it necessary to revise your will and estate plans. Perhaps you can benefit from lifetime gifts, trusts, and other devices long used by the wealthy to "disinherit" the IRS. (See "How to Play Santa and Trim Taxes, Too" in Chapter 1.)

Caution. Your estate planning can prove meaningless if you transfer property to someone who dies before you do and leaves everything to you. In that event, the property reverts to your estate and stays there unless you transfer it to someone else. For this reason, the recipient of a gift of property should leave it to someone other than the donor.

MAKING OUT A WILL IS NOT ENOUGH

You have lots of company if you are reluctant to make a will. Only a third of all persons with property to pass after they die have wills, according to surveys taken by bar associations.

If you are too busy or superstitious to write a will that spells out who is to get what when you die, your assets will pass in accordance with your state's intestacy laws. These laws are always impersonal and inflexible. They decide where property goes when a person dies without a will, regardless of what the family prefers and whether it makes sense from a tax standpoint.

For example, the intestacy laws could disinherit someone that you particularly wanted to benefit and send your property to someone that you never intended to benefit. Or the laws could cause your property to be divided in a way that gives most of it to a relative who is already wealthy.

The only way to avoid these occurrences is to have a will or some other advance arrangement, such as joint ownership of property with "the right of survivorship." This means that when one joint owner dies, the other automatically becomes the owner.

Many couples mistakenly think that there is no need to bother with wills because they own most of their property jointly. Or they think that only the husband needs a will because the property automatically goes to the wife on his death or because she has little property in her own name.

These couples do not think about what could happen if they are both involved in an accident, in which he dies and she lives for a short while. All of their joint holdings (bank accounts and stocks, to cite some common examples) will become hers. Because she left no will, the assets would then pass under the intestacy laws to her family. Forget the couple's understanding, say, about setting money aside for the education of his children from a former marriage. So a husband and wife *both* need wills even though they own their property jointly.

Caution.   Are you unmarried and want the person with whom you live to inherit some of your property? For that to happen, you need a will.

Tip.   Yet another drawback is that being without a will often means that your estate will be burdened with unnecessary administrative expenses and taxes. That is why it is inexcusable to put off making a will.

Even if you have a will, you need to review it periodically and keep it up-to-date. Check with an attorney experienced in estate planning to see whether any changes are necessary to carry out your actual intentions and to avoid confusion, family wangles, expensive legal fees, and unnecessary taxes during the settlement of your estate.

Planning Pointers

Here are some reminders on typical events in life that may signal the need to go over your will. Check those that apply to you. Then contact your attorney.

A substantial change in your financial situation.   If your estate grows or shrinks significantly, you may want to distribute it differently. Consider this situation: You drew a will that provides specific amounts for charities, with the balance going to your children. But now, for whatever reason, your net worth has dropped significantly. Unless you change your will, the specified amount must be paid to the charities. Only the shrunken remainder goes to your children.

Changes in your family status.   Chances are, your will needs redoing if you have married, divorced, or legally separated since you wrote it. Your property intentions normally change when your marriage ends. And a remarriage also increases the complications, particularly when each spouse has children from previous marriages.

Death of a beneficiary. What if your will leaves some of your property to, say, your favorite niece and she unexpectedly fails to outlive you? Don't assume your bequest to her becomes void. Unless you close that gap in your will, the property may end up with someone you loathe. So be certain your will explains clearly what you want to happen in case your niece dies before you do. Incidentally, it is also prudent to designate contingent beneficiaries for your insurance policies, in case a beneficiary you've named in a policy predeceases you.

Sale of an asset mentioned in your will. If you sell a valuable asset mentioned in your will or buy one not mentioned, your will probably needs revising. Let's say that when you wrote your will, you intended to leave your son a vacation home in Vermont. Now you plan to sell that home and replace it with one in Maine. Update your will if you intend him to get the Maine place instead.

Death or disability of your executor. One important purpose of your will is to name an executor—the person assigned to bring together all your assets, pay all bills and charges (including any taxes assessed against the estate), and distribute the remaining property in accordance with the terms of your will. But you may have named as executor someone who has died or is no longer able to effectively serve in this potentially time-consuming and demanding position of managing the disposition of your estate, because of age, disability, a move to a distant town, or some other reason.

If so, you need to name a replacement now. Otherwise, when the time comes to do so, the court may select someone who does not measure up to the person you would have picked for the job. Worse yet, this could result in your estate being saddled with unnecessary costs. Also, it is a good idea for your will to designate an alternate executor who can step right in to handle things in case your first choice becomes unable to serve. To cut the costs of settling an estate, your will can specify that the executor need not post a bond. (For more on the responsibilities of an executor, see "Choose Carefully When You Name an Executor for Your Will" later in this chapter.)

Change of guardian. Suppose the person your will nominates to serve as guardian of your minor children declines or is unable to serve. In that case, the court has to name someone else unless your will nominates a successor guardian.

A move to another state. There are 50 sets of state laws involving wills, all of which read differently. The law of the state in which you last resided controls your will, even if you signed it in another state. If you move, the law in your new location may affect the validity of some provisions in your will. Another problem is that the person you named executor may no longer be eligible to serve in the new state.

What can really complicate things is when a couple moves to one of the nine states that have a community property system from a state with a common law system, or vice versa. The community property states are Arizona, California, Idaho, Louisiana, Nevada, New Mexico, Texas, Washington, and Wisconsin. In general, these states assume that a husband and wife each own half of all property during their marriage, except inherited property and gifts from third parties.

The other states have common law systems, in which, as a general rule, a husband and wife are considered to be separate owners of whatever they have independently purchased from their own funds. Property rights of spouses in community property states may conflict with the instructions in wills written in common law states. For that reason, a move to another state calls for checking with a lawyer in the new location on whether any changes in your will are necessary to carry out your intentions.

A change in your will.   You may have written a will five or fifteen years ago that is no longer up-to-date. Not to worry. You can rethink, redo, or revoke your will at any time because it does not take effect until your death. And you do not have to redo the entire will every time you want to change it.

Suppose, for instance, that the change is as simple as naming a new executor or guardian, or adding or eliminating a beneficiary. You can do it by having your lawyer draw up a codicil—the legal term for a document that modifies or adds to a will. Whether you make a new will or merely add a new codicil, the change is not legally effective unless you do it with the same formalities that were required for your original will—signing and dating by you in the presence of witnesses, and signing by witnesses who are not beneficiaries under the will.

Safeguarding Your Will

Make sure to safeguard your will in a place where it can be easily found. Steer clear of anyplace where your will can be stolen, forgotten, misplaced, or lost. If your will cannot be found, it does not matter how carefully you worked out the details contained within

it; your property will probably pass under the intestacy laws just as though you died without a will.

One possibility is to keep the original will with your lawyer or your executor. It's also wise to keep a copy of your will at home in the place that your family will look first. But it is not wise to keep the original will in your safe deposit box, even one that you hold jointly with another person, like your spouse.

The often-overlooked point is that many states require the bank to seal the box temporarily as soon as it receives notice of the death of a boxholder. In such situations, nobody is supposed to enter the box until a representative of the state tax authority is present to witness an inventory of the contents. This could delay access to the box just when the will is needed. To avoid an unnecessary hardship at a difficult time, the box should *not* be used to safeguard original wills, life insurance policies, a deed to a cemetery plot, burial instructions, and similar items. Even if a co-holder or deputy gains access after the holder's death because the bank was unaware of it, the record of this visit may prompt embarrassing questions from the state tax collector.

To sidestep these snags, some couples rent two boxes, one in the husband's name, the other in the wife's name. She stores in her box important papers that might be needed quickly should the husband die first; he keeps similar documents that belong to her. The extra rental outlay is certainly worthwhile if the box helps minimize some of the many problems that inevitably come up when a person dies.

Another completely legal way to avoid sealing is to put the will in a box rented in the name of a corporation, rather than an individual—a maneuver that is available to persons who have incorporated their businesses or professions.

Another view on who is the best custodian for your will. Near the start of this discussion, I pointed out that you can keep the original will with someone other than the attorney who prepared it. But a persuasive argument can be made for sticking with the preparer. I got that good advice from Benedict Ginsberg, a nationally recognized attorney who practices in New York City, was already providing sage counseling on estate planning when the stock market crashed in 1929, and can provide some educated guesses on why Judge Joseph Force Crater decided to take an extended walk. What follows is his advice.

Leaving your will in the custody of your lawyer has a value that you might not have considered. Anyone who can get his (or her) hands on your will, upon your death, will read it—and might conclude, correctly or not, that he (or she) will fare better under the intestacy laws or under a prior will, and be tempted to destroy it. Once destroyed, a will cannot be probated. A destroyed will is dead. Not even an exact copy can be probated.

Some lawyers retain the original and give the client an exact copy with a notation on the cover that the lawyer has the original. This discourages destruction in a circumstance such as described above.

Leaving the will with your lawyer does not mean you are directing your executor to retain him or her to handle the estate, unless you say so in the will itself. In many states, whoever has custody of a will is required, promptly upon learning of the death of the maker, to deliver the will to the clerk of the probate (sometimes called orphan's or surro-

gate's) court. So your executor will have no problem in proceeding with probate.

What the Lawyer Will Charge

How much can you expect to pay for legal help when you write or revise a will? And how do you find a competent lawyer with the right rate for your pocketbook? I'll answer those questions in reverse order.

Your best bet is the way most people find an affordable attorney: word-of-mouth recommendations. Obvious sources include relatives, friends, or business acquaintances who have had good experiences with an attorney. Legal-referral services run by local bar associations are another option.

Now let's get down to dollars. Your session with an attorney should be straightforward—a discussion of your assets, heirs, and wishes. Most lawyers are up-front about their charges for preparing wills. If yours is not, don't hesitate to ask. Fees vary widely, depending on the complexity of the document you need.

On the low end, some legal clinics advertise that they charge as little as $75 to draft simple wills for relatively small, uncomplicated estates. In such a will, each spouse typically leaves everything to the other, or, should they die simultaneously, to the surviving children. But if the children are minors, you no longer have a simple will situation.

Many attorneys, however, do charge more for simple wills; though there is no average price, you'll find that fees ranging from $150 to $250 are common. On the plus side, lawyers often draw up wills for a husband and wife at the same time for less than the usual fee for drawing up each spouse's will separately.

Understandably, you can expect the charges to escalate considerably if you have a sizable estate or if you have property complications and want to use the services of an attorney who specializes in wills, trusts, and estate planning.

Tax deductions.   Ordinarily, there is no deduction for a will-preparation fee. You may, though, be able to salvage a write-off for the part of the fee allocable to tax advice on estate planning.

Tax reform limits the deductions allowed itemizers for most miscellaneous expenses, a category that includes what you spend for tax advice. These outlays are allowable only to the extent that their total in any one year is greater than 2 percent of your AGI, short for adjusted gross income. AGI is the amount you list on the last line of page 1 of Form 1040.

Example.   You have an AGI of $50,000 and miscellaneous expenses of $1,500. The 2 percent floor shrinks your deduction to just $500—what is left after the $1,500 is offset by $1,000, which is 2 percent of $50,000.

Tip.   If your attorney's services include counseling on strategies to lower taxes, remind the attorney to prepare a bill that shows the breakdown between the nondeductible portion charged for will preparation and the amount charged for tax advice, which is the deductible part that you can include with your other miscellaneous expenditures. That way, assuming you surpass the 2 percent floor, you are able to substantiate your deduction in the event that you are au-

dited. (For a discussion of miscellaneous deductions, see Chapter 9.)

LETTER OF INSTRUCTIONS

In the best of all worlds, we would know exactly what to do when someone close dies. Our loved one would have informed us where to find instructions setting forth funeral arrangements, the location of the will and any life insurance policies, a list of all property and assets, and the name of the deceased's lawyer. Any minors would be provided for in the will. No one would challenge the authority of the executor—the person named by the deceased to make sure the terms of the will are met. Probating an estate, an often grueling court process, would be completed smoothly and quickly. In the real world, such a well-ordered process almost never occurs.
    —*Money* magazine, August, 1986

When you make out a will or bring one up to date, it is also the practical time to write what lawyers call a "letter of instructions." Don't be intimidated by the formal title; the letter is just an informal document that is not legally binding. Usually, it is addressed to your surviving spouse, one of your adult children, your lawyer, or your executor. (For the duties of an executor, see the next section of this chapter.)

Why is it worthwhile to go through the chore? So your heirs are made aware of what your assets are and where they are, as well as how you want your personal affairs handled. There are important details that can change quickly and are usually impractical to put into a will.

At the very least, your letter of instructions should spell out the exact location of all your important personal papers and also note any personal requests that you want to make. To help you organize a letter that can be as necessary as your will, here are some reminders on what sort of information to include.

Who gets what. Let your heirs know how much they can expect when you die. List all benefits due them from your employer or your business. These include life insurance, 401(k) (see Chapter 10), profit sharing, accident insurance, or other fringes, as well as benefits from Social Security, the Veterans Administration, or other sources.

People to contact. Put in the names, addresses, and phone numbers of persons and organizations to notify in case of your death—relatives and friends, attorneys, accountants, employers, and banks, for instance.

The places you keep personal papers. Indicate the whereabouts of your personal papers, particularly your will, birth and marriage certificates, diplomas, military records, naturalization papers, and similar vital documents. Be specific about these locations. Use language like "in my safe deposit box at the Fifth National Bank" or "in the bottom left-hand drawer of my desk." There is an added plus if you have yet to file your papers properly: Making out this letter will force you to do so before they go astray.

Checking and savings accounts. List all of them— their numbers, the banks and their addresses, names of the owners, and location of the passbooks. Each year, banks and other financial organizations advertise for missing depositors who forgot their accounts or died without informing relatives about them. Your letter can avoid this.

Tip. Tell, too, where you keep canceled checks, credit card slips, and the like that, among other things, supply the information that you rely on at Form 1040 time to justify the amounts that you show as income, deductions, exemptions, and other return figures. In the event that the Internal Revenue Service questions those figures and the substantiating records are unavailable, your estate may be drastically diminished by assessments for additional taxes, interest charges, and, perhaps, penalties. (See Chapter 11 for IRS audits.)

Chances are that you use credit cards to pay for many items, including meals, travel, and purchases at stores. Your listing of cards should include a reminder to cancel the cards or convert them to your spouse's name.

Insurance. For each insurance policy, whether it be life, accident, car, household, medical, or mortgage, list the name of the insurer, policy number, agent, and location. Don't overlook those group insurance policies acquired through your employment or by joining professional or fraternal associations.

To illustrate, suppose someone dies while traveling on business. His fringe benefits might include an accidental-death policy, and he also might have coverage for a specified amount if he is a member of an automobile club. Moreover, some credit cards provide casualty insurance with tickets that are charged.

Stocks and bonds. List all stocks, bonds, and other investments. If you trade stocks frequently, keeping a current list would be inconvenient; so simply list their location. If you have an account with a stockbroker, include his or her name and address and your account number.

Safe deposit box and debts. Record information about the box's contents, the location of the key to the box, and debts, whether owed by or to you. List the details about the information needed to sell your year-round residence, vacation retreat, or other dwelling. That should include such key documents as deeds, statements of real estate closings, and mortgages. For example, explain whether insurance automatically pays off a mortgage at your death. Don't forget things like money due—say, a loan made to a sister, but not openly discussed.

Funeral arrangements. Add a separate page to explain your specific wishes about such matters as the education of your children or burial or cremation arrangements. Spell out how elaborate or simple a funeral you want and whether you have already bought a burial plot, made arrangements with a specific funeral home, and desire the service to be religious or secular. Remember, the reading of a will usually is not until after the burial.

Tip. Although it might sound morbid, you need to write a letter sufficiently clear to be understood by a complete stranger, should a car accident or other disaster wipe out your family.

Strategy. Writing the letter ought not to be a daunting chore. Still, it is tedious to organize the needed records that clutter up your desk drawers, closets, and other storage spaces. What I advise clients is to break the work of sorting through financial papers into segments of no more than a couple of hours at a time—insurance one evening, investments another, and so on.

There is a side benefit to this do-it-yourself project: Your desk will be less cluttered, and you wind up tossing out lots of stuff as you organize your records.

Tip. Make several copies of your letter and attach one to a copy of your will, leaving it wherever your family will look first. Attach another one to the original will. (For where to keep the original will, see "Safeguarding Your Will" earlier in this chapter.)

Resolve to keep your letter up to date. Revise it whenever important changes occur, such as a job change or marriage. Unlike a will, your letter is not a legal document. That is why you remain free to revise it as frequently as you wish to without the formalities required for a will to be legally effective—signing and dating by you in the presence of witnesses, and signing by witnesses who are not beneficiaries under the will. (For more on keeping records, see "Make Tax Planning a Year-Round Job" in Chapter 1.)

Avoiding a nightmare. Unless they have a letter of final instructions, the heirs will have to reconstruct the assets without guidelines. The result is a situation that can be nightmarish, cause family disputes and significantly increase legal and other expenses.

Like other lawyers, I have often been called in to help heirs search for property. My most memorable case was that of a much-married widow with children from each of her marriages. After her death, the half brothers and half sisters found themselves scavenging for such documents as a will, insurance policies, stock certificates, and bank statements.

It was not until years afterward that the squabbling siblings stumbled upon stock certificates hidden away in the mother's armoire. Worse still, missing jewelry had them eying one another distrustfully until they finally discovered the gems behind a loose board in the closet of a summer home that, fortunately, had remained in the family.

Tip. To speed things up and lessen their expenses, I advised the children, as I do all heirs, of several long-standing techniques for reconstructing assets that they could employ without assistance from me. For starters, all they had to do was monitor mom's mail during the filing season for 1099 forms, from banks, brokerage outfits, and other financial institutions. That would show interest, dividends, and other income sources. As anticipated, the 1099s eventually enabled them to track down much of her property.

Another reminder: The children might be able to reconstruct other assets from her tax returns. The possibilities included the existence of retirement plans and the ownership of real estate for which she had claimed deductions for property taxes. Unfortunately, that method was unavailable, as they found that she had not filed 1040s for years.

What if the mother had filed 1040s, but copies were unlocatable? Then the fastest way to obtain them is from her return preparer, assuming she used one. The law, in most cases, requires preparers to keep copies for at least three years after the filing deadline. Failing this, the children can get copies from the IRS by submitting Form 4506 (Request for Copy of Tax Form). But figure on at

least 45 days for the IRS to send copies. (For more information on Form 4506, see "Paperwork" in "Coping with the IRS after April 15" in Chapter 14.)

Meanwhile, the needlessly protracted search continued, as a consequence of which, my fee, though based on an hourly rate that I deemed moderate, continued to swell—a circumstance that discomforted the children and comforted my creditors.

CHOOSE CAREFULLY WHEN YOU NAME AN EXECUTOR FOR YOUR WILL

A chore that most people put off is first, writing a will, and, second, keeping it up-to-date to reflect changed circumstances. If your will needs to be written or revised, consider carefully when you select or replace an executor—the legal term for the person who is the key figure in the settlement of your estate.

The executor's job is a potentially time-consuming and demanding position that requires a lot more work than many people realize. An executor has four major functions to perform:

1. Assemble and value assets. It can be a formidable task to assemble those records of bank accounts; automobiles; loans to family members or others; Individual Retirement Accounts (see Chapter 10); 401(k)s (see Chapter 10) and retirement plans at work; brokerage accounts; mutual funds; insurance policies; other assets like real estate, jewelry, or artworks; debts; mortgages;

and tax returns, and determine the location of safe deposit boxes.

2. Pay all bills and charges, a task that often requires professional help as it includes the timely filing of returns for federal estate taxes, state inheritance taxes, final income taxes for the deceased, and current income taxes for the estate, as well as payment of those levies.

3. Distribute what is left of the property in accordance with the will.

4. Account to the probate—sometimes called orphan's or surrogate's—court for everything that he or she has done.

Hiring lawyers, accountants, or other professional advisers to help does not get executors off the hook, as many thousands of them have discovered the hard way. When something goes wrong with, say, federal taxes, the executors get personal bills from the IRS.

What can go wrong? Among other things, the executor is *personally* responsible when assets are distributed and taxes remain unpaid or forms are filed late.

Consider the predicament of Kenneth Leigh, production manager of a dress business. Because of his familiarity with the business, Kenneth became the court-appointed administrator of the estate of the owner, who died without a will. The manager knew nothing about administering an estate but retained an attorney in whom he had complete confidence.

He tried to read estate documents presented to him for signature; by and large, however, he blindly relied on the lawyer's competence. Several days before Kenneth's final accounting and request for an order to distribute the assets was to be filed with the probate court, the attorney asked him to sign an amended estate tax return, which listed assets overlooked in the original return.

Kenneth saw that the amended return's cover page showed an additional $27,000 due; but he signed without questioning the lawyer about the amount due.

The probate court approved the accounting, although it did not reflect the additional estate tax. To wind things up, or so Kenneth thought, he went ahead with a distribution of the remaining assets to the heirs.

Not long afterward, he received an IRS notification. Sorry, it said, but Kenneth was personally liable for the $27,000, as he was aware that taxes were due at a time when the estate had sufficient assets to pay them.

Apparently, Kenneth was unable to get the heirs to take care of the taxes. So the dispute wound up in the Tax Court, which rejected his argument that, as a layman inexperienced with estate matters, his reliance on competent counsel relieved him of the duty to inquire as to the proper disposition of the estate.

The court cited his awareness of the general obligation of estate taxes, signing of the original tax return, payment of the tax, and signing of the amended return—circumstances that indicated actual knowledge on his part of the existence of the debt. He had an obligation, said the court, independent of any reliance on his attorney, to look at the face of the amended return to see whether any additional tax was due. Then a reasonable inquiry of the lawyer would have revealed that the tax was still unpaid. Because Kenneth failed to do those things, he was personally liable for the taxes.

The need to obtain proper tax advice also was made expensively clear to the son and daughter-in-law of Henry Lammerts, who had designated them as his executors. On Henry's death, his son took over leadership in settling the estate. Although under the impression that a tax return had to be filed for his father, the son was unaware that it was also necessary to file an income tax return for the estate. This is where matters stood until his accountant discovered that no return had been filed reporting income received by the estate. The filing was eventually made seven months after the due date.

The IRS exacted a nondeductible penalty from the estate, as well as the usual interest charges. The executors offered the counterargument that they were new at this sort of thing and had relied on their accountant and the estate's lawyer to do whatever was necessary.

But the accountant, in his own defense, testified that there was nothing in his past services to the family to suggest that, on his own initiative, he would have to file an income tax return for the estate. Similarly, the estate's lawyer pointed out that neither of the executors had asked him for a rundown of the responsibilities attached to being an executor. Consequently, the Second Circuit Court of Appeals upheld imposition of the penalty.

QUESTIONS AND ANSWERS

Q. *My estate planner recommends that I use a living trust. What are the advantages? How much will I save in income and estate taxes?*

A. With this type of trust, which is also known as a "revocable" trust, it is possible to transfer property in a simple, relatively painless way that avoids some of the headaches of probate and reduces administrative expenses for your estate.

Also, it is more difficult for someone to challenge a trust than it is to challenge a will.

But unlike other types of trusts that are de-signed primarily to save income or estate taxes (such as a trust that shifts investment income for a specified period of time from yourself to a lower-bracket beneficiary), you gain no income or estate tax advantages with a revocable living trust. For income tax purposes, the trust is ignored. You remain liable for income taxes on income from property put in the trust.

Where an estate is sizable enough to require the filing of an estate tax return (taxable estate above $600,000), the return must list all the trust assets and the tax that falls due is the same as would be due without the trust. It makes no difference that the assets go directly to your heirs and are not subject to the probate process for property that passes under your will.

Caution. A living trust is not necessarily suited for everyone. Moreover, even if you use one, you still need a will to provide for the disposition of assets not put in the trust.

Q. *United States Savings Bonds are among the assets that I intend to place in a living trust. Do I have to report the accumulated interest when the bonds go in the trust?*

A. No. An IRS ruling says that you continue to be viewed as the owner of the bonds and not in receipt of the benefit of the deferred interest at the time of the transfer.

Q. *My estate will be well above the current exemption of $600,000 from estate taxes. As part of my estate planning, I use custodian accounts to handle gifts of stock or cash to my youngster. Taxwise, does it make any difference whether I name myself or someone else as custodian?*

A. Your child acquires full legal title to the property once the gift is made. But the IRS counts custodian account assets as part of your taxable estate if you fail to steer clear of a tax trap that has closed on many parents. Don't name yourself custodian for the account. The IRS can still include the assets if you die before your child comes of age at 18 or 21, depending on state law.

The catch is that, as custodian, you keep an impermissible string on the gift—the right to use the assets to take care of your legal obligation to support your child. This holds true even though there is little likelihood of your tapping the assets for support. To avoid that trap, just make sure to name your spouse or some other trusted person as custodian. If you are transferring assets held by you and your spouse as community property, name someone other than yourself or your spouse as custodian.

Tip. Custodian accounts provide an easy and inexpensive way to irrevocably transfer assets to your children, without the bother and expense involved in outright gifts, guardianships, or trusts. You simply set up a custodian account to hold the property until your child reaches the age of majority at 18 or 21, depending upon the law in the state where you live.

You can establish an account in a few minutes, and it costs nothing to arrange. In the case of, say, savings accounts or stocks, all you need to do is open the account or register the stock in the name of the custodian who will handle the assets until the child grows up and takes over. Be mindful, though, that you cannot name more than one child as beneficiary of a custodian account. You must start a separate account for each child. Your banker or broker will fill you in on the details and the forms to use.

Example. Typically, the savings account or stocks would be registered as follows: Account of Zelda Miller as custodian for Nadine Miller, a minor, under the New York Uniform Gifts to Minors Act."

Caution. There are drawbacks that outweigh any tax savings from custodian accounts, which is why you should weigh your other options before you move assets into custodian accounts. As soon as you establish such accounts, you make irrevocable gifts, and you can use those assets only for your children's benefit. You cannot get them back while your children are minors, nor after they reach the age of majority, unless, as adults, they are willing to give them back. Put another way, once the law confers control on your children, they are free to use the property as they wish, whether for college or cocaine. Consequently, consider your future financial position before you bid a permanent farewell to your property.

You might find it well worth the risk to allow your child at age 18 to gain complete control over some property. It should give good guidance as to how capably he or she might manage heftier sums later on. Yet you might be unwilling to run the risk of having the child take full responsibility at that age for what could turn out to be a sizable chunk of property—and then not using it as you had wished. If that is your concern, you might think about channeling the assets into a trust, which can give you a better shot at making certain that your intentions are carried out.

Dependency exemptions. Setting up a custodian account for your child need not jeopardize your claiming that child as a dependent on your return. No matter how much income he or she receives from the account or from other sources, you are still entitled to the dependency exemption, provided you furnish over half of the child's total support for the year and he or she either (1) will not reach the age of 19 this year or (2) is a full-time student for at least five months (not necessarily consecutive) and will not reach the age of 24 this year (see Chapter 2).

Caution. Don't confuse custodian accounts with "in trust for" or "guardian" accounts, or any similar arrangement where you, not your child, continue to be the owner of the money in the account and can withdraw it for your own use. Under these arrangements, you remain liable for income taxes on the interest from the account. It is immaterial that the money passes automatically to the child on your death or that the child's Social Security number is used for the account.

Q. *Will my wife have to report life insurance proceeds received on my death?*

A. No. Life insurance proceeds paid to her because of your death do not count as taxable income. Nor does taxable income include money or other assets she receives as gifts or inheritances. But your wife does have to reckon with the IRS on any dividends, interest, rents, or other earnings that she later receives from investing the property.

Q. *What about a settlement she receives from the children of my first marriage for agreeing not to contest my will?*

A. Settlements similarly escape income taxes, just like inheritances.

Q. *To save on estate taxes, I plan to transfer ownership rights in a life insurance policy to my daughter. Can I retain the right to use the policy as security for a loan?*

A. No. To insulate insurance proceeds from estate taxes, you have to relinquish all policy rights to the new owner. That includes the right to borrow against or collect its cash surrender value.

Q. *When my daughter was born, I bought a sizable amount of United States Savings Bonds and named myself and her as co-owners. Last week, I handed the bonds over to her. Does this remove them from my taxable estate?*

A. Treasury Department regulations clearly spell out how co-owned bonds are supposed to be transferred and there is only one way: Redeem them and have the Treasury reissue the new bonds in your daughter's name alone.

Be aware that you must report the interest that built up on these bonds before you redeemed them. But any later interest is taxed to your daughter.

Moreover, you need to consider gift taxes when you redeem bonds and have them reissued in the name of the co-owner. Fortunately, it is usually possible to get around gift taxes, thanks to annual exclusions of $10,000 ($20,000 when your spouse consents to "gift splitting," which treats a gift of property owned by only one spouse as though half was given by the husband and half by the wife) and a credit for gift and estate taxes that provides the equivalent of an exemption of $600,000. Your financial adviser can fill you in on how to use these breaks to erase any gift tax that would otherwise be due. (For more on United States Savings Bonds, see "Timing Receipt of Income" in Chapter 1.)

INDEX

NOTES

NOTES

NOTES

NOTES